BREAKING
THE ABORTION
DEADLOCK

345

BREAKING THE ABORTION DEADLOCK

From Choice to Consent

Eileen L. McDonagh

New York   Oxford
OXFORD UNIVERSITY PRESS
1996

Oxford University Press

Oxford   New York
Athens   Aukland   Bangkok   Bogota   Bombay
Buenos Aires   Calcutta   Cape Town   Dar es Salaam
Delhi   Florence   Hong Kong   Istanbul   Karachi
Kuala Lumpur   Madras   Madrid   Melbourne
Mexico City   Nairobi   Paris   Singapore
Taipie   Tokyo   Toronto

and associated companies in
Berlin   Ibadan

Copyright © 1996 by Oxford University Press, Inc.

Published by Oxford University Press, Inc.,
198 Madison Avenue, New York, New York 10016

Library of Congress Cataloging-in-Publication-Data
McDonagh, Eileen L.
Breaking the abortion deadlock : from choice to consent
/ Eileen L. McDonagh.
p.   cm.   Includes index.
ISBN 0-19-509141-8; ISBN 0-19-509142-6 (pbk.)
1. Abortion—Government policy—United States.   2. Abortion—Law
and legislation—United States.   3. Abortion—Moral and ethical
aspects.   4. Human reporduction—Moral and ethical aspects.
5. Pregnancy—Moral and ethical aspects.   6. Women's rights—United
States.   I. Title.
HQ767.5.U5M373   1996
363.4'6'0973—dc20   95-25899

Eileen L. McDonagh, "Good, Bad, and Captive Samaritans: Adding-In Pregnancy and Consent to the Abortion Debate," co-published simultaneously in *Women and Politics*, vol. 13, no. 3/4 (1993), pp. 31–49 (The Haworth Press, Inc.), and *The Politics of Pregnancy: Policy Dilemmas in the Maternal-Fetal Relationship* (ed. Janna C. Merrick and Robert H. Blank), The Haworth Press, Inc., 1993, pp. 31–49. Copyright © The Haworth Press, Inc.

Eileen Lorenzi McDonagh, "Abortion Rights Alchemy and the U.S. Supreme Court: What's Wrong and How to Fix It," *Social Politics* (Summer 1994), pp. 130–156. Copyright © Board of Trustees of the University of Illinois.

Eileen L. McDonagh, "From Pro-Choice to Pro-Consent in the Abortion Debate: Reframing Women's Reproductive Rights," *Studies in Law, Politics and Society*, vol. 14 (1994), pp. 245–287. Copyright © JAI Press Inc.

1 3 5 7 9 8 6 4 2
Printed in the United States of America
on acid-free paper

*With thanks to Edward McDonagh, who showed
me how to see with the mind's eye,
and in loving memory of Louise McDonagh,
who consented to bring me into the world.*

Preface

A book is an enterprise, like life itself, generated by relationships. I embarked on this project without realizing it in the mid-1970s when asked to teach a course on the conceptual foundations of social science. As I reviewed the many differences between the social and natural sciences, such as the inability of social science to formulate theories that are as precise and predictable as those we think govern the motion of stars and molecules, I concluded that the key difference, the one that truly separates these sciences, is *ethics*. We can never study human beings without considering the ethical dimensions entailed in such research. To get this point across to my students, in the context of an issue, of political if not personal significance for them, I assigned the classic article by Judith Jarvis Thomson, "In Defense of Abortion."

Over the years of teaching, I grew increasingly convinced that Thomson was right in arguing that the notion of women being obligated to "give" themselves to a fetus, rather than getting an abortion, far exceeds what would constitute a reasonable demand from a good samaritan. So I began to watch for the "Thomson logic" in newspaper reports about abortion, but stories about good and bad samaritan issues almost never mentioned abortion, and reporting about abortion only rarely drew on good and bad samaritan justifications.

About this time, I began to conduct surveys of my students' attitudes toward "coerced" samaritan behavior. When they were asked if a person should be *legally forced* to give even a pint of blood to a close relative, such as a sister, they consistently said no. From these classroom experiments, I gathered that there well might exist a public wellspring of support for abortion rights within the framework of samaritan issues. With the encouragement of my graduate students, especially Lisa Ginsberg and Christina Kulich, I then began the long and arduous task of figuring out how to switch abortion rights from a principle of choice to a principle of consent, with the goal of securing for women not only the right to an abortion but also the right to abortion funding.

In developing the ideas in this book, I have accumulated many debts. Martha Minow was one of the first to provide a forum for my work at a discussion meeting of FemCrits, an association of law scholars, lawyers, and others interested in legal issues. The polarized reaction at that meeting was a harbinger of things to come. It is safe to say that everyone there supported a woman's right to an abortion. What was at issue was portraying a "nonconsensual pregnancy" as the aggressive intrusion of a woman's body by a fertilized ovum. For some, such an approach was offensive, if not threatening, to deeply felt emotions and attitudes, while others expressed approval of such a reframing of abortion rights.

Friends, such as Mary Katzenstein, provided critical support at significant preliminary stages. Marcia Angell and Sandy Levinson also backed this project early on from their respective perspectives of medicine and law. At later stages Laurence Tribe gave vital encouragement, as did Kathleen Sullivan, whose time and advice were as generous as they were crucially on point.

In the seven years between the beginning and end of writing this book, the network of associates and assistants who helped me through its pitfalls expanded considerably. I am very grateful to all those who took the time to read preliminary papers and engage in probing, if not troubling, conversations, all of which were grist for the mill. My enduring thanks go to Kathyrn Abrams, Holly Alderman, Leslie Berlowitz, John Brigham, Nonnie Burnes, Robert Cord, Nancy Cott, Michael Dukakis, Susan Eaton, Ellen Fisher, Catherine Fisk, Isabel Freeman, Jack Freeman, Christine Harrington, Richard Harris, Nancy Hirschmann, Hilda Hein, Ted Jelen, Leonard Laster, Thomas Kempner, Sally Kenney, Paul Maeder, Marty Mauzy, Edward McDonagh, the late Louise McDonagh, Sidney Milkis, Stephen Nathanson, Ruth O'Brien, Julie Pavlon, Lea Pendleton, Edward Price, Robert Price, Marie Provine, Steven Quatrano, Susan Okin, Molly Shanley, Austin Sarat, Mary Segers, Reva Siegel, Susan Silbey, Cass Sunstein, Ann Tickner, Michael Tolley, Joanna Weinberg, Mary Wolf, the late Fred Worden, Kay Worden, and Gwill York. For reading drafts of the book, offering insights, and suggesting improvements, I offer special thanks to Mary Becker, Guido Calabresi, Barbara Craig, Cynthia Daniels, Martha Field, Adrienne Fulco, Nicki Nichols Gamble, David Garrow, Robert Gilmour, Frances Kamm, Sylvia Law, Sandy Levinson, Lisa Manshel, Mark Munger, Karen O'Connor, Karen Orren, Deborah Rhode, Jamie Sabino, Mary Segers, and Susan Webber. For their especially helpful detailed crtiques of the book, I thank Susan Appelton, Stuart Banner, Bob Davoli, Laura Jensen, Andrew Koppelman, Edward McDonagh, Tony Martin, Carol Nakenoff, Karen O'Connor, and Suzanne Ogden.

I also have been privileged to work with students whose enthusiasm contributed to the project along with their research skills. Thanks go to Lisa Burton-Radzely, Rachel Harris, Lisa Holmes, Jennifer Kinnear, and Susan Lee, and special appreciation is due Autumn Elliott and Eunice Park for their recent research assistance. For excellent legal research, I am indebted to Sarah Barney, Kim Christensen, Katie Fallow, Michele Kisloff, Virginia McVarish, and Adam Wolff. I am also grateful for the efforts of those responsible for transforming words into print, particularly David Roll for taking a chance on this book, Gioia Stevens for backing it, Peter Knapp and Cynthia Garver for piloting it through production, and Virginia LaPlante for her expert editing. I also thank my good friend and photographer Carol Newsom for the many extra miles she went to provide her photographic contribution for the book cover.

This project was written and completed under the auspices of the Murray Research Center at Radcliffe College where the interviews conducted by Kristin Luker for *Abortion and the Politics of Motherhood* are housed and were made available to me. I gratefully acknowledge the Center's help. Thanks also to Director Anne Colby for creating such an intellectually productive haven at the Murray Center, and for including me within its compass as a visiting scholar, thereby making this book possible, and to Evelyn Liberatore and Marty Mauzy for imbuing each day with warmth and humor.

Finally, I extend heartfelt thanks to my family, who have lived and breathed through this work with me. My parents deserve much credit for their patience and interest; although my mother died before the book's publication, she was one of its staunchest supporters. My sons, Edward and Robert, gave me not only their support but their love, packaged with an inimitable combination of humor and advice, including how to avoid sounding like a "man-hating radical feminist." And my husband, Bob Davoli, deserves thanks not only for starting my day with offerings of morning coffee and the latest *Wall Street Journal* articles on abortion but, most important, for his confidence and love, without which this book would never have been written.

Cambridge, Massachusetts   E. L. M.
April 1996

Contents

BREAKING
THE ABORTION
DEADLOCK

1

Where Do We Go from Here?

More than a generation has passed since the Supreme Court first ruled in 1973 in *Roe v. Wade* that a woman has a constitutional right to an abortion.[1] During this time, the abortion issue has become "one of the most hotly debated issues" in the country,[2] and the exercise of abortion rights has become progressively limited. Though the Supreme Court has firmly upheld in principle a woman's right to an abortion,[3] it has just as firmly undermined a woman's ability to exercise that right, by ruling that there is no constitutional obligation for the state to fund abortions for women who cannot afford them, to make facilities[4] or personnel available for the performance of abortions,[5] or even to provide information about abortions as an option in family planning.[6]

The Court has also chipped away at the right to an abortion by declaring that states may impose strict regulations that inhibit a woman's ability to obtain an abortion as long as these restrictions do not pose an undue burden preventing her from actually obtaining one.[7] It is constitutional, for example, for a state to require a twenty-four-hour waiting period, despite the hardship posed for women who must travel long distances;[8] to compel women to receive information about adoption options, regardless of how carefully they have already considered these alternatives; and to force on women information about the exact stage of fetal development involved in their abortion, even when they have already shown sensitivity to the ethical issues involved in the process.[9] Medical programs now offer less training than ever before to new physicians in abortion techniques, thereby contributing to the dearth of personnel qualified to implement women's right to abortion.[10] In many parts of the country the growing shortage of doctors competent to perform abortions goes hand in hand with an increasing lack of facilities equipped to provide abortions, and mounting harassment, including murder, of those who provide or facilitate abortions.

In the years since *Roe*, therefore, abortion rights have become little more than a meaningless abstraction for millions of women who lack the means to pay for an abortion, are incapable of traveling great distances to obtain one, or are unable to wait a long period before having one. The current conservative climate, highlighted by the 1994 elections, has further exacerbated the way government policies are undermining the constitutional right to an abortion. After the 1994 midterm elections, the Republican majority on the House Appropriations Committee voted to overturn a 1993 law that allowed the federal Medicaid program to pay for abortions for indigent women in cases of pregnancies that endangered their health or were subsequent to rape or incest.[11] As Patricia Schroeder, a long-time House representative in Congress, noted, a woman can no longer count on a majority vote for such fundamental pro-choice positions as legislative guarantees for access to abortion clinics. And as President Bill Clinton found out the hard way, regardless of the legal confirmation of abortion rights, the nomination of a physician for the post of surgeon general who has performed abortions as a regular part of his gynecology and obstetrics practice still fans the fire of public controversy about the morality of abortion. The abortion rights issue also remains central to 1996 electoral politics.

This book attributes responsibility for the enduring conflict over and persistent undermining of abortion rights to the Supreme Court's position on these rights. The Court based women's right to an abortion on the right of privacy, defined as decisional autonomy, or the right of people to make choices about their personal and reproductive life without interference from the state. Prior to *Roe*, the Court had ruled that the right of privacy encompasses such choices as whether to use contraceptives,[12] whom to marry,[13] where to send one's children to school,[14] and what materials to read.[15] In *Roe* the Court expanded this right of privacy to include "a woman's decision whether or not to terminate her pregnancy."[16]

At the same time, however, the Court noted in *Roe* that decisional autonomy in the context of abortion differs from the context of whom to marry or what to read because a woman who is pregnant "cannot be isolated in her privacy."[17] By this, the Court presumably meant that although a person's decision concerning the use of contraceptives obviously affects others, one's sexual partner has the right to consent to those effects by agreeing to a sexual relationship contingent on the use (or disuse) of contraceptives. Similarly, while the choice of whom to marry affects the person who is chosen, one's marriage partner has the right to consent to those effects by agreeing to be married (or not).

While it is clear that one's privacy choices ordinarily affect others, pregnancy is notable for the degree to which it involves another entity: the fetus. As the Court put it, a pregnant woman "carries an embryo and, later, a fetus."[18] Because a pregnant woman's privacy is "no longer sole," it is legitimate for the state to restrict her decision-making autonomy in order to protect the fetus.[19] In an attempt to balance a woman's right to choose what to do with her own body and the state's interest in protecting the fetus from the consequences of that choice, the Court ruled that prior to viability, or before the fetus can survive outside the womb, no state may prohibit a woman from terminating her pregnancy.[20] After viability, however, the state's interest in the well-being of the fetus becomes more compelling than its interest in protecting the woman's right to choose. At that point in fetal development, therefore, it is constitutional for the state to proscribe an abortion to protect the fetus as potential life unless the woman's own life or health is endangered by pregnancy.[21]

What is more, as the Court ruled in cases subsequent to *Roe*, it is constitutional for the federal government and the states to protect the fetus by removing abortion funding from medical policies for indigent women and by restricting the use of public funds and resources to perform abortions.[22] Even if a woman faces permanent damage to her health due to the pregnancy, it is constitutional for the state to withhold funds for an abortion in order to protect the fetus. Respected constitutional law authorities further contend that it would be constitutional for states to protect the fetus by withholding abortion funds even if a woman's life were in danger due to pregnancy.

Although a woman would have a constitutional right to obtain an abortion to save her life, that right would not necessarily include a constitutional right to public funding to obtain one, even if she could not afford to pay for one herself. To date, of course, Congress and the states consistently make abortion funding available when a woman's life is threatened by pregnancy, even while restricting that funding when it is only her health that is at stake. Significantly, therefore, currently a woman's access to public funds to save her life from a medically abnormal pregnancy stems not from a constitutional right to such funds, but only by virtue of particular legislative decrees that are subject to change at any point.

The state's protection of what the fetus is as human life, even to the degree of preferring to let a woman be bedridden and crippled for life as a result of health damage suffered while pregnant rather than fund an abortion, reflects a general tendency in the abortion debate to assume that women's rights to an abortion and to abortion funding stand or fall on the human status of the fetus.[23] Although women have a right to make choices, obviously the effect of those choices cannot include inadvertently killing a human being—hence pro-choice claims that the fetus is not a person and thus an abortion does not kill a person. Were pro-life advocates to challenge this claim successfully, many contend that abortion rights as currently framed would be fatally undermined. As some say, "What is the debate over abortion about, indeed, if not the question of when, precisely, a being assumes a human form."[24] The inordinate attention directed to this question by pro-choice and pro-life advocates, even though they reach opposite answers, affirms the primacy of the humanity of the fetus as the principle that determines women's right to an abortion.[25] The resulting conundrum—as Laurence Tribe terms it, the "clash of absolutes" between the belief of pro-life advocates that the fetus is a person and the belief of pro-choice advocates that it is not—has sustained the conflict between the two camps for over twenty years.[26]

To find a solution to the abortion conundrum and a way to secure for women the right not only to an abortion but also to abortion funding, this book reexamines and reframes the basic principles underlying the abortion issue. It does so by shifting attention from what the fertilized ovum "is," as it develops into a fetus and eventually into a baby, to what the fertilized ovum "does," as it causes preg-

nancy by implanting itself in a woman's body and maintaining that implantation for nine months.[27]

Intrusion Confusion

This reframing shows that the key right involved in abortion is not merely a
woman's right to decisional autonomy to choose what to do with her own body
but also, and more important, her right to bodily integrity and the liberty to consent to what another private party, the fetus, does to her body when it causes
pregnancy. Rather than a woman's freedom from the state, the key issue in abortion then becomes a woman's right to the assistance of the state to stop the fetus
as a private party from intruding on her bodily integrity and liberty without consent. These factors have long been missing in the abortion debate. While many
have noted the coercive dimension of a pregnancy that a woman seeks to terminate, they have failed to identify the actual coercer: the fetus.

When trying to locate the source of coercion, pro-choice advocates sometimes
identify the state as the coercer of an unwanted pregnancy when it either refuses
to legalize a woman's choice to have an abortion or prohibits public funding for
it. This sentiment is expressed in such bumper stickers as "GET THE STATE OUT OF
MY UTERUS." Yet the state is not the one in a woman's uterus, making her pregnant, nor has any state ever passed legislation that requires a woman to become
or remain pregnant or that conscripts a woman's body for pregnancy service.[28]

At other times, both pro-choice and pro-life advocates identify men as the
coercers of an unwanted pregnancy if they impose sexual intercourse on women
without their consent. Yet this recognition also misdirects attention from the primary agent of coercion, the fetus, which actually makes a woman pregnant, to
a secondary agent, the man, when he exposes a woman to the risk that a fertilized ovum will subsequently be conceived and will implant itself.[29] Whether sexual intercourse is consensual or not, no man implants himself in a woman's
uterus to make her pregnant. A woman seeking to terminate her pregnancy does
not wish to expel the coercive imposition of a man on her body. On the contrary,
she seeks to expel the coercive imposition of the one and only agent capable of
making her pregnant: the fetus.[30]

This book shows that founding abortion rights on the conditions under which
sexual intercourse occurs prior to pregnancy misses the point. The fetus is the
direct cause of pregnancy, and if it makes a woman pregnant without her consent, it severely violates her bodily integrity and liberty. Our culture, courts, and
Congress have all ignored the fetus as the agent of pregnancy, with one telling
exception: when the fetus threatens a woman's life. Even in the repressive environment of the late nineteenth century, virtually every state legislative policy on
abortion explicitly guaranteed for women the right to kill the fetus by having an
abortion when it threatened her life. Even the Texas statute at issue in 1973 in

Roe allowed abortions when the fetus, which causes pregnancy, endangered a woman's life.[31]

Self-defense

Abortion as self-defense in this limited context of a life-threatening fetus is the illusive common ground we have all been seeking, because it enjoys broad recognition and support from pro-life and pro-choice advocates alike. Even such a vehemently pro-life proponent as Rep. Henry Hyde implicitly endorses a woman's right to use deadly force to stop a fetus that endangers her life. What is more, he believes that the state should pay for an abortion in those cases. Embedded in his position are two key components of the new way in which this book reframes abortion rights. First, the right to an abortion is founded on what the fetus does to a woman, not what it is; second, the state's job is to assist a woman in her self-defense against a fetus's injury.

This book, therefore, breaks the abortion deadlock over the personhood of the fetus by expanding the common ground already established in law and accepted by pro-choice and pro-life advocates alike. It does so by showing why we must make protections offered by law to pregnant women consistent with those offered to others in our society. The latitude for the use of deadly force in self-defense in our culture and legal system extends beyond threats to one's life alone and includes threats of serious bodily injury and the loss of liberty, as in rape, kidnapping, or slavery. This book shows how we must extend to a pregnant woman this same latitude for self-defense when a fetus intrudes on her bodily integrity and liberty against her will.

Even in a medically normal pregnancy, the fetus massively intrudes on a woman's body and expropriates her liberty. If a woman does not consent to this transformation and use of her body, the fetus's imposition constitutes injuries sufficient to justify the use of deadly force to stop it. While it is not usual to think of pregnancy as an injury, that is exactly how the law already defines it when it is imposed on a woman without her consent. For example, when men or physicians expose women to the risk of pregnancy by means of rape or incompetent sterilization, and a pregnancy follows, the law clearly acknowledges that women have been seriously injured. The term the law uses for such a coerced pregnancy is *wrongful pregnancy*, and the law holds the perpetrators responsible for the injuries entailed by it. This book expands the concept of wrongful pregnancy to include what the fertilized ovum does to a woman when it makes her pregnant without her consent. It is the only entity that can make a woman pregnant, and when it does so without her consent, it imposes the serious injuries of wrongful pregnancy even if the pregnancy in question is medically normal.

As this book shows, to the extent that the law protects the fetus as human life, the law must hold the fetus accountable for what it does.

Having Your Cake and Eating It Too

If the state chooses to include abortion funding in health policy benefits, of course, then the abortion funding issue becomes moot. But once the state removes abortion funding from publicly funded health programs as a means for protecting the fetus as human life, then the state must also hold the fetus accountable for what it does as a human life and stop it when it makes a woman pregnant against her will. Just as the state's protection of born people stops short of allowing them to intrude upon the bodies and liberties of others, whatever might be their need or kinship relations to others, so, too, must the state's protection of fetuses stop short of allowing them to intrude upon the bodies and liberties of women without consent. As this book shows, to the extent that the state treats the fetus as human life, it must not only protect it from harm but also stop it from causing harm to others. Consequently, to the degree that the state stops human life from intruding upon the bodies and liberties of others, the state must stop the fetus from imposing pregnancy upon women without consent.

Currently, the federal government and most states remove abortion funding from health policies, not because they lack the funds to pay for abortions or because abortions are more costly than resources alloted for childbirth. To the contrary, it costs less for the state to fund abortions than to fund childbirth. Congress and state legislatures, therefore, remove abortion funding from health policy benefits as a *means* for protecting the fetus, and it is the legal foundation of this situation that this book investigates in its reframing of the abortion issue.

This book shows how the Court has allowed the state to get away with having its cake and eating it too. Currently, the state removes abortion funding from publicly funded health programs in order to protect the fetus as human life, and then the state fails to hold the fetus accountable for what it does as human life when it harms a woman by imposing nonconsensual pregnancy on her. The Court has failed to consider, however, the obligation of the state to stop the fetus in its capacity as state-protected human life from causing harm to women to the degree that the state protects others from harm imposed by human life.

This book, therefore, reveals new legal grounds for evaluating abortion funding policies that give the state two options. The state can include abortion funding in health policy benefits and fund abortions to the degree that it provides funds for other health needs. Or, if the state removes abortion funding from health policies as a means for protecting the fetus as human life, then the state must also stop the fetus as human life from intruding upon the body and liberty of a woman, much as the state stops other state-protected human beings from intruding upon others. Either way, the bottom line is that when a fetus makes a woman pregnant without consent, not only is she entitled as a private person to terminate that pregnancy, she is entitled to public funding to assist her to obtain an abortion, either as a health benefit provided by the state or as the state's exercise of its police power to stop the fetus as human life from intruding upon the body and liberty of a person without consent.

What is more, this new framing of women's rights not only to abortion but also to abortion funding establishes the right to public funding for all women, not just indigent women. To the degree that the state provides health benefits to everyone, such as in a national health care plan, it must provide abortions to all women. Similarly, to the degree that the state stops human life from harming others, it must stop fetuses from harming any and all women, not just indigent women. Casting the right to abortion funding in these terms both (1) gains the affirmative assistance of the state to provide benefits and protection to all women and (2) removes class and race as factors associated with women's differential abilities to exercise their right to abortion.

When a fetus makes a woman pregnant, it has no conscious intentions, of course, and cannot control its behavior. It is also dependent on the woman for its survival and growth. Yet this is not to say that the fetus is innocent. Although the fetus is innocent of a conscious intent to cause pregnancy, it is the only entity that can do so. Its only innocence resides in its lack of conscious intentions and its inability to control its behavior, similar to a person who is mentally incompetent because of insanity, retardation, or youth. Born people who are mentally incompetent cannot be held legally responsible for the harm they inflict on others. Nor does a person's need for another's body or body parts entitle him or her to take another's body without consent. Our legal system operates to restrict people from intruding on the bodies and liberties of others, whatever their competency to be held legally responsible for their behavior or their need to preserve their own life.

So, too, with fetuses. This book shows that the standards in place for born people reinforce, rather than diminish, women's abortion rights, a point philosopher Frances Kamm also makes from the perspective of moral norms.[32] Pro-life advocates claim only that fetuses should be accorded the same rights as born people, not that they should have more rights. Since no born people have a right to intrude massively on the body of another, neither do preborn people, much less fetuses who may or may not yet be people. Concomitantly, to the degree that the state stops people from harming others by intruding on their bodies and liberty, including the mentally incompetent or those in dire need of the body parts of others, similarly the state must stop fetuses that intrude on women's bodies without consent.

Reasons versus Justification for Abortion

The purpose of this book is not to argue that abortion is an intrinsically valuable experience. As Sarah Weddington, who argued *Roe* before the Supreme Court, said, "I don't hear anyone advertising that a 'neat' thing to do on a sunny

Saturday would be to get an abortion."[33] Yet abortion is necessary for some women at some point in their lives, despite the difficulty many have in reconciling it with deeply held values,[34] and women seek an abortion for various reasons. Pro-life advocates are prone to stress frivolous, unethical, uncaring reasons, such as a desire to go on vacation or to avoid more responsible methods of birth control. Pro-choice advocates understandably stress the more serious, ethical, and caring reasons, such as the wish to be good mothers to children they already have, to advance their educational and employment opportunities, or to postpone motherhood until they are better able to meet its demands.

This book goes a step further than both sides by differentiating the many reasons for seeking abortions from the justification for killing a human life. Even if the fetus were a person, a woman is justified in killing it because of what it does to her when it imposes wrongful pregnancy, whatever might be her personal reasons for doing so. In this way, the distinction between reasons versus justification for stopping the fetus from imposing pregnancy parallels the distinction between reasons and justification for a woman stopping a man from imposing sexual intercourse on her, or for any person stopping another from imposing on one's bodily integrity and liberty. A woman, for example, may not consent to sexual intercourse with a man because of his hair or skin color, his social class background, or the tone of his voice—or because she just does not like him. We can morally classify her reasons as good or bad based on a normative schema, but what justifies her right to use deadly force to stop a man from raping her, according to law, is not the reasons she might have for saying no to his imposition on her, but rather the invasiveness of the imposition itself.

Similarly with nonconsensual pregnancy. We can classify a woman's reason for saying no to a pregnancy relationship with a fetus as good or bad, but that classification does not negate the primacy of her justification to terminate pregnancy based on the invasiveness of the fetus's imposition on her body and liberty. Perhaps a woman learns, for example, that the fetus is chromosomally impaired, or that, based on her preferences, it is the wrong sex. While reasons such as these for terminating pregnancy raise serious moral questions, a woman nevertheless is still justified in obtaining an abortion based on the invasive extent to which any and every fetus intrudes upon her bodily integrity and liberty. Even if the fetus is constructed to be a person, it gains no right to take over a woman's body against her will. And if and when it does, she has a right to say no, whatever might be her reasons for activating that right.

In this sense, by showing how the fetus's status as human life actually justifies the use of deadly force to stop it from imposing wrongful pregnancy, this book uses pro-life premises to get to pro-choice conclusions. Yet this approach does not diminish the nurturing and caretaking activities that women contribute when they consent to be pregnant. Such women may be viewed as *good samaritans*, who donate their bodies and liberty to needy fetuses so that new lives may be born. But we need not, and must not, go the next step, that is, *requiring* women to be good samaritans by giving themselves to fetuses. To the contrary, as philosopher Judith Jarvis Thomson pointed out long ago, the enormous donations required from women to sustain the fetus far exceed those required for moral behavior in any other relationship.[35] As an analogy, she argued that if upon waking one morning, you found yourself attached to a violinist who would die if you severed that connection, you would not be morally obligated to stay physically joined with the violinist, because acquiescence to a need of such magnitude exceeds what one person can morally demand from another. Donald Regan and Frances Kamm confirm that women have a legal and moral right to be a *bad samaritan* by refusing to donate their bodies to a fetus, much as they have a moral and legal right to refuse to donate blood or a kidney to a needy relative.[36]

This book identifies yet a third kind of samaritan involved in the abortion issue. When a fetus imposes wrongful pregnancy on a woman, it does not allow her to decide whether to be either a good or bad samaritan. On the contrary, it puts her in the position of being a *captive samaritan* by taking her body and liberty against her will to serve its own needs. Abortion, therefore, does not stop the giving activity of the woman as a good samaritan, nor does it present women with the option of being a bad samaritan who refuses to donate to a fetus. Rather, abortion stops the fetus from taking the woman's body and liberty without her consent, thereby freeing her from the captive samaritan status imposed by the fetus.

Regardless of a woman's reasons for seeking an abortion, her right to kill a fetus is based on her primary right of privacy to be free from intrusions of her body and liberty by other private parties. This principle would be immediately apparent if a born person were to do to another born person the equivalent of what a fetus does to a woman, even in a medically normal pregnancy. The same principle applies to preborn human life. To the degree that our laws protect the fetus as human life, our laws must also restrict the fetus as human life.

This book breaks the deadlock over abortion rights created by the clash of absolutes over the personhood of the fetus by recentering the abortion issue on a premise of self-defense, which is the common ground that can unite pro-life and pro-choice forces alike. It does so by expanding the latitude for self-defense accorded to pregnant women to match the latitude recognized by law to others in our society. In addition, this book draws on constitutional doctrine to argue that once we reframe abortion rights in terms of women's right to consent to be pregnant, the obligation of the state to provide abortions becomes clear. That is, to the degree that the state takes over the job of self-defense for those under its jurisdiction, it must take over the job of pregnant women's self-defense. To the degree that the state stops born people from intruding on the bodies and liberties of others, it must stop a fetus from intruding on the body and liberty of a woman by imposing a wrongful pregnancy.

Some might suggest that the solution to coercive pregnancy is simply for the woman to wait until the fetus is born, at which point its coercive imposition of pregnancy will cease. This type of reasoning is akin to suggesting that a woman being raped should wait until the rape is over rather than stopping the rapist. Nonconsensual pregnancy, like nonconsensual sexual intercourse, is a condition that must be stopped immediately because both processes severely violate one's bodily integrity and liberty. For a woman who does not consent to pregnancy to have to wait twenty-four hours, much less nine months, before stopping the fetus who is coercing her runs counter to our law's fundamental premises, which guarantee people's right to be free from private aggression.

A consent-to-pregnancy approach to abortion rights opens new doors for assessing the role of the state in relation to abortion funding. Establishing the fetus as the cause of wrongful pregnancy redefines the primary privacy issue at stake in the abortion debate as women's right to be free from the fetus's intrusion as a private party. The key constitutional issue is not a woman's right to freedom from state interference but the state's response to the private injury imposed by a fetus. To the degree that the state assists victims of private injury, so it must assist pregnant women who are undergoing the injuries of wrongful pregnancy.

A consent-to-pregnancy foundation for abortion rights, therefore, shows how state tolerance, permission, and sanction, as well as an explicit preference for the fetus's imposition of wrongful pregnancy, involves the state in the fetus's private aggression. Such state involvement transforms the private action of the fetus into an unconstitutional form of state action that violates due process guarantees. Equally telling, even without any explicit policy that endorses such intrusion, a simple failure by the state to protect women from the fetus's imposition of wrongful pregnancy violates equal protection guarantees as long as the state extends to others protection from intrusions by private parties. The consent-to-pregnancy approach to abortion rights, by providing new grounds for abortion rights, also provides grounds for the right to abortion funding.

Ethical Models

The consent-to-pregnancy justification for abortion requires the expansion of the continuum we use to depict pregnancy. On the positive end of the spectrum is the symbiotic union of mother and child, epitomizing love and bonds of care. On the negative end is the serious legal injury that occurs when pregnancy is imposed on a woman without her consent. While a consent-to-pregnancy approach to abortion may appear to focus too narrowly on the negative end of the pregnancy spectrum, the reality is that abortion terminates, rather than sustains, the pregnancy relationship between a woman and a fetus. The fetus's massively coercive imposition upon a woman can transform the bonds of love into a form of bondage, which justifies the use of deadly force. Rather than dehumanizing the pregnancy experience, therefore, abortion as self-defense does just the opposite.

Justifying abortion rights and funding on a consent-to-pregnancy principle does not require that the fetus be a subhuman entity. Rather, the pro-life premise that the fetus is a person strengthens rather than diminishes women's right to an abortion and also to abortion funding. Using standards already in place in the law, the fetus's status as a person would confer no right to use another person's body without consent since no born person possesses such a right.[37] While the consent-to-pregnancy approach does portray the fetus as an aggressive intruder, thereby stretching the usual understanding of pregnancy, this way of framing abortion rights does not necessitate devaluing the fetus by dehumanizing it. In this sense, it opens the door to greater, not less, respect for the fetus. A woman's right to kill a fetus depends not on the fetus's lack of value because it is not yet born or is not yet a person but rather on a consideration of what it does to a woman by coercively imposing pregnancy.

Basing abortion rights on women's right to consent to what another private entity, the fetus, does to them, stands in stark contrast to the utilitarian lifeboat ethics commonly employed to justify abortions as a way to maximize the greatest good for the greatest number. According to these ethics, the mother and fetus are joined together in a common space and context marked by a scarcity of resources. The mother feels bonds of care toward the fetus and empathy for its needs. Because there are others in the lifeboat, however, such as other children or the mother herself, who needs to acquire education, skills, and employment to be a responsible adult, there is a shortage of resources to go around. In such a scene, to be a good mother, if not a good person, the woman has to make a choice: she has to sacrifice someone in the lifeboat in order to nurture her other children or to pursue her own development as an adult, and the sacrifice turns out to be the fetus rather than a born child or even her own goals. The appeal of the lifeboat ethics is that everyone remains connected to everyone else in bonds of love without any inherent conflict or adversarial relationship, and the only problem is the scarcity of resources, which requires a sacrifice. The fetus ends up going overboard, not because it is an intruder on the woman's body, much less because the woman has frivolous reasons for getting rid of it, but only because the boat lacks room for all.

To sacrifice the fetus while declaring an empathic connection to it, however, does not necessarily establish a more ethical relationship than the norm of self-defense offered by the consent approach. To throw the fetus instead of someone else out of the boat requires ranking the fetus as less valuable than the born people or than the woman's aspirations. For some, of course, embracing such an assumption is easy because the fetus, while valuable, does not rank at the level of a born person. For others, however, defining the fetus as only a quasi person is unethical regardless of any residual feelings of love toward it, particularly if that definition is the rationale for choosing to sacrifice it in lieu of others, much less in lieu of educational and employment goals.

As some would argue, you cannot kill a person, albeit an unborn one, simply to go to law school or get a better job. You cannot claim to be a good mother by killing your unborn child in order to take better care of your born children. Even while the lifeboat model is attractive because it avoids depicting pregnancy in adversarial and conflictual terms, it nevertheless is extraordinarily unpalatable to those who believe the fetus is a person because this model devalues the fetus, getting us right back to Laurence Tribe's conundrum of abortion as a "clash of absolutes."[38] As pro-life advocates point out, people are never justified in making a private choice about how to live their own lives if that choice inadvertently kills another person. Those in the lifeboat must instead draw straws to decide who goes overboard.

Some see this conflict around abortion laws as analogous to the laws that support slavery. As pro-life legal scholar Mary Ann Glendon notes, for much of American history, many states legalized slavery, and in 1857 the Supreme Court in *Dred Scott* reinforced the constitutionality of slavery by holding that Congress lacked the authority to ban slavery in the western territories and that a slave taken to a free state for a short time did not thereby become free, thus allowing slavery to be constitutional.[39] Yet abolitionists claimed that there is a higher law than those passed by any particular state at any particular time, whereby all people have inalienable rights simply by virtue of being human and that they should defy and break particular laws in conflict with these basic, natural rights. We view those who broke the law by helping slaves escape, sheltering them, and refusing to return runaway slaves to their masters as being courageous and morally sound.

Opponents to abortion often feel the same way. The fact that abortion is legal and that the Supreme Court has ruled it to be constitutional is irrelevant to them in comparison to the higher law that recognizes the inherent rights of all people, born or unborn, however old, handicapped, helpless, or defenseless. For them, arguments that the fetus has not yet developed sufficiently to be covered by legal and constitutional guarantees do nothing more than "cheapen life."[40] They see the fetus as just as deserving of legal protection as any born person. For such pro-life advocates, *Roe* only legalized the daily murder of "4,000 innocent human lives" by a "me generation" impervious to the needs or value of others, a terrible "way of constructing reality . . . [based on] lethal logic" akin to euthanasia and eugenics policies. The Court in *Roe* did little more than create a "crisis of moral legitimacy," which has been sustained for over twenty years.[41] For this reason, some pro-life supporters consider it a moral imperative to break the laws that support abortion by trespassing on abortion clinics, harassing women who enter clinics, and even murdering those who provide abortion services, all in the name of protecting the natural rights of unborn people.

Those in the pro-choice camp are forced by the current rationales for abortion rights to dismiss such pro-life claims as emanating from fanatics, if not the insane. Surely it appears that some pro-lifers use arguments about the fetus's personhood merely as an excuse for committing acts of violence, discharging more general feelings of hate and contempt. And courts to date generally have refused to allow those who commit murder on behalf of fetuses to use the defense that the fetus is a person.[42] Yet this book develops another response to pro-life claims by focusing on what the fetus does to a woman, rather than on what it is. While it might seem difficult to have empathy and respect for the fetus while using deadly force to expel it, some self-defense traditions embody exactly that combination.

As Robert Jay Lifton has shown, societies enmeshed in or reeling from such experiences as those produced by Nazi Germany, Hiroshima, and the Vietnam War may experience psychic numbing, a pathological condition in which people become unable to relate to others or even to events happening around them.[43] This malady is caused not by people killing others so much as by their dehumanization of those they kill. The process of dehumanization, not the conflict or killing per se, is what destroys people's ethical and empathic sensibilities. When applied to abortion, this suggests that a self-defense model that justifies abortion rights holds more, not less, promise for meeting ethical standards than a lifeboat model based on the dehumanization of the fetus.

Another advantage of the self-defense approach is that it opens new doors for abortion funding. Standards in place for born people give a woman a personal right of self-defense to stop a fetus from imposing pregnancy on her. More important, to the degree that the state takes on the task of defending people against the private intrusion of others, the state is obligated to expel a fetus on her behalf. This translates into the right to abortion funding. This right has been obscured because of assumptions about women's inherently "giving" nature as good samaritans, what Carol Gilligan and others have observed to be women's tendency to frame issues in relational dimensions of care and responsibility rather than in instrumental terms of rights and boundaries.[44]

The premise that women are naturally good samaritans produces as an alternative only the premise that women who refuse to give are bad samaritans. This view appears in the pro-choice emphasis on securing for women the right to be bad samaritans by refusing to give their bodies to fetuses. People's refusal as bad samaritans to give their bodies, their liberty, or their property to others in need, however, involves the state only if others take people's bodies, liberty, or property without consent. This view has been missing from the abortion debate. The state must stop a fetus from making a woman a captive samaritan by taking her body without her consent, much as the state would stop a born person from so intruding on another.

The Use of Deadly Force

At the core of the abortion issue lie not only women's rights but also issues of life and death. Something is killed in an abortion, and at the very least, that "something" has the potential to become a human being.[45] Pregnancy, therefore, like perhaps no other relationship, encapsulates the way in which the men and women in our culture count on women to care for others. Abortion, by contrast, stands for the reality that we all could be abandoned and rejected, even when we are most in need of help. While pregnancy triggers our deepest sentiments of love and care, abortion triggers our deepest fears of being annihilated by others rather than sustained and nurtured.

One way to guard against the fear of annihilation is to portray women as having been born to be pregnant, as being such natural nurturers that there is no question of abortion. Yet as this book shows, pregnancy means not merely that a woman must give to a fetus, but also that the fetus must take what it needs from a woman's body. While we all want to live, we might not want to do so at the price of intruding on our own mother's body without her consent. Even if our lives depended on it, presumably most of us would feel at least some reluctance to capture our parents, force massive physical intrusion on them, and deprive them of their liberty in ways that violated their natural rights. We need to rephrase the pro-life bumper sticker that asks, "What would you do if your mother had aborted you?" to the more relevant question, "Would you massively intrude on your parents' bodies and imprison them for months without consent to save your life?"

At the very least, raising that question cautions us about assuming that the only alternative to women's ability to give is their right to refuse to give. In addition to giving and refusing, there is the issue of taking. And it is this issue that has been missing from the abortion debate. When a woman seeks an abortion, it is not that she is merely refusing to give her body to the fetus; it is also that she is refusing to have her body and liberty taken without her consent by its imposition of wrongful pregnancy. The issue is the woman's right to be free from a captive status, not merely her right to refuse to give her body to the fetus in the first place.

The history of women's rights is one of freeing women from classes of people viewed by culture and law as having an automatic right of access to women's bodies. Husbands are a case in point since it is only within the last few decades that legal reformists have been successful in freeing women from the assumption that husbands have a right of sexual access to their wives' bodies.[46] Blindness to the way fetuses take women's bodies when women do not consent to pregnancy is a contemporary version of the same old problem. As with assumptions about sexual access, the first step in liberating women from their captive status is to recognize the problem for what it is. This means we must recognize women's victimization as a condition for freeing women from that status.

While some may balk at portraying pregnant women as being victimized by a fetus, it is only after the problem of victimization has been defined that a liberating solution can be forged. Before women could be protected and freed from the injuries of sexual harassment, for example, their victimization had to be articulated. So, too, with wrongful pregnancy imposed by a fetus. Identification of women as the victims of wrongful pregnancy is a necessary first step in the process of freeing them from this situation. Such an approach does not make women passive damsels in distress, waiting for the state to rescue them from the private intrusion of the fetus; but on the contrary, it places women on an equal footing with others in our society whose rights include calling on the state for assistance when private parties intrude without consent on their bodies and liberty.

How to Get from Here to There

In recent years public opinion and public policy on abortion have not moved. From their fixed positions, activists on both sides remain intractable and unable to find common ground. Anna Quindlen, previously a columnist for the *New York Times*, who claims to have written more about abortion than about any other issue, asks, "Where in the world do we go from here?"[47]

This book is a map that shows both where we must go and a new route for getting there. The goal is an ambitious one, to secure for women the right not only to an abortion but also to public funding. The journey is a difficult one, challenging treasured assumptions about pregnancy and core values associated with women's role. It tolerates the possibility that the fetus is a person, thereby conceding rather than contesting the most precious premise of pro-life advocates. It shows that this concession need not undermine women's reproductive rights, as pro-choice proponents may fear, but in fact strengthens them.

Others may balk at this book's contention that consent to sexual intercourse does not imply consent to pregnancy, or they may reject or be offended by the idea that the fetus can be an aggressor and the woman a victim in cases in which she does not consent to pregnancy.[48] Constitutional law scholars, even when sympathetic to pro-choice goals, may resist the claim that the state is obligated to stop a fetus from imposing a wrongful pregnancy. Yet these components of the consent-to-pregnancy approach draw on accepted legal principles and values of the American political tradition. The only novelty is to apply them to the context of pregnancy as a means for securing for women not only the right to an abortion but also the right to public funding.

It has been a mistake to view the personhood status of the fetus as the key issue in the debate. Such an assumption produces a fetus-centered approach to abortion rights, which examines only what the fetus is, not what the fetus does. This book moves from a fetus-centered approach to a woman-centered approach. It is the woman who is pregnant, not the fetus. It is what the fetus does to a woman that justifies her right to terminate that condition, as well as the state's obligation to assist her to the degree that it provides protection to others against nonconsensual intrusion by private parties.

It is how we think about pregnancy, therefore, not merely how we think about the fetus, that justifies abortion. As Kristin Luker observed, many pro-choice advocates feel empathy and respect for the fetus they abort, even while believ-

ing adamantly that they have a right to abortion.[49] This book illuminates why
women are justified in aborting a fetus based on what the fetus does. By so doing,
this book answers the position taken by Justices Rehnquist's and Scalia's criticism that the current constitutional basis for the right to an abortion fails to
address the central issue: the destruction of the fetus. As they note in their dissent in *Casey*,

> One cannot ignore the fact that a woman is not isolated in her pregnancy, and that
> the decision to abort necessarily involves the destruction of a fetus. . . . To look "at
> the act which is assertedly the subject of a liberty interest in isolation from its effect
> upon other people [is] like inquiring whether there is a liberty interest in firing a
> gun where the case at hand happens to involve its discharge into another person's
> body."[50]

The liberty interest at stake in abortion, however, resides not in a woman's
right to fire a gun into another's body but rather in her right to be free from intrusion. That right includes her right to fire a gun in self-defense into the body of a
person who is massively intruding on her own body and liberty. What is more,
the issue includes the obligation of the state to fire that gun on her behalf.

The question is now no longer, "Where do we go from here?" but, "How do
we get there?" This book shows how to reach new destinations which not only
strengthen women's right to an abortion but also secure public access to it. It
does so by employing what some will label as typically masculine concepts, such
as autonomy, the right to be let alone, and the role of the state as a provider of
law and order. It establishes that the fundamental liberty at issue in abortion
debate is a woman's right to consent to pregnancy. As a corollary, to the degree
that the state stops the wrongful acts of private parties, the state must stop a fetus
which violates a woman's body and deprives her of her liberty. Such a reframing, while not the only way to portray the abortion issue, is nonetheless well
suited to the masculine biases encoded in law. Whereas some seek to change
those legal principles and processes, this book accepts them as givens in order to
find a more immediate route to abortion funding.

From Legal Formalism to Policy Outcome

For some, of course, the utility of this new framing may be only as a heuristic
device, a formalistic fashioning of legal principles which, while discovering a
new way to think about abortion rights, nevertheless must be distinguished from
what is "'true' or 'real' about pregnancy."[51] Yet this book's proposal for getting
from here to there is as practical as it is theoretical. Part of what is "real and true"
about pregnancy is that the current legal formalisms developed by the Court to
establish women's constitutional right to an abortion have meant, at a practical

level, that a woman suffering from even a health-crippling pregnancy has no constitutional right to public funds to terminate that pregnancy, and most likely no constitutional right to state assistance even if she is threatened with death. Far from detached from reality, this book addresses that reality, and its formalism derives from and is a response to the formalism already established and used by the Court to determine abortion rights. Some locate that formalism in the Court's affirmation of assigning to potential life a protected legal status, which treats the fetus as if it were a distinct entity with interests of its own. Rather than perpetuate debate over this issue, however, this book instead requires that we answer key questions raised by the Court's formalistic identification of the welfare of the fetus as a legitimate state interest.

How can the state, for example, choose to implement its protection of pre-born potential life by extracting abortion funding from health policies, even in situations where the fetus causes a medically abnormal pregnancy threatening to cripple a woman for life, when the state's protection of born life never entails such a withdrawal of public funds allowing the infliction of bodily injuries upon others, much less crippling ones? In general, how can the state justify using its police power to stop state-protected born people from taking or damaging others' property, much less from imposing bodily injuries, on the one hand, but on the other hand, refuse to stop state-protected preborn life from massively intruding upon a woman's body and liberty for a protracted period of nine months, much less threaten her with permanent damage to her health?

Self-defense versus Self-sacrifice

The answers, of course, derive from our culture as reflected in law, which attribute self-defense norms as appropriate to men and self-sacrifice norms to women. When a man's home, family, much less his body is intruded upon, our laws and our culture do not expect his response to be self-sacrifice—that is, giving his home, his family, or his body to benefit the intruder. To the contrary, manly self-defense norms affirm his right not only to refuse to give himself to an intruder but also to use deadly force to stop that intruder from taking his house, family, or body without consent. What is more, the primary purpose of the state as envisioned by founders of the American nation is to stop intruders on behalf of those they threaten. Rather than freedom from the state, therefore, the public analog of a man's personal right of self-defense is his right to state assistance to help him defend himself against those who intrude upon him.

The opposite is true for women, however, who are most often associated in our culture and our laws with self-sacrifice and giving norms rather than self-defense norms. A case in point is abortion. It is assumed that to be a mother, if not a woman, entails sacrificing and giving yourself to others, including giving oneself to a fetus when pregnant. Consequently, when women seek to terminate pregnancy, abortion is viewed as the stopping of a woman's giving activity to a fetus—that is, as a woman's refusal to sacrifice herself for the benefit of potential life.

This book, however, asks us to imagine the policy consequences that accrue when we stretch the way we depict pregnancy to include recognition of how the fetus takes a woman's body, if it makes her pregnant without consent. Abortion, accordingly, then becomes the way a woman stops the taking of her body and liberty by a fetus. When we expand in this way how we view pregnancy, we see abortion as the only means possible for defending a woman's body and liberty against a fetus which massively intrudes upon her without consent. Even more significant, to the degree that the state protects the fetus as potential life, it becomes incumbent upon the state to stop the fetus from so intruding upon the bodily integrity and liberty of a woman. Rather than freedom from the state, the key constitutional issue becomes women's right to state assistance to help her defend herself against those who intrude upon her, including state-protected fetuses.

This book's discovery of new implications embedded in the legal formalisms already characterizing the abortion debate, therefore, connects legal theory with powerful policy outcomes. By moving from choice to consent, this book reframes abortion rights in terms of both a woman's right to choose what to do with her own body and a woman's right to consent to what another entity, the fetus, does to her body when it makes her pregnant, as well as her right to state assistance to stop a fetus on her behalf. Whether this view "will play in Peoria," as the saying goes, remains to be seen. Yet before rejecting the promise of this perspective or marginalizing it as a theoretically-interesting-but-practically-useless heuristic device, let us first explore how its tolerance of pro-life premises affirming the personhood of the fetus in combination with a strengthening of pro-choice goals resolves the "clash of absolutes" identified by Laurence Tribe. Let us, therefore, think about pregnancy in new ways, as the first step down a road that breaks the abortion deadlock by moving from choice to consent, thereby achieving critical policy objectives for women seeking an abortion, as well as abortion funding.

2

Immaculate Pregnancy

In *Roe v. Wade* the Supreme Court in its majority opinion noted the American Bar Association's definition of abortion as the "termination of human pregnancy with an intention other than to produce a live birth or to remove a dead fetus."[1] In the years since *Roe*, it has been common to focus on the last part of this definition, which concerns the fetus. Debate has centered on whether the fetus is a person and the extent to which its personhood affects the right of a woman to remove it "with an intention other than to produce a live birth." Insufficient attention has been paid to the first part of this definition, which refers to the condition of pregnancy that abortion terminates. Despite the many cases in which the Court has considered the abortion issue, it has yet to evaluate pregnancy in a formal, systematic, or complete way from either a medical or a legal perspective.

In *Roe*, the Court devoted seventeen pages to exploring the legal status of the "fetus and the history of attitudes and practices regarding abortion since ancient times in Greece."[2] The result was an impressive journey, encompassing the attitudes of Hippocrates and Aristotle, English common law, and the American medical profession, to mention only a few. A comparable history of medical, religious, and philosophical opinions about pregnancy, however, was conspicuously absent.[3]

The Court concluded in *Roe* that the fetus cannot be considered a person entitled to constitutional protection under the Fourteenth Amendment primarily because it has not yet been born, and the Fourteenth Amendment explicitly refers to "born" people.[4] As the Court stated,

> The Constitution does not define "person" in so many words. Section 1 of the Fourteenth Amendment . . . in defining "citizens," speaks of "persons born or naturalized in the United States." The word [person] also appears both in the Due Process Clause and in the Equal Protection Clause. "Person" is used in other places in the Constitution. . . . But in nearly all these instances, the use of the word is such that it has application only postnatally. None indicates, with any assurance, that it has any possible prenatal application. . . . All this, together with our observation that throughout the major portion of the 19th century prevailing legal abortion practices were far freer than they are today, persuades us that the word "person," as used in the Fourteenth Amendment, does not include the unborn.[5]

However, the Court refused to rule on the more general question of when life begins:

> We [the Court] need not resolve the difficult question of when life begins. When those trained in the respective disciplines of medicine, philosophy, and theology are unable to arrive at any consensus, the judiciary, at this point in the development of man's knowledge, is not in a position to speculate as to the answer.[6]

Instead of analyzing precisely what constitutes the condition of pregnancy, the Court referred to this condition with only the most loosely constructed metaphors—so loose and so culturally derived, in fact, that the Court's terms replicate what many of my undergraduate students say when first asked to define pregnancy. Both the students' and the Court's definitions of pregnancy, like most other cultural depictions of it, fit into five categories: women as vessels, fetal development, caused by sex, burdensome condition, and value to society. The Court's use of these cultural metaphors has transformed them into correlative legal doctrines that have had devastating consequences on guaranteeing abortion rights.

Women as Vessels

One of the most common cultural depictions of pregnancy is in terms of women as vessels. The basic idea underlying this metaphor is that women are containers for fetuses and that women carry fetuses around when they are pregnant. As one student put it, "Pregnancy is having a living person inside of you." The power of this cultural metaphor for limiting women's rights appears from the very outset of the Court's 1973 reasoning about the constitutionality of abortion rights in *Roe*. In that case, where the Court expanded the right to privacy—otherwise defined as the right of decisional autonomy, or the right to make choices about private matters without interference from the state—to include the right to terminate a pregnancy, the Court stated, when a woman is pregnant, she "carries an embryo and, later, a fetus."[7] The Court's use of this metaphor for pregnancy is cited again and again throughout subsequent abortion rulings. In 1977 in *Beal v. Doe*, an abortion-funding case, the Court quoted the district court's distinction between "indigent women who choose to carry their pregnancies to birth and indigent women who choose to terminate their pregnancies by abortion."[8] Later in the case, the Court noted that a pregnant woman "normally will either have an abortion or carry her child [to] full term."[9]

The women-as-vessels metaphor also figures prominently throughout the 1992 *Planned Parenthood v. Casey* decision in a variety of contexts. When affirming the right to an abortion, the Court noted,

If indeed the woman's interest in deciding whether to bear and beget a child had not been recognized as in *Roe*, the State might as readily restrict a woman's right to choose to carry a pregnancy to term as to terminate it, to further asserted state interests in population control, or eugenics, for example.[10]

When restating the state's legitimate interest in the fetus, the Court referred to the fetus as the "potential life within her [the pregnant woman]."[11]

Similarly, when upholding regulations that require a woman to be informed about pregnancy assistance and the status of the fetus before having an abortion, the Court stated that these are "reasonable" measures "to insure an informed choice" of a woman deciding whether "to carry the [her] pregnancy to full term."[12] When assessing the relative impact on men and women of abortion restrictions, the Court noted, "[i]t is an inescapable biological fact that state regulation with respect to the child a woman is carrying will have a far greater impact on the mother's liberty than on the father's."[13] And when striking down the spousal notification regulation, the Court remarked that the "husband's interest in the life of the child his wife is carrying does not permit the State to empower him with this troubling degree of authority over his wife."[14] Similarly, when Justice Stevens questioned the majority ruling that upheld a [twenty-four hour waiting period] before obtaining an abortion, he noted that a "woman who decides to terminate her pregnancy is entitled to the same respect as a woman who decides to carry the fetus to term."[15]

These are only a few examples of the Court's pervasive and persistent reliance over the nineteen years spanning *Roe* and *Casey* on the cultural definition of pregnant women as vessels. The stunning legal consequence of the Court's codification of this metaphor for pregnancy has been a legal doctrine that restricts the very right of privacy established for women in *Roe*. Specifically, the Court concluded that because a woman carries a fetus when she is pregnant, her privacy is no longer "sole,"[16] meaning that she can no longer be viewed as an individual separated from others but rather as a person in a relationship with another private party, a potential life. Hence, a pregnant woman's right to choose what to do with her own body is inherently linked to the consequences of that choice for the fetus.

As the Court put it in *Roe*, because a pregnant woman "carries [potential life] within her,"[17] she "cannot be isolated in her privacy" and her "privacy is no longer sole."[18] A pregnant woman's privacy, is, therefore, "inherently different" from other examples of privacy, such as "marital intimacy, or bedroom possession of obscene material, or marriage, or procreation, or education," all of which refer to the privacy rights of an autonomous individual rather than to a relationship between individuals.[19] As the Court states, because a pregnant woman carries a fetus, "any right of privacy she possesses must be measured accordingly."[20] In other words, the state's interest in protecting a pregnant's woman's right of privacy to make choices about her own body must be limited by, or balanced against, the state's interest in protecting the fetus that she carries. When figuring out how to balance these two interests, the Court turned to yet another cultural metaphor for pregnancy: fetal development.

Fetal Development

Another common way in which our culture depicts pregnancy is as a time period marked and calibrated by the developmental stages of fetal growth, which eventually culminate in a baby's birth. As one student expressed this idea, pregnancy is a "joyous nine-month incubation period that a woman must go through in order for a child to be born." So, too, does this definition of pregnancy figure prominently in Supreme Court reasoning in the abortion debate. It was bedrock to the *Roe* decision and has underpinned the Court's assessment of women's abortion rights ever since.

In *Roe*, for example, the Court referred to the "developing young"[21] a woman carries when pregnant, and as Justice Blackmun said in the majority opinion, "[I]t is reasonable and appropriate for a State to decide that at some point in time in [fetal development] another interest, that of the health of the mother or that of the potential life becomes significantly involved."[22] The legal consequence of the Court's adoption of this definition of pregnancy is the use of the trimester system and viability for determining abortion rights. The trimester system divides up the nine-month period of pregnancy into three equal periods that correspond to the major phases of fetal development.[23] Viability is the point at which the fetus is "potentially able to live outside the mother's womb, albeit with artificial aid."[24] At the fetal stage of viability, the Court has decided, the balance between the state's interest in protecting potential life and its interest in protecting a woman's right of privacy to choose an abortion tips in favor of the fetus.[25]

In *Roe*, the Court ruled that the Texas statute at issue violated the due process clause of the Fourteenth Amendment because it made abortion a criminal act "without regard to pregnancy stage."[26]

> For the stage prior to approximately the end of the first trimester, the abortion decision and its effectuation must be left to the medical judgment of the pregnant woman's attending physician . . . [f]or the stage subsequent to approximately the end of the first trimester, the State . . . may . . . regulate the abortion procedure in ways that are reasonably related to maternal health . . . [and] [f]or the stage subsequent to viability, the State in promoting its interest in the potentiality of human life may . . . regulate, and even proscribe, abortion except where it is necessary, in appropriate medical judgment, for the preservation of the life or health of the mother.[27]

Quoting an earlier case, Chief Justice Rehnquist in *Webster* noted that:

> For both logical and biological reasons, we indicated in [Roe] that the State's
> interest in the potential life of the fetus reaches the compelling point at the stage
> of viability. Hence, prior to viability, the State may not seek to further this inter-
> est by directly restricting a woman's decision whether or not to terminate her
> pregnancy.[28]

Chief Justice Rehnquist went on to say that after viability the state's interest in
protecting potential human life becomes compelling and that the state may then
restrict a woman's decision to terminate her pregnancy.[29]

The Court carried this clear idea of fetal development as a measure or marker
of pregnancy to its 1992 *Casey* decision, where it noted that *Roe* established "that
the Constitution protects a woman's right to terminate her pregnancy in its early
stages"[30] and that women have a constitutional right "to choose to have an abortion before viability and to obtain it without undue interference from the State."
"Before viability, the State's interests are not strong enough to support a prohibition of abortion or the imposition of a substantial obstacle to the woman's
effective right to elect the procedure."[31] The Court at the same time confirmed
the primacy of fetal development as a definition of pregnancy by ruling that the
state has the "power to restrict abortions after fetal viability."[32]

In *Casey*, the Court noted that the original trimester framework established
in *Roe* had to be modified, both because of "advances in maternal health care,"
which "allow for abortions safe to the mother later in pregnancy than was true
in 1973," and because of "advances in neonatal care," which have "advanced viability to a point somewhat earlier."[33] Yet the Court affirmed that the cutoff point
of viability itself was still sound[34]:

> *Roe*'s central holding . . . [is] that viability marks the earliest point at which the
> State's interest in fetal life is constitutionally adequate to justify a legislative ban
> on nontherapeutic abortions. The soundness or unsoundness of that constitutional
> judgment in no sense turns on whether viability occurs at approximately 28 weeks,
> as was usual at the time of *Roe*, at 23 to 24 weeks, as it sometimes does today, or at
> some moment even slightly earlier in pregnancy, as it may if fetal respiratory
> capacity can somehow be enhanced in the future. *Whenever it may occur, the
> attainment of viability may continue to serve as the critical fact.*[35]

In Justice Blackmun's words, "[T]he viability standard takes account of the
undeniable fact that as the fetus evolves into its postnatal form, and as it loses
its dependence on the uterine environment, the State's interest in the fetus'
potential human life . . . becomes compelling."[36] The pregnant woman's liberty
is restricted, therefore, not because of what is happening to her body but because
of what is happening to the fetus's body at particular stages of its development.
If the fetus has not developed to the point at which it can survive outside her
womb, she is allowed to terminate her pregnancy. Once the fetus has developed
to that point, however, she cannot terminate her pregnancy.

The Court affirmed this reasoning in *Casey* by noting that

> woman's liberty is not so unlimited . . . that from the outset the State cannot show its concern for the life of the unborn, and at a later point in fetal development the State's interest in life has sufficient force so that the right of the woman to terminate the pregnancy can be restricted."[37]

The Court clarified the meaning of viability, stating that

> the concept of viability . . . is the time at which there is a realistic possibility of maintaining and nourishing a life outside the womb, so that the independent existence of the second life can in reason and all fairness be the object of state protection that now overrides the rights of the woman [to choose to terminate her pregnancy by means of an abortion].[38]

Pregnancy depicted in terms of fetal development was thus transformed by the Court into the controversial trimester system and viability standard, according to which the stage of the fetus's development defines the parameters of the woman's liberty and privacy. Yet the Court was also willing to consider contexts of pregnancy in which the general rules laid down in *Roe* must be modified. In so doing, the Court invoked yet another representation of pregnancy as a condition caused by sex.

Sex Causes Pregnancy

The association of sex with pregnancy is virtually a cultural icon. In the inimitable words of one student, "Pregnancy is what happens to a woman when she has sex with a man and his sperm fertilizes her egg." So, too, did the Supreme Court adopt the idea as early as *Roe* that sexual intercourse is the cause of pregnancy. Accordingly, a key criterion in determining a woman's right to terminate her pregnancy is whether she consented to the sexual intercourse assumed to have caused it. If she did not consent to sexual intercourse, as in rape or incest, then in the eyes of the law she is given greater latitude for an abortion, such as access to public funding; but if she did consent to sexual intercourse, she is given less, such as the withdrawal of public funds for an abortion.

Justice Blackmun in *Roe*, for example, cited the American Bar Association's 1972 Uniform Abortion Act, which states that an abortion may be performed after 20 weeks "if the physician has reasonable cause to believe . . . that the pregnancy resulted from rape or incest, or illicit intercourse with a girl under the age of 16 years."[39] His uncritical acceptance that sex causes pregnancy illustrates not only how the law has formalized such cultural assumptions but also how the Supreme Court has embedded them into its reasoning on abortion. In *Doe v.*

Bolton, a 1973 companion case to *Roe*, Chief Justice Burger referred to "nonconsensual pregnancies" as "those resulting from rape and incest."[40] According to the Court in a later case, the Georgia statutes at issue in *Bolton* were "somewhat less onerous" because they allowed abortions for women "in which the pregnancy was the result of rape."[41] The problem with the Court's assumption that nonconsensual pregnancies result from nonconsensual sexual intercourse is that it implies the obverse, namely, that consensual pregnancies result from consensual sex.

In one form or another, the Court has maintained the view for over nineteen years that sex causes pregnancy, or more specifically, that a man's impregnation of a woman causes her pregnant condition. In 1980, in *Harris v. McRae*, for example, Justice Marshall, in his dissent from the Court's ruling that it is constitutional to deny public funds to indigent women who seek abortions, expressed the equation of sex with pregnancy when he stated that the "Hyde Amendment denies funding for the majority of women whose pregnancies have been caused by rape or incest."[42] Similarly, in the 1983 case of *Simopoulous v. Virginia*, Justice Stewart in dissent noted that under Virginia law, in-hospital abortions were "unlawful" unless the "pregnancy was the product of rape or incest."[43]

This supposition that sex causes pregnancy is perhaps the most familiar of all cultural assumptions about what constitutes the condition of pregnancy. And the Supreme Court has consistently relied on it, never questioning its validity as a basis for state-level and federal legislation. In *Casey*, for example, though the Court struck down a Pennsylvania regulation that requires a woman to notify her spouse that she intends to obtain an abortion, it took no exception to the language of the statute where the assumption that sex causes pregnancy was embedded:

> Section 3209 of Pennsylvania's abortion law provides [that] no physician shall perform an abortion on a married woman without receiving a signed statement from the woman that she has notified her spouse that she is about to undergo an abortion. The woman has the option of providing an alternative signed statement certifying that *her husband is not the man who impregnated her* . . . [or] that the *pregnancy is the result of spousal sexual assault* which she has reported.[44]

The dissenting justices who believed that the spousal notification in *Casey* should be upheld specifically referred to the language of the Pennsylvania statute and, by so doing, reasserted the principle that sex causes pregnancy. Chief Justice Rehnquist, for example, noted that a woman did not need to expose herself to possible violence from her spouse since the statute specified that "a woman need not notify her husband if the pregnancy is the result of a reported sexual assault."[45]

The Court has allowed the cultural presumption that sex causes pregnancy to become state policy conditioning a woman's right to terminate her pregnancy by the context of the sexual intercourse that preceded it. Even highly restrictive measures that prohibit state funding of abortions, for example, assume that sex is the cause of pregnancy by recognizing exceptions for pregnancies subsequent to nonconsensual sexual intercourse, such as rape and incest. As the Court noted in *Harris*, with the passage of the Hyde Amendment in 1976, Congress prohibited[46] "the use of any federal funds to reimburse the cost of abortions under the Medicaid program except under certain specified circumstances,"[47] one of which was when women are the "victims of rape or incest."[48]

The Court's acceptance of the idea that sex causes pregnancy focuses attention on the consensual nature of the sexual relationship between a woman and a man, not on the consensual nature of the pregnancy relationship between a woman and a fetus. Once a woman had consented to a sexual relationship with a man, therefore, even though the Court respectfully noted the extreme burdens entailed by pregnancy, it had no way to attribute those burdens to the fetus as the cause of pregnancy. As a result, in the context of consensual sex, in the Court's view, it is as if the burdens of pregnancy passively come out of nowhere, attributable to no private party.

Burdensome Condition

The way in which our culture depicts pregnancy as a burdensome condition ranges from mere inconvenience to major sacrifice. As one student stated, "Pregnancy is a strain for a female who must go through the pain and agony of the nine-month process." From its first review in 1973 of a woman's constitutional right to an abortion, the Supreme Court has also incorporated into law views of pregnancy as a burdensome condition for a woman. In *Roe* these burdens were recognized as "the specific and direct medical harm medically diagnosable even in early pregnancy," which "may be involved" in pregnancy.[49] In *Casey*, the Court recognized that pregnancy entails "anxieties," "physical constraints," "intimate and personal . . . suffering," and "pain," which only the pregnant woman bears.[50] "These sacrifices," the Court stated, "have from the beginning of the human race been endured by woman with a pride that ennobles her in the eyes of others."[51] The Court views these burdens of pregnancy, no matter how dramatically depicted, as *normal* as long as they do not threaten a woman's health or life. From the Court's vantage point, the burdens experienced while pregnant can be sufficiently taxing to ennoble the women involved, but they never constitute medical harm unless they pose serious, if not permanent, damage to her health or become life threatening. As Justice Stevens stated in his dissenting opinion in *Harris*, "Surely the government may properly presume that no [medical] harm will ensue from normal childbirth."[52]

In the 1976 case of *General Electric v. Gilbert*, when ruling on whether prohibitions against sex discrimination, as defined by Title VII of the Civil Rights

Act, mandated medical benefits for pregnancy in a private insurance program, the Court noted that the district court had defined "normal" pregnancy as "not necessarily either a 'disease' or an 'accident'"[53] and had regarded normal pregnancy as "disabling" only for a period of six to eight weeks, "which time includes the period from labor and delivery, or slightly before."[54] The district court did view as disabling approximately 10 percent of pregnancies terminated by miscarriage and another 10 percent "complicated by diseases which may lead to additional disability."[55] By so isolating only specific contexts of pregnancy to be disabling, courts in effect are defining all other contexts of pregnancy as normal or as nonintrusive in character.

The Court in *Gilbert* also quoted an opinion expressed in a letter by the general counsel of the Equal Employment Opportunity Commission that distinguishes pregnancy from other forms of illness or injury because "maternity is a temporary disability unique to the female sex and more or less to be anticipated during the working life of most women employees."[56] Recognition by the Court that pregnancy is a burdensome condition need not, therefore, entail recognition that the burdens of pregnancy are abnormal. The medical burdens of pregnancy that pose emergencies that threaten to kill a woman or permanently impair her health are viewed by the Court as abnormal. All other burdens imposed by pregnancy are viewed by the Court as the *normal* accompaniments of pregnancy and hence as nonproblematic since they do not threaten a woman's life or health.

The Court has used the definition of pregnancy as a burdensome condition to develop the notion of therapeutic and nontherapeutic abortions. If a woman is experiencing only the normal burdens of pregnancy—defined as anything and everything short of a threat to her life or permanent injury to her health—her abortion is considered medically "unnecessary" and therefore "nontherapeutic." Even while recognizing in *Casey* that these normal burdens of pregnancy entail sacrifice and suffering,[57] the Court views the means that would end this suffering as unnecessary. Not until a pregnant woman's suffering reaches life-threatening proportions does the Court view an abortion as medically necessary and concomitantly as therapeutic. As the Court said in *Beal*, "treatment for therapeutic abortions" constitutes "necessary medical services," but treatment for "elective abortions" does not.[58]

Many cultural assumptions underpin the notion that pregnancy is a normal condition, no matter how burdensome. Of all of them, perhaps none is more fundamental than the view that pregnancy is a value to society, a concept adopted by courts in connection with abortion rights.

Value to Society

Whatever the burdens of pregnancy, no one would be alive if women did not assume them. Pregnancy, therefore, has serious value for all, which for some is expressed in spiritual or religious terms. Students expressing the latter depict pregnancy as a "gift from God" or "the way society reproduces, a role given to women as a link to the growth of society." So, too, does the Court adopt cultural valuations of pregnancy as necessary for the very existence of society. This definition of pregnancy was stated outright in *Roe* when Justice Blackmun, writing for the majority, referred to the fact that pregnancy is something the Court has to deal with because it "often comes" to women, and, significantly, it must come "if man is to survive."[59]

Recognition by the Court of how the nation's very existence depends on women's reproductive labor in the form of pregnancy and childbirth dates back centuries. In a classic late-nineteenth-century case, *Minor v. Happersett*, the Court noted that without a people, there would be no nation, and the only two ways to add new citizens to a nation were "first, by birth, and second, by naturalization."[60] The value of pregnancy and childbirth goes to the very heart of the survival of society and the political community that constitutes the United States. Clearly, if women were not pregnant and did not bear children, there would be no more people and, consequently, no more nation.

The use by the Court of the cultural definition of pregnancy as a value to society is the foundation for its construction of a doctrine that favors childbirth. It is reasonable, the Court maintained in *Beal* and *Maher v. Roe* in 1977, for a state "to further this unquestionably strong and legitimate interest in encouraging normal childbirth,"[61] which is "an interest honored over the centuries."[62] Pregnancy as a value to society, therefore, results in the legal doctrine of a preference for childbirth, which means that the state may withhold funds for abortions even while providing funds for childbirth.

As the Court stated in *Maher*, *Roe* "implies no limitation on the authority of a State to make a value judgment favoring childbirth over abortion, and to implement that judgment by the allocation of public funds."[63] A regulation that fails to fund abortions for indigent women even while funding childbirth is therefore constitutional because it is "rationally related to and furthers its [the state's] 'strong and legitimate interest in encouraging normal childbirth.'"[64]

Policy Consequences of Cultural Codification

Whereas the public, including pro-life and pro-choice advocates alike, and the Court base their stance on abortion in terms of one or more of these five cultural metaphors for pregnancy, the Court alone has had the judicial power to transform them into a powerful doctrinal edifice that has devastating policy consequences, as table 2.1 summarizes. The cultural depiction of women as vessels is the basis for the Court's legal doctrine that a pregnant woman's privacy is not sole. The policy consequence is that the Court then balances her right to privacy against the value of potential life without ever considering why

Table 2.1 Policy Consequences of the Court's Codification of Culture

Cultural Assumptions about Pregnancy	Legal Doctrines	Policy Consequences
Women as vessels	Pregnant woman's "privacy is not sole"	Privacy rights of pregnant woman balanced against value of potential life
Fetal development	Viability as the stage of fetal development having legal significance	Viability of fetus as point where legal protection switches from woman's right of privacy to state's protection of potential life
Sex causes pregnancy	Rape and incest exceptions to abortion restriction	Abortions allowed and/or funded when preceded by rape or incest
Burdensome condition	Normal/abnormal pregnancies; concomitant nontherapeutic/therapeutic abortions	State funding provided only for therapeutic abortions terminating abnormal pregnancies
Value to society	Preference for childbirth	It is constitutional for state medical benefits to cover pregnancy and childbirth but not abortions

SOURCE: Eileen McDonagh, "Abortion Rights Alchemy and the U.S. Supreme Court," *Social Politics*, 1:2 (Summer 1994), pp. 130–156.

her privacy is transformed from one that is sole to one that is not by a pregnancy-causing fetus.

The cultural representation of pregnancy in terms of stages of fetal development has become the foundation of the Court's viability doctrine. The policy consequence of this doctrine is that viability is the point in fetal development at which the state's legal protection of a woman's right of privacy switches to the state's protection of potential life, albeit without any consideration of what it is that the fetus does to a woman when it causes pregnancy in her body. The cultural assumption that sex causes pregnancy was never questioned by the Court when reviewing rape and incest exceptions to restrictions on abortion funding. The policy consequence is the inference that consent to sex implies consent to pregnancy, thereby undercutting claims to abortion funding when pregnancy is subsequent to consensual sex.

Cultural understandings of pregnancy as a burdensome condition have been transformed by the Court into a legal doctrine that categorizes pregnancies as entailing medically normal and medically abnormal burdens. The policy consequence of this ranking is to produce a vocabulary that obscures the unacceptable imposition of the burdens involved in all coerced pregnancies, whether medically normal or not. Finally, the Court transformed the cultural depiction of pregnancy as a value to society into its preference for childbirth doctrine. The devastating policy consequence of this doctrine is the Court's ruling that it is constitutional for state medical benefits to cover pregnancy and childbirth but not abortion, even abortions necessary to preserve the health of the woman.

It is not that these five metaphors of pregnancy are completely wrong and irrelevant, of course. Clearly when women are pregnant, they do carry a fetus, it develops over a nine-month period, sexual intercourse usually (though not always) precedes pregnancy, pregnancy poses burdens ranging from minimum to maximum, and pregnancy generally has a value to society. Yet these five metaphors omit the most significant dimension of pregnancy for women's legal rights: the fertilized ovum as the cause of pregnancy.

The Fertilized Ovum

Roe has been criticized on many grounds, but the most serious one has been virtually ignored: the Court's failure to use formal legal or medical definitions of pregnancy that identify the fertilized ovum as its cause. According to a standard law dictionary, pregnancy is the "condition *resulting from the fertilized ovum . . .* beginning at the moment of conception and terminating with delivery of the child."[65] The key aspect of this definition is that pregnancy is a condition in a woman's body that results from something else—in this case, the fertilized ovum throughout its developmental stages.

Introducing this definition of pregnancy into the abortion debate recasts immediately the issue of women's rights. Rather than a woman's fundamental right to *decisional autonomy*, that is, a right to choose what to do with her own body, the fundamental right invoked is a woman's right to *bodily integrity* and *liberty*, that is, her right to consent to what is done to her body by another entity, the fertilized ovum. When a woman is pregnant, it is not merely that she "carries" the fetus or that it "grows" and "develops" while she carries it or that society "values" her "carrying" of it. To the contrary, pregnancy refers to a condition in the woman's body, not a condition in the fetus's body. It is the woman who is pregnant, not the fetus, and what makes a woman pregnant is the presence and effect on her body of the fetus. As long as the fetus is in her body and affecting it, she remains pregnant. The only way to terminate her pregnant condition is to terminate the presence and influence of the fetus.

For this reason, the key issue in pregnancy is not what the fetus is in terms of its personhood status but rather what a fetus does to a woman when it makes her pregnant and maintains this condition in her body. Pregnancy, in short, is not merely a condition that happens to a woman, which she must endure, but a condition brought about by another entity—the fertilized ovum—that affects her.

Her body is pregnant because the fertilized ovum implants itself in her body and maintains that implantation over a protracted period of nine months.[66]

The Court's failure to identify the fertilized ovum as the cause of a woman's pregnancy results in its notion of *immaculate pregnancy*, that is, the view that pregnancy is a condition that simply "comes to a woman," without any clear identification of the physical agent that brings about this pregnant condition. Throughout subsequent decades the Court continued to ignore the fertilized ovum as the cause of pregnancy. In 1992 in *Casey*, for example, the Court depicted the pregnant woman in this way: the "mother who carries a child to full term *is subject* to anxieties, to physical constraints, to pain that only she must bear."[67] These words exemplify the Court's passive construction of pregnancy, that is, its failure to identify the active agent, the fetus, which makes a woman pregnant. Obviously a pregnant woman is subject to burdens. The real question, however, is who or what subjects her to these burdens of anxiety, physical constraint, and pain — in other words, who or what is the causal agent that is responsible for her pregnant condition.

It is not sufficient merely to portray the burdens of pregnancy without attributing their cause to the fetus. Yet unfortunately even the most stunning critiques of abortion rights perpetuate a passive, rather than an active, attribution to the causes. In their brilliant message to Sandra Day O'Connor, for example, legal scholars Susan Estrich and Kathleen Sullivan quote Chief Justice Rehnquist, who observed that "pregnancy entails 'profound physical, emotional, and psychological consequences.'"[68] The authors then enumerate the many ways in which pregnancy impinges on a woman: by increasing her "uterine size 500–1000 times, her pulse rate by ten to fifteen beats a minute, and her body weight by 25 pounds or more."[69] As they note,

> [Even] the healthiest pregnancy can entail nausea, vomiting, more frequent urination, fatigue, back pain, labored breathing, or water retention. There are also numerous medical risks involved in carrying pregnancy to term: of every ten women who experience pregnancy and childbirth, six need treatment for some medical complication, and three need treatment for major complications. In addition, labor and delivery impose extraordinary physical demands, whether over the six to twelve hour or longer course of vaginal delivery, or during the highly invasive surgery involved in a Caesarean section, which accounts for one out of four deliveries.[70]

Yet in this list of burdens, the agent responsible for causing the condition of pregnancy, the fetus, is notably invisible. This failure results in a social and legal construction of pregnancy as if it were an immaculate condition that occurs in the absence of any identifiable physical agent.[71] Yet there is an agent that directly causes pregnancy: the fertilized ovum.

The Fetus as Agent

The Supreme Court has ruled in no uncertain terms that it is constitutional for the state to have a profound interest in the protection of potential life from the moment of conception.[72] As the Court stated in *Casey*, "[T]he State has legitimate interests from the outset of the pregnancy in protecting . . . the life of the fetus that may become a child."[73] As *Roe* ruled, after viability the State's interest in protecting potential life becomes compelling, which is why a woman may be prohibited from obtaining an abortion unless her life or health is in danger.[74]

In this sense, the fetus is a human being even if it is not a person covered by the Fourteenth Amendment, or even a person at all. The distinction between a human being and a person is not arbitrary but refers to one's biological classification. Put simply, if you are conceived by human parents, you are human, leaving open the question of when you might become a person. Some answer that question as does pro-life advocate John Noonan Jr., who by stressing the salience of biological processes and species membership, concludes that to be human is to be a human being or person.[75] As he points out, the "entire argument for permitting experimentation on the unborn rested on the contention that they were members of the human species."[76] Yet others, such as pro-choice Tristram Engelhardt, note that into the category human being, we can put the fetus, along with zygotes, embryos, brain-dead human life, and other forms of human life that "give no evidence of being person."[77] To say that the fetus is a human being, therefore, is not to say that it is a person, and for some, what is important is not one's species but whether one is a person.

From the standpoint of the law, however, one's species is important, for the Court protects the fetus precisely because it is, as potential life, a member of the human species on its way to becoming a child, if not a person. It is because the fetus is a potential life that may become a child that it shares the attributes of a person. From the vantage point of the law, for the fetus to share the attributes of a person means that the behavior of the fetus, its movement and its effects on others, can be evaluated in terms of its mens rea, or guilty mind. Clearly the fetus has no conscious intentions and cannot control its movements. For this reason, the law evaluates its mens rea as incompetent. To the degree that fetuses act, therefore, they act like mentally incompetent human life.

In its most general sense the verb *to act* refers to all bodily movements, including involuntary actions such as might occur when one is asleep or unconscious. In its more narrow sense, *to act* refers only to voluntary bodily movement.[78] The law recognizes that both nonvoluntary and voluntary acts can cause harm and injury to other people and that the nonvoluntary characteristic of an action does not give its perpetrator any right to inflict harm or injury. As the *Model Penal Code* notes, "People whose involuntary movements threaten harm to others may present a public health or safety problem."[79]

Charges against perpetrators of actions that cause harm can be brought in two ways. In civil proceedings, or torts, courts weigh the various interests of the private parties involved and their claims of injury in order to assess who, if anyone, is responsible for damages and how much compensation will be made.[80] Criminal proceedings, however, refer to efforts by the state "to protect the public against harm, by punishing harmful results of conduct or at least situations (not yet resulting in actual harm) which are likely to result in harm if allowed to proceed further."[81] In criminal cases the state itself initiates proceedings against the perpetrators of harm to protect the public interest.

In both tort and criminal contexts, people who cause harm involuntarily lack the mens rea to be held legally responsible for their behavior. When people are asleep, for example, or in a clouded state between sleeping and waking, their actions are not considered voluntary. A person who kills someone in such a state, therefore, cannot be considered guilty of murder.[82] Similarly, sleepwalkers may have purposive behavior, but since they are unaware of their purposes, the law considers their actions while sleepwalking to be unconscious.[83] Most courts have also held that there is no voluntary act when movement or action follows unconsciousness or uncontrollable seizures, as when people have been hypnotized or suffer epileptic seizures.[84]

What is more, an act can be said not to be voluntary when the person in question is underage. In common law, for example, when children were younger than seven years old, they were presumed to be without criminal capacity, in contrast to those who had reached the age of fourteen and were treated as fully responsible. Children between the ages of seven and fourteen were in a limbo category where the presumption of incapacity could be rebutted.[85] This did not mean that underage children could not harm other people. To the contrary, there was consensus that children can perform atrocious acts. It was merely that prior to the age of discretion, the law recognized that youthful defendants did not have the ability "to distinguish between good and evil," and for this reason they could not be held criminally culpable, however abominable might be their behavior. Age, therefore, is a factor much like unconsciousness, insanity, epileptic seizure, or any other involuntary act, or autonomism, a defense that rendered people incapable of having the mens rea necessary to make them legally responsible for crime.[86]

When their actions are involuntary, regardless of how seriously they might harm others, people are not held legally responsible for what they do. They can kill, physically injure, capture, and kidnap others, for example, but if they do so without conscious intent they cannot be criminally liable for their actions, no matter what damages and injuries they might cause. While the state will make every effort to stop them, it cannot bring them to trial as criminally responsible for those injuries.

In this sense, the fetus is innocent. Its innocence does not mean that the fetus is a passive, inert mass of material that does not do anything to a woman. To the contrary, it is a vital, living, active entity with tremendous power. It alone has the power to transform a woman's body from a nonpregnant to a pregnant condition. The very fact that the fetus is portrayed as innocent underscores its status as human life, even though it is incompetent human life. Fires that destroy vast plots of property or earthquakes that bring devastation are not called innocent, nor are cancerous tumors that kill people or viruses that cause diseases. Rather, it is seen that these entities possess no human attributes at all, even in a potential, much less actual, form. When people describe the fetus as innocent, therefore, they are recognizing that it is in a category with other human beings who, though they seriously affect the well-being of others, remain innocent of criminality because they lack control of their behavior and have no conscious intentions. The law views such people as the objective cause of their actions, even though they cannot be held legally responsible for them.[87]

The fetus's behavior nonetheless falls into that category of action in which the law assigns objective fault even without the presence of conscious intention. Some statutory requirements, for example, when defining the crime of receiving stolen property, read, "[W]hoever receives stolen property" is guilty of receiving stolen property whether they had reason to know or do know that the property is stolen.[88] In this sense, people can be objectively at fault whether or not they have the mental capacity or requisite knowledge to know that their behavior is criminal.[89] In this same way the fetus's behavior is objectively at fault for causing pregnancy, even though it has no knowledge, consciousness, or intention of so doing.

The portrayal of the fetus as any type of actor, even an incompetent one, may offend those who see pregnancy as merely a set of biological processes more akin to other kinds of physiological processes, such as circulating blood, focusing the eye, or digesting food. Yet this is not how the Court has defined pregnancy. Rather than a set of biological processes involving only one individual, a woman, the Court in Roe established that pregnancy is a condition in which there are two recognizable entities, the woman and the fertilized ovum throughout its developmental stages. The state protects both of them. For this reason it is insufficient to think of pregnancy as merely a set of physiological processes void of human agency. To the extent that there are two human entities in pregnancy, the state protects two human interests and therefore two human actors, even if one of them, the fetus, is an incompetent actor.

Consent to Fetal Intrusion

Recognition of the fertilized ovum as an incompetent actor who makes a woman pregnant opens the door to a new way of evaluating the legal significance of what the fetus does when it imposes even a medically normal pregnancy on a woman. To the degree that the fetus shares the attributes of a person, its imposition of normal pregnancy against a woman's will is an invasion of her right to be let alone from other private entities. The fetus acquires no entitlement to intrude on a woman simply because it lacks the mens rea to make it criminally responsible for what it does.[90]

To categorize the fertilized ovum as an incompetent actor that intrudes on a woman's bodily integrity and liberty provides a new way to evaluate the state's response to this private aggression, whether its imposition involves a medically normal or abnormal pregnancy. Specifically, even if the state has a legitimate interest in protecting the fetus, on what grounds can it allow the fetus, as an incompetent actor, to intrude on the bodily integrity and liberty of another private party, the woman, as a means for attaining its objective? But because the Court has not yet evaluated the legal significance of what the fetus does to a woman when it coerces her to be pregnant, the Court has not yet addressed the constitutionality of the state's response to that intrusion, including the use of that intrusion as a means for accomplishing the state's goal: the protection of the fetus.

Rather than developing the legal parallels between a pregnancy relationship and other types of relationships, our courts and culture more commonly emphasize what makes pregnancy different from other relationships, if not unique.[91] As the Court stated in *Casey*, the "liberty at stake in abortion cases is 'unique to the human condition and so unique to the law.'"[92] To segregate and isolate pregnancy as a unique condition to which no other laws are relevant, however, is to rob women of the protection of laws designed exactly to guarantee the bodily integrity of people from nonconsensual intrusion by other people, much less potential people. The danger of the uniqueness view is evident in its application by the pro-life advocate Rep. Christopher H. Smith of New Jersey (R), who defines pregnancy as "fundamentally different than any other condition that a woman in her lifetime will experience" and then uses this distinction as grounds for restricting abortion rights.[93]

The value of potential life, however, as represented by the fetus, is similar to, if not the same as, the value placed on all born human life. The issue in abortion rights is, therefore, not the state's interest in protecting potential life but rather the state's justification for offering greater protection of potential life than of born life. In other words, the issue is not the legitimacy of the state's interest in potential life but rather the state's justification for granting to preborn potential life a greater right of access to another person's body than it grants to born life.

It is because the Court has failed to identify the fertilized ovum as the cause of a woman's pregnancy that it has also failed to develop the idea of the right of a woman to consent to the way in which a fertilized ovum penetrates her body. By definition, a woman who seeks an abortion does not consent to let the fertilized ovum make her pregnant. The right to an abortion, therefore, ultimately derives from a woman's right to consent to the way others intrude on her body and her liberty, which includes the right to consent to the way a fertilized ovum intrudes on her body and liberty when it transforms her body from a nonpregnant to a pregnant condition.

Abortion rights involve women's right to consent to what is done to their bodies by fertilized ova that make them pregnant. Women are not inert material to be used by a fetus at will, nor are they passive vessels where fetuses may reside while growing and developing. Women's human status is not defined by how their wombs may be of use to others, nor does a woman's sexual identity imply an automatic right of access by private parties who may need her body for their own survival and development.

To the contrary, as human beings protected by the full scope of the law, women possess the right to consent to how their bodies are intruded on and used by other private parties. Even if the fetus were a person and even if state protection of the fetus were construed as equal to that of a born person, the fetus nevertheless would not acquire a legal right to intrude on a woman's body without her consent since no born person has such a right. And if the fetus is not a person, whatever rights it might have are further diminished, not enhanced. The fetus as a potential life can, therefore, have no legal right of access to a woman's body. And when it intrudes on and expropriates a woman's body for its own benefit, it is hardly the case that it is doing nothing of legal, medical, or cultural significance to her; on the contrary, to the degree that it shares the attributes of a person, what it is doing has enormous legal implications and multifaceted significance.

Viewing pregnancy in terms of consent places pregnancy in the larger legal framework established to deal with privacy, or the right to be let alone from nonconsensual physical intrusion by other people. This view broadens the implications of abortion rights to include the law's protection not only of women but also of all people who are intruded on by private parties. While all men and some women are not vulnerable to the specific intrusion of a fertilized ovum, all people are vulnerable to physical intrusion by other private parties. It is this comparison that we must apply to abortion rights. To say that a woman does not have a right to stop the fetus as a private party from intruding on her is comparable to saying that men and women do not have a right to stop private parties from intruding on them. And to say that a state is under no obligation to help a woman stop a fetus from intruding on her is comparable to saying that the state is under no obligation to help anyone stop private parties from intruding on them.

A consent-to-pregnancy approach provides a way to situate men and women more equally by reframing pregnancy as the right to consent to have one's body intruded on by private parties, including preborn ones.[94] When reframed in these terms, pregnancy is no longer a unique experience relevant only to the bodily integrity of some women but rather part of a universal category of experiences relevant to everyone's right of bodily integrity. That the law has failed to provide pregnant women with rights to bodily integrity equal to those guaranteed to others testifies not to the uniqueness of women in general or pregnant women in particular but rather to the way in which cultural assumptions about pregnancy have contaminated the Court's application of legal principles to abortion rights.

For too long the abortion debate has been governed by the issue of the personhood status of the fetus. Consequently, the basic issue has remained undetected: the fetus as the cause of the pregnant condition in a woman's body that abortion terminates. Recasting abortion rights in terms of a woman's right to consent to what the fetus does to her body will show that the fundamental liberty at stake in the abortion debate is not merely women's right to choose what to do with their own bodies but, more important, their right to consent to what another private party, the fetus, does to their bodies and their liberty when it makes them pregnant. To reach this point we must understand not only what the fetus does to a woman in pregnancy but also what the man does not do.

3

Separating Sex from Pregnancy

It is common to depict men as impregnating women, and thus to equate sex with pregnancy. But because pregnancy is the condition in a woman's body caused by a fertilized ovum, there are actually two relationships involved in reproduction: a *sexual relationship* between a man and a woman and a *pregnancy relationship* between a fetus and a woman. Whereas a man can cause a woman to engage in a sexual relationship with him, a man cannot cause a woman's body to change from a nonpregnant to a pregnant condition; the only entity that can do that is a fertilized ovum when it implants itself in a woman's uterus.[1] Thus, although a man and a woman can have a sexual relationship, they cannot, reproductively speaking, have a pregnancy relationship. Concomitantly, although a fetus and a woman can have a pregnancy relationship, they cannot have a sexual relationship. And to state the obvious, a fetus and a man can have neither a sexual nor a pregnancy relationship.

For this reason, although a sexual relationship between a man and a woman usually precedes a pregnancy relationship between a fetus and a woman, these two relationships are by no means the same.[2] What is more, not only is it the fertilized ovum, rather than a man, that joins with a woman in a pregnancy relationship, but it is the fertilized ovum, not a man, that is the primary cause of that relationship. The only way a woman will ever be pregnant is if a fertilized ovum implants itself and stays there, and the only way to terminate the condition of pregnancy in a woman's body is to remove the cause of that pregnancy: the fertilized ovum (or at later stages of development, the fetus). Under the law, therefore, it is the fertilized ovum or fetus, not a man, that is the primary cause of pregnancy.

The Legal Cause of Pregnancy

How to assess causality, whether of pregnancy or of any other matter, is one of the most complex questions in the legal field. Often the law must determine cause in order to assess who or what is responsible for events or damages.[3] The law makes that determination by assessing causal links, that is, by identifying the sequences of events, or chains, that explain how or why an event occurred.[4] Because it is possible to trace chains of events back to the beginning of time and to imagine effects continuing into the future through eternity,[5] courts set up practical, if arbitrary, starting and ending points for explaining causality. The law tries, therefore, to consider only those causes that are "so closely connected with the result"[6] that it makes sense to regard them as responsible for it. In the process, courts distinguish between two main types of causes: *factual causes*, which explain in a broad context why an event occurred, and *legal causes*, which constitute the sole or primary reason for an event's occurrence.[7]

A factual cause can be thought of as a necessary but not a sufficient cause of an event.[8] Guido Calabresi differentiates between two types of factual causes: causal links and "but for" causes. The former increase the chances that another event will occur but do not cause the actual event itself,[9] and the latter are acts or activities "without which a particular injury would not have occurred,"[10] yet not sufficient in itself for its occurrence. If women jog in Central Park at ten o'clock at night, for example, although such activity increases the chances they will be raped, beaten, and killed, it does not actually cause those events to occur; someone else has to do the raping, beating, and killing. Exposing oneself to the risk of injury, therefore, while it may be a necessary, factual cause of that injury, does not mean it is the sufficient, legal cause. The people who actually do the raping, beating, and killing are the necessary and sufficient cause of the injuries, and thus also the legal cause.

Among the virtually infinite number of necessary factual causes, therefore, the task in law is to locate the one necessary and sufficient cause of an event, that is, the legal or proximate cause.[11] The proximate cause is "that which is nearest in the order of responsible causation . . . the primary or moving cause . . . the last negligent act contributory to an injury, without which such an injury would not have resulted. The dominant, moving or producing cause."[12] The legal cause is, therefore, both a necessary and sufficient condition to explain why an event occurred.

The distinction between factual and legal causes relates nicely to the distinction between sexual intercourse, caused by a man, and pregnancy, caused by a fertilized ovum. A man, by virtue of being a cause of sexual intercourse, becomes a factual cause of pregnancy. By moving his sperm into a woman's body through sexual intercourse, he provides a necessary but not sufficient condition for her body to change from a nonpregnant to a pregnant condition. Not until a fertilized ovum is conceived, however, does its presence actually change her body from a nonpregnant to a pregnant state. For this reason, since pregnancy is a condition that follows absolutely from the presence of a fertilized ovum in a woman's body, we can identify the fertilized ovum to be the legal cause of a woman's pregnancy state.[13]

In the case of most pregnancies, men and sexual intercourse are a necessary condition that increases the chances of pregnancy by putting a woman at risk to become pregnant, but the conception of a fertilized ovum in a woman's body and its implantation are the necessary and sufficient conditions that actually make her pregnant. What men cause in sexual intercourse is merely one of the factual sequential links involved in pregnancy: the transportation of sperm from their body to the body of a woman. Moving sperm into a woman's body, however, is not the legal, or most important, cause of a woman's pregnant condition. It is merely a preceding factual cause that puts her at risk for becoming pregnant.

Both men and women are causally related to pregnancy in terms of their roles as part of a long chain of events. Somewhere in that chain, men must transfer sperm out of their bodies and into some other container. For conception to occur, the container must also have ova in it from a woman. Usually men and women accomplish this process by means of sexual intercourse, which puts sperm inside a woman's body that contains ova. After a man ejaculates his sperm into the vagina of a woman, however, there is nothing more he can do to affect the subsequent causal links that lead to pregnancy. There is no way he can cause his sperm to move, or not to move, to the site of fertilization, nor can he control whether his sperm will fuse with an ovum or not. For this reason, it does not make sense to say that men cause conception, much less that men cause pregnancy. Until a fertilized ovum conceives and implants itself in a woman's body, pregnancy cannot occur. Sexual intercourse, therefore, although commonly a factual cause of pregnancy, cannot be viewed as the "controlling agency" or legal cause of pregnancy. The fertilized ovum's implantation accomplishes that task.[14]

While the deposit of a man's sperm in the vagina of a woman by means of sexual intercourse sets in motion a possible sequence of events that may or may not lead to the implantation of a fertilized ovum in the woman's uterus, the law does not identify events that set things in motion as the legal cause of eventual consequences. For example, a Louisiana Court of Appeals considered the claim of a cattleman that his cattle had died from lack of water because, with his permission, a gas pipeline company had dug a canal in his pasture, thereby isolating his cattle from fresh water and additional grazing land. The court ruled that although the cattleman's loss was "set in motion" by the company's action, that action was not the legal cause of the cattle's death because their death need not have followed absolutely from the digging of the pipeline.[15] The cattleman could have moved his cattle or could have otherwise provided for them.[16]

Similarly, when a man deposits sperm inside a woman's body by means of sexual intercourse, this event in and of itself does not make it absolutely necessary that her body will change from a nonpregnant to a pregnant condition. Men and sexual intercourse do not by necessity either define or produce a pregnant condition in a woman's body, any more than the digging of the canal necessarily entailed the death of the cattle. The sperm may or may not move to the site of fertilization. An ovum may or may not also move to the site of fertilization. Even if sperm and ovum do move to a common site of fertilization, they may or may not unite. And even if an ovum and a sperm unite, the fertilized ovum may or may not move to a woman's uterus, much less implant itself there.[17]

Under the law, therefore, men cannot impregnate women. All that men can do is to be crucially involved in pregnancy as one of many necessary factual, "but for" causes. Without men, there would be no sperm; "but for" sperm, there would be no fertilized ova; "but for" fertilized ova, there would be no implantations in women's uteruses; "but for" implantations by fertilized ova in women's uteruses, there would be no sustained pregnancies.

However, a woman is not pregnant until, or unless, a fertilized ovum does something to her body by its presence and the maintenance of its implantation in her body. In the eyes of the law, therefore, the fertilized ovum should be the legal cause of a woman's pregnancy. The way it affects her body most involves the idea of absolute necessity, the idea that pregnancy must follow as a condition in her body. All other causes of pregnancy are merely factual causes, being necessary but not sufficient.

The association between sexual intercourse and pregnancy, however, might lead some to claim that pregnancy is a foreseeable event subsequent to sexual intercourse. As such, some might assert that a woman could be held responsible for the harm that ensues when a fetus makes her pregnant against her will. As the *Restatement (Second) of the Law of Torts* establishes, "where the negligent conduct of the actor creates or increases the foreseeable risk of harm through the intervention of another force, such intervention is not" enough to eviscerate the first actor's liability.[18] Applied to pregnancy, this would mean that if the man and woman's sexual conduct created a situation—that is, placing sperm and ova in proximate locations to each other, that they could foresee would give rise to harmful conduct by a fertilized ovum, or, its imposition of pregnancy on the woman—then the man and women both could be viewed as negligent, that is, as contributing to their own harm.

By negligence, the law means "conduct which creates an undue risk of harm to others. Contributory negligence is conduct which involves an undue risk of harm to the actor himself."[19] The idea of contributory negligence is the idea of "contributory fault."[20] If a woman suddenly runs into a street, for example, and a man driving a car hits her, the driver could claim contributory negligence, that is, that she contributed to her own harm, and, hence, he is not at fault for hitting her. Before deciding who is at fault, of course, we would need to know how fast the driver was going, how visible the woman was before she was hit, and whether the driver tried to avoid hitting her, or, once seeing the opportunity, intentionally hit her. In the latter case, the issue of negligence is moot, since to be negligent assumes that there is no intention to harm. Once the driver of the car intends to harm the woman by hitting her, whatever she might have done to make this intentional harm easier for him to impose is beside the point in terms of what might be her contributory negligence to her own harm.

Where there is intent to harm, therefore, contributory negligence does not apply. If a woman walks down a street late at night, for example, and a man rapes her, he cannot claim contributory negligence—that is, that she contributed to her own harm by placing herself in a foreseeable situation where he could rape her easily without bystanders or police to stop him. Rather, he is held responsible for attacking her, however she might have contributed to the situation that enabled him to do so. If the rapist is insane, on drugs, or otherwise lacking the mens rea for mental competence, of course, he will not be held legally responsible for the harm he causes even though he is objectively the cause of that harm.

When we apply these distinctions to pregnancy, we find that men and women who contribute to a situation in which it is foreseeable that a fertilized ovum might be conceived and make a woman pregnant against her will contribute no more to the woman's harm than does a woman who walks down a street late at night contribute to her own rape. Having sexual intercourse is not like running out in front of an oncoming car which then hits you, for at least one major reason: pregnancy serves the fertilized ovum's interests.

When a fertilized ovum is conceived subsequent to sexual intercourse, and when it harms a woman by imposing pregnancy upon her, it does so to serve its own interests. In this way, the harm it imposes upon a woman is not like an accident. When the driver of a car hits a victim unintentionally, that hit serves no interest of the driver, much less of the victim. The opposite is true of the fertilized ovum. It is not as if it imposes pregnancy without its own interests being involved. To the contrary, it will die if it does not impose pregnancy. And it will die if it does not maintain that pregnancy. The fertilized ovum, therefore, is not like the driver of a car that would rather not hit a person; to the contrary, the fertilized ovum must impose pregnancy upon a woman if it is to survive and develop.

The fertilized ovum, of course, has no conscious intentions and no control over its behavior, but that is not to say that when it causes pregnancy, it does not serve its own interests. While it cannot directly articulate those interests, it is precisely to protect the fetus's interests in maintaining pregnancy in a woman's body that serves as current legal justification for regulating, restricting, and even prohibiting a woman from terminating pregnancy. In this sense, a fetus making a woman pregnant without consent is similar to a rapist intruding upon and taking another's body in pursuit of his own interest, to the detriment of the woman's interests, in contrast to a car driver who has no interest in hitting a person who steps out in front of the car.

Were the fetus to articulate its intentions, presumably it would intend to make and keep a woman pregnant to serve its own interests. At least, that appears to be the state's presumption, as evidenced by the means the state uses to protect the fetus as preborn human life. Since the harm the fetus imposes presumably would be intentional, if it were mentally competent, contributory negligence does not apply to the pregnancy it causes. Men and women who engage in sexual intercourse, therefore, cannot be held as contributing to the harm imposed on a woman by a fertilized ovum making her pregnant without consent.

The Medical Cause of Pregnancy

The medical profession reinforces the identification of men as the factual cause and fetuses as the legal cause of pregnancy by distinguishing between two major phases of reproduction: sperm and egg transport versus pregnancy. For a sperm and ovum (male and female gametes) to unite, they must move closer together, which is termed *gamete transport*. The most common form of gamete transport involves sexual intercourse, in which a man deposits his sperm inside the vagina of a woman. While it is unlikely that many romantic evenings have begun with the query, "How about a little gamete transport tonight?" nevertheless, from the standpoint of the reproductive process, this is the major utility of sexual intercourse.

Most women do have sexual intercourse with a man prior to pregnancy, but some women use artificial insemination, which enables them to put sperm inside their bodies with sperm-filled syringes. If a sperm and ovum subsequently join and the fertilized ovum implants itself, a woman becomes pregnant without ever having had sexual intercourse with a man.

Other women use in vitro fertilization (IVF).[21] In this procedure sperm and ova are extracted from men, and women, respectively, and put in a petri dish. The joining together of the sperm and ova in what is known as fertilization or conception then occurs outside the woman's body. After a few cell divisions in the petri dish, fertilized ova, now termed *embryos*, are then put inside a woman's uterus in hopes that at least one will implant itself in her uterus. In this case a woman becomes pregnant not only without having had sexual intercourse but also without having had sperm inside her body prior to fertilization or conception.

Normal egg transport in a woman "encompasses the period of time from ovulation to the entry of the egg into the uterus." During this period "the egg can be fertilized only during the early stages of its sojourn in the fallopian tube."[22] To reach the fertilization site, an ovum comes out of, or is "shed by," an ovary. Usually the ovum is "picked up" from the surface of the ovary by a multitude of complex processes that involve the oviduct and the egg, which funnel the ovum toward and to the fertilization site in the oviduct.[23]

Of the approximately 200 to 500 million sperm normally deposited by a man into the vagina of a woman during sexual intercourse, as few as 200 sperm are left after reaching the fertilization site.[24] The main reason so few sperm reach the oviduct fertilization site is that "in comparison to the cervix, the uterine environment [through which the sperm must pass on the way to the oviduct] is relatively hostile to sperm." A woman's "immunological system responds to sperm as a 'foreign' protein." In the uterus a woman's "body responds by killing these cells, much as it would respond to bacteria or a tissue graft from an unrelated individual."[25]

Fertilization or conception occurs when the male element, or spermatozoon, and the female element, or ovum, fuse together,[26] either inside a woman's body subsequent to sexual intercourse or artificial insemination or outside her body when in vitro techniques are employed. When conception occurs inside a woman's body, most medical practitioners consider her to be pregnant[27] because a fertilized ovum inside her body affects it, meaning that it transforms her body from a nonpregnant to a pregnant condition. Some tests can detect whether a woman is pregnant within one to two days after coitus; other tests can produce a finding five days after conception.[28]

Conception that occurs in a petri dish does not make a woman pregnant since her body is not affected in any way by the fertilized ovum. Similarly, a man who relocates his sperm in a woman's body by means of sexual intercourse does not by this act alone make her pregnant since no fertilized ovum exists at that point. Only when a fertilized ovum affects a woman's body by its presence in her body, its implantation, and its maintenance of that implantation does a woman become pregnant. It is the fertilized ovum, therefore, that is the only necessary and sufficient cause of a woman's pregnant condition.

This recognition does not take men and sex out of the picture altogether; it merely clarifies the distinction between men and sperm as necessary, factual causes and the fertilized ovum as the only necessary and sufficient, legal cause of pregnancy. When we see a group of pregnant women walking down the street, most of us would assume that they have all had sex with a man, yet this assumption could very well be wrong. All or some of them might have used artificial insemination or IVF, thus bypassing sexual intercourse altogether on the road to pregnancy. The one and only thing that can be said with certainty about all pregnant women is that fertilized ova have caused pregnancy by initiating and maintaining their bodies' transformation from a nonpregnant to a pregnant condition. Although a man's sperm as well as a woman's ovum are necessary conditions for pregnancy, only a fertilized ovum is actually both the necessary and sufficient cause of a woman's pregnancy.[29]

We must distinguish, therefore, between necessary but not sufficient factual causes of pregnancy, and the fetus as the one necessary and sufficient legal cause of pregnancy. While men, women, sperm, ova, some form of gamete transport, and conception all must be present as factual causes of pregnancy, none is sufficient alone to produce that condition in a woman's body. Rather, it is only when conception of a fertilized ovum takes place within a woman's body and the fertilized ovum implants itself there that pregnancy is initiated and maintained, as table 3.1 summarizes.

The Fetus as a Separate Entity

Identifying the fertilized ovum as the cause of a pregnancy draws attention to a controversial issue in the abortion debate: whether the fetus is part of a woman's

Table 3.1 Causes of Pregnancy

Necessary (but Not Sufficient) Factual Causes of Pregnancy	Necessary and Sufficient Legal Cause of Pregnancy
Men	
Sperm	
Women	
Ova	
Gamete transport	
Sexual intercourse	
Artificial insemination	
In vitro fertilization	
Conception	
Fusion of sperm and ovum	
	Post-conception effects of fertilized ovum in a woman's body

body or a separate entity. The answer holds profound legal and political significance. Currently, abortion rights rest on a woman's right of privacy to make choices about her own body, not about the body of another entity. Many advocates for women's reproductive rights stoutly claim that there is no body other than the woman's to consider in the abortion issue. They adamantly reject depictions of the fertilized ovum as an entity separate from the woman, much less as an entity with the full status of a person.[30] Their assumption is that such a construction of the fetus undermines women's autonomy by implying that fetuses have interests separate from their mothers and that those interests are grounds for restricting abortion, which destroys the fetus.

By declaring that the woman's privacy is "no longer sole" when she is pregnant, however, the Supreme Court in 1973, in *Roe*, accorded the fetus an identity and body separate from the pregnant woman's such that she necessarily shares her privacy with another.[31] Also, though the Court ruled that the fetus is not covered by the Fourteenth Amendment, it did so not on the grounds that the fetus is not a person so much as on the grounds that it is not a born person, as specified by the Constitution.[32] In addition, the Court ruled in *Casey* that the state has "legitimate interests from the outset of the pregnancy" in protecting the life of the fetus, and that these interests become strong enough after viability to prohibit women's right to an abortion, unless their health or lives are endangered, because of the negative impact of this choice on the fetus.[33]

For this reason, the view of the fetus as an entity separate from its mother, with its own interests, already is solidly embedded in Supreme Court reasoning about abortion rights. Pro-life advocates elaborate on these premises by declaring that the fetus is also a person with the same rights and interests as a born person. Surely, they argue, people have no right of privacy to make choices about their own bodies if by so doing they murder another person. When a woman has an abortion, according to pro-life views, she is necessarily making a choice that involves another entity separate from her, who deserves the same respect and protection as a born person. While she might have a right to choose what to do with her own body, she does not have a right to decide what to do with the other entity's body, particularly when that decision involves destroying it.

There is a way to bridge these pro-life and pro-choice perspectives and reach some kind of consensus. Pro-life views that the fertilized ovum throughout its developmental stages is a separate entity from its mother can in fact lead to pro-choice conclusions that women have a right to abort that separate entity. Rather than impairing women's right to an abortion, pro-life premises can actually expand that right to include a woman's right both to an abortion and to its public funding.

In one case, where the fertilized ovum is in a petri dish, there is patently no question that it is a separate entity from its mother. It is not then considered to be part of a woman's body since it is outside, and has never been inside, her body. Yet it is the very same entity as a fertilized ovum within her body. The fertilized ovum in a petri dish may never even end up inside a woman's body, unless the woman consents to allow it to be surgically placed in her uterus. Furthermore, a fertilized ovum in a petri dish is composed of both a man's sperm and a woman's ovum, so that if it were thought to be part of a woman's body, it also would have to be considered part of a man's body, thereby being in two bodies at once, which is an absurdity.

Locating the fertilized ovum inside a woman's body cannot in and of itself, however, define it as part of her body. If everything inside a person's body were held to be an integral part of that body, a thimble swallowed by someone would be part of that person's body by virtue of being inside it. If we removed the thimble, it would then be akin to removing an arm, a leg, or some other part of that person's body. Clearly, many things that are not part of a person's body can get inside that body. For this reason it makes no sense to define the fertilized ovum as part of its mother's body merely on the basis of its location within it.

Another faulty basis for viewing the fertilized ovum as part of a woman's body is its genetic link to her body. Half of the chromosomes that make up the fertilized ovum come from the woman and half from the man. On this basis, it is possible to say only that the fertilized ovum is composed of part of a woman's body and part of a man's body. The genetic identity of a fertilized ovum itself is thus no reason to consider it to be solely a part of the woman's body. Common genetic identity alone, for example, does not suffice for identification of a common body in the case of identical twins. People are termed identical twins precisely because they have the same genetic composition; during early cell division, a single fertilized ovum splits into two, thereby producing two individuals, each of whom has exactly the same chromosome composition. Yet no one would think to maintain that identical twins share a common body or that the body of one identical twin is part of the body of the other. This genetic principle extends to kinship groups that share a gene pool. The genetic heritage of children derives from parts of both parents' bodies, yet the children are not considered literally to be part of either parent's body. They are viewed as having bodies and identities of their own.

Children's separate identities, however, are not based on their physical separation from their parents. The mere separation of physical parts of one's body is not grounds for claiming a separate identity for such parts. If we sever a finger or an arm, that physical separation alone does not mean that these entities are no longer parts of the body from which they came. For this reason, the separation itself of children from their mothers' bodies is not sufficient grounds for transforming them into different bodies from their mothers.[34]

It is neither the fact of physical attachment or detachment nor the location inside or outside a body nor the genetic composition of a person that determines whether someone is part of another person's body or is a separate self, with a body and identity of its own. Rather, such a determination is a product of cultural, political, and legal constructions. While it has been common in the abortion debate to assume that the view of the fetus as a separate entity from a woman, much less a person, necessarily undermines women's reproductive rights, that is far from the case. Ironically, recognition of the fetus as a separate entity facilitates distinguishing the significance of what it "is" from what it "does."

Risks versus Consequences

Despite medical and legal perspectives that point to why we must separate sexual relationships between men and women from pregnancy relationships between fetuses and women, the heritage of our culture and our laws has been to confuse and mistake one for the other and also to fuse them together, as if they were one and the same. Recognition that a man can cause a woman to have a sexual relationship with him is taken to mean that he can cause her to be pregnant. Yet sexual intercourse of a man and a woman at most only puts her at risk that a fertilized ovum will be conceived and make her pregnant. While men, and usually sexual intercourse, are indeed involved in a chain of events that makes it possible for a fertilized ovum to make a woman pregnant, men are not the primary legal cause of pregnancy; fertilized ova are.[35]

Men, for all women, and sexual intercourse, for most women, are factual causes of pregnancy, which create the risk or probability that a fertilized ovum will be conceived and make a woman pregnant. In this way, when a woman has sexual intercourse with a man, she is exposing herself to the risk of pregnancy, much as a woman who jogs alone in New York City at ten o'clock at night exposes herself to the risk of mugging and rape. The probability of being mugged and raped is affected by how people expose themselves to those risks. To jog in Central Park alone at night instead of in your own apartment on a treadmill increases the probability that you will be mugged and raped.

Yet exposure to this risk still needs to be distinguished from the actual acts.[36] For this reason, when people expose themselves to risks, their behavior constitutes a necessary, but by no means a sufficient, cause for a mugging or rape to occur. As a necessary, factual cause, their behavior sets up the probability that they will be mugged or raped but does not actually make that occur without muggers or rapists to do the job. Only the mugger and the rapist are both the necessary and the sufficient causes of mugging and rape. The phrase *necessary cause*, then, refers to the risk that something will happen, whereas a *necessary and sufficient cause* points to the absolute necessity that something will happen.

The extremely close identification of sex with pregnancy might lead to the assumption that the probability of pregnancy following sexual intercourse is so high as to make these two events virtually one and the same. Granted, some women bypass sexual intercourse, but most do not. For those women who do engage in sexual intercourse, many might think it is nothing but a meaningless abstraction to separate sex and pregnancy in terms of risks and consequences.

At first glance, it might seem reasonable to equate risks with consequences if and when they are linked by extremely high probabilities. Yet on further examination, this is not the way it works, at least when the issue involves the intrusion of one private party on another. Even when the probability is very high between two events, people do not lose their right to distinguish between risks and consequences if and when the consequences involve harmful actions directed against them by other private parties. Even if people knew the probability was .99, for example, that they would be mugged when jogging in Central Park, they still would not lose their right not to be mugged, even though it was an all but certain consequence of exposing themselves to the risk of mugging. What is more, the police are held responsible for enforcing the laws that prohibit private people from mugging others, even when the victims voluntarily have exposed themselves to the risk that such events will occur.[37]

Similarly, even if the probabilities were .99 that a fertilized ovum would be conceived subsequent to sexual intercourse, women would not lose the right to separate sexual intercourse from pregnancy, any more than people lose the right to separate jogging in Central Park from muggings that occur there. And in the case of pregnancy, the probability that it will follow sexual intercourse most likely is considerably less than the probability that a person will experience a mugging while jogging alone at night in Central Park.

Although it is common to think that unprotected sexual intercourse leads to the virtually certain result that pregnancy will ensue, that is far from the case. Charlene Pacourek, for example, tried for seven frustrating years to get pregnant, to no avail. By the age of forty-five, after three unsuccessful IVF procedures, she had almost given up hope. Then an embryo conceived with eggs donated by a friend at last implanted itself in yet another in vitro go-round, and at last she was pregnant. By now, however, her life included not only pregnancy but also a sex, pregnancy, age, and disability discrimination suit against her employer, who had fired her from the job she had held for eighteen years as she underwent infertility treatments.[38]

Charlene Pacourek is only one example. For other couples there is little or no risk of pregnancy after sexual intercourse because of infertility problems. Infertility is defined as "one year of unprotected coitus without conception," and it "affects approximately 10–15 percent of couples in the reproductive age group."[39] During 1982, nearly one in five ever-married women of reproductive age reported that they had sought professional help for infertility problems. Medical experts report that in the 1980s there was "no significant change in the proportion of infertile couples." In 1988, 13.9 percent of married couples, when the wife was in the childbearing range (excluding those who were surgically sterile), were considered infertile. Approximately 25 percent of women are expected to experience an episode of infertility during their reproductive life,[40] and 35 percent of infertility problems are accounted for by male factors.[41] Modern medicine, however, has made great strides in diagnosing and treating infertility. All but 90 percent of the cases of infertility can be diagnosed, and many of these can be successfully treated with drugs or surgical procedures.

Age is one of the key factors in infertility. Maternal age increases the risk of spontaneous abortion. This risk increases from about 10 percent up to age thirty, to 18 percent in the late thirties, to 34 percent in the early forties. Women thirty years or older are also more susceptible to a number of diseases and other factors that interfere with fertility.[42] The onset of menopause in the late forties to early fifties renders women completely infertile, though in rare instances menopause does not occur until the late fifties or even sixties.[43]

The number of factors that affect the probabilities that link sexual intercourse with pregnancy, therefore, reinforce the necessity of distinguishing sexual relationships between men and women from pregnancy relationships between fetuses and women. Researchers point to how it is the timing of sexual intercourse in relation to women's ovulatory cycles, not sexual intercourse per se, that is the important factor for predicting whether pregnancy will ensue. An ovary of a fertile woman releases an ovum approximately once every twenty-eight days, thereby constituting the ovulatory cycle. The only time, therefore, that a woman's body has an ovum in it that can join with a sperm is on the day of ovulation when an ovary has released an ovum. For this reason, "[c]onception can occur only near the time of ovulation."[44]

When sexual intercourse occurs too far away from ovulation, therefore, the probability that conception will occur is zero because there is no ovum present or about to be present to join with a sperm. As sexual intercourse occurs closer to the day of ovulation, the probability that conception will occur increases, of course, since at least an ovum will be present in a woman's body even if it does not join with a sperm. There is uncertainty about how close to ovulation sexual intercourse must occur in order for there to be at least some probability for conception, but recent reports indicate that "nearly all pregnancies" occur subsequent to sexual intercourse that occurs "during a six-day period ending on the day of ovulation."[45]

What this means is that for all but six days of a woman's ovulatory cycle, the probability is zero that conception will follow sexual intercourse. Even during the six-day period when conception is possible, the probability is not as high as popular assumptions linking sex and pregnancy might indicate. The probability that conception will follow sexual intercourse is only .10 when intercourse occurs five days before ovulation and is a maximum of only .33 for the one day of the month when ovulation itself actually occurs.[46] This means that even when women engage in sexual intercourse at the absolutely most maximum probable time for conception to occur, the one day of ovulation, it does so only for 33 out of 100 women. What is more, conception itself does not always lead to a sustained pregnancy. Even when conception does occur, only two-thirds of those conceptions followed in a controlled study culminate in a live birth. The probability that a sustained pregnancy will be subsequent to sexual intercourse, therefore, ranges from a minimum of .00 to a maximum of .22, the latter representing the probability that a woman who has sexual intercourse on the one day of ovulation will have a live birth.[47]

Women do not always know, of course, the day of ovulation or even the length of the period surrounding the day of ovulation. Sometimes this lack of knowledge is due to ignorance; sometimes irregular cycles may make it difficult or impossible to know the day of ovulation in order to calculate the odds that conception might follow sexual intercourse. If we were to ask, therefore, what are the odds that one incident of sexual intercourse will lead to conception on a day of the ovulatory cycle selected at random, we find very low odds linking the incident of sexual intercourse to conception. The maximum probability that conception will occur is only .012 when the day selected at random happens to be the day of ovulation.[48] That probability drops to .004 when the day selected at random is the fifth day before ovulation, and of course, the probability is .00 that conception will follow sexual intercourse for all randomly selected days outside the six-day fertile period of the ovulatory cycle.[49] The average probability linking sexual intercourse and conception for one incident of intercourse in a randomly chosen day out of the twenty-eight-day ovulatory cycle is only .05.[50] The probabilities linking sex and conception are exceptionally low, therefore, for women who randomly engage in one incident of unprotected sexual intercourse without benefit of information about how the timing of that intercourse corresponds to the six-day period of their ovulatory cycle when conception is possible.

Other studies have shown that if a woman engages in multiple incidents of unprotected sex throughout her twenty-eight-day cycle, with an intention to have sexual intercourse during her peak fertility periods, the odds of being pregnant after one month are only .25, or 25 percent. This means if one hundred women engage in multiple incidents of unprotected sex throughout their ovulatory cycle, with an intention to have sexual intercourse during their most fertile periods, twenty-five of them will become pregnant after a month. The reason women become pregnant, therefore, is not because a high probability of pregnancy is associated with any single incident of unprotected sexual intercourse, or even with a month of unprotected sex. Rather, it is because couples engage in multiple acts of sexual intercourse, thereby increasing a woman's exposure to the risk of pregnancy. Yet the probability that pregnancy will follow sexual intercourse rises to only a 57 percent chance, or slightly better than 50–50, after three months of unprotected sexual intercourse.[51] And these are the figures for couples trying to maximize the probability that pregnancy will follow sexual intercourse, not for random sexual activity, much less for couples attempting to minimize the probability that pregnancy will follow sexual intercourse.

As medical experts note, "Couples need to be aware that there is a normal time requirement to achieve pregnancy." Even after one month of concerted effort to become pregnant, only one out of four women in the reproductive age range will become pregnant following sexual intercourse. For most couples, it requires six months of unprotected sex before pregnancy ensues.[52] In addition, even after a fertilized ovum is conceived, there is no guarantee that it will implant itself and remain implanted for the duration of the time needed for the birth of a child. About 50 percent of fertilized ova do not progress to a viable stage of pregnancy, and up to 30 percent of pregnancies spontaneously abort between implantation and the sixth week.[53]

Another way of putting the probabilities is to say that of all the conceptions that occur, only one-third result in a live birth. Over 50 percent of the fertilized ova that are conceived are lost so early in pregnancy that they go without a trace, and another 15 percent are lost as a result of spontaneous abortions or stillbirths.[54] According to one estimate, 31 percent of all fertilizations end in miscarriages, and two-thirds of these miscarriages occur before the woman or her doctor is even aware that conception has taken place.[55] Another authority estimates that only 20 percent of all fertilized ova produce a live baby, and 31 percent, or close to a third, of all implanted embryos do not result in a live birth.[56] Even after conception, the odds of a viable pregnancy resulting in a live birth are far less than even a 50–50 proposition.[57]

The odds linking sex and pregnancy, therefore, do not make pregnancy such a certainty that it is reasonable to say that sex with a man causes pregnancy, or that a woman's sexual relationship with a man is one and the same thing as her pregnancy relationship with a fetus. On the contrary, the odds linking sex and pregnancy point to why we must separate, not combine, sexual relationships from pregnancy relationships. While a sexual relationship puts a woman at risk that a pregnancy relationship will follow, that risk is too low to assume that one follows the other as a certainty.

It is critical to respect these odds, even though they are low, since any risk of pregnancy is too much if a woman does not intend to consent to that state. Much like rape and mugging, the best strategy is to minimize the risk that pregnancy will occur to the degree one can, if that is one's goal. Men and women should use contraceptives when engaging in sexual intercourse to reduce the risk of pregnancy to its absolute lowest. Yet we must not go overboard in the other direction, and we must recognize that pregnancy does not follow so automatically as a consequence of unprotected sex that we absolutely must equate the two.

Some view the distinctive feature of law to be its provision of opportunities to debate important issues rather than its rules and its commands. As such, the power of the law is as a "stylized form of discourse," which focuses not so much on "what people are" but rather on what people do.[58] Yet the abortion debate has focused primarily on what fetuses are, not on what fetuses do. We must change this focus in order to place the abortion issue in step with how the law treats other forms of causation and how it operates as a powerful discursive medium in our culture. To focus on what the fetus does, we must recognize the legal significance of the distinction between a woman's sexual relationship with a man and her pregnancy relationship with a fetus. Recommendations by some that we create a typology of different "types of pregnancy" based on different "types of sexual relationships" only perpetuate confusion and erroneous conclusions that pregnancies "caused by rape" give women more entitlement to abortion rights than pregnancies "caused by the recklessness" of women who do not use contraceptives.[59]

To speak in these terms mistakenly conflates the two relationships. When a man rapes a woman, he no more causes a subsequent pregnancy than does a man who engages in consensual sex with a woman. Both types of sexual intercourse set up the risk that a fertilized ovum will be conceived and make a woman pregnant, but they are not the sufficient condition for that pregnancy to occur. Obviously, a woman must have the right to consent to the risk that a fertilized ovum will act on her body to make her pregnant, so the distinction between rape and consensual sexual intercourse is a crucial one. It is not a causal distinction, however.

Similarly, when a woman recklessly engages in sexual intercourse without contraceptive protection, she is clearly exposing herself to a higher risk that a fertilized ovum will be conceived and make her pregnant. Yet the higher probability of pregnancy is no more a cause of that occurrence than is walking alone in Central Park the cause of a beating or mugging. Sexual intercourse, whatever its context, is a necessary but not sufficient condition for pregnancy to occur.

It is precisely pro-life proponents' insistence that the fetus is a separate entity from the woman that emphasizes the identification of the fetus, not a man, as the cause of pregnancy. As pro-life advocates stated in their amicus briefs in *Webster*, from the very moment of conception, the fetus is "in charge of the pregnancy," that is, "in charge of the woman's body" in which it "organizes pregnancy," even to the point of deciding when to be born.[60]

Resistance to Separating Sex from Pregnancy

Distorted comparisons of men's and women's roles in procreation abound not only in our culture but also in the very way the law refers to each role. A contemporary law dictionary defines a father to be the "procreator of a child," and procreation is defined as the "generation of children."[61] The same dictionary defines a mother to be a "woman who has borne a child," and born is defined as the "act of being delivered or expelled from a mother's body."[62] Contemporary legal definitions of what it means to be a mother, therefore, do not refer to the notion of procreation or the generation of children. On the contrary, to be a mother extends only to the act of having a child in and expelling a child from your body.[63]

Against such cultural and legal backdrops, to reframe abortion rights around the identification of the fetus as the cause of pregnancy requires the modification of assumptions about the power of men to generate children. It necessitates the recognition of genetic parity between men and women since both generate, or procreate, children by contributing their respective sperm and ova. While men have an obvious stake in the way their genetic material is involved in pregnancy, women have the same comparable stake. What differentiates men and women, therefore, is not their genetic contributions to children but the way in which a fertilized ovum makes women, but not men, pregnant.

For some people there is something funny, even disturbing, about separating sex from pregnancy. Resistance to the idea that the fertilized ovum, not a man, impregnates a woman most likely comes from resistance to changing what are usually rigid notions of male power and prerogatives, which for centuries have elevated and inflated the reproductive role of men in comparison to women and fetuses. The fixity of male power in our views of sexuality and reproduction is shown by comparing the meaning of such common terms as *to father* and *to mother*.

In biological terms, men and women are equal genetic reproductive agents. Both men and women contribute an equal set of chromosomes to produce a new human being. To father a child and to mother a child are therefore biologically equivalent, with both terms referring to men's and women's contribution of an equal set of genes that defines a new human being. Yet our culture assigns quite different meanings to these terms in nonbiological contexts.

The elevation of men appears in the asymmetry of the meaning of words used to identify the respective contributions of men and women in creative if not specifically biological contexts. When we say that men father children, we rarely mean that men nurture and care for children. On the contrary, *to father* ordinarily refers to the power of men biologically to regenerate the human species. To father a child means to produce that child, to give the child its biological life. *To father* refers to the biological potency of men's reproductive agency.

Attributing to men's reproductive agency the idea that they impregnate women spills over into other cultural representations of men's power. In a more general sense, *to father* means "to originate, to bring into existence" or "to be the author of" a doctrine or a statement.[64] As Tennyson said in *Love and Duty*, "Shall Error in the round of time Still father Truth?"[65]

The equation of fathering with a direct, empowering agency also appears in the notion that *to father* means "to appear or to acknowledge oneself as the author" of a work, to take "responsibility" for something, or "to represent oneself as the owner" of a thing. Consider these statements: "he was not the . . . author of it [a written report], but another did it, and got him to father it";[66] "No other writer should be sought for to father any of the Psalms, when David will suffice";[67] and a man's reference to a "singular letter from a lady, requesting I would father a novel of hers."[68] The meaning of these statements is lost if *to mother* is substituted for *to father*: "She was not the . . . author of it, but another did it, and got her to mother it"; "No other writer should be sought for to mother any of the Psalms, when David will suffice"; and a "singular letter from a lady, requesting I would mother a novel of hers."

Despite the biological equality of fathering and mothering, the verbs are not interchangeable because *to father* represents men's reproductive agency as the cause of a new person or, more generally, as the element that gives definition and identity to a new person or creative work. The reason for this is the cultural, not biological, reflection of the way our culture designates men to be the active agents who create our social and political life. In Judeo-Christian religious formulation, men are thought to be the very agents of creation itself: a male God created the heavens and the earth, all the flora and fauna, and human beings to boot. In its secular version, men are the fathers of the American nation, the creators of our intellectual and political world, and the impregnators of women.

The cultural distortion of men's procreative powers is starkly apparent in the meaning of the verb *to mother*. This term refers to responding to the needs of others through birthing, nurturing, protection, and care. The contrast between *to father* and *to mother* appears in the sentence "[He] is not fathered by the castle, nor mothered by the Church,"[69] which attributes fathering to creation and mothering to care. Similarly, the idea that mothering means to care for someone or something appears in the sentence "You would like to take Lizzie Reed into our house, for a time, and mother her till something can be found for her."[70] This statement would make no sense if it read, "You would like to take Lizzie Reed into our house, for a time, and father her till something can be found for her."

The value of mothering rests not with the mother herself but with the beneficiary of her mothering. Since *to mother* means to be of service to others, how well one mothers is measured by how much benefit the person or object receives from the mothering activity. This leads to the idea of "bad mothering," for which there is no parallel of "bad fathering." Bad mothering is usually defined as either too little care and nurturing or too much, as in the statement "Some mothers mother their children too much."[71] Again it would make no sense to say, "Some fathers father their children too much."

In the case of pregnancy, men are simply not as powerful as our culture assumes. When men father a child, it means that men contribute their genetic material to a child, in the same way that women contribute their genetic material to a child. As legal scholar Sherry Colb notes, "Once a man has contributed genetic material, his biological task is essentially complete."[72] Since contributing genetic material does not define the condition of pregnancy, *to father* a child does not mean that a man has directly caused a woman to be pregnant.[73] It means only that he has caused his sperm to move to a location closer to one or more ova as part of a long sequence of events that set in motion conditions that are necessary but not sufficient for pregnancy to occur.

Yet we see the elevation of men's procreative roles embedded even in the way questions are worded in public opinion polls that ask people about their attitudes toward abortion. It is common to inquire, for example, whether people think it should be legal for a woman to obtain an abortion if "pregnancy is the result of rape."[74] And as legal scholar Kathleen Sullivan and others note, many people opposed to abortion nevertheless favor exceptions when pregnancy is subsequent to rape and incest. Indeed, President Bush himself differed with the Republican party platform on this point.[75]

Yet pregnancy does not result from rape or any other form of sexual intercourse. To the contrary, as a law dictionary defines pregnancy, it is a condition in a woman's body that results from a fertilized ovum. What would happen, we can only imagine, if this idea took over. How would the public respond to the question "Do women have a legal right to terminate a pregnancy imposed on them by a fertilized ovum without their consent?"[76]

It is difficult, if not impossible, of course, for some people to separate sex from pregnancy. As one critic of my approach remarked, "You will never get the American public to accept the notion that 'men do not make women pregnant.'" Or as a law student commented on this point, "You've got to be kidding." Men have understandable reasons for resisting the separation of sex from pregnancy since they lose their empowerment as the impregnators of women once the fertilized ovum is acknowledged as the cause of pregnancy. Not only do men have reason to envy women's unique reproductive capacity, what Sherry Colb terms "fetus-envy,"[77] but also women's greater role in reproduction makes men envious as it threatens them. Since the vast amount of reproductive processes that lead to childbirth takes place inside a woman's body, not a man's, men may be unaware they have even become the genetic father of a child or that they are really the genetic father of one that is born. Attesting to men's feelings of reproductive vulnerability, one male friend even asked me, "Is it really 'necessary' for your reframing to take men out of the picture?"[78]

But identifying fertilized ova rather than men as the cause of pregnancy does not take men out of the picture; it merely clarifies the picture. Men and women are vitally involved in the reproductive process, as are fertilized ova. To say that the fertilized ovum causes a woman's body to change from a nonpregnant to a pregnant condition is not to say that men are not parents. Rather, it is to distinguish among different types of parenthood.

Different Types of Parenthood

The separation of sex from pregnancy holds out the promise of improving our understanding of parenthood.[79] Traditionally, fathers are held economically responsible for their children because they are presumed to be the primary cause of a woman's pregnancy. Identification of the cause as the fertilized ovum reveals that the source of men's and women's responsibility for their offspring is based instead on different types of parenthood: genetic, pregnancy, and social.

Both men and women share equally in genetic parenthood when they contribute their sperm and ovum to the processes of reproduction. Men and women are, therefore, equal as genetic parents and incur parental obligations simply because of their genetic contributions to new life. Men incur legal parental obligations on this basis because the law is prone to elevate genetic parenthood above all other types of parenting. Men who become the genetic parent of an offspring by virtue of contributing their sperm are held just as legally responsible for their genetic offspring as are women.

The law's elevation of genetic parenthood appears in the case of Jessica, a child two-and-one-half years old who had been given up for adoption at birth by her unwed mother. Her unwed genetic father, who had not been informed of her birth, later successfully sued for custody of Jessica on behalf of himself and Jessica's genetic mother. To the horror of much of the nation, Jessica was taken away from her adoptive parents, the only parents she had ever known, to be returned to her genetic parents, whom she had virtually never seen.[80]

Genetic parenthood in the law is, therefore, a powerful force that works both for and against men. It can empower men by serving as the basis for their parental claims to custody of their offspring, but it can also hold them economically responsible for their genetic offspring against their wishes. Some critics, such as legal scholar Elizabeth Bartholet, contend that the law should reduce the rights and presumably the obligations attendant on genetic parenthood and substitute instead the rights of "true family ties" that "have little to do with blood" but much to do with the "bonds of love."[81] Until this happens, however, fathers are included in the parenthood picture by virtue of their genetic contributions alone.

Pregnancy parenthood, sometimes referred to as gestational parenthood, refers only to women who are made pregnant by a fertilized ovum.[82] Men and women are the cause of genetic parenthood, whereas fetuses are the cause of pregnancy parenthood. Pregnancy parenthood is the stage in reproduction where the key issue is the way a fetus causes a woman's body to change from a nonpregnant to a pregnant condition.

Of all of the ways to be a parent, none is more significant and important than producing the social bonds of care and nurturing, or social parenthood. Men and women share the ability to be social parents, so that separating sex and pregnancy in no way impinges on men's interest in their empowerment as progenitors. Although *to father* traditionally meant "to generate" and "to create," separating sex and pregnancy shows that it is better to think of this verb as meaning "to nurture and care." In this sense, men and women can share more equally in the critical lifetime activities involved in rearing children.

Separating sex from pregnancy puts the reproductive picture in focus by highlighting men's roles as genetic and social parents and underscoring the relationship between the fetus and the woman during pregnancy parenthood. While men are critical to reproduction, their role does not extend over all phases. Only through recognition that a fetus alone can cause a woman's body to change from a nonpregnant to a pregnant condition is it possible to redirect attention to the overriding issue in the abortion debate: a women's right to consent to the way a fetus makes her pregnant.

4

Consent to Pregnancy

The concept of consent has figured centrally in the abortion debate, as in the right of minors to obtain an abortion without the consent of a parent or parental surrogate, the right of a woman to give her informed consent to abortion procedures, and the right of husbands to consent to abortions by their wives. The one type of consent that is completely missing from the abortion debate, however, is the right of a woman to consent to a pregnancy relationship with a fertilized ovum. Yet identification of the fertilized ovum as the cause of a woman's pregnancy makes her consent to its implantation the key issue in the abortion debate. It reframes her fundamental right as the right to consent to be pregnant rather than merely the right to choose an abortion.

Consent

Consent means legally to "express consent," or that which is "directly given, either *viva voce* or in writing."[1] Such consent "is positive, direct, unequivocal . . . requiring no inference or implication to supply its meaning."[2] Consent is an "act of reason," which must be a "voluntary agreement by a person in the possession and exercise of sufficient mental capacity to make an intelligent choice to do something proposed by another."[3] More simply, consent is the willingness that "an act or an invasion of interest shall take place" based on "a choice between resistance and assent."[4] In the context of pregnancy, consent means a woman's explicit willingness, based on her choice between resistance and assent, for the fertilized ovum to implant itself and cause her body to change from a nonpregnant to a pregnant condition.

A woman's right to consent to physical intrusion by a fertilized ovum depends on acknowledgment of the personhood attributes of the fetus. If the fertilized ovum were merely a physiological mass of cells, like a force of nature, the legal meaning of consent, defined as a concurrence of wills, would become an unnecessary and a meaningless concept. It makes no sense, for example, to say that people consent to the way in which their blood circulates or their eyes focus or that they consent to rain. If people want to reroute their blood circulation, as in bypass surgery, or to alter surgically the way in which their eyes focus, they are not restricted by the right of their blood to circulate in their bodies in a particular way or the right of their eyes to operate within their bodies. Similarly, if physiological masses of cells are identified by people as alien to their bodies, as in the case of cancer, no one is going to restrict people's right to eradicate the presence and action of those cells on their bodies because of the cells' "right to life" or right to use people's bodies.

So, too, with the fetus. If it is viewed as a natural force, much like a fire or flood, or as a mere physiological mass of cells, the concept of consent makes no sense. If a fire is burning your house, it is foolish to say that you do not consent with the fire to allow it to burn your house. It only makes sense to say that you do not choose to let the fire, as a natural force, burn your house. Based on that choice, you will call the fire department to stop the blaze, but surely not the police department to stop the fire from breaking the law by burning. Natural forces cannot break laws. Hurricanes, fires, floods, earthquakes, diseases, and other natural forces, although they often cause enormous damage, killing people and destroying property, do not break laws when they do so. The law is relevant only to people, the state, or juridical entities such as corporations, and only when entities such as these become involved in the damages or injuries caused by natural forces are laws applicable.[5]

Pro-life advocates are prone to embrace the slogan that "The natural choice is life,"[6] by which they mean that pregnancy is not only a normal but also a natural process. Yet the word *natural* refers to processes that occur without human intervention, like hurricanes, floods, fires, earthquakes, diseases, and death. If a person becomes involved in these processes, they are no longer regarded as natural but, rather, as caused at least in part by human agency. If a person sets a fire or murders someone, for example, even if that person is insane, the resulting fire or death is no longer regarded by the law as the result of natural forces; it is rather an event that obliges the involvement of the police, even if the mental incompetence of the perpetrator precludes holding her or him legally responsible for the action.

Ironically, therefore, it is precisely the claim of pro-life forces and others that the fetus must be considered to be a person that starkly contradicts any depiction of pregnancy as natural. To the extent that pregnancy is initiated and maintained by an entity that is a person, it is a product of human agency, not the product of forces of nature. Similarly, although it might seem to be natural for a man and a woman to have sexual intercourse, from the standpoint of the law, sexual intercourse between people is the product of their human agency, not the product of natural forces. If a woman refuses to consent to sexual intercourse, it is not lawful for a man to impose himself sexually on her by claiming that he is a natural force or that he is mentally incompetent. His imposition of sexual intercourse on a woman without her consent is the crime of rape, whatever may be our cultural attitudes toward the naturalness of heterosexual relationships, much less the rights of those who are mentally incompetent.

So, too, with pregnancy. The condition of pregnancy is initiated and maintained by an entity that the Court has declared to be human life under the protection of the state. Pro-life forces insist that the fertilized ovum from the moment of conception is an actual person, just like a born person. Some states, such as Missouri, have declared that the fetus is a person from the moment of conception onward, and other states, such as Massachusetts, Nebraska, Oklahoma, and Pennsylvania, have passed legislation that explicitly or implicitly classifies early embryos as human beings.[7] Louisiana passed a statute that gives rights to embryos as juridical persons and requires courts to resolve disputes about them in accordance with their "best interests."[8] What is more, some legal scholars do not think that the Fourteenth Amendment prohibits a state from asserting that the fetus is a person.[9]

Because the fetus cannot be a natural force and a person at the same time, to the extent that when the fetus attains a human status it loses its status as a natural force. When it causes pregnancy, it acts more like a mentally incompetent person than like a natural force.[10]

From the standpoint of the law, therefore, pregnancy is not a natural process precisely because it is initiated and maintained by an entity, the fetus, that is protected by the state as human life, regardless of whether that human life has yet attained the status of a person. A woman's right to consent to what the fetus does to her when it makes her pregnant, therefore, derives directly from the state's designation of the fetus as protected human life. While it makes no sense to say that you consent to a natural force, such as fire, to burn your house, it does make sense to talk about whether you consent to let a person, or some other juridical agent, burn your house. Equally important, should you not consent, it is appropriate to call not only the fire department to put out the fire but also the police department to stop the person from breaking the law by setting fire to your house against your will.

If the state were instead to categorize the fetus as a mass of living cells void of human identity, of course, the issue of consent would disappear, but so, too, would the state's removal of abortion funding from health policies as a means to protect the fetus as human life disappears. Once the state declares the fetus to be under its protection as a form of human life, however, the issue no longer is merely women's right to choose what to do with their own bodies, but rather women's right to consent to what the fetus as a form of state-protected human life does to their bodies. This is so because whereas choice refers to only one individual,[11] consent necessarily refers to a relationship between two entities, both of whom have at least some attributes of a person or a juridical system. Consent is an agreement between two such entities that signifies that one agrees to let the other invade her, his, or its interests.

The distinction between choice and consent emerges when Congress, for example, passes bills by unanimous consent in order to omit the usual roll-call votes by which members register their yea or nay choices. Unanimous consent is not merely an aggregate of individual choices but also something more. It is recognition of an agreement among members of Congress that they consent to forego their roll-call options since they have all made the same choice to vote yea on a particular piece of legislation. Yet such a vote is not called unanimous choice but rather unanimous consent, thereby acknowledging that their votes hinge on their prior agreement to relinquish their right to a roll-call tally.

Not only does consent subsume choice, but it is also the basic concept underlying our form of government.[12] Modern conceptions of the state following the Enlightenment are built on the idea that the only way to make the exercise of power legitimate is to base it on the consent of the governed. "In this sense, consent is a value prior to any constitution, for it is the value upon which the legitimacy of the state and the constitution itself rest."[13] As Sanford Levinson and Nancy Hirschmann note, the liberal heritage of the American state emphasizes consent as the basis for political obligation, however difficult it has been to determine it.[14] For the laws and government of the United States to be legitimate, therefore, people must consent to them. In most cases consent is inferred by a lack of action,[15] but electoral processes give people the opportunity to express their choice of whom to elect to office. For an election to be valid, there must be a real choice between candidates, but the rationale for elections also provides a mechanism by which those who govern by holding office do so on the basis of the consent of the governed.

Reframing women's abortion rights in terms of their consent to be pregnant rather than their choice to have an abortion taps into the very cornerstone of the American political system: consent. To gain recognition of women's right to consent to pregnancy, rather than merely their choice to have an abortion, enormously strengthens their claims within the context of the American legal system, not so much because consent substitutes for choice as because consent subsumes and is built on choice. Since consent legally is an agreement for a person's interests to be invaded by another, a person must have the choice of whether to consent or not. If people do not have a choice, the invasion of their interests is coercive, which is the antithesis of consent. Although there can be choice without consent, as when people make decisions that refer only to themselves, there can be no consent without choice because consent refers to a relationship between two people, one of whom invades the interest of the other. Without choice, that invasion is necessarily coercive, not consensual.

While there can be meaningful choice without consent, there can be no meaningful consent without choice. People can make individual choices without in the process consenting with others. On the one hand, if you *choose* to use contraceptives, that act refers only to yourself and is meaningful to the extent that you have a real choice of whether to do so or not. If, on the other hand, you *consent* to use contraceptives, it implies not only that you have a real choice of whether to use them or not but also that you have chosen to use them as part of an agreement with others. Specifically, you have agreed to an invasion of your interests by others, based on a valid choice between assenting or not.

Consent is, therefore, built on choice. There can be no valid consent unless there is valid choice; when choices are undermined, so, too, is the validity of consent.[16] If and when people lack meaningful options, or the choice of whether to say yes or no, the validity of their consent to agree to an invasion of their interests must be questioned. Feminists have long articulated this point in the context of legitimizing relationships in the American political and legal culture. They question the ultimate utility of the concept of consent when women are embedded in a patriarchal society characterized by contextual constraints and laws that so severely limit women's choices that the very concept of choice, and hence consent, is virtually meaningless.[17] Catharine MacKinnon, for example, argues that women's subordination to men on the basis of patriarchal social structures, buttressed by law, renders distinctions between rape and consensual sexual intercourse so ephemeral as to be nonexistent; thus all sexual intercourse is in a sense rape.[18] So, too, does Carole Pateman question the validity of consent as a basis for women's rights on the grounds that the paucity of choices or opportunities for women undermine any possibility of consent.[19] Nancy Hirschmann points out that women's obligations historically have derived from nonconsensual bonds defined by their familial relationship. As she notes, if "a woman has a child against her will but comes to love it . . . she may recognize an obligation without fulfilling the necessary criteria for consent."[20]

These criticisms of consent underscore the necessity that choice must be the foundation of consent for agreements between parties to be valid. Yet application of the principle of consent to abortion rights uncovers an even more critical problem than limited range of choices available to women. Instead the major problem is that a woman's right to consent to a pregnancy relationship with a fetus has been almost completely absent from the abortion debate. Rather than examining the way in which women's limited choices may undermine their right to consent, we need to reframe the abortion debate by introducing women's right to consent to pregnancy in the first place.

Reframing abortion rights in terms of consent to pregnancy obviates the problem many have noted when applying consent theory to women's lives: the mistake of assuming that women's submission is a sign of their consent, when submission is the very opposite of what is meant by consent.[21] The act of seeking an abortion stands for a woman's lack of consent to be pregnant since abortion is a procedure that terminates pregnancy. A woman who chooses an abortion, therefore, is not submitting to a pregnancy caused by a fetus. To the contrary, she is stopping a fetus from making her pregnant by having an abortion.

Consent to Fetal Intrusion

Since our culture makes the mistake of designating men rather than fetuses as the cause of pregnancy, it commonly makes the correlative mistake of assuming that a woman's consent to sex signifies her consent to pregnancy. Whether because of our Puritan heritage or our dominant, bourgeois middle-class morality, many people identify sexual intercourse with pregnancy not only empirically but also normatively. They think that women who consent to sexual intercourse have actually consented to pregnancy, and moreover, that they should. To many, the idea of recreational sex, detached from any commitment to a subsequent pregnancy, is an anathema. Even decades after the sexual revolution of the 1960s, separating consent to sex from consent to pregnancy strikes a dissonant chord in the sensibilities of many in American culture.

The reluctance to separate sex and pregnancy is a major source of opposition to abortion. Allowing, much less assisting, women to have abortions only reinforces the ability of people to engage in sex without the reproductive consequences entailed by pregnancy and childbirth. As David Garrow explains, the conflation of consent to sex and pregnancy by abortion opponents leads them to the moral conclusion that pregnancy is an appropriate punishment for women who consent to engage in sex.[22] In this view, enabling a woman who has consented to sexual intercourse to have an abortion does nothing more than facilitate her escape from the utterly just punishment of a subsequent pregnancy. It is for this reason that the abortion issue stands for much more than merely protection of the fetus; it also stands for protection of sexual mores assumed to be vital to the well-being of society.[23]

Yet despite the range of cultural attitudes about the connection between sexual intercourse and pregnancy, there are still two relationships involved for a woman, not one. A man never has a pregnancy relationship with a fetus, and a fetus never has a sexual relationship with a man. By contrast, women have both sexual and pregnancy relationships, but not with the same person, to the degree that we think of the fetus as a person. A woman's pregnancy relationship with the fetus is distinct from her sexual relationship with a man. Her bodily integrity and liberty must, therefore, be assessed in the context of two relationships, each with a different private party, not one relationship with one private party.

A woman must have a right to consent to the way in which a man necessarily intrudes on her body and liberty when he has a sexual relationship with her, and so, too, must she have a comparable right to consent to how a fetus necessarily intrudes on her body and liberty when it has a pregnancy relationship with her. While people may hold philosophical and religious views that connect consent to sexual relationships with consent to pregnancy relationships, such beliefs do not alter the reality that each of these relationships involves different private parties, men and fetuses, respectively. For this reason, women must consent to the two relationships, not one, that are involved in their experience of reproduction.

The Supreme Court affirms the separation of sex and pregnancy, even in the absence of an explicit consent-to-pregnancy doctrine, by ruling that people have a constitutional right to disaggregate consent to one from consent to the other.[24] A woman who consents to sexual intercourse need not consent to pregnancy, and the constitutional right to use contraceptives is evidence of the legal recognition of her right to separate the two. Another way is for a woman simply to voice her lack of consent to pregnancy, much as she might voice her lack of consent to sexual intercourse. Seeking an abortion explicitly expresses a woman's lack of consent to pregnancy, much as a woman's call to the police to stop a man from raping her explicitly expresses her lack of consent to sexual intercourse.

Proponents of abortion rights need a more fully developed consent-to-pregnancy doctrine that more explicitly distinguishes between sexual intercourse and pregnancy. Sexual intercourse is only one of a long sequences of events that can lead to the conception of a fertilized ovum and its subsequent implantation in a woman's uterus. Sexual intercourse merely causes the risk that pregnancy will occur, and consent to engage in sexual intercourse with a man, for any and all fertile women, implies consent to expose oneself to that risk.

Consent to expose oneself to the risk that one will be injured by a private party, however, is not a legal proxy for consent to the actual injuries, should they occur. On the contrary, the law recognizes just the opposite. Consent to jog alone in Central Park does not stand as a proxy for consent to be mugged and raped, should others so attack you. The law instead recognizes in many ways how people can consent to factual, necessary causes of accidents and injuries imposed by other people without consenting to the legal causes of accidents. The "mere fact that one is willing to incur a risk that conduct in deliberate violation of the rules of a sporting contest will be committed," for example, "does not mean that one is willing for such conduct to be committed."[25] For this reason, just because normal, that is, consensual sexual intercourse precedes pregnancy does not mean that a woman has consented to that pregnancy any more than it means that because normal, that is, consensual jogging precedes a mugging and rape that the jogger has consented to a mugging and rape.[26]

Consent to incur the risk of pregnancy by engaging in sexual intercourse, of course, must be distinguished from other forms of risk assumption, such as when a person engages in dangerous sports (such as rock climbing), participates in dangerous amusement park rides (such as roller coasters), or incurs such routine risks as traveling on airplanes or in cars. All of these examples illustrate how people who consent to the risk of engaging in an activity by themselves may lose some rights to claiming damages, should they be injured. Yet even when they assume such risks, people do not lose their right to be free of nonconsensual injuries from others. Consent to incur the risks of rock climbing, for example, pertains only to the dangers incurred by one's own skill, or lack thereof, in rock climbing, but not to be thrown off the mountain and injured by another person. Similarly, consent to ride a roller coaster pertains only to the dangers that activity incurs in relation to the rider's own strengths or weaknesses, such as respirator and pulmonary problems, but not to be thrown out of the roller coaster by another person, nor even consent to injuries stemming from the negligent maintenance of the roller coaster by another person.

The distinction between the assumption of risk and contributory negligence is that the former is viewed as serving one's interests, while the latter is action that does not serve one's interest. While it may serve people's interests to engage in dangerous sports, such as rock climbing, for example, it does not serve their interests to engage in such dangerous activities as stepping into the street in front of an oncoming car. For this reason, the former is an assumption of risk, should people accidentally harm themselves while rock climbing, while the latter is contributory negligence, should people accidentally be hit by an oncoming car.

Women who assume the risk of pregnancy, therefore, must be viewed as acting in their own interest for the assumption of risk analysis to apply. One way they can be said to have assumed the risks of pregnancy is if they have given their express consent to that condition.[27] In this case, of course, a woman is not being harmed by a fetus imposing pregnancy against her will. She may be harmed as a result of the condition of pregnancy itself, but she does not endure harm by virtue of the imposition of pregnancy upon her against her will. Surgeons, for example, might operate without consent and even improve the condition of people's health, but if they do so without consent, they also harm people.

Another way to evaluate the assumption of risk is to think of it in terms of a relationship of duty.[28] Here we might think of a woman who voluntarily enters into a pregnancy relationship with a fetus, knowing full well that this relationship may entail harmful effects upon her. This might be like someone agreeing to play a dangerous game with others, such as boxing, with the understanding that one's opponent will make no effort to protect one from harm, and, in fact, may be intent on imposing harm. Such a relationship involves the consent to be harmed, however implicitly or tacitly it may be given. Presumably, that consent is revocable, however; if one wishes to stop boxing by breaking the relationship, one's opponent is not entitled to continue to inflict harm. Should an opponent continue to inflict harm after the relationship is broken, the victim would be entitled at that point to state assistance to stop the perpetrator.

If we apply this notion of assumed risk to pregnant women, we note that most women seek to terminate pregnancy at the earliest point possible, prior to establishing any relationship with the fertilized ovum. No tacit agreement, therefore, between the woman and the fertilized ovum ever existed because the woman never consented to the pregnant condition imposed upon her. And even if there were a relationship, and the woman decided to rescind her assumption of risk, she would be entitled to do so. If that were the case, the fertilized ovum's imposition upon a woman would then be unjustified because she no longer agrees to assume the risks of being harmed.

The assumption of risk also can be seen in cases where people realize others have created risks, yet they voluntarily exposes themselves to those risks.[29] A person who sees that someone has left dangerous objects on a sidewalk, for example, but nevertheless chooses to walk down the sidewalk, can be said to have assumed the risk of that activity and cannot hold the person responsible for debris contributing to an injury. If we apply this idea to a pregnant woman, it would mean that if she voluntarily agrees to be pregnant, she cannot hold the fetus responsible for harming her. On the other hand, of course, if she does not agree to be pregnant, the fetus's harm of her falls outside the parameters of her assumption of risk.

In general, even if a woman can be said to have assumed the risk that a fertilized ovum will harm her, since people are not bound to continue their assumption of risk, neither would she be so bound. People who agree to box with others are allowed to stop boxing when the harm exceeds their tolerance. Even if we were to apply an assumption of risk analysis to pregnancy, therefore, it would not entitle the fertilized ovum to harm a woman unless she has consented to that harm.

The law also recognizes the idea of implied consent, involving "an inference arising from a course of conduct or *relationship between the parties,* in which there is mutual acquiescence or a lack of objection under circumstances signifying assent."[30] If a woman does not explicitly say no to sexual intercourse, for example, her lack of objection can signify her implicit consent to sexual intercourse. So, too, with pregnancy. If a woman acquiesces to the way in which a fetus makes her pregnant and expresses no objection, one can infer her implicit consent to that pregnancy relationship.

Yet once a woman does say no to sexual intercourse, it is no longer possible to infer her implicit consent.[31] To the contrary, "no means no," and at that point a man imposing sexual intercourse on her is committing the felony of rape. So, too, with pregnancy. A woman who seeks an abortion by definition is seeking the termination of the pregnant condition imposed on her body by the fetus. Such a woman explicitly is saying no to pregnancy; she does not consent to be made pregnant by a fertilized ovum. And just as "no means no" in relation to sexual intercourse, so, too, does "no mean no" in relation to a pregnancy.[32]

There are thus two reproductive relationships, sexual intercourse and pregnancy, and consent to one does not stand for consent to the other.[33] Each relationship requires a woman's specific consent: the woman must explicitly consent to engage in *sexual intercourse with a man,* and she must also explicitly consent to engage in *pregnancy with a fertilized ovum.* A woman's consent to pregnancy means that she agrees to allow the fetus to invade her interests as represented by her body and her liberty. A woman who seeks an abortion gives explicit notice that she does not consent to engage in a pregnancy relationship with a fetus. By seeking an abortion, she is actively expressing her explicit objection, not her implicit assent. Once a woman actively objects to a relationship with the fetus, there are no longer any grounds for inferring from her conduct that she implicitly consents to that relationship. Quite the opposite is true: her conduct explicitly asserts that she does not consent to a pregnancy relationship with the fetus.

Consent to Quantitative Intrusion

Central to the concept of privacy is a person's right to bodily integrity and liberty. People related by kinship ties do not have the right to take even a pint of blood from each other's bodies without consent. To do so would be viewed in the law as imposing an injury. Yet some intrusions are so minimal that they warrant no legal claim of injury. On the one hand, if a person merely brushes your arm while passing on a sidewalk, such a brief and cursory physical contact does not constitute an injury even in the absence of consent. On the other hand, if a person knocks you down and breaks your leg, kidnaps, or rapes you, such an intrusion on your body and liberty is a serious injury, sufficient to invoke the power of the law and the state to stop it.

The question is whether the fetus merely inconveniences a woman when it causes a normal pregnancy, much as someone might do who brushed against you while passing, or whether the fetus intrudes on a woman's body and liberty so greatly as to qualify in the law as imposing significant injury when it makes a woman pregnant without her consent. The Court's opinion, as expressed in *Casey*, is that the pains and burdens of normal pregnancy attain all but mythical proportions, which would categorize pregnancy from the standpoint of the law as a serious injury when imposed without consent rather than as a mere inconvenience.[34] And the opinion of the medical profession is that normal pregnancy is an extraordinary condition, in which "the physiologic alterations" that the fetus causes "in all organ systems in the pregnant woman are among the most remarkable events in normal biology."[35] What unborn potential human life does to a woman when making her pregnant, therefore, demonstrates that pregnancy is a condition far exceeding mere inconvenience. On the contrary, when a fetus makes a woman pregnant, even in a normal pregnancy, it intrudes on her body and liberty in multiple and extensive ways.

Once a fertilized ovum is conceived and implants itself in a woman's body, for example, she begins to experience massive physical alterations.[36] One medical dictionary defines pregnancy as a condition that "sets up great changes, not only in the womb, but throughout the whole body."[37] While most of the changes in a normal pregnancy subside about a month after birth, a "few minor alterations persist throughout life."[38] The right of a woman to consent to pregnancy is underscored simply by looking at the sheer quantity of changes the fetus causes, portrayed by medical texts as a product of the fertilized ovum's intrusion and aggression.[39]

When the fertilized ovum[40] first "adheres to the endometrium," or tissue lining of the uterus, its "cells secrete an enzyme which enables" it "to literally eat a hole in the luscious endometrium and become completely buried within it."[41] The "erosive implantation" of the fertilized ovum in a woman's body allows it "to readily absorb nutrients" from the woman's "endometrial glands and blood vessels." Secretions of its cells[42] almost immediately following its implantation also maintain its implantation.[43]

During the early weeks of gestation, the cells of the fertilized ovum "stream out," "penetrate," and "extensively colonize" areas of the woman's uterus. Its cells also "destroy and replace the endothelium [lining] of the maternal vessels" and then "invade the [woman's] media with resulting destruction of the medial elastic and muscular tissue." The end result of the fertilized ovum's [44] "invasion of, and attack on" the woman's blood vessels is that her "thick-walled muscular spiral arteries are converted" into flaccid vessels, "which can passively dilate in order to accommodate the greatly augmented blood flow through this vascular system which is required as pregnancy progress."[45]

Around the eleventh day, the "advancing" fertilized ovum[46] "penetrates a maternal capillary and initiates a flow of blood" into a primitive placenta.[47] Among the many ways in which a fetus alters a woman's body to serve its own interests and needs, the placenta is unique. It is a new tissue structure, more complicated than a lung, that grows inside a woman's body only and specifically in response to a pregnancy.[48] It grows the entire time a woman is pregnant, eventually attaining a size of approximately 15 centimeters in diameter and 2 centimeters in thickness. At birth, the placenta may weigh 300 to 1200 grams. Because the fetus "depends on the growth of the placenta for its welfare . . . the growth of the placenta must keep pace with that of the fetus. Should the placenta fail, the fetus must either be delivered or experience intrauterine starvation or asphyxiation."[49]

Even these rudimentary glimpses of what the fetus does to a woman in normal pregnancy attest to her right to consent to be pregnant. If a born person were to invade, destroy, colonize, or otherwise intrude on your body so extensively, the law would be quick to assert your right to consent to that intrusion. Similarly, if a born person were to stimulate and maintain the growth in your body of a new, large organ, one more complex than your lung, the law would defend your right to consent to such an addition to your body.

Yet this is not all the fetus does when it initiates normal pregnancy. Compounding these physical intrusions, the fertilized ovum reroutes a woman's circulatory system so that her blood is available for its own needs and uses.[50] As a result, blood plasma volume increases 40 percent, cardiac volume increases 40 percent, heart rate increases 15 percent, stroke volume increases 30 percent, peripheral resistance increases 25 percent, and diastolic blood pressure increases 15 percent.[51] The total blood flow through the umbilical cord, which attaches the fetus to the placenta, is on the average about 125 milliliters per kilogram of body weight per minute, and at term it is about 500 milliliters per minute.[52] The amniotic fluid, which surrounds the fetus and is composed largely of maternal plasma filtrate and fetal urine, undergoes constant exchange between fetus and mother. At term, this exchange of water is approximately 3500 milliliters per hour in each direction.[53]

Other complicated exchanges between the fetus and the woman take place across the placenta. Substances that maintain biochemical homeostasis or protect against sudden fetal death, such as electrolytes, water, and respiratory gases (oxygen and carbon dioxide), are transferred at a rate of milligrams per second and rapidly diffused. Substances that are necessary to maintain fetal nutrition, such as amino acids, sugars, and most water-soluble vitamins (such as riboflavin), are exchanged in milligrams per minute. Substances that modify fetal growth and maintain pregnancy in a woman's body, such as the hormones thyroxine, estrogen, and progesterone, are exchanged in milligrams per hour. Finally, substances that have immunologic importance, such as plasma proteins, are exchanged in milligrams per day.[54]

All of these exchanges, which occur as part of a condition initiated and maintained by the fetus, take place in a woman's body on a second-by-second, minute-by-minute, hour-by-hour, and day-by-day basis. The saying that no woman can be "a little bit" pregnant could not be more true. Pregnancy is a massive, ongoing set of processes, caused by a fertilized ovum, which keeps a woman's body physically operating and changing every second, minute, hour, day, week, and month for nine months.

From the perspective of a woman's right to terminate a nonconsensual pregnancy, the key comparison is to the position of the state if a born person imposed such physical transformations on another born person's body. Such impositions would not be viewed as merely an inconvenience. To the contrary, their massive quantitative character would be apparent. No born person has such a right to impose such physically invasive processes on the body of another person, nor does any preborn potential person. To the degree that the Court protects the fetus as if it had personhood attributes, the Court also must restrict the fetus as if it had personhood attributes. For it is not merely that the fetus embeds itself in a woman's uterus, causes a complex new organ to grow, initiates and maintains multiple transfers of liquids, and reroutes her circulatory system, but also that it impacts dramatically on her endocrine system by affecting her glands and hormonal secretions.

Glands and other organs increase dramatically in size and weight when a fetus makes a woman pregnant. The pituitary gland progressively enlarges during pregnancy and by term is double its nonpregnant weight.[55] In addition, hormonal levels in a woman's body drastically change, making them an easy way to diagnose whether a woman is pregnant. One of the most dramatic transformations is the monumental elevation of some hormones to over 400 times their normal levels. The developing fertilized ovum so drastically alters the woman's endocrine system that her menstrual cycle completely stops, which is a crucial step to maintaining her pregnancy.[56] In addition, the fertilized ovum[57] produces pregnancy-specific concentrations of some substances[58] that reach the maternal bloodstream, thereby providing another accurate test for whether a woman is pregnant.[59]

Common symptoms of pregnancy reflect the enormity of the transformations of a woman's body involved. Not only does her cardiac volume, stroke volume, heart rate, and pulse increase significantly, but because her blood flow in pregnancy is obstructed by the large uterus on the iliac vens and interior vena cava, the rate of blood flow to her lower extremities decreases. For this reason, in a normal pregnancy women are predisposed to edema in the lower extremities, as well as to varicosities and sometimes to thrombophlebitis.[60]

A woman's respiratory system also undergoes may changes in a normal pregnancy, including hyperventilation, characterized by frequent sighing. About 50 percent of pregnant women experience breathlessness by twenty weeks' gestation, and more do so as their pregnancy approaches term. Blood volume flowing through a pregnant woman's body increases about 45 percent over non-pregnant levels, which can lead to physiologic anemia. A woman's white blood cell count also increases in pregnancy, as do factors required for blood coagulation. Because pregnancy alters a woman's gastrointestinal tract anatomically and physiologically, as many as 90 percent of pregnant women are bothered by gastrointestinal symptoms at some point in pregnancy. Since the hormonal changes of pregnancy change the soft tissues, smooth muscle, and epithelial surfaces of the oral cavity, as many as 75 percent of pregnant women bleed from the gums or oral pharynx during a medically normal pregnancy.[61]

Nausea and vomiting are so common during early pregnancy that they have become presumptive evidence of pregnancy. Changes in appetite also characterize pregnancy, including not only decreases and increases in the intake of food, but also cravings for particular types of food as a result of changes in the threshold for all forms of taste (salt, sour, sweet, and bitter). A pregnant condition decreases the tone of a woman's lower esophagus, which can lead to symptoms of heartburn. A woman's skin also responds to the physical and hormonal alterations constituting a pregnant condition, which often increase pigmentation. About 70 percent of all pregnant women experience such pigmentation changes, usually on the forehead, cheeks, bridge of the nose, and chin. The blotchy appearance of pregnant women's faces that result is known as the "mask of pregnancy." Estrogen increases during pregnancy have dramatic effects on hair growth, both during pregnancy and immediately afterward, resulting in increased shedding of hair during the first three to four months after giving birth.[62]

While all of these transformations are normal to pregnancy, they are nonetheless extraordinary. Possibly some people think of such intrusions as mere inconveniences, but by legal standards they must trigger concern. To the degree that the fetus imposes these massive physical transformations on a woman's body in its capacity as a potential human being, rather than as a natural force or a disease, the key legal issue becomes a woman's right to consent to how a fetus as a private party makes her pregnant.

Consent to Qualitative Intrusion

There is yet another dimension to normal pregnancy, which is qualitative rather than quantitative. It is not merely that a fetus physically transforms a woman's body in massive ways when making her pregnant, but also that in so doing it necessarily intrudes on her liberty. Liberty has many meanings, and in terms of the law it usually refers to the fact that a state may not intrude on the fundamental rights of a private party. While no one has immunity from "reasonable regulations and prohibitions" imposed by the state in order to protect the interests of the community, people nevertheless have a right to be free from "arbitrary restraint" by the state.[63]

The right to liberty that is guaranteed and protected by the state refers to "freedom from unauthorized physical restraint" and to a range of ways in which an individual must be free to "use and enjoy his faculties" in lawful ways; to acquire knowledge; to marry and establish a home, including procreation and the rearing of children; to exercise religious conscience and preferences freely; to "live and work" where one chooses; and to "engage in any of the common and lawful occupations of life . . . and generally to enjoy those privileges long recognized at common law as essential to the orderly pursuit of happiness by free people."[64] In addition to relationships between the state and individuals, guarantees of liberty extend to relationships between individuals.

Freedom from intrusion by other private parties of one's body, person, property, ability to move about, capacity for work, and even one's personality is basic to the idea of what the law recognizes as the right to liberty. Intrusion on one's privacy by private people was defined by Louis Brandeis and Samuel Warren as a basic violation of the right to liberty, or the "right to be let alone" by other private people, not merely by the state.[65] As Laurence Tribe notes, first and foremost *Homo sapiens* is a social animal, yet "the concept of privacy embodies the 'moral fact that a person belongs to himself and not others nor to society as a whole.'"[66] Belonging to yourself means that no other private person may intrude on your right to make decisions about your life, liberty, and property in violation of the law.

The right to be let alone by the state and by other private people derives from the natural law heritage of our political system, which asserts that there is a natural standard of justice for human behavior that predates any particular society and its laws, so that unjust laws legislated or adjudicated by the government need not bind one's conscience. According to this doctrine, people possess an inalienable right to life, liberty, and the pursuit of happiness, which is more fundamental than any system of government or actual law. People's right to natural liberty therefore precedes their right to liberty in relation to the state. Natural liberty is the

> power of acting as one thinks fit, without any restraint or control. . . . The right which nature gives to all mankind of disposing of their persons and property after the manner they judge most consistent with their happiness . . . [without interfering] with an equal exercise of the same rights by other men.[67]

The idea of inalienable rights, which precede the establishment of any particular government, deeply influenced the founders of the American state, as reflected in the American Declaration of Independence and Constitution. Since people possess these rights prior to the founding of a state, the fundamental duty of the state, once established, is to protect people's inalienable right to life, liberty, and property—hence the constitutional prohibitions against state interference in people's liberty without due process, which derive from a general recognition of people's right to their natural liberty in relation to the state and to other private people.[68]

The way in which liberty extends to prohibitions against intrusions by private parties shows up most vividly in the case of slavery. Although the Constitution in general regulates the relationship between the state and the individual, a notable exception is the Thirteenth Amendment, which the Supreme Court interprets as forbidding the state and private parties from imposing slavery. The amendment reads,

> Section 1. Neither slavery nor involuntary servitude, except as a punishment for crime whereof the party shall have been duly convicted, shall exist within the United States, or any place subject to their jurisdiction. Section 2. Congress shall have the power to enforce this article by appropriate legislation.

Thus the Constitution prohibits the state from imposing either slavery or involuntary servitude and grants to Congress the power to regulate private conduct in order to prohibit the imposition of slavery.[69] The law defines slavery as a civil relationship between two private parties in which one "has absolute power over the life, fortune, and liberty of another,"[70] which means that one person's freedom of action, person, and services is "wholly under the control of another."[71]

This definition casts what the fetus does to a woman in normal pregnancy in a new light. The fetus causes a massive physical transformation of a woman's body, and it also wholly controls her body, her freedom of movement, and her reproductive services. When a woman is pregnant, as the Court noted, her privacy is no longer sole. She can go nowhere without the fetus; every action she takes necessarily includes the fetus. The circulation of her blood, her endocrine system, and her menstrual cycles are now controlled by the fetus. As long as it maintains a pregnant condition in her body, for up to nine months she is decidedly not let alone, and she is anything but free.

As Nicky Hart notes, "Creating new human life is a costly material process" in which the fetus draws on the woman's energy, nutrition, and labor, and although it conventionally has been set apart from productive forms of capitalist labor, that has been a mistake. When women are pregnant, they are at work.[72] The fetus uses its mother's blood to obtain all its nutrients and to dispose of all its wastes. Every breath a woman takes must be done in relationship with the fetus, as must every meal that a woman eats while pregnant. The fetus uses the mother's food reserves, even when her own nutrient resources are low.[73] While it has been common for biologists to assume that "a mother and her fetus have an underlying harmony of interests," it is not always the case that what is best for the fetus is best for the woman.[74] Though infants are dependent on their mothers, they can at times survive without them. When childbirth becomes life threatening to a baby and its mother, therefore, we can expect the baby to struggle for its own survival even if this increases the risk of death or permanent injury to its mother. In addition to mutuality, there is also as much evidence for socially constructing the fetal-maternal relationship in terms of conflict, and it is conflict that typifies a pregnancy relationship; this conflict includes the fetus's intimate imposition on a woman, which is to say, her virtual enslavement by it.

The fetus, therefore, uses a woman's body and appropriates her reproductive labor for its own benefit, thereby intruding on her liberty in a serious qualitative way when initiating and maintaining even a normal pregnancy. If the fetus makes a woman pregnant without her consent, it deprives her of her liberty, that is, her inalienable rights. People's right to liberty means that they have a right to freedom of action and to the control of their own selves without intrusion and control from others. They have a right to be let alone from nonconsensual restrictions of their liberty.

If a woman does not consent to pregnancy, the fetus has intruded on her liberty in a way similar to that of a kidnapper or slave master. If people invite you to take a trip with them, for example, and you consent, we call that a vacation, wish you bon voyage, and expect to receive a postcard extolling your adventure. But if you refuse to go on a trip with another private party, and that person coerces you and takes you away against your will, that same trip is transformed into the crime of kidnapping because your liberty has been invaded by a private party. Rather than waiting for postcards, we would call on the police to stop the kidnapper from so intruding on your right to freedom of action.

So, too, with normal pregnancy. If a woman consents to the way in which a fetus transforms and uses her body when it makes her pregnant, the issue of coercion and violation of her liberty does not arise. If, however, she refuses to consent to pregnancy, the fetus is then imposing on her in a way that violates her right to liberty. Its control of her body, her freedom of action, her person, and her reproductive services, as distinguished from the sheer quantity of its physical intrusion per se, is a serious qualitative violation of her inalienable rights.

For good reason, we call the process by which a woman gives birth, or actually bears a child, labor, thereby recognizing the effort and work involved in the task. So, too, is pregnancy throughout its duration reproductive work. Without consent, the totality of the fetus's appropriation of a woman's body for its own sake is, therefore, involuntary servitude if not enslavement.[75] When the fetus takes over a woman's reproductive capacities against her will, it becomes the master of her body and her liberty, putting her in the position of its slave.

It has been common in the abortion debate for pro-life, rather than pro-choice, advocates to invoke analogies with slavery.[76] The claim is that aborting fetuses on the grounds that they are not persons devalues their humanity in much the same way that slavery devalues the humanity of those under its oppression. What is more, the pregnancy relationship lasts only nine months for a woman in comparison to a lifetime of entrapment for people caught in the evil grip of slavery as an institution. To turn the slavery principle completely around, some might contend that it is not merely the abortion of the fetus that invokes slavery principles but also the pregnancy relationship itself. While a woman has the choice to abort the fetus, it has no ability to exercise a conscious intention to remain, or not to remain, in that relationship.[77] For this reason, it is the fetus that is entrapped and enslaved by the woman. Yet it is the fetus that causes pregnancy, not the woman. What is more, pregnancy is a condition that serves the fetus's need for survival and growth, not the woman's. While reproduction ensures the continuation of the human species and more specifically of kinship groupings, no person has to engage in reproduction in order to secure the continuation of his or her own life as an individual. No woman needs to be pregnant, therefore, in order to continue living as an individual. Pregnancy, in fact, poses physical risks to her life, not physical benefits.

Precisely the opposite is true for the fetus. It is exactly because the termination of pregnancy harms the fetus, destroys it in fact, that women's rights to terminate pregnancy have been limited by the Court. Since pregnancy benefits the fetus, therefore, it is difficult to construe that condition as a form of enslavement at odds with its own interests. To the contrary, it is the woman's liberty, not the fetus's, that is at stake in pregnancy. Nine months compared to a lifetime is not a long period, but in principle pregnancy can be considered a form of enslavement if it is imposed on a woman without her consent for that period. It is not only the way that pregnancy affects a woman's physical body that is at issue in the abortion debate, therefore, but also the way that it appropriates her reproductive labor and her very liberty.

Consent to Absolute Intrusion

The massive physical intrusions and qualitative invasions of a woman's liberty caused by a fetus in normal pregnancy are not the end of the story, however, for the fetus can also cause an abnormal pregnancy, producing additional injuries. A medically abnormal pregnancy is one in which the quantitative physical effects of the fetus reach proportions that threaten severe impairment of a woman's health, perhaps for the rest of her life, or even death. Sometimes life or death crises occur because the pregnancy exacerbates a health vulnerability the woman already has. At other times the pregnancy creates a new threat to a woman's life and health. The increase in the size and weight of the pituitary gland caused by the fetus, for example, can stimulate the growth of tumors in a woman's body. Such tumors are associated with 17 percent of the medical complications during pregnancy. When these tumors press on surrounding structures, they can produce acute symptoms, such as headaches, "visual defects, impaired cranial nerve function, and prolonged nausea and vomiting."[78] Whereas in normal pregnancy the growth of the woman's uterus "causes some degree of ureteral obstruction," in abnormal pregnancy the obstruction can cause renal failure, in which a woman's kidneys stop functioning.[79]

The changes in a woman's cardiovascular system caused by the fetus can lead to serious symptoms that mimic heart disease, such as a decrease in cardiac output. When a woman is in a supine position, this decrease in cardiac output can lead to a decrease in blood pressure, which causes such symptoms as lightheadedness, nausea, and even fainting.[80] In some cases the cardiovascular changes of normal pregnancy can aggravate an underlying heart condition, and then a normal pregnancy can become an abnormal pregnancy that threatens a woman's life. Another potentially fatal problem associated with the changes wrought by the fetus is thromboembolic disease, "the leading cause of nonobstetric postpartum maternal mortality." The risk of deep vein thrombophlebitis is five times higher for pregnant than nonpregnant women.[81] A normal pregnancy can also become life threatening if septic pelvic vein thrombophlebitis develops.[82] These are only a few of the many ways in which a normal pregnancy can become abnormal, threatening a woman with death.

Some women, of course, will choose to consent to a medically abnormal pregnancy even though it entails even higher levels of intrusion on their bodily integrity, liberty, and well-being than that imposed by medically normal pregnancies. Yet even the Court in *Roe* went out of its way to make it clear that women have a constitutional right to say no to a medically abnormal pregnancy at every stage of pregnancy, whatever might be the state's interest in protecting the fetus. Embedded in this ruling is recognition that pregnancy can be an extremely threatening condition for women, and the only flaw is the Court's use of a medically abnormal pregnancy as a standard for defining those threats. To say that a medically normal pregnancy does not intrude on a woman's bodily integrity and liberty to the same degree as a medically abnormal one is not to say that the former is merely an inconvenience. On the contrary, it also massively and seriously violates a woman's bodily integrity and liberty when imposed on her without consent, even if it does not threaten to permanently damage her health or to kill her.

Duty of Care

The fertilized ovum is usually genetically related to the woman, and thus, by making her pregnant, it makes her its genetic parent. As the parent of the fertilized ovum, a woman might seem to have a duty to care for the fetus, but however that duty is defined, it does not override the woman's right to consent to the pregnancy in the first place. Though parents do have a duty to care for their children, that duty does not include the use, or taking, of a parent's body. Once born, children do not have the right to intrude physically on the bodies of their parents, regardless of what their needs might be. A born child who kidnaps a mother and forcibly extracts a pint of blood, in conditions simulating pregnancy, would not be protected by the law. Rather, the law would view the parent as the victim of the child's coercive physical intrusion on her bodily integrity and liberty.

A woman is thus not bound by parental duty to give the kind of care that includes donating her body to a fertilized ovum, as its parent, even if the fertilized ovum is thought to have the same status as a born child.[83] And whatever the personhood status of the fetus, it surely has no right to take a person's body without consent. There are no legal grounds, therefore, for empowering preborn potential life, which may not yet be a person, to take a woman's body and liberty without her consent, whatever might be a woman's duty to care for her offspring and whatever might be the needs of preborn life.[84]

Also, to say that a woman who carelessly risks pregnancy by engaging in sexual intercourse without protection "tortiously endangers" the fetus and therefore would have a "clear legal duty to aid the endangered person"[85] puts the cart before the horse. As Sissela Bok notes, "Ceasing bodily life support *of a fetus or of anyone else* cannot be looked at as a breach of duty except where such a duty has been assumed in the first place."[86] Before assessing a woman's duty of care, we first must assess whether she has consented to the pregnancy initially.[87] And before assessing how the woman affects a fetus by having an abortion, we must first establish what it is that the fetus does to a woman when it makes her pregnant. If a woman does not consent to be pregnant, the fetus imposes huge quantitative and qualitative injuries on her body and liberty, if not the absolute injury of death. Any injury a woman inflicts on a fetus necessarily is in response to its injury of her. Rather than a duty of care, she has a right to defend herself against the fetus's serious injury.

What is more, pregnancy is an ongoing condition, defined by a series of ways in which the implanted, fertilized ovum initiates and maintains massive bodily changes in the woman. As such, it requires not just a woman's initial consent but also her ongoing consent in tandem with the ongoing bodily changes involved. Pregnancy based on consent, therefore, does not constitute either a binding contract or a binding promise—what the law calls an estoppel by promise.

The law views a promise by one person as binding, and hence requiring enforcement to avoid injustice, only when it induces action or forbearance on the part of another person who will be harmed if the promise is not kept.[88] If friends promise you a job, for example, thereby causing you to quit your present employment, sell your house, and move to the new employment location, all on the basis of their guarantee that their promise will be kept, the law might hold your friends responsible for making good on the promise to the extent that they can.

Pregnancy, however, does not qualify as a binding promise to a fetus when a woman does not consent to the pregnancy because she has promised nothing to a fetus and cannot be bound by promises she never made. To the contrary, a fertilized ovum is imposing a pregnancy relationship on a woman that she has never agreed to accept. Even if a woman has consented to be pregnant at one time, this does not bind her to continue to consent in the future, given the changing conditions defining the experience of pregnancy. A woman who consents to marry a man, for example, is not required to stay married to him for the rest of her life, particularly if the conditions of that marriage change. Similarly, the promise to give someone a job does not bind an employer to continue employing a person if his or her work changes and becomes unsatisfactory.

A woman who initially consents to pregnancy might change her mind as the pregnancy progresses and she experiences its bodily alterations. This raises the question of abortion in late pregnancy and the possible limits to a woman's right to withdraw her consent to be pregnant. No private person has the right to intrude on the body of another private person without his or her consent. In a technical, strictly legal sense, a pregnant woman retains the right to withdraw her consent to the use of her body by a fetus throughout pregnancy. This does not mean, however, that the result would be abortion in late pregnancy, for as a pregnancy progresses, the techniques for removing a fetus do not necessitate killing it. The termination of late pregnancies therefore converges with birth itself, not abortion. The definition of an abortion is the "termination of human pregnancy with an intention other than to produce a live birth or to remove a dead fetus."[89] If the intention in the termination of a late pregnancy is to preserve the life of the fetus, this is not, strictly speaking, an abortion at all. Rather it is a preterm termination of pregnancy.

A preterm termination of pregnancy, with the intention to produce a live fetus, raises many other questions, such as the use of artificial means of support to keep a viable fetus alive in lieu of the pregnant woman. It also means that women who choose to withdraw their consent to pregnancy late in term may find that they become biological mothers, even though they have refused to continue to be pregnant. As philosopher Judith Jarvis Thomson argues, the right to withdraw samaritan support for a needy recipient is not coterminous with the right "to be guaranteed his death."[90]

While women retain the legal right to consent to pregnancy throughout its duration, in the context of women's abortion rights, late abortions are not a policy problem because women's own interests are best served when they can seek and obtain needed abortions at the earliest, not the latest, stages of pregnancy. As Laurence Tribe notes, "early abortion . . . is statistically a far safer procedure for a pregnant woman than carrying her pregnancy to term."[91] Richard Posner concurs that the earlier an abortion is performed, the stronger the woman's interest in having an abortion because she will be "spared more of the risks and inconveniences of pregnancy"; the later the abortion is performed, the weaker is the woman's interest "because she has borne more of the burdens of pregnancy already."[92] We could add that a woman's interest in terminating a medically normal pregnancy also becomes significantly more costly to her in terms of the invasiveness of the abortion techniques required. For this and other reasons, the overwhelming number of women do just that: if they choose an abortion, they seek and obtain one as early as possible into their pregnancy. This holds true even in countries such as Canada, where women have the right to terminate pregnancy at later stages."

Although it is not in women's self-interest to postpone a needed abortion, if they do so, the medical techniques used for terminating late-term pregnancies can be the same as those used for preterm births, such as induced labor and Caesarean surgery. Since it is also not in a woman's self-interest to give birth prematurely, women seeking to terminate their pregnancies choose the earliest date possible. Canadian law, which has long made abortions "legal to the moment of live birth," does not cause women to wait as long as possible to obtain one.[93]

No woman becomes pregnant in order to procure an abortion, much less to wait as long into pregnancy as possible before doing so. Currently, prohibitions on abortion funding, however, have the effect of producing more, not fewer, late abortions. This occurs when the state denies public funds to indigent women in early pregnancy, but subsequently makes those funds available later in pregnancy, if it becomes a threat to her health or life, depending on the public policies in force. The policy goal, therefore, is to secure public funding for women in medically normal as well as abnormal pregnancies, so that women may obtain abortions *early* in pregnancy before the fetus is viable in lieu of being forced to wait until late in pregnancy to obtain public funds to terminate pregnancies that become severely threatening to their health. The policy impact of the consent-to-pregnancy approach to abortion rights accomplishes just that. Moving from choice to consent as the grounds for women's right to an abortion provides the legal basis for the right not only to an abortion but also to abortion funding early in pregnancy, even if it is medically normal, thereby reducing the number of late-term pregnancies.

Consent to Altruism

To explain what the fertilized ovum does to a woman to make her pregnant requires the use of metaphors, which reflect the values and worldviews of those who tell the stories we then call reality. Since the dominant stories have been constructed by men, there is the danger that what we learn about reality captures masculine and male, rather than feminine and female, perspectives. As anthropologist Emily Martin demonstrates, the metaphors used to describe and explain the biological process of conception have long recapitulated the stereotypical views of how men relate to women, including men's active pursuit of, competition for, dominance over, and possession of women.[94] Similarly, English professor Robert Baker finds that the common idea that men penetrate women during sexual intercourse is not validated by the anatomical distinctions between the sexes.[95] Rather than thinking that a penis "penetrates" a vagina, we could as easily think that a vagina "engulfs" a penis. Our linguistic choice of *penetration* reflects and reproduces men's social and political power over women, not their anatomical differences per se.

The biological representation of pregnancy employs a parallel metaphor. The language of penetration and aggression attributed to the fetus can be viewed as simply the product of a male profession, medicine, which imposes its own social stereotypes on women, who are typically conceptualized as the "objects" of male aggression. As a result, the social construction of pregnancy merely extends the penetration metaphor to include three phases of reproduction: in sexual intercourse a man penetrates a woman, in conception a sperm penetrates an ovum, and in pregnancy a fertilized ovum penetrates a woman by implanting itself in her body.[96]

Alternatives to the penetration metaphor avoid the cultural stereotypes of biological reproductive processes and of social and political relationships between the sexes. Instead of saying that the sperm penetrates the ovum, for example, we could say that the two "join" together to become a fertilized ovum. Similarly, instead of saying that the fertilized ovum implants itself in the body of a woman, intrudes on her, or uses her body when it makes her pregnant, we could say altruistically that the fertilized ovum "gives" itself to a woman, "bestows" itself on her, and "activates" her capacity to be pregnant.[97] When this symbiotic view of pregnancy is carried to its logical extreme, the body of the mother and the fetus become one, rather than two, which many pro-choice advocates believe reinforces women's right to choose whether to be pregnant, based on their right to make decisions about their own body rather than worrying about injury to the fetus's separate body.[98]

Yet even if we frame pregnancy in these maternalistic, nurturing, altruistic ways, the issue still must be whether a woman consents to receive the gift of pregnancy from the fetus or to have her body transformed by union with the fetus. Someone might well say, "Have I got a present for you!" but the question remains whether a person consents to be the recipient of that present, particularly when the present in question transforms her body and liberty so massively. The language of altruism to depict what occurs when a fetus makes a woman pregnant does not guarantee the woman's consent. A woman must have the right to consent to maternalism in particular and to altruism bestowed by a fetus in general.

Just as the law allows no born person to take someone else's body without consent, so, too, the law allows no born person to impose altruistic behavior on another person without consent. It might be considered altruistic, for example, to donate a pint of blood or a body organ to a person in need, yet even when that need is dire, the potential receiver must consent to such an altruistic body transfer. People who have signed living wills may need such a donation to live but may refuse to receive the donation because they do not wish to prolong their lives.[99] In such a case, without consent, it is not lawful for one born person to impose an altruistic gift on another. If the fetus is treated as a born person, therefore, as pro-life advocates demand, a woman still must consent to the way in which it makes her body pregnant, even when altruistic metaphors replace penetration metaphors to depict that process.

The view of pregnancy as a form of intrusive aggression against a woman by a fertilized ovum does not preclude other depictions of pregnancy as a symbiotic union of mother and child.[100] No species would survive if mothers viewed offspring solely as aggressors. The key word here is *solely*. The view of pregnancy as intrusive aggression by a fetus does not substitute for all other views but rather expands the continuum of legal and social constructions of pregnancy so that it, too, has the same latitude as other intimate relationships, such as sexual intercourse.[101]

It is time now to reframe pregnancy, much as sexual intercourse has already been reframed, into an experience that requires at a minimum a woman's explicit consent in order to be legal, leaving a wide scope for whatever else is required to impart maximum value.[102] Sexual intercourse runs the gamut from positive to negative extremes. Highly romanticized under some conditions, intercourse is a criminal offense in other contexts. What makes the difference between a valentine, on the one hand, and a law suit, on the other, is consent. The fact that sexual intercourse without consent is recognized not only as a crime but also as a degrading, intrusive, and violent injury does not in any way detract from the positive dimensions of the physicality of this act under consensual, as well as ecstatically romantic, conditions.

So it is with pregnancy. As Dorothy Roberts and Martha Fineman point out, motherhood is a problematic concept and experience that can result in women's subordination, not liberation or fulfillment.[103] Surely all human beings must have a right to say no, with the full support of the state, to such a massive quantitative and qualitative invasion as is imposed by a fertilized ovum when it causes pregnancy. Yet the right to say no to a fertilized ovum does not negate a romantic attitude toward pregnancy. When a woman not only consents to be pregnant but also actively wishes and seeks to be pregnant, this surely serves as the ideal. That this is not always the situation, however, requires legal recognition. There is room for romance in our attitudes toward both intercourse and pregnancy, even while adding legal guarantees to ensure that no woman must experience either without her consent.

5

Wrongful Pregnancy

In *Roe v. Wade*, the Supreme Court ruled that protecting the fetus as a form of human life is a profound state interest from the moment of conception, which increases to a compelling interest by the time of fetal viability.[1] While the fetus's status as a person may be in a potential rather than an actual stage, the law nonetheless does not treat the fetus as if it were a subhuman species, such as a dog or a cat, or a natural force, such as a disease, hurricane, fire, or flood. To the contrary, the state protects the fetus as human life, albeit unborn human life, which may or may not be an actual person. When the fetus causes pregnancy, it does so in its capacity as valuable, state-protected human life. But if a woman does not consent to the fetus's imposition of pregnancy, it causes what the law terms a *wrongful pregnancy*.

When men rape women or physicians incompetently perform sterilizations, even though they had no intention to put a woman at risk for pregnancy, they nevertheless are held responsible for coercing a woman to be pregnant should that condition ensue. *Wrongful pregnancy*, also known as wrongful conception, is a legal term that refers to a private party's imposition of a pregnant condition on a woman, or even the risk of a pregnant condition, against her will.[2] When the fetus imposes not merely the risk but also the actual condition of pregnancy on a woman without consent, therefore, from the standpoint of the law what it is doing in its capacity as a state-protected form of human life is imposing wrongful pregnancy.

Wrongful Pregnancy as Serious Injury

Justice Stevens stated in his dissent in *Harris v. McRae*, "Surely the government may properly presume that no harm will ensue from normal childbirth."[3] Even though Justice Stevens made this statement in the context of support for abortion funding, he undercut the justification for all aspects of women's abortion rights by failing to recognize that the law already categorizes normal pregnancy as a serious bodily injury when imposed on a woman without consent.

Recognition that even normal pregnancy is a serious injury when imposed on a woman without consent was the basis for the Court's decision in *Michael M.*

v. Superior Court of Sonoma County,[4] which held that it was constitutional for a state to penalize a male, but not a female, in statutory rape on the grounds that pregnancy entails harmful consequences to women that men do not face. As the Court stated,

> Only women may become pregnant . . . [and] Because virtually all of the significant harmful and inescapably identifiable consequences of teenage pregnancy fall on the young female, a legislature acts well within its authority when it elects to punish only the participant who, by nature, suffers few of the consequences of his conduct. It is hardly unreasonable for a legislature acting to protect minor females to exclude them from punishment. Moreover, the risk of pregnancy itself constitutes a substantial deterrent to young females. No similar natural sanctions deter males.[5]

The law's recognition that a normal pregnancy is a serious bodily injury when forced on a woman is becoming more and more apparent because of the growing percentage of women choosing sterilization as their preferred form of contraception. In 1988, for example, 28.3 percent of all women chose sterilization, making it the most popular form of contraception, and recent studies show that 23.6 percent of couples who used birth control chose sterilization.[6] Consequently, increasing numbers of women or couples are successfully suing physicians for damages caused by wrongful pregnancy subsequent to negligent sterilization. The damages typically include the costs of the pregnancy and of rearing the child, even when there are no injuries to the woman or child over and above the nonconsensual character of the pregnancy itself.[7] In a unanimous decision in *Marciniak v. Lundborg* in 1990, for example, the Wisconsin Supreme Court ruled that the "costs of raising the child to the age of majority may be recovered by the parents for damages caused by a negligently performed sterilization operation."[8] What is more, the court concluded that "these costs may not be offset by any benefits conferred upon the parents by virtue of the presence of the child in their lives."[9]

When a physician fails to sterilize a man or woman competently and a child is subsequently born, almost every legal jurisdiction considers this to be serious malpractice. This holds even if the pregnancy entails no medical complications, the child that is born is completely healthy, and the woman opts to keep it. In a Georgia case in 1984,[10] for example, Brenda Stroup underwent a sterilization procedure performed by Dr. Herbert Shessel. A month later she discovered she was pregnant, and subsequently she gave birth to a healthy child. Later the Stroups sued Shessel for malpractice, seeking damages.

The court affirmed in this context that pregnancy is a legal injury.[11] *Black's Law Dictionary* generally defines injury as a "wrong or damage done to another, either in his person, rights, reputation, or property. The invasion of any legally protected interest of another."[12] There was nothing to indicate that Brenda Stroup had suffered an abnormal pregnancy since it presented no medical complications and she gave birth to a healthy child. Yet because she did not consent to her pregnant condition, she was judged by the law to have suffered injury.

A woman must have informed choice if her consent to be pregnant is to be valid. It is also an injury if a woman does not receive information pertinent to choosing whether or not to consent to pregnancy. In this sense, choice necessarily underlies both consent in general and a woman's consent to pregnancy in particular.[13] The Ohio Supreme Court emphasized the critical dimension of choice by explaining how normal pregnancy becomes an injury when it is coerced:

> In order to establish malpractice, appellants must prove that the injury complained of, here the denial of their right to make an informed choice about pregnancy termination, was directly and proximately caused by a practice that a physician of ordinary skill, care or diligence would not have done . . . . A physician's failure to disclose material information regarding a patient's condition within the time necessary to effectively treat the condition certainly constitutes a claim of malpractice . . . . Failure to diagnose and/or disclose information which is crucial to the exercise of this right [of choice whether to procreate] is actionable as medical malpractice.[14]

A Florida court also defined wrongful pregnancy to include a birth subsequent to a "negligently performed abortion procedure."[15] Similarly the Supreme Court of Alabama defined "wrongful birth" as having

> nothing to do with whether the defendant caused the injury or harm to the child, but, rather, with whether the defendant's negligence was the proximate cause of the parents' being deprived of the option of avoiding a conception or, in the case of pregnancy, making an informed and meaningful decision either to terminate the pregnancy or to give birth to a potentially defective child.[16]

Rape statutes and court rulings, which recognize that a woman has been injured more severely if she becomes pregnant subsequent to rape than if she does not, also establish that normal pregnancy is an injury when it occurs without a woman's consent. A Wisconsin statute, for example, specifically lists pregnancy as one of the conditions, along with disease, used to determine the "extent of injury" suffered in the aftermath of sexual assault.[17] Similarly, California courts have established that normal pregnancy constitutes "great bodily harm" when it occurs subsequent to rape or incest,[18] and that such harm must be evaluated as an additional injury to the rape itself.

State statutes link nonconsensual pregnancy with harm when evaluating the "degree of sexual assault" or the "extent of injury suffered" by a woman as the result of sexual assault. The greater the degree of sexual assault and the greater the extent of injury suffered by the victim when normal pregnancy results, the higher the degree of punishment for the perpetrator of the assault. The Wisconsin statute, for example, stipulates that if a defendant is accused of sexual assault, "Evidence of specific instances of sexual conduct showing the source or origin of semen, pregnancy or disease, for use in determining the degree of sexual assault or the extent of injury suffered" is admissible in court.[19] Wisconsin thereby classifies normal pregnancy as an injury over and above the injury of the sexual assault itself, much as a beating sustained during sexual assault is considered to be an additional injury.

The same reasoning appears in a strong dissent to a 1942 California case, *People v. McIlvain*.[20] The victim, a woman, had attended a dance with three men. After the dance hall closed at 1:30 A.M., one of the men offered to drive the woman home. Enroute the man drove off the highway to a secluded place and stopped the car. For the next four or five hours, he raped the woman, threw her from the front seat to the rear and onto the floor of the car, and repeatedly struck her. She suffered bruises, laceration of the wall of her vagina as a result of the insertion of the defendant's fingers, and pain. The jury found the man guilty of two crimes, rape committed with force and violence and assault by means of force likely to produce great bodily injury.[21] In a notable dissent in this case, Presiding Justice Schauer took issue with the idea of two distinct crimes because in his opinion "forcible rape" necessarily includes the "offense of 'assault by means of force likely to produce great bodily injury.'"[22] He specifically cited normal pregnancy as an example of "great bodily injury."[23] Although the plaintiff did not become pregnant, forcible rape itself constitutes great bodily injury, he noted, because it includes "not only physical, mental, and psychic shock, but also a likelihood of causing the victim to become pregnant . . . . Surely [normal] pregnancy as a result of forcible rape is great bodily injury."[24]

Although Justice Schauer wrote in the dissent in this case, his evaluation later became the standard in California for defining normal pregnancy as great bodily injury if and when a woman does not consent to a pregnancy that is subsequent to rape. In 1975, for example, the California Court of Appeals specifically quoted his view that nonconsensual normal pregnancy is great bodily injury to support its position that forcible rape in and of itself constitutes great bodily injury because of the possibility that pregnancy may result.[25] In 1978 another California court, while ruling that rape itself does not constitute great bodily injury, specifically noted that it did "not take issue" with the view that "as a general matter . . . pregnancy as a result of forcible rape is great bodily injury."[26]

The implication of these decisions that nonconsensual pregnancy, even when normal, is great bodily injury, even if the rape preceding it is not, was confirmed in *People v. Caudillo*. Here a California court interpreted great bodily injury to mean "significant or substantial physical injury[27] . . . incurred in addition to that which must be present in every case of rape."[28] The court singled out normal pregnancy as one of the additional injuries attendant to rape that "can easily be equated with a high level of injury."[29] Subsequent California cases declared even more clearly that normal pregnancy, when it occurs without a woman's consent, is a "significant and substantial bodily injury or damage." In 1978 in *People v. Sargent*, for example, the court declared that a man who raped a woman had "clearly inflicted on his victim great bodily injury," not so much because of the rape itself but because of the normal pregnancy resulting from it.[30]

These court decisions make a sharp distinction between the effects of nonconsensual sex and nonconsensual pregnancy. The injuries attendant to each are assessed as discrete and separable by the law. Pregnancy is clearly recognized in the law as an injury a victim may experience in addition to the injury of rape itself.[31] Even when the forcible rape does not itself inflict great bodily harm, if the victim does not consent to the normal pregnancy that may ensue, that pregnancy constitutes an injury in addition to the injury of the rape. What is more, when a medically normal pregnancy is nonconsensual, the bodily injury it causes, according to the law, is "great."

As the court put it in *Sargent*,

"bodily injury involved in a [normal] pregnancy . . . [is] significant and substantial. Pregnancy cannot be termed a trivial, insignificant matter. It amounts to significant and substantial bodily injury or damage . . . . Major physical changes begin to take place at the time of pregnancy. It involves a significant bodily impairment primarily affecting a woman's health and well being."[32] This ruling raises normal, but nonconsensual, pregnancy to the level of "significant and substantial" injury. The three possible outcomes of pregnancy are childbirth, abortion, or miscarriage, each of which the court characterized as severe injuries, adding that normal but nonconsensual childbirth is a particularly "agonizing experience."[33]

In *People v. Superior Court (Duval)*,[34] the vice principal of a high school became sexually involved with two minor students. One, Sonia, became pregnant. When the vice principal was tried, the issue was whether Sonia's pregnancy constituted an additional injury over and above that caused by illicit sexual intercourse with a minor. The California Court of Appeals ruled that pregnancy does "constitute injury significantly and substantially beyond that necessarily present in the commission of an act of unlawful sexual intercourse."[35] Quoting *Sargent*, it reiterated that normal "[p]regnancy cannot be termed a trivial, insignificant matter. It amounts to a significant and substantial bodily injury or damage."[36]

Michigan courts also affirm that nonconsensual normal pregnancy is a serious injury. In 1993 in *People v. Brown*,[37] the defendant was convicted of first-degree criminal sexual conduct, which is defined as "force or coercion used to accomplish sexual penetration" with the infliction of "personal injury."[38] The Michigan Court of Appeals included pregnancy in the range of injuries used to specify "personal injury," which it defined as "bodily injury, disfigurement, mental anguish, chronic pain, pregnancy, disease, or loss or impairment of a sexual or reproductive organ."[39]

The law's definition of normal pregnancy as an injury also shows up in rape shield laws, which are designed to protect rape victims from admission of evidence deemed irrelevant to the crime but potentially damaging to the victims, such as their past sexual history. These prohibitions have motivated many states to pass legislation that explicates what evidence is admissible in rape trials. State statutes permit the inclusion of normal pregnancy as admissible evidence of injury. The Wisconsin rape shield law, for example, specifies that pregnancy is admissible as evidence in court to determine either the "extent of injury suffered" by the victim of rape or the "degree of sexual assault" itself.[40] Similarly, Connecticut lists evidence as to "pregnancy" along with "injury" as admissible evidence in a rape trial in order to determine the guilt of the defendant.[41] So do Virginia[42] and Mississippi.[43] In Louisiana, the court acknowledged the state's legitimate interest to protect "young females from [normal] pregnancy."[44]

Through these rulings the courts have already recognized that normal pregnancy, posing no medical threat to women, nevertheless constitutes a serious injury and harm when nonconsensual. Justice Stevens's statement notwithstanding, the law is clear that a woman is the victim of serious injury when pregnancy is imposed on her without her consent. What is more, law cases dealing with wrongful pregnancy affirm that a key aspect of a woman's right to consent to be pregnant is access to information that makes her choice valid. Her consent to be pregnant must be a real choice based on relevant information that offers an alternative to pregnancy, such as abortion.

Normal Pregnancy as Serious Injury

Medically, a normal pregnancy is an extraordinary condition,[45] but the legal significance of the extraordinary way in which a fetus transforms a woman's body in even a normal pregnancy is that it is an extraordinary injury if a woman does not consent to pregnancy. Identification of the fertilized ovum as the cause of pregnancy, and therefore as the cause of wrongful pregnancy if a woman seeks an abortion, provides a new way to evaluate what the fetus does to a woman when it coerces her to be pregnant: namely, the fetus seriously injures her, even in a medically normal pregnancy, by forcing pregnancy on her against her will.

In the context of abortion, however, the Supreme Court has failed to grasp either that a medically normal pregnancy is a serious injury when coerced or that the fetus is responsible for that injury as the coercer. That is, the Court has failed to develop a systematic analysis of how the fetus causes pregnancy, much less wrongful pregnancy. On the contrary, the Court's reliance on its depiction of pregnancy as an immaculate condition uncaused by any private party hides how the fetus acts as a private party when it makes a woman pregnant, and as a private party that imposes serious injury when it does so without the woman's consent.

Yet for the Court merely to chart the burdens of pregnancy without examining how a fetus coercively imposes them fails to address what the law recognizes as the key component of all injuries: coercion. When people consent to engage in an activity such as sexual intercourse, the law views it as noninjurious. Without consent, the very same activity becomes the crime of rape. Similarly, if one person travels with another, that is called a vacation. But if one person coerces another to travel, that is called kidnapping. The legal distinction between the two hinges on consent. The behavior of traveling itself is not what legally defines either a vacation or a kidnapping but whether or not the behavior in question is being coerced by another. So, too, with pregnancy. From the standpoint of the law, a woman who consents to a normal pregnancy is not being injured; a woman who is coerced to be pregnant, however, is a victim of the serious injury of wrongful pregnancy.

As Justice Holmes said, "The absence of lawful consent . . . is part of the definition of an assault." And as legal scholars note, the "same is true of false imprisonment, conversion, and trespass."[46] Because consent is the defining component of all types of injuries within human relationships,[47] the presence of coercion is the most salient characteristic in defining any and all injuries. The law defines an injury in terms of a lack of consent as "any wrong or damage done to another, either in his person, rights, reputation, or property . . . [the] invasion of any legally protected interest of another."[48] The key word is *invasion*. Defining what constitutes an injury from the standpoint of the law depends not so much on what one private party specifically does to another as on whether the other person consents to it. Without consent, it becomes an invasion of the person's legally protected interest, and thus an injury.

It might appear that one person injures another when that person makes deep incisions with sharp instruments into the other person's body. Yet if the person who is using the instruments is a surgeon, and even more important, if the patient has consented to the actions of the surgeon, cutting into a person's body, far from being an injury, can be a life-saving behavior. Without consent, however, regardless of the success of the operation from a medical standpoint, it is a legal injury.[49] Similarly, while it is normal and natural to die, physicians who let people die without appropriate treatment, unless a living will expressly consents to that course, are liable for serious injury. However, physicians who keep people alive without their consent also impose legal injuries if the people in question have signed a living will that expresses their lack of consent to such procedures. It is not possible, therefore, to decide what is and is not an injury solely by looking at what one private party does to another. Rather, the key element from the standpoint of the law is to identify whether or not the people in question have consented to what others are doing to them.[50]

Harm, therefore, is the "basic commonsense notion . . . that a person is made worse off" by another person.[51] In wrongful-life tort cases, a person claims to have been harmed by being conceived and brought into existence, that is, by being born. In these cases, however, it is very difficult to prove that one's life is worse than not being born at all, so courts have been reluctant to recognize damages.[52] The traditional view, as represented in *Zepeda v. Zepeda*,[53] is that life cannot be an injury. In cases where courts do recognize wrongful life as a cause of action, such as *Curlender v. Bio-Science Laboratories*,[54] they have limited damages to recovery for the pain and damages endured during the life of the child, not to an assessment of birth itself as a damage. As the California Supreme Court ruled in *Turpin v. Sortini*,[55] a wrongful life cause of action cannot lead to a recovery of general damages, as can a wrongful death action, but wrongful life plaintiffs can recover special damages for the expenses necessary to treat them during their lives.[56] The Arizona Supreme Court went even further in *Walker v. Mart*[57] by choosing not to recognize wrongful life as a claim at all. The court reasoned that wrongful life was not analogous to the parents' wrongful birth claim, since no choice was improperly taken from the fetus.

While courts do not view birth itself to be an injury, therefore, the same is not true of pregnancy. Courts have clearly recognized that pregnancy itself is an injury when imposed on a woman without consent, even if the pregnancy in question is normal by medical standards. To say, as Justice Stevens did, therefore, that normal pregnancy constitutes "no harm," without taking into consideration whether a woman consents to be made pregnant by a fertilized ovum, runs counter to the law. If a woman consents to be pregnant, the fertilized ovum does not injure her. If a woman does not consent to be pregnant, it seriously injures her, and this is the starting point for assessing a woman's legal right to terminate pregnancy by means of an abortion, which stops the fetus from imposing the injuries of wrongful pregnancy.

Two Modes of Privacy

In *Roe* the majority opinion concluded that the

> right of personal privacy includes the abortion decision . . . but that . . . the State does have an important and legitimate interest . . . in protecting the potentiality of human life . . . [which] becomes "compelling" . . . at viability . . . . If the State is interested in protecting fetal life after viability, it may go so far as to proscribe abortion during that period except when it is necessary to preserve the life or health of the mother.[58]

By this statement, the Court established not one, but two, modes of privacy as a foundation for women's constitutional right to an abortion.

First, the Court ruled that a woman's right of personal privacy to make decisions includes her constitutional right to choose an abortion without interference from the state. This right of privacy, however, applies only to that stage of pregnancy when the fetus is not yet viable; after viability, it is constitutional for the state to restrict a woman's right to choose an abortion. Second, the Court ruled that women have a constitutional right to preserve their health and life. This right of privacy applies to every stage of pregnancy, even when the fetus is viable. If the fetus's imposition of pregnancy threatens a woman's health or life, no state may prohibit her from obtaining an abortion to stop it from so injuring her, even if the state's interest in protecting the fetus is compelling.

That people possess a constitutional right to preserve their lives and health is a generally accepted principle. In most contexts, this means that it is unconstitutional for a state to prohibit a person from calling on physicians for assistance in dealing with their illnesses or to prohibit people from obtaining or refusing medical treatments of their choice.[59] Abortion, however, introduces an important additional element because it is a medical procedure that necessarily involves destroying the state-protected form of human life, namely the fetus, that is the cause of the threat to one's health or life. In principle, if one could remove this cause without destroying it, the most contentious aspects of the abortion debate would go away. Currently, however, medical technology provides no such option. To preserve one's health and life in an abnormal pregnancy requires the death of the fetus.

In the context of pregnancy, therefore, the preservation of women's health and life involves not only the right to procure a needed medical treatment but also the right to destroy state-protected human life to stop it from imposing serious injuries. The Court's affirmation that a woman has a constitutional right to kill the fetus at any stage of a medically abnormal pregnancy, therefore, extends the right of privacy to a right to use deadly force in one's self-defense. Embedded in *Roe*, therefore, is the Court's recognition not only that the fetus can seriously injure a woman but also that she has a right to use deadly force to stop it from imposing those injuries in its capacity as state-protected human life.

As established in *Roe*, a woman's right of personal privacy as defined by her decisional autonomy is governed and limited by what the fetus is, not by what it does. As long as the fetus is previable, justification for a woman's right to an abortion rests simply on whether she chooses to have one or not. No other factors need be present, and the reason why she chooses to have an abortion is irrelevant to her right to choose one. As long as the fetus is previable, a woman may choose an abortion because she cannot afford to have another child; because she wishes to go to law school; or as some pro-life advocates would have us believe, because she chooses to engage in frivolous behavior, such as trips to a beauty parlor or vacations in Bermuda. Once the fetus is viable, however, a woman no longer has the right to exercise personal privacy by choosing an abortion, and a state may prohibit her right to choose one.

By contrast, a woman's right of self-defense in relation to the fetus as established in *Roe* is governed and limited by what the fetus does, not by what it is. At any point in pregnancy, regardless of whether the fetus is or is not viable, if what it does imposes a sufficient amount of injury on the woman, no state may prohibit her from using deadly force to stop it, even if the state has a compelling interest to protect it. Since a woman is justified in killing the fetus to keep it from injuring her, the key criterion in this context is the degree of injury the fetus imposes; it must be sufficient to justify killing a state-protected human life.

Latitude for Self-defense

Basing women's right of self-defense on the degree of injury imposed by a fetus is typical of how the law in general regulates the use of deadly force in self-defense. Deadly force is justified not merely by the need to preserve one's own life and health but also by the level of injury being threatened or actually imposed by the private party in question.[60] From a review of state statutes and the *Model Penal Code*, we can discern three types or dimensions of injury that justify the use of deadly force in self-defense: absolute threats to one's life; quantitative threats of large amounts of physical injury to one's body; and qualitative threats to one's liberty and dignity, such as entailed in rape, kidnapping, or slavery.[61]

All states affirm the right of people to use deadly force to defend themselves from absolute threats to their life. (See table 5.1. for a summary and the appendix for a more complete list.) States also affirm that people have a right to use deadly force to stop private parties from imposing serious amounts of quantitative injuries, even if these injuries stop short of actually threatening death. Forty-two states, for example, have passed statutes that explicitly affirm people's right to use deadly force when another private party threatens them with a sufficient quantity of bodily injury, referred to variously as "serious bodily harm," "serious physical injury," "great bodily harm," "great personal injury," "in peril of bodily harm," "grievous bodily harm," or as in the case of Michigan, "brutality."[62]

The law also recognizes the right of people to use deadly force when threatened with qualitative injuries that intrude on their basic liberty or bodily integrity even while threatening no objective physical injuries per se, much less threatening their lives. Thirty-six states explicitly affirm a person's right to use deadly force when threatened with forcible rape, even when that rape is not aggravated by physical injuries.[63] Thirty-five states legislatively recognize the right to use deadly force against kidnapping. Only one of these states, Indiana, stipulates that the kidnapping must occur with the use or threat of force; kidnapping alone is sufficient in the other states. Twenty-seven states specifically affirm the right to use deadly force when threatened with slavery, either by explicit reference to their own state constitutions or to the federal Constitution. In addition, some states affirm the use of deadly force when threatened with assault, robbery, arson, burglary, and any other forcible felony.[64]

So, too, does the *Model Penal Code* affirm a latitude for self-defense that encompasses the absolute injury of death and also serious quantitative and qual-

Table 5.1   Summary of State Laws: Injuries Permitting the Use of Deadly Force in Self-defense by Legislative Statute

State	Absolute Injury: Death	Quantitative Injury: Serious Bodily Harm	Qualitative Injury: Forcible Rape, Kidnapping, or Slavery
Alabama	yes	no*	yes
Alaska	yes	yes	yes
Arizona	yes	yes	no*
Arkansas	yes	no*	yes
California	yes	yes	yes
Colorado	yes	yes	yes
Delaware	yes	yes	yes
District of Columbia†	yes	yes	yes
Florida	yes	yes	yes
Georgia	yes	yes	yes
Hawaii	yes	yes	yes
Idaho	yes	yes	yes
Illinois	yes	yes	yes
Indiana	yes	yes	yes
Iowa	yes	yes	yes
Kansas	yes	no*	yes
Kentucky	yes	yes	yes
Louisiana	yes	yes	yes
Maine	yes	no*	yes
Maryland†	yes	yes	no*
Massachusetts†	yes	yes	no*
Michigan†	yes	yes	no*
Minnesota	yes	yes	no*
Missouri	yes	yes	yes
Montana	yes	yes	yes
Nebraska	yes	yes	yes
Nevada	yes	yes	yes
New Hampshire	yes	yes	yes
New Jersey	yes	yes	yes
New Mexico	yes	yes	yes
New York	yes	yes	yes
North Carolina	yes	yes	no*
North Dakota	yes	yes	yes
Ohio	yes	yes	no*
Oklahoma	yes	yes	yes
Oregon	yes	yes	yes
Pennsylvania	yes	yes	yes
Rhode Island	yes	yes	no*
South Carolina	yes	yes	no*
South Dakota	yes	yes	yes
Texas	yes	yes	yes
Utah	yes	yes	yes
Vermont	yes	yes	yes
Virginia	yes	yes	yes

Table 5.1   (*continued*)

State	Absolute Injury: Death	Quantitative Injury: Serious Bodily Harm	Qualitative Injury: Forcible Rape, Kidnapping, or Slavery
Washington	yes	yes	yes
West Virginia	yes	yes	no*
Wisconsin	yes	yes	yes
Wyoming	yes	yes	no*

*No specific reference in text of a statute; this does not mean, however, that the right to use deadly force in self-defense would not prevail in court.

†Common law state; no statutory provisions for self-defense with the use of deadly force.

itative injuries to one's body and liberty. The code states that deadly force in self-protection is justified when a person believes that

> such force is necessary for the purpose of protecting [herself] himself against the use of unlawful force by such other person . . . [such as] against death [absolute injury], serious bodily injury [quantitative injury], kidnapping or sexual intercourse [qualitative injury] compelled by force or threat.[65]

The *Model Penal Code* also notes that people have a duty to avoid the use of deadly force, if possible, by retreating. The duty to retreat, however, does not apply in all situations. If people are attacked in their homes or places of business, such an attack is so personal an intrusion on one's privacy that people may use deadly force instead.[66] If a person

> knows that he [she] can avoid the necessity of using such force with complete safety by retreating or by surrendering possession of a thing to a person asserting a claim of right thereto or by complying with a demand that he abstain from any action which he has no duty to take, [the use of deadly force is not justified unless the person is threatened in] his dwelling or place of work.[67]

The latitude recognized in law for the use of self-defense with deadly force, established by both state statutes and the *Model Penal Code*, clearly encompasses absolute threats to one's life, quantitative threats to one's health, and qualitative threats to one's liberty. Although the Court in *Roe* used a principle of self-defense with deadly force to establish women's constitutional right to an abortion, the Court did not go far enough in securing for pregnant women the same latitude as is currently in place for others in our society.

While the Court's use of decisional autonomy to establish women's constitutional right to an abortion was a novel extension of a right that may or may not exist in the Constitution, no innovation was needed to base this right on a principle of self-defense. One of the oldest and least contested of all the grounds for abortion is the fetus's threat of causing death. Even an arch-conservative, pro-life advocate, such as Henry Hyde, who believes that the fetus is a person, nevertheless contends that a woman must have a right to an abortion when the fetus threatens her death. And even in the repressive legislative environment of the nineteenth century, when states first began to regulate women's right to an abortion, the overwhelming majority of states explicitly stated that a woman has a right to kill the fetus by means of an abortion if it threatens her life.[68]

Justice Rehnquist acknowledged as much in his dissent in *Roe*, where he noted that in 1868, when the Fourteenth Amendment was ratified, "[T]here were at least 36 laws enacted by state or territorial legislatures limiting [but not banning] abortion."[69] To put it another way, in 1868 twenty-six states explicitly allowed abortions when the fetus threatened a woman with death (see table 5.2).[70] Nine states, including conservative southern bastions such as Maryland, Mississippi, Missouri, and West Virginia, explicitly affirm by legislative statute that a woman has a right to an abortion before quickening, regardless of whether her life is in jeopardy. As Justice Rehnquist himself added, "There apparently was no question concerning the validity" of these statutes, which affirm that women have always had a right to defend themselves with deadly force when sufficiently threatened by the intrusion of a fetus.[71]

The Texas statute at issue in *Roe* is a case in point. It did not ban abortions but, rather, limited them to circumstances in which the fetus threatens a woman with death. There was no need in *Roe*, therefore, for the Court to rule that it is unconstitutional for a state to deny to woman a right to use deadly force to stop the threat of death since the Texas statute in question did not do so, and in fact affirmed such a right. Yet the Court expanded that latitude to include threats of quantitative injury to her health as well. The Court ruled that regardless of whether the fetus is previable or viable and regardless of whether the state has a profound or compelling interest in protecting it, no state may deny to a woman the right to use deadly force at any point in her pregnancy when the fetus imposes not only absolute injuries threatening her life but also quantitative injuries threatening her health.

This expansion moved the right of self-defense for pregnant women closer to the standards in place for other people in our society. Yet the Court did not go far enough, for absolute threats to one's life or quantitative threats to one's health are not the only threats that according to law justify the use of deadly force in self-defense. Also included are qualitative injuries that threaten one's liberty.

Innocent and Weak?

Probably one of the most overworked adjectives applied to the fetus by pro-life advocates is *innocent*. Yet the fetus is innocent only of conscious intentions.

Table 5.2 Abortion Statutes Cited in *Roe v. Wade* (1973) in
Justice Rehnquist's Dissent

State or Territory	Date	Exception: Threat to Mother's Life	Exception: Before Quickening (*) or Threat to Mother's Physical Safety (†)
Alabama	1843	yes	
Arizona	1864	yes	
Arkansas	1837	yes	yes*
California	1850	yes	
Colorado	1861	[yes]	
Connecticut	1821	yes	yes*
Florida	1868	[yes]	
Georgia	1837	[yes]	
Hawaii	1850	yes	
Idaho	1863	yes	
Illinois	1827	[yes]	
Indiana	1838	yes	
Iowa	1838–1839	[yes]	
Kansas	1855	yes	yes*
Louisiana	1856	[yes]	
Maine	1847	yes	
Maryland	1868	yes	yes*+
Massachusetts	1854	lawful	
Michigan	1846	yes	yes*
Minnesota	1851	yes	
Mississippi	1848	yes	yes*
Missouri	1840	yes	yes*
Montana	1864	yes	
Nevada	1862	yes	
New Hampshire	1848	[oversight omission]	
New Jersey	1849	[yes]	
New York	1829	yes	yes*
Ohio	1841	yes	
Oregon	1866	yes	
Pennsylvania	1860	[yes]	
Texas	1859	yes	
Vermont	1845	lawful	
Virginia	1848	yes	
Washington	1854	yes	
West Virginia	1870	yes	yes*
Wisconsin	1849	yes	

NOTE: [ ] = not explicitly stated but most likely in effect.

The fetus imposes extraordinary injury on a woman much as a born person imposes injuries while mentally incompetent because of drugs, sleepwalking, mental retardation, or other such factors. From the legal standpoint, the fetus is innocent only in the sense that it is not competent to be held legally responsible for what it does, even though it is the objective cause of a woman's injuries.

This does not mean that a woman loses a right to defend herself against a fetus just because it does not know what it is doing to her. To the contrary, self-defense rights apply even to the killing of an innocent person[72] when by innocence we mean only that the person does not know what he or she is doing.

It is misleading, therefore, to claim, as many do, that because the fetus is innocent of conscious intentions, there are no grounds to keep it from harming a woman by means of an abortion. To the contrary, the degree of injury the fetus imposes on a woman meets legal standards for the use of deadly force to stop it, and its status as "innocent" refers only to its lack of conscious intent.[73] Imagine how people would respond if a born person did to them what a fetus does to a woman when imposing even a medically normal pregnancy without consent: capture for nine months, injection of 400 times the base level of hormones, destruction of tissues, growth of new organs, rerouting of the blood system, and so on. Most likely they would be quick to say that they were suffering sufficient quantitative and qualitative injuries to justify the use of deadly force to stop the perpetrator, regardless of how "innocent" the intruder might be and even if death or permanent damage to their health were not imminent.[74] What is more, these people would expect the state to step in to stop the private aggressor on their behalf because the most fundamental purpose of the American state as conceived by its founders was to provide for law and order by stopping private parties from intruding on the lives, liberty, and property of others.[75]

Founders of the United States believed that one's right to be let alone by other private people was a natural right, an inherent, inalienable right that predates the establishment of any particular form of government.[76] According to the American political heritage, the purpose of the state is not to deny, but rather to protect, people's natural rights.[77] The primary purpose of the state is to stop the wrongful injuries imposed by private parties on others.[78] As legal scholar Sheldon Gelman writes, when the Due Process Clause guaranteeing "life, liberty, or property" was added to the Constitution, the meaning of the term *"life"* expansively included "more than mere biological existence; it also encompassed [bodily] physical integrity, 'health' . . . and even a minimum quality of life."[79] To intrude on people's bodily integrity, therefore, is to intrude on their life, as well as on their liberty.

In a state of nature, void of political institutions, of course, people have absolute freedom to do whatever their brute force enables them to do, including taking others' property and imposing serious quantitative injuries and even death. The result is extreme conflict and insecurity for all involved. To solve the insecurity created by the conflict in a state of nature, the founders of this country envisioned agreement on a social contract that established civil society, including its political institutions and form of government.

The law and order of civil society replaces life in a state of nature. The laws, as executed by the state, set parameters around the exercise of freedom by preventing people from killing one another, imposing injury on one another, and taking one another's property.[80] The state's provision of security reduces physical conflict in a civil society as compared to a state of nature, and it is this trade-off that more than compensates for the switch from absolute freedom to regulated freedom.[81]

Freedom from State Intrusion

The founders worried, however, that the state itself might intrude too much on bodily integrity, life, and liberty, thereby posing threats as serious to people's security as those imposed by private parties, which the state was created to stop. To guard against too much state intrusion, in 1791 they added to the Constitution the Bill of Rights, ten amendments that for the most part spell out ways in which the federal government may not intrude on its citizens.[82] In 1868 the Fourteenth Amendment was added to the Constitution, thereby guaranteeing further protections not only from the federal government but the state governments as well.[83]

The Constitution regulates the relationship between people and the state, particularly ensuring that the state does not intrude too much on people's lives as it exercises its police power to provide law and order for the public welfare. The police power of the state is an "essential attribute," referring to the "exercise of the sovereign right of a government to promote order, safety, security, health, morals, and general welfare within constitutional limits."[84] It is the police power of the state, as delegated to the individual states and in turn to the local governments by the Tenth Amendment, that authorizes government

> to establish a special department of police; adopt such laws and regulations as tend to prevent the commission of fraud and crime, and secure generally the comfort, safety, morals, health, and prosperity of its citizens by preserving the public order, preventing a conflict of rights in the common intercourse of the citizens, and insuring to each an uninterrupted enjoyment of all privileges conferred upon him or her by the general laws.[85]

A state that cannot provide even this minimal service of protection from the private aggression of other people is arguably no state at all.

The American legal system can be thought of as a dynamic seesaw, in which the Constitution must grant to the state sufficient power over people's lives to provide for the public safety, and yet at the same time must restrict the power of the state from too much intrusion to preserve fundamental rights. For this reason, although people have some right to be let alone by the state, they do not have an absolute right.

The question that constantly comes before the Court is whether the state is intruding too much or not enough. Over the years the Court has established guidelines in answer to that question. In all instances, the Court has scrutinized closely whether the state intrudes on people's bodies and liberties, whether the state has a compelling interest to justify such intrusion, and whether the state is using the most narrowly tailored means to obtain its objectives.

Sometimes the Court determines that the state has intruded excessively, and it rules that such intrusion is unconstitutional. In a landmark case, *Rochin v. California*,[86] Antonio Richard Rochin was arrested on suspicion of possessing a "preparation of morphine," whereupon law enforcement officers ordered doctors to pump his stomach to obtain the swallowed morphine, even though this clearly was against the will of the suspect. When a California court convicted Rochin, he appealed on the grounds that the evidence used against him—the stomach-pumped morphine—had been obtained through means that violated his fundamental rights as protected by the Constitution.[87]

The Supreme Court reviewed the case and agreed with him, overturning his conviction in an eight-to-zero vote. Justice Frankfurter, writing the majority opinion, said that pumping Rochin's stomach without his consent was a means that "shocks the conscience."[88] Frankfurter compared nonconsensual stomach pumping to forms of torture, such as the "rack and screw," whose purpose and effect is purely to produce pain and whose use is open-ended in terms of duration.[89]

This ruling reflects the Court's general reluctance to give wide leeway to the state to intrude on people's bodily integrity even when the people are suspected of criminal activity.[90] As Laurence Tribe points out, the degree with which the Court takes seriously the intrusion on a person's bodily integrity, including those suspected of serious criminal activity, indicates that an "aspect of personhood" is at stake. For this reason, the "government's burden" is "to provide more than minimal justification for its action" of intruding on the body of a person, even when the person in question is suspected of crimes against the state.[91]

This is not to say that the state does not have the right to intrude at all on people's bodily integrity or liberty.[92] The right to be free from interference from the state is far from absolute. People do not even have an absolute right to do with their own bodies as they choose. It is constitutional for the state to prohibit one's choice to engage in homosexual activity, to contract for prostitution services, and to sell one's organs. In addition, it is constitutional for the state to require people to obtain vaccinations in order to prevent the spread of disease[93] and to be conscripted for military service.[94]

Freedom from Private Intrusion

While the right to be let alone from intrusion by the state is not an absolute right, the right to be let alone from private parties is. According to the American tradition, it is to protect themselves from nonconsensual private injuries that people consent to move from a state of nature to civil society in the first place. Although the state may coerce a person to obtain a vaccination, no private person has the right to coerce another to do so. While the state may conscript one's body for public service, no private person may do so. While the state may in a limited way intrude on one's body, even physically breaking one's skin, no private party has a right to invade physically the body of another.

It was the fundamental right to be let alone from private parties that Louis Brandeis and Samuel Warren used in their classic article that expanded the right of privacy from merely the right to be let alone from private intrusion of one's body and property to the right to be let alone from private intrusion of one's very personality.[95] According to them, the most fundamental right to privacy is the right to be let alone from private parties. In their analysis of privacy rights, therefore, it is not the state's interference in people's lives that raises privacy issues but rather private people's interference in others' lives. Rather than causing the problem, it is the state that provides the remedy and solution by stopping private intrusion. As legal scholar Mary Ann Glendon notes, it is Brandeis and Warren's articulation of this right to privacy that eventually found acceptance in American tort law and later migrated to the Supreme Court, where it became the right to be free of state interference, not merely the more fundamental right to be free of private intrusion.[96]

Privacy, therefore, "defines a sphere of individual dominion"[97] into which private parties may not intrude without consent. Rather than dominion over things, as legal scholar Daniel Ortiz points out, privacy is the right to have "dominion over oneself."[98] The right to be free from private intrusion is absolute. By criminalizing such intrusion, the state transforms acts of private aggression into acts of aggression against the state. If a private party physically intrudes on the body or even the property of another, imposing injuries by mugging, raping, or robbery, for example, these acts of aggression not only violate the victim as a private party but also are crimes against the state. The victim has recourse to sue the aggressor, and so, too, can the state act to stop the aggressor. In situations in which the state is unable to come to the aid of a victim of private aggression, of course, states recognize the right of the victim to use deadly force in self-defense.

The state's criminalization of private aggression and affirmation of the right of self-defense are evidence that people do not have a right to intrude on the bodily integrity, liberty, or even property of other private people. If the states did not criminalize private aggression, these acts would revert to common law restrictions as a basis for outlawing them.[99] Common law is that which is produced by custom, tradition, and the adjudication of courts in contrast to positive law legislated by the state.[100] The list of common law crimes, though reading more like the residue of what is left over after the states have passed statutes, nevertheless affirms the primacy of people's right to be let alone from the private aggression of other private parties.[101]

Both positive law legislated by the state and common law as adjudicated by the courts affirm that no private person may take another's body, liberty, or even property[102] without consent and also that no private party may coerce others to give or donate their bodies to others without consent. This holds true even if the life of the person needing the body parts of another is at stake, even if kinship ties link the potential donor and recipient, and even if the bodily intrusions involved are only minimally invasive physical procedures such as blood tests.

In what is known as a 'good samaritan' case, the Illinois Supreme Court upheld this view when ruling that consent was necessary before two children could even take a blood test to determine if they were suitable donors of bone marrow to their half-sibling, who was dying of leukemia.[103] Despite challenges that the blood tests were "minimally invasive and harmless," the court ruled that

> [n]o right is held more sacred, or is more carefully guarded by the common law, than the right of every individual to the possession and control of [the individual's] own person, free from all restraint or interference of others, unless by clear and unquestionable authority of law,[104]

which includes the right to refuse consent even to a blood test.

The primacy of donor consent, as an example of the primacy of people's right to be let alone by others, is also evident in cases involving good, rather than bad, samaritan behavior, particularly when the people in question are under the age of consent or legally incompetent. One of the best-known cases is *Strunk v. Strunk* in 1969, involving a kidney donation from a twenty-seven-year-old man, who had the mental capacity of a six-year-old, to his twenty-eight-year-old brother, whose life depended on the donation.[105] The donor's mother and the Department of Mental Health both recommended that the transplant take place. They based their claims not on the need of the recipient but on the best interests of the donor, claiming that the donor was "greatly dependent upon [his brother], emotionally and psychologically," and that the donor's "well-being would be jeopardized more severely by the loss of his brother than by the removal of a kidney," a position affirmed by the donor's psychiatrist.[106] Before such good samaritan behavior could take place, the case was sent to the Kentucky Court of Appeals, which in a close (4-to-3) decision eventually upheld the lower court's decision to approve the transplant.[107]

The American public is decidedly in favor of explicit consent in samaritan situations. Forty-two percent, for example, think it is unethical even to ask a child under the age of eighteen to give up a kidney for a relative. Only 15 percent say that they would apply emotional pressure to a relative to get him or her to donate an organ, even to a family member. Even more interesting, only a minuscule 6 percent would take legal action to force a relative to donate an organ against his or her will.[108]

Good samaritan principles, which guarantee that no body parts of a donor will be taken or used without consent, regardless of the need of the recipient, also cover parent-child relationships, if and when the children are outside the womb. The child outside its mother's womb has no legal right to take the blood of its parent, much less any other body part, without that parent's consent.[109] Parents' legal obligations to provide for their children's material needs, once born, stop short of any legal requirement to donate parts of their body, however minimal that donation might be or however great might be the severity of the child's need.[110]

Five states in the United States and sixteen European nations have passed good samaritan legislation that requires people to aid others, but this aid does not entail exposing oneself to injury or to the required donation of body parts to others.[111] There is nothing to prevent a state, of course, from passing more demanding forms of good samaritan legislation, for example, requiring parents to donate blood or organs to their born children, but such legislation would be closely scrutinized by the Supreme Court, and legal scholars question whether the Court would find it constitutional, particularly if it exceeded the level of blood donation.[112] Since courts have ruled that it is too invasive even to require a blood test between relatives, most likely the Supreme Court would rule that it is unconstitutional for the state to require donation of a pint of blood.

Yet even if the Court did rule such legislation constitutional, it is unlikely that a state could go much further without violating the Constitution. We could expect the Court to rule that it is unconstitutional for the state to demand that people donate their bone marrow or their organs or sustain massively invasive use of their bodies for prolonged periods of time. Also the Court would probably rule that it is unconstitutional for a state to demand good samaritan behavior from people when that behavior threatens them with medical emergencies or even with death, as medically abnormal pregnancies do. While it is constitutional for the state to demand minimal good samaritan behavior, therefore, the massive donations to the fetus required of a pregnant woman surely exceed levels the Court would uphold as constitutional.

Instead, courts affirm that the right of a person to be free from intrusion by another person is absolute. There are no exceptions. Even when facing death or when dead, people retain their right to bodily integrity in relation to another private party. The Court has ruled, for example, that people have the right to consent to bodily intrusions by physicians, even if that intrusion is required to maintain their life.[113] The Supreme Court established the constitutionality of this right in 1990, in *Cruzan v. Director, Missouri Department of Health*,[114] when it recognized the right of a competent individual to be "free of unwanted medical treatment."[115] The Court left it up to the states to determine how to regulate this right for incompetent patients. Long before the *Cruzan* decision, California was the first state to pass a living will statute, in 1976,[116] and in the aftermath of this decision, virtually every state has now passed legislation that requires people to make formal statements of their preferences regarding the use of medical treatment if they become so ill that they can no longer make their wishes known.[117] What is more, without expressed written consent to have parts of one's body used for the benefit of others after death, the body parts of those who have died remain sacrosanct, even if such use is necessary to sustain the life of a living, potential recipient.[118]

It is telling that the exceptions to the doctrine that the state may not force a person to be a good samaritan are found in cases dealing with pregnant women. Although in *Roe* the Court protected a woman's right in general to be a bad samaritan by refusing to donate her body to a fetus, there are notable, if not scandalous, examples of how states have endeavored to coerce women to be good samaritans by forcing them to undergo invasive surgery as a means for protecting the well-being of a fetus. Perhaps the most dramatic is the travesty imposed upon twenty-seven-year-old Angela Carder who, when six months pregnant and in the terminal states of lung cancer, was admitted to George Washington University Hospital in Washington, D.C. Facing death, she had arranged with her doctor to have a Caesarean section, only if she lived to the point when the fetus was twenty-eight weeks old and viable. During the twenty-fifth week, however, she took a turn for the worse, becoming unconscious at times and in a failing condition. In consultation with her husband, family, and physician, she decided not to undergo a Caesarean on the grounds that the fetus most likely would not survive and, thus, the surgery would do nothing but hasten her own death.

Hospital administrators, however, upon learning of her decision, turned to the courts, which provided separate legal counsel for all the parties involved, including the fetus. The court ordered a Caesarean, thereby overriding the testimony presented by Carder's own physicians that they were opposed to the surgery. A three-judge appellate panel upheld the court order, her attending physician refused to do the surgery, and so another physician was called in, who performed the Caesarean. The fetus died within two hours after surgery, and so did Angela Carder, two days later, but not before she had regained enough consciousness to learn that the fetus had died. Angela's family sued the hospital for violation of her civil rights, and in 1990 the U.S. Court of Appeals upheld her rights, arguing that "the lower court 'erred in subordinating Angela Carder's right to bodily integrity in favor of the state's interest in potential life.'"[119] In 1991, the Court ruled in *UAW v. Johnson Controls*[120] that forcing women to be a good samaritan by requiring a woman to avoid risks to the fetus in the context of her employment options is a form of sex discrimination that violated Title VII of federal law.[121]

Stranded in a State of Nature

The right of privacy, in short, involves not merely the right to be let alone by the state but also the right to be let alone by other private parties. And while the right to be let alone by the state is not absolute, the right to be let alone by private parties is. Further, the purpose of the state is to stop private parties from intruding on the bodies and liberties of other private parties. A state that does not do this is arguably no state at all, and living in such a condition of anarchy would be akin to returning to the state of nature that civil society was intended to replace. From this perspective, the main privacy issue involved in women's constitutional right to an abortion is not their right to be free from interference by the state, since the state does not directly make women pregnant, but, rather, the right to be free from the intrusion of the fetus as a private party on their bodily integrity and their liberty.

The constitutional question thus centers on how the state responds to the way in which the fetus, as a private party, interferes with a woman's bodily integrity and liberty when it imposes wrongful pregnancy. Women must have a right of self-defense to use deadly force to stop the fetus from imposing such injuries, and the Court was correct in affirming this constitutional right in *Roe*.[122] Yet self-defense is not enough. If a man is raping a woman or a mugger is inflicting a severe beating on someone or one private party is killing another, of course the victims have a right of self-defense to try to stop that injury themselves, but they also have a right to state assistance to stop the private parties on their behalf. It is the job of the state to protect victims of wrongful private acts by stopping the perpetrators. The right of self-defense is meant to be a fall-back option for those times when the state cannot do its job because it lacks the necessary resources or personnel; it is not a policy preference.

When a fetus seriously injures a woman by imposing a wrongful pregnancy, therefore, of course she has a right to stop it from injuring her, but she also has a right to state assistance in stopping it on her behalf. This is to say that to the degree that it is the job of the state to protect the fetus as human life, it becomes the job of the state to restrict the fetus as human life from intruding on the bodily integrity and liberty of others. Women's right to use deadly force must be viewed by the law as only the fall-back option applicable to those limited situations in which the state is unable, but not unwilling, to do its job. To suggest otherwise is to deny women the protections of civil society, thereby stranding them in the proverbial state of nature.[123]

Many attempts have been made to depict the abstract, fantasylike place known as a state of nature, which civil society replaces.[124] The difficulty derives from the anthropological impossibility of actually finding a time in history when human relationships were so untouched by principles of law or justice that brute force alone ruled the day and the strongest individuals could invade at will the bodies, liberties, and property of others. Presumably no such stage in human civilization ever existed, and the concept of a state of nature is only an artifact of human ingenuity, a technique for emphasizing the value added by civil society to human life.[125]

Yet we need look no further than current abortion-funding policies to find the principles of a state of nature exemplified. State policies that systematically prohibit the use of public resources to help a woman defend herself against the injuries of a fetus, even while constitutionally guaranteeing her right to defend herself because the injuries in question are so severe, allow the brute force of the fetus to impose itself physically on her body as if in a state of nature. Her injuries are limited by nothing more than her own material resources to stop it, unassisted by state protection. Such policies not only ostracize women from civil society and the protection of the state but also violate the Constitution.

6

Abortion Funding and Due Process

When the Supreme Court established a woman's constitutional right to choose an abortion in *Roe*, it did so on due process grounds.[1] As framed in the Fourteenth Amendment, the Due Process Clause specifies, "No State shall . . . deprive any person of life, liberty, or property, without due process of law."[2] In previous cases, the Court had ruled that due process rights guarantee freedom from government interference when people are making choices about such private activities as whether to use contraceptives, whom to marry, what materials to read, and where to send their children to school.[3] In *Roe*, the Court ruled that this right to privacy, guaranteed by the Due Process Clause, "is broad enough to encompass a woman's decision whether or not to terminate her pregnancy" without interference from the state.[4]

This landmark ruling was a tremendous gain for women because it made constitutional their right to obtain abortions prior to fetal viability even when the pregnancy in question was a medically normal one, thereby striking down a myriad of state statutes that had criminalized such abortions.[5] Yet there is a problem about basing the right to an abortion on due process grounds. Some legal experts question whether such a right to privacy actually exists in the Constitution or, even if it does, whether it covers the right to an abortion. For this reason, as legal scholar Laurence Tribe notes, since the right to privacy is not specifically enumerated in the Constitution, it has been difficult to establish whether it is sufficient for providing a fundamental right to an abortion.[6] It certainly has not been sufficient for preventing states from imposing restrictive regulations, such as twenty-four-hour waiting periods and transmitting information to women about the stages of fetal development and how an abortion destroys the fetus. As long as such state regulations do not pose an undue burden that actually prevents a woman from obtaining an abortion, the Court ruled in 1992, in *Casey*, that they are constitutional.

While many pro-choice advocates rightly decry the Court's ruling that such regulations are constitutional, an even more serious problem with the Due Process Clause as the foundation for abortion rights is that it is what is known as a negative right. That is, it specifies how the state will not act to interfere with life, liberty, and property, but it does not specify how the state must act to protect these rights. The due process guarantee that people have a right to use contraceptives without state interference, for example, does not mandate that the state must fund the purchase of contraceptives for those people who cannot afford to buy them. Similarly, the right to read a book or send your children to the school of your choice does not imply, on due process grounds, that the state must buy the book of your choice or pay your child's school tuition.[7]

When it came time for the Court to consider the right to public funding for abortion, therefore, the establishment of the right to an abortion on negative, due process grounds proved to be disastrous. Consistent with the way the Court has ruled in other privacy contexts, it concluded that the right to an abortion only entitles women to be free from state interference when exercising that right, not entitlement to assistance from the state in order to obtain one. The right to choose an abortion without state interference, therefore, according to the Court, no more entitles women to public funding of abortions than the right to choose whom to marry entitles one to public funding of one's wedding.

As the Court stated unequivocally in *Harris v. McRae*,

[I]t simply does not follow that a woman's freedom of choice carries with it a constitutional entitlement to the financial resources to avail herself of the full range of protected choices . . . . Although the liberty protected by the Due Process Clause affords protection against unwarranted government interference with freedom of choice . . . it does not confer an entitlement to such funds as may be necessary to realize all the advantages of that freedom . . . we hold [therefore] that a State . . . is not obligated . . . to fund . . . [even] medically necessary abortions.[8]

By extension, it would apparently be constitutional for the state to refuse to help an indigent woman obtain an abortion when the wrongful pregnancy imposed by the fetus threatens her with death. Justice Stevens criticized the reasoning of the Court, noting that its holding would constitutionally justify a denial of "funding to a medically and financially needy person even if abortion were the only lifesaving medical procedure available."[9]

Over the years, the Court has snuffed out all possibility of a constitutional right to state assistance for obtaining an abortion. Beginning in 1977, in *Beal*,[10] *Maher*,[11] and *Poelker*,[12] the Court ruled that it is constitutional for the state to deny funds and access to public hospitals to help a woman obtain an abortion in a medically normal pregnancy. Even when faced with dramatic examples of women whose health was in serious jeopardy because they were suffering from a medically abnormal pregnancy and were too poor to pay for the abortion that their physicians recommended, the Court nevertheless held firm that although the Due Process Clause guarantees women a right to choose an abortion without state interference, it does not entitle a woman to public support for that abortion. In 1980, in *Harris*, for example, the Court was fully aware of the severity of injuries suffered by one of the injured parties, a twenty-five-year-old married woman with children who had developed a serious case of phlebitis after the birth of her third child, from which she never fully recovered.[13] For this reason her physician, who feared that her fourth pregnancy would greatly aggravate her medical condition by increasing the risk of blood clots to her lungs, recommended an abortion, which the woman could not afford to pay for herself. But the Court supported the state, which rather than stepping in to help the woman stop the fetus from imposing such severe injuries, prohibited the use of public funds for an abortion.

The Court also was fully informed about another woman whose plight was at issue in *Harris*, a thirty-eight-year-old woman who had nine previous pregnancies and a history of varicose veins and thrombophlebitis, or blood clots, of the left leg caused by her multiple pregnancies. When she was pregnant for the tenth time, her physician feared that the weight of her uterus on her pelvic veins would increase the blood pressure in the veins of her lower extremities, thereby dilating those veins, impairing her blood circulation, and producing blood clots. In a previous pregnancy the blood clots had become so severe that they had required surgical removal. To prevent the recurrence of new blood clots during the woman's current pregnancy and therefore the necessity for a second operation to remove them, her physician recommended an abortion on the grounds that a second operation would so seriously impair her circulation that she could require prolonged hospitalization with bed rest.[14] When she could not afford an abortion, the state, as supported by the Court, prohibited the use of public resources to provide one.

In *Webster v. Reproductive Health Services* in 1989, the Court expanded the way in which the state may fail to act by ruling that it is constitutional for a state to prohibit the use of all public facilities, public personnel, and public funds for abortions not necessary to save a woman's life.[15] The Court's acceptance in Missouri statutes of the unusually broad definition of these terms—facilities are said to include everything "owned, leased, or controlled" by the state; public personnel to include all public employees; and public funds to include all monies allocated for "encouraging or counseling abortions"—gave a sweep to the constitutionality of the state's failure to act that left pro-choice advocates reeling.[16] In *Rust v. Sullivan* in 1991, the Court ruled that it is constitutional to prohibit even the discussion of abortion as part of federally funded family-planning programs.[17]

Thus, the Court has ruled that it is constitutional for the state to withhold information, funds, facilities, and personnel for medically normal and medically abnormal pregnancies. By implication, most likely the Court would rule that it would even be constitutional for the state to withhold all assistance to women who seek an abortion to save their lives.[18] For thousands of women too poor to pay for abortions, therefore, the right to have one as guaranteed by the negative rights of the Due Process Clause is a meaningless abstraction. While the Due Process Clause guarantees women's right to choose an abortion without state interference, it does not provide women with the means to do so when they are too poor to afford one.[19]

No State Obstacles

The Court has stuck to its position over the years on the Due Process Clause that the state is not acting when it fails to fund abortions or otherwise provide public resources. And if the state is not acting, by definition, it cannot be violating the Due Process Clause since that clause mandates only how a state must *not act* to deprive people of their lives, liberty, or property, not how the state *must act* to assist people exercise their right to life, liberty, and property. It is not the state that is acting to create an obstacle preventing women from choosing an abortion, according to the Court, but women's poverty.

As the Court put it in *Harris*, state restriction on abortion funding, whether by means of a statute passed by Congress or by a state legislature, "places no governmental obstacle in the path of a woman who chooses to terminate her pregnancy."[20] And as the Court noted in *Harris*, the Hyde amendment, which prohibits federal funds for most abortions, "leaves an indigent woman with at least the same range of choice in deciding whether to obtain a medically necessary abortion as she would have had if Congress had chosen to subsidize no health care costs at all."[21] The Court concluded, therefore, that the Hyde amendment does not impinge "on the constitutionally protected freedom of choice [or on] . . . the due process liberty recognized in [*Roe*]."[22] Or as the Court noted in *Webster*, a state's "refusal to allow public employees to perform abortions in public hospitals leaves a pregnant woman with the same choices as if the State had chosen not to operate any public hospitals at all."[23]

Abortion Is Different

Yet there is a way in which the state's failure to act to provide an abortion becomes a form of unconstitutional state action that does violate the Due Process Clause: abortion is different from the choice of whom to marry, whether to use contraceptives, what materials to read, or where to send your children to school. The Court itself has noted over and over again in *Roe* and its progeny that abortion is different. As stated in *Roe*, the "pregnant woman cannot be isolated in her privacy" because she "carries an embryo and, later, a fetus," and the "situation therefore is inherently different from marital intimacy, or bedroom possession of obscene material, or marriage, or procreation, or education . . . [and since] [t]he woman's privacy is no longer sole . . . any right of privacy she possesses must be measured accordingly."[24] Yet the measurement the Court applied only considered how a woman injures a fetus by choosing an abortion, not how a fetus injures a woman by causing wrongful pregnancy in the first place. According to the Court, abortion is different because it is a choice made in the context of a relationship with another entity, the fetus, while other privacy choices are made in the context of a single individual, and it is a choice that necessarily destroys the other entity in the pregnancy relationship: potential life. As the Court put it in *Harris*, "[a]bortion is inherently different from other medical procedures, because no other procedure involves the purposeful termination of a potential life."[25]

The Court is correct that pregnancy is a relationship; no woman would ever be pregnant if another entity, potential life, did not make her so. But although the Court obviously understands how a woman injures the fetus by choosing an abortion, it has failed to recognize how the fetus injures the woman by causing wrongful pregnancy. For this reason, the Court has recognized only how abortion uses deadly force to destroy a fetus, not how the use of deadly force is justified to stop the fetus from imposing the serious injuries of wrongful pregnancy. While the Court has recognized that a woman is not sole when she is pregnant, it has not recognized the implications of her right to be sole in relation to a fetus that physically imposes itself on her bodily integrity and liberty.

The abortion-funding consequences of the Court's interpretation of due process guarantees, therefore, reflect the basic fallacy that underlies its analysis of abortion rights: failure to identify the fetus as the cause of pregnancy and as the cause of wrongful pregnancy if a woman does not consent to pregnancy. The issue in wrongful pregnancy is not women's right to be free from the state because it is not the state that is coercing them to be pregnant. Rather it is women's right to be free of the serious injuries imposed by the fetus as a private party. The primary constitutional issue, therefore, is the state's response to the private injuries imposed by a fetus on a woman, not the state's interference in a woman's decision-making process as a single individual.[26]

What the Court has failed to recognize is that abortion is different from other privacy choices, such as what book to read or whom to marry, because it is a procedure for stopping one private party, the fetus, from injuring another, the woman. Abortion is not merely a choice but a self-defense response of one private party, the woman, to another private party, the fetus, that is causing serious injury to her. While other privacy contexts involve only one individual who is making choices about how to live his or her own life, abortion concerns a pregnancy relationship in which the fetus is imposing injury by making her privacy "not sole" against her will.

Abortion, therefore, is not comparable to a person's choice to take a vacation; rather, it is comparable to a person's right to use deadly force to stop his or her own kidnapping. While the state is not obligated to fund people's vacations, the same is not true of the state's response to kidnapping. When people are being kidnapped, the constitutional issue is not their right to be free of state interference to exercise their right to travel nor the state's direct intrusion into their lives to make them travel. Rather, the constitutional issue is the state's response to how a private party is making them travel against their will.

It is this frame that must be used to interpret the state's response, or lack of response, to the fetus's imposition of wrongful pregnancy. The constitutional issue is the state's response to the private injury the fetus is imposing by initiating and maintaining wrongful pregnancy. Specifically, the constitutional problem the Court has failed to address, much less solve, is whether it is constitutional for the state to fail to stop the fetus from imposing serious injuries on the woman as a means for protecting it; or in other words, whether it is constitutional for the state to encourage not merely pregnancy but also the fetus's imposition of the injuries of wrongful pregnancy, including medically abnormal wrongful pregnancies, which threaten women with permanent damage to their health or even with death.

Due Process and State Action

The application of due process guarantees to the state's response to the fetus's private injury of a woman is complicated because generally, due process guarantees refer only to the right of an individual to be free from intrusion by the state, not intrusion by a private party.[27] For this reason, generally, when private parties injure others, no constitutional issues are involved, nor does the failure of the state to stop private injury immediately trigger constitutional rights. Imagine, for example, that you are sitting in your kitchen, eating dinner with your family, when suddenly a group of strangers break down your front door and storm into your house. They are private people, who may have responded to an urge to invade your home, or they may merely lack control of their behavior because of the influence of drugs or insanity. Whatever the reason, they ransack your rooms, take your belongings, rape and beat you, and kill members of your family. Despite their savagery, these people have not violated your constitutional rights because they are private people depriving you and your family of life, liberty, and property, not the state imposing such deprivations.[28]

Because the Due Process Clause refers to state action, not private action, pro-choice advocates have turned their attention to how the state does act to compel a woman to be pregnant when it passes legislation that restricts her right to an abortion and/or the use of public resources to obtain one, thereby intruding on her due process right to privacy. Legal scholars Susan Estrich and Kathleen Sullivan adopt that tack, for example, when they compare state restrictions on abortion to the state's intrusions on a person's bodily integrity entailed by forced stomach pumping. Although

> abortion laws do not literally involve "laying hands on a woman" . . . this . . . should make no difference: the state would plainly infringe its citizens' bodily integrity whether its agents inflicted knife wounds or its laws forbade surgery or restricted blood transfusions in cases of private knifings.[29]

Yet by claiming that the state intrudes on a woman's body by restricting abortion funding, Estrich and Sullivan miss the even more basic point about how abortion-funding restrictions allow a state-protected private party, the fetus, to intrude on a woman's body, capture that body, and take that body without consent to serve its own needs. The proper analogy, therefore, is not whether it would be constitutional for the state to restrict people from giving or receiving blood transfusions to help someone who had been knifed but whether it would be constitutional for the state to allow private parties to capture people and take their blood from them without consent. Whereas it is highly unlikely that it would be constitutional for the state to restrict blood donations from one person to another, it defies the imagination to believe that state policies that allowed private people to take the body parts of others without consent would be constitutional, whatever might be the needs of the recipients of that blood.

Yet that is precisely the current policy used by states to protect preborn life. The state's refusal to fund abortions allows preborn life to take and use a woman's body without her consent for an extended period of nine months, even if such use threatens her with permanent injury to her health, simply because the fetus needs that body for its own survival. To protect by allowing the fetus to use a woman's body, even when she does not consent to its use, however, goes way beyond anything the state allows as a means for protecting born people. Regardless of born people's need for others' bodies or body parts, the state not only does not require people to donate their bodies to others but also criminalizes the intrusion of others, regardless of the intruder's need or kinship status to others. The state does not even allow born people to take the bodies of the dead without a form of consent, such as living wills or the agreement of family members, even if such a taking would save the life of a living person.

The constitutional issue in restrictive abortion-funding policies, therefore, is not the legitimacy of the state's interest in protecting preborn life but the means the state uses to implement that interest. When the state allows the fetus to take a woman's body without consent, it uses means that offer greater protection to preborn life than to born life by sanctioning preborn life to do to a person what the state does not allow born life to do, namely, to intrude on another's body and to use that body without consent to serve its own needs. If state policies did allow born people to intrude in this way, presumably those policies would violate the Constitution on procedural if not substantive grounds.

Procedural guarantees require the state to use fair and just processes when it imposes burdens on individuals. If the state needs to barge into your home, for example, in all but extraordinary cases it must first have a search warrant. If the state must restrict your liberty by imprisonment, it must do so in a way that assures you of procedural guarantees, such as informing you of the charges, giving you a chance to respond, and making sure that state officials engage only in appropriate conduct.[30]

While procedural due process guarantees control the manner in which the state may act, substantive guarantees restrain the type of intrusions the state may make. Substantive due process guarantees restrict the type of deprivations that the state may constitutionally impose. Regardless of how evenhanded the state's procedures may be, the Constitution restricts the state from making certain types of deprivations of life, liberty, and property unless there is an overriding need, and the means used by the state are the narrowest necessary for achieving its compelling state objective.[31]

It is difficult to pinpoint substantive, or fundamental, rights because they are not specifically enumerated in the Constitution, but over the years the Court has identified many of them in the area of reproductive activity, such as the right to engage in sexual intercourse with the use of contraceptives, the right to choose whom to marry,[32] the right to bear children, and the right to make educational decisions for one's children. Protection of the substantive due process guarantees means that, regardless of the state's adherence to strict due process procedures, some actions by the state can still be unconstitutional simply because of the type of deprivation involved. We can only assume that if it is unconstitutional for the state to coerce people to marry or not to marry, surely it is unconstitutional for the state to coerce women to be pregnant or not, whatever procedural guarantees might be instituted to implement such policies.

Yet, since no state has passed legislation that either requires or forbids women to be pregnant, the relevant issue of state action, or inaction, in the abortion debate does not center on how the state itself directly intrudes on a woman by conscripting her body for pregnancy service, requiring her to use contraceptives, or mandating an abortion. Nor does it even center on how the state deprives women of needed welfare benefits to help them maintain their health against diseases or other natural forces. Rather it centers on how the state responds to the fetus's imposition of injury as a private party protected by the state as human life. The constitutional issue in abortion funding is how the state, on the one hand, removes abortion funding from welfare benefits on the grounds that it is protecting the fetus as preborn human life and then, on the other hand, stands by and allows the fetus as preborn human life to impose serious and even severe injuries on a woman, which the state allows no born human life to do. The key due process question, therefore, is the state's response to the private injury imposed on the woman by the fetus as state-protected human life.

From Private Action to State Action

Generally, of course, when private parties injure others, no constitutional issues are involved, nor does the failure of the state to stop private injury immediately trigger constitutional rights because due process guarantees generally cover only overt state action, not inaction. These guarantees limit the ways in which the state may act, but they do not prescribe how the state must act. For this reason, most of the time, when the state simply fails to act, it does not violate due process guarantees even when, as a consequence of that failure, people are imposed on by others.

The leading case on this point is the notorious *DeShaney* case.[33] Joshua DeShaney, a five-year-old child, was in the custody of his father, whom social workers had suspected of child abuse for over three years. Finally, Joshua was so severely beaten by his father that he suffered irreversible brain damage, which required him to receive institutional care for the rest of his life.[34] Despite the social workers' suspicions that the child was constantly at risk, the Department of Social Services had left Joshua in the custody of his father, in jeopardy of continued abuse, which eventually all but killed him.[35] Joshua's mother sued the state, asserting that it had an obligation to protect Joshua from his father's beating. The Court ruled, however, that the state's failure to act on Joshua's behalf as a victim was not unconstitutional.

Whereas the right to due process guarantees that the state will not intrude too much on privacy rights, it requires no affirmative government action.[36] As a result, while the state itself may not deprive a person of life, liberty, or property without due process, the state has no duty to protect the victims of such deprivation. As the Court stated, in general the right to due process confers "no affirmative right to governmental aid, even where such aid may be necessary to secure life, liberty, or property interests of which the government itself may not deprive the individual."[37] For this reason, the state is not required "to protect the life, liberty, and property of its citizens against invasion by private actors."[38] The critics of the *DeShaney* decision are legion. Many proclaim it to be a flat-out wrong decision.[39] Yet the *DeShaney* decision is consistent with the Court's interpretation of state action to mean that "[g]overnment need not establish police or fire departments"[40] or any other mechanisms for stopping private aggressors.[41]

The *DeShaney* case, therefore, might suggest that when the fetus imposes wrongful pregnancy on a woman, although the Constitution empowers the state to stop the fetus, the Constitution does not obligate the state to do so. The fetus's imposition of wrongful pregnancy is simply the private action of a private party. As private action, it does not come under the purview of the Constitution, any more than do other private actions. Furthermore, even though the Constitution empowers the state to use its police power to stop private wrongful acts, the Due Process Clause does not mandate that the state do so. In sum, although a woman has a constitutional right to defend herself against the serious injuries imposed by a fetus, and although it is the purpose of the state to stop wrongful private acts, the Constitution does not obligate the state to stop the fetus on her behalf. According to this line of reasoning, the state is under no constitutional obligation to provide public funds, personnel, or facilities to help a woman obtain an abortion as a means for stopping the fetus from seriously injuring her.

The constitutionality of state inaction, however, is premised on the assumption that when private people suffer from the wrongful acts of others, the victims have recourse to the institutions of the state for redress.[42] The Court expressed this view in 1883 when ruling on the Civil Rights Act[43] passed by Congress in

1875, which made it illegal for private individuals to interfere with the rights of other private individuals to use the accommodations, facilities, and privileges of inns, public conveyances, and theaters on the basis of their race. The Court held this statute to be facially unconstitutional because the Fourteenth Amendment authorizes Congress to prohibit only state action, not private action.[44] Yet at the same time, the Court noted that if a state failed to regulate private conduct in accordance with the Fourteenth Amendment, such failure to act "could constitute 'state action' justifying federal intervention."[45]

The constitutionality of state inaction assumes, therefore, that when the state does not act, its failure to do so does not stem from state policies that tolerate or allow, much less sanction, the wrongful acts of private parties, thereby systematically cutting off the victims of those acts from the protection of the state.[46] Most of the time this is a safe presumption because, far from tolerating, allowing, sanctioning, or preferring to let private parties injure others, the state criminalizes private wrongful acts and stops private aggression. Although occasionally the state may fail to act in a particular, isolated instance, as in DeShaney, such a failure ordinarily does not imply, much less explicitly rest on, state policies that prefer private aggression over stopping it.

Certainly in the DeShaney case, there is no evidence that a state policy of preferring parental child abuse was the reason the state did not act to protect Joshua from his father. To the contrary, the state's policy was to stop parental child abuse. The state explicitly criminalized child abuse and used its public resources to stop it by setting up the Department of Social Services. Once it was clear to the state, moreover, that Joshua's father had violated his child's bodily integrity and liberty, the state did act to redress the victim's grievances by trying and convicting Joshua's father of child abuse.[47] The consequences of the state's failure to protect Joshua from the risk of a beating are horrendous. Yet as tragic as is the outcome of the state's failure in this particular case, the rationale for the state's failure to act does not imply a state policy of tolerance, permission, or sanction of child abuse by parents as a means of achieving a state goal, such as preservation of the family unit or protection of parental rights.

In other, relatively rare instances, however, the state fails to act because it does in fact tolerate, sanction, or favor injuries to others by private parties in preference to stopping them.[48] When this occurs, the Court has ruled that the state's failure to act not only transforms private action into state action but also transforms private wrongful action into unconstitutional state action. As the Court ruled in 1883 in the Civil Rights Cases, the private "wrongful act of an individual . . . is simply a private wrong or a crime of that individual; an invasion of the rights of the injured party . . . affect[ing] his person, his property, or his reputation," but such a private wrongful act is not an action by the state, unless "sanctioned in some way by the State, or . . . done under State authority."[49]

By this the Court means that as long as the state does not tolerate or sanction, much less prefer, the wrongful acts of private parties, the injured parties have access to the support of state institutions, such as courts and legislatures, to redress those injuries, and therefore private action does not involve constitutional issues. Once the state itself, however, fails to stop wrongful private actions because it sanctions them, by so doing the state deprives the injured parties of the use of state institutions to redress their grievances. State inaction that involves such a deprivation can violate the Constitution, including the Due Process Clause.

Although the field of state action is complex, if not confused, there are at least three ways the state can become so involved in private action that the law views the action of a private party to be the action of the state. This can happen when the state delegates public authority to a private actor, so that the actions of the private actor become the actions of the state; when the state establishes such a close relationship with a private party and insinuates itself with a private actor that the private action then takes on the character of state action; and when the state fails to stop private action because of its tolerance or sanction of that private action such that state sanction of private action renders it a form of state action.[50]

We can apply this typology of state action to the private action of the fetus when it imposes wrongful pregnancy. The state, of course, does not directly delegate authority to the fetus to capture a woman and take her body without consent to serve its own needs.[51] Yet what the state does do is tolerate, if not sanction, the fetus's imposition of the injuries of wrongful pregnancy by explicitly legislating statutes that prohibit the use of state resources to stop it. By such legislation the state uses a policy of state inaction as a means for protecting the fetus. The state prohibits itself from acting to stop the fetus from intruding on a woman's bodily integrity and liberty, even when the fetus's injury of a woman reaches health-threatening proportions entailed by a medically abnormal pregnancy.

As such, we can apply to abortion-funding restrictions precedents set by the Court that make state sanction of private wrongful action an unconstitutional form of state action. To the degree that it is unconstitutional for the state to sanction private wrongful acts by a policy of failing to stop them, it is an unconstitutional policy for the state to sanction the fetus's imposition of wrongful pregnancy by prohibitions against the use of public funds to stop it. To the degree, therefore, that it is unconstitutional for the state to insinuate itself with private actors who impose wrongful acts on others, much less to execute policies that sanction private wrongful acts, it is unconstitutional for the state to insinuate itself with the fetus's imposition of injury or to sanction that injury by means of policies that prohibit the state from stopping it.

In *Lynch v. United States,* the 5th Circuit Court of Appeals ruled, for example, that it is unconstitutional state action for the police to allow private people to beat a prisoner while they passively look on.[52] In *Reitman v. Mulkey* in 1967, the Court ruled that it is unconstitutional state action for the state of California to fail to act to prohibit private housing arrangements that are racially discriminatory.[53] Californians had amended their state constitution to outlaw government intervention in the private discrimination of an individual's sale or lease of residential property.[54] The Court held that such an amendment was unconstitutional state action because it improperly "encouraged" private racial discrimination by guaranteeing that the state would not intervene to stop it.[55]

Similarly, in *NAACP v. Alabama* in 1958, according to Professor Laurence Tribe the Court ruled that the state is "responsible for private injuries likely to be triggered when it withdraws protection of anonymity,"[56] thereby leaving people vulnerable to private parties who seek to injure them. The state's failure to act to protect a person's anonymity is thus unconstitutional state action. Courts also have ruled that if the state becomes involved in private action, that involvement can transform the private action into state action subject to standards set by the Constitution. This occurs when the state insinuates itself with a private actor by granting a license to a private actor or by enforcing a private action.[57] When the state becomes sufficiently involved in private action by establishing such a close relationship with the private actor, the action of the private actor may be fairly treated as that of the state itself;[58] or when the state actively encourages, either overtly or covertly, the activities of a private party, then the state itself is a "party of that action," and the action of the private party becomes state action.[59]

The Court ruled, for example, in *Burton v. Wilmington Parking Authority*, in 1961, that leasing space to a private restauranteur by the state in a building financed by public funds established such a close nexus between the restaurant owner and the state that actions of the private owner could be fairly said to be state action.[60] The restaurant owner had refused to serve an African-American, an action that if done solely between private parties is not unconstitutional. As the Court noted, the Fourteenth Amendment "erects no shield against merely private conduct, however discriminatory or wrongful."[61]

But, the Court ruled, by leasing space to the restaurant, the state established such a close relationship with the private owner that the owner's private action became a form of state action because the state, as lessor, had done nothing to prohibit the owner from establishing racially discriminatory policies against patrons of the restaurant.[62] It made no difference whether such state action was done in "good faith" or whether the state intended to discriminate on the basis of race.[63] The Court ruled further that the state, by failing to prohibit the restaurant owner from discriminating by race, "not only made itself a party to the refusal of service" but also "elected to place its power, property and prestige behind the admitted discrimination of the private actor" by actively leasing the property to him.[64] In this way, the Court concluded, the

> State has so far insinuated itself into a position of interdependence with Eagle [the restaurant owner] that it [the state] must be recognized as a joint participant in the challenged activity, which, on that account, cannot be considered to have been so "purely private" as to fall outside the scope of the Fourteenth Amendment.[65]

In other words, the financial relationship between the private owner and the state transformed the owner's private discriminatory action into unconstitutional state action.

In a similar case, *Shelley v. Kraemer*,[66] in 1948, the Court ruled on the constitutionality of a state's failure to prevent private parties from agreeing among themselves to restrict the rental and sale of their property to African-Americans and Asians. While private parties may exercise racial and ethnic discrimination in the conduct of their own private associations, state action that discriminates on the basis of race violates the Constitution. The Court ruled that the state, by recognizing the legitimacy of property transfers based on private restrictive covenants and by enforcing property rights established on the basis of those covenants, had established a sufficiently close relationship with these private actions of individuals to transform them into state action.[67]

The Court noted that recognition and enforcement of such covenants by the state encourages private parties to engage in the discriminatory actions, secure in the knowledge that their ensuing property transfers would be recognized as legitimate and lawful by the state.[68] Even though the state in no way acted to create or mandate the restrictive covenants, it enforced them by recognizing their legitimacy, thereby making the state a party to them and responsible for them.[69] Consequently, restrictive covenants agreed to by private parties became state action and, as such, became unconstitutional state action, which violated the equal protection clause of the Fourteenth Amendment.[70] Similarly, the Court ruled in 1946, in *Marsh v. Alabama*,[71] that a privately owned company town invoking trespass laws equaled state action and, as such, could not restrict First Amendment rights by regulating the dissemination of religious literature.

There are countercases, of course, making it difficult to generalize about how private action can become state action. The Court ruled in 1974, in *Jackson v. Metropolitan Edison*,[72] for example, that state licensing of and regulating a privately owned company does not make its private action state action. Similarly, in 1978, in *Flagg Brothers v. Brooks*,[73] the Court ruled that a state statute that allowed a warehouse to sell furniture owned by people who had not paid their bills was not a form of state action.

Yet as Laurence Tribe notes, a basic principle of the American republican system of government is the equality of the rights of all citizens. If within its power, "[e]very republican government is in duty bound to protect all its citizens in the enjoyment of this principle."[74] This duty resides with governments at the state level, and the obligation of the federal government, as established by the Fourteenth Amendment, is "to see that States do not deny the right."[75] As Judge Woods stated in *United States v. Hall*, in 1871, state denial of the protection of the Fourteenth Amendment "includes inaction as well as action, and . . . the omission to protect, as well as the omission to pass laws for protection."[76]

This standard applies to state and federal policies that mandate state inaction in providing public resources to women who seek an abortion. When the fetus injures a woman by imposing the wrongful act of nonconsensual pregnancy, the key constitutional question is not how the state itself directly injures a woman by coercing her to be pregnant but rather how the state responds to the private, wrongful acts of the fetus. If the state in isolated instances fails to stop those wrongful acts but has no policy of tolerating, allowing, sanctioning, or preferring them, probably no constitutional issue is raised. But if the state's failure to stop the fetus from imposing a wrongful pregnancy stems from state policies that tolerate, allow, sanction, or prefer its injury, the state's failure to act becomes a form of state action under the purview of the Constitution. The question then becomes whether the state's sanction of the fetus's private injury is a constitutional means for protecting it.

State Sanction of Private Injury

To sanction means "to assent," and one form of assent is to acquiesce.[77] *To acquiesce* means to give "implied consent to an act . . . by one's mere silence or without express assent or acknowledgement."[78] *To acquiesce* is in turn related to the meaning of *permit*, as when one permits something by acquiescing to it. And permission, according to law, is a form of tolerance.[79] At the very least, current abortion-funding restrictions express the state's tolerance of the imposition of pregnancy. The evidence that the state tolerates the fetus's injury of a woman lies in the legislation that expressly prohibits the use of state resources to stop the fetus. Even when the state is fully aware that a medically abnormal pregnancy severely threatens a woman's health, the state nevertheless explicitly allows the fetus to impose the serious injury of wrongful pregnancy by legislatively withholding public funds, facilities, and personnel to stop it by means of an abortion.

What is more, the state not only tolerates the fetus's imposition of serious injury, but also expressly prefers that injury to stopping the fetus. As the Court ruled in *Harris*, it is constitutional for the state to encourage childbirth as an "alternative activity . . . by means of unequal subsidization of abortion and other medical services"[80] in order to protect "the potential life of the fetus" by making "childbirth a more attractive alternative than abortion for persons eligible for Medicaid."[81] Or as the Court stated in *Maher v. Roe*, [T]he right in *Roe* "implies no limitation on the authority of a State to make a value judgment favoring childbirth over abortion, and to implement that judgment by the allocation of public funds."[82]

The issue, however, is not the state's preference for childbirth but the means it uses to encourage that preference. Certainly, it is constitutional for the state to offer economic benefits to women who consent to be pregnant. More controversial is whether it would be constitutional for the state to mandate that women must be pregnant by conscripting their bodies for pregnancy service. Some contend that such state intrusion into people's bodily integrity would violate the Due

Process Clause on substantive grounds because people have a fundamental right to be free of state coercion in such reproductive activities as contraception, sterilization, and pregnancy.[83] This means that the government cannot directly dictate to people whether to use or not to use contraceptives, to be or not to be sterilized, and presumably to be or not to be pregnant.

State requirements that pose unusually large burdens on a minority of people are usually accompanied or followed by compensatory measures for the sacrifices exacted. Forced conscription into the armed services, for example, brings with it generous economic and educational benefits to balance the extremity of the demands made by the state on those drafted.[84] Yet even if the state instituted an elaborate procedural apparatus so that women could appeal their pregnancy conscription by the state, and even if the state provided generous forms of compensation for their coerced pregnancy service, such as economic, educational, and employment benefits, it would still probably be an unconstitutional form of state action to directly require women to be pregnant.[85]

Only in an emergency of science-fiction proportions might the constitutional outcome differ. If the American population were reduced, for example, to five fertile women and five fertile men, and if all human life in the United States would become extinct unless those five couples engaged in reproductive activity, then it would perhaps be constitutional for the state to require those five couples to maximize their reproductive odds of producing children. Such state action would require women to increase the odds that a fertilized ovum would make them pregnant and, if that occurs, to allow a fertilized ovum to continue to do so. We have never faced such an emergency, however, and hopefully we never will.[86] For that reason, it is difficult to imagine what compelling state interest could justify state action that deprives women of their liberty, if not their lives, by legislative statutes that mandate the conscription of their bodies into state-coerced pregnancy service.

When the state encourages pregnancy without a woman's consent, it encourages wrongful pregnancy, a condition already recognized by law to be a serious bodily injury. By so doing, the state also sanctions that injury. In this sense the state's failure to stop the fetus represents its tolerance of fetal coercion and its sanction of and preference for a pregnancy that is coercively imposed on a woman by a fertilized ovum. As Laurence Tribe notes, if we conceive of liberty as "a sphere of private autonomy free from both governmental and private infringement [then] a government decision not to protect individuals from private infringements will plainly be a species of unconstitutional state action."[87]

While it is constitutional for the state to encourage childbirth, it is not constitutional for the state to use as a means the sanction of the fetus's private injury of a woman. Before determining whether state policies that encourage childbirth are constitutional, therefore, the Court must first establish whether the childbirth in question is consensual or nonconsensual. If, on the one hand, a woman consents to let a fetus make her pregnant, surely it is constitutional for the state to encourage that childbirth by providing funds to support the pregnancy. If, on the other hand, a woman does not consent to let a fetus make her pregnant, it is not constitutional for the state to encourage wrongful pregnancy by prohibiting the use of state resources to stop the fetus from injuring her because such a means makes the state a party to the fetus's imposition of harm.

This holds even when the state has a compelling interest in protecting the fetus after viability, much less a profound interest before viability. Whatever the degree of interest the state has in protecting the fetus, that interest does not make it constitutional for the state to encourage the fetus to impose a wrongful pregnancy as a *means* for protecting it because to do so is tantamount to state *encouragement* of private violence, not merely a neutral stance by the state in response to private violence. The Court has ruled that even when the state has a compelling interest, it must not use means to accomplish its objectives that violate the Constitution, such as the encouragement of private violence, and there must be a rational relationship between the goals of the legislation and the means used to attain them.[88]

In *McCulloch v. Maryland*,[89] in 1819, the Court emphasized the necessity for the state to use constitutional means to achieve its legitimate purposes. As Chief Justice John Marshall stated in the Court's opinion, for a statute to be constitutional, its end must be legitimate and fall within the scope of the Constitution, and "all means which are appropriate, which are plainly adapted to that end, which are not prohibited, but consistent with the letter and spirit of the constitution, are constitutional."[90] As Laurence Tribe notes, though Marshall's rational connection requirement is primary, it is not definitive: "It sets a minimum standard only; in many circumstances, legislation must pass more rigorous tests in order to survive constitutional challenge."[91]

The purpose of the state is to stop private aggressors from intruding on the bodies, liberty, and property of other private people, and the Constitution grants to states the police power to achieve this goal. State policies that tolerate, allow, sanction, or prefer the private intrusion of one party on another as a means for achieving a state goal, however, subvert the police power of the state as set up by the Constitution by sanctioning the very type of private wrongs the Constitution empowers the state to stop. Such policies do not merely exemplify the failure of the state to exercise its police power; they exemplify the state's subversion of its police power.

As Laurence Tribe notes, the Court was even more specific in an early case limiting governmental power to intrude upon "natural rights" reserved to the people.[92] In *Calder v. Bull*, in 1798, the Court stated that the "obligation of a law in governments established . . . on republican principles" is to prohibit certain "acts of legislation," such as a "law that destroys, or impairs, the lawful private contracts of citizens."[93] Natural rights are considered by many constitutional law scholars to be a relic of the past, yet they continued to be invoked in modern times by Supreme Court Justices who use them as a framework for "delineating the reach of the liberty clause of the fourteenth amendment."[94] What is more, some claim that rather than dropping natural rights, the Court instead has merely substituted another word for them, fundamental rights.[95] While the specific content of *Calder* was overruled by the Court in the Roosevelt era of the New Deal, the notion that there are limits to the degree to which the state may substantially intrude on people is far from dead.

Surely a law that prohibits the state from stopping one private party from imposing aggression on another impairs, if not destroys, the lawful relationship between the private parties involved. Current state polices that prohibit abortion funding, therefore, violate due process guarantees because they sanction the fetus's private injury of a woman as a means for protecting the fetus. While it is dubious that it would be constitutional for the state itself to coerce a woman to be pregnant, it is surely not constitutional for the state to sanction coercion by a private party.

The unconstitutionality of such state policies would become obvious if the current means that the state uses to protect preborn life were used to protect born life. Imagine the following scene. Private persons who seek to obtain from you needed body parts to sustain their own health and life aggressively intrude on your bodily integrity and liberty. They hook you up to blood transfusion machines to reroute your blood through their own bodies, they invade your tissues by taking your bone marrow, and they impose a host of physical invasions against your will, perhaps even threatening permanent damage to your health or even your death—all for the prolonged period of nine months and all because they must have your body in order to live.

You call on the state to stop these private intruders from so egregiously invading your bodily integrity and life. But not only does the state fail to act to stop their private wrongful acts against you, but also the police present you with the following rationale for their failure. They acknowledge that you are being severely injured by private parties—so severely, in fact, that the state and the Court affirm your right to use deadly force to stop the intruders yourself. The state also acknowledges that it has the resources to stop people from intruding on your body and liberty. Yet the state chooses not to stop born people from appropriating your blood, bone marrow, and body on the grounds that it prefers to protect them. The means the state uses to protect born people who capture you is to allow them to continue that capture by prohibiting the use of state resources to stop them. Although the state allows you to use deadly force to stop them, the state itself will not do so.

Such a state policy would be not only ludicrous if applied to born life but also unconstitutional because it would be a form of state action depriving you of your right to life and liberty in violation of the Constitution's Due Process Clause. State protection of born life does not entail the imposition of injuries on others, no matter how great the need. The current method, or means, the state uses to protect fetuses as preborn life therefore allows the fetus to do to women what the state allows no born person to do to another. Not only is this preposterous, but also it violates the Due Process Clause on procedural if not substantive grounds.

Ultimately the state's failure to stop the fetus stems from the impossibility of having one's cake and eating it too. The state wishes to protect the fetus as pre-born human life, but it does not wish to restrict the fetus in the same way that it would restrict born human life. Even when the state recognizes that a fetus can severely damage a woman's health, it does not want to stop the fetus from doing so, even though the state's protection of born people does not allow them to impose such injuries on others. This situation raises constitutional issues because, although the state may encourage consensual childbirth, encouragement of private wrongful injuries violates due process guarantees; by sanctioning the fetus's private wrongful acts, the state itself becomes involved in the fetus's deprivation of a woman's liberty and, possibly, her life.

While it is constitutional on due process grounds for the state simply to fail to act, it is not the case that the state simply fails to act when it passes legislation prohibiting the use of state resources to stop the fetus as a private party from imposing the serious injuries entailed even in a medically normal pregnancy. Such state policies are state actions that sanction harm caused by fetuses imposing wrongful pregnancy. Reframing abortion rights in terms of women's right to consent to pregnancy, therefore, illuminates the hidden way in which current legislation that prohibits the use of public resources for abortions violates due process guarantees. The state's tolerance, sanction, and preference for the fetus's deprivation of a woman's liberty transform private action into state action, and concomitantly wrongful private deprivation of women's liberty into an unconstitutional state deprivation that violates the Due Process Clause.

7

From Due Process to Equal Protection

The right to an abortion is a necessary but not sufficient condition for obtaining one. Abortions also must be available. Medical personnel must be trained to perform them, clinics must be able to operate to provide them, and women must be able to afford them. It is this last factor that is the most serious impediment to the reproductive rights of thousands of indigent women who lack the funds to pay for an abortion.[1] Although the constitutional right to an abortion appears to be secure after the Court upheld it in *Casey*, the job of ensuring women's reproductive rights is far from done. At the top of the list of things still to be accomplished is establishing the constitutional grounds that guarantee the right to abortion funding.[2]

It is not sufficient, therefore, as the Court did in *Roe*, merely to affirm a woman's constitutional right to make private decisions about her own reproduction options without state interference and her right to use deadly force to stop the fetus from imposing the serious injuries entailed in medically abnormal pregnancies. A fetus's imposition of even a medically normal pregnancy exceeds the latitude recognized in the law for one person to intrude on the bodily integrity and liberty of another. Even a medically normal pregnancy constitutes sufficient intrusion to justify the use of deadly force to stop a wrongful pregnancy.

Therefore, the right of self-defense applies to medically normal pregnancies as well. To rule otherwise implies that there is no legal significance to the fetus's initial intrusion of and implantation in a woman's body as well as its maintenance of that implantation. If the state viewed the fetus merely as a mass of alien cells that intruded on a woman's body, a woman would have access to health benefits to remove it, as she would any other type of cellular intrusion, such as cancer, and the legal significance of the fetus's intrusion as state-protected human life would disappear.

This, however, is not what the state does. Rather, the state omits health benefits to cover the cost of an abortion precisely to protect the fetus, as human life, from the harm of its removal. Treatment of the fetus as state-protected human life, however, must work both ways. If the fetus is to be protected from harm, it must be restricted from causing harm. Legally, what the fetus does to a woman even in a medically normal pregnancy constitutes massive harm if she does not consent to its implantation and transformation of her body from a nonpregnant to a pregnant condition. To wait until the fetus threatens to permanently damage a woman's health or kill her before recognizing that it is imposing harm hides the serious harm the fetus imposes on a woman from the very moment it makes her pregnant, if it does so without her consent. This harm would be immediately apparent if born people were to simulate the imposition of a medically normal pregnancy on others by injecting them with hormones, using their blood, destroying their cells, and growing new organs in their body, all over the prolonged period of nine months and all without consent.

Concrete Intrusion

Legal scholar, and Solicitor General during President Reagan's administration, Charles Fried, in oral argument before the Court, declared "concrete intrusion" to be a standard for the Court's evaluation of privacy rights.[3] The fetus meets the concrete intrusion test. There is nothing abstract about being made pregnant by a fetus. It is a concrete intrusion that massively changes and transforms a woman's body for the prolonged period of nine months. It is high time, therefore, for the Court to recognize that preborn human life, much like born human life, harms others when it massively uses and transforms their bodies without consent. Even a medically normal pregnancy causes serious harm when imposed nonconsensually, as the law already recognizes in contexts other than abortion.

Obviously the state must not tolerate, allow, or sanction, much less prefer, the fetus's concrete intrusion without consent as a means for protecting it as human life. To the contrary, it is the state's job to defend people against private intrusion of their bodily integrity and liberty. The right to self-defense is meant to be a fallback option for when the state cannot do its job, not a preferred policy of the state.[4] This means that the state must provide for abortions as the means for stopping the fetus from harming women, much as the state stops born human life from harming others.[5]

Over the years since *Roe v. Wade*, many pro-choice advocates have looked for affirmative grounds that would obligate the state to provide abortions. They have done so by shifting their attention from the negative rights guaranteed by the Due Process Clause to the positive rights guaranteed by the Equal Protection Clause.[6] Whereas negative rights guarantee freedom from state interference, positive rights guarantee the affirmative assistance of the state. The Equal Protection Clause of the Fourteenth Amendment states that no "State shall . . . deny to any person within its jurisdiction the equal protection of the laws."[7] This means that the state is affirmatively obligated to provide to all people the equal protection of the laws. To the extent that laws protect people from the private injuries of others, the Equal Protection Clause affirmatively obligates the state to protect people equally from the private injuries of others. Some legal scholars interpret the Equal Protection Clause to be an absolute affirmative right to state protection against private wrongful acts; others believe that it guarantees only a contingent affirmative right, which means that to the degree that the state protects some people from private injury, it must then protect others who are similarly situated.

Absolute versus Contingent Affirmative Rights

A classic interpretation of the Equal Protection Clause as an absolute right to state protection from private injury is that of Jacobus tenBroek[8]: the "equal protection of the laws is violated fully as much, perhaps even more, by private invasions made possible through failure of government to act as by discriminatory laws and officials."[9] In this sense, the denial of protection by the state against the wrongful acts of private parties is a denial of equality.[10] This means that the state must stop private aggressors from violating the natural rights of other people, such as their right to life and liberty. If a private person threatens to murder, rape, rob, or otherwise seriously injure another, according to some, the Equal Protection Clause guarantees that the state must stop those wrongful acts.[11]

That the Equal Protection Clause guarantees an absolute affirmative right to state protection from private injuries is confirmed by the oath that public officials swear upon assuming office. From the president of the nation on down, all state officials swear that they will uphold the laws of the state (see table 7.1). They do not contingently swear that if they uphold the laws for some, they will then uphold the laws for others. Rather, they swear to do so in absolute terms, thereby acquiring what we might think of as an absolute obligation to execute the laws of the state.

The Constitution, for example, not only requires presidents to take an oath of office but also mandates what that oath must be; according to article II, section 1, clause 8 of the Constitution, the president-elect must recite the following before assuming the presidency: "I do solemnly swear [or affirm] that I will faithfully execute the Office of President of the United States, and will to the best of my Ability preserve, protect, and defend the Constitution of the United States."[12] Supreme Court Justices of the United States, as well as other federal judges, also must swear to an oath of office, promising that they will "administer justice without respect to persons, and do equal right to the poor and to the rich," and will "impartially discharge and perform all the duties incumbent" upon them according to "the Constitution and laws of the United States."[13] So, too, do the vice president, attorney general, and governors of the states take an oath of office in which they swear to uphold the laws. In Boston, for example, police officers must swear to uphold and defend the Constitution of the United States of America and the Commonwealth of Massachusetts.[14]

Table 7.1   Oaths of Office

Presidential Oath of Office

The Constitution requires presidents to take an oath of office. Article II, section 1, clause 8, of the Constitution requires the president-elect to recite the following oath before assuming the presidency:
"I do solemnly swear (or affirm) that I will faithfully execute the Office of President of the United States, and will to the best of my Ability preserve, protect, and defend the Constitution of the United States."

Vice Presidential Oath of Office

I pledge to "support and defend the Constitution of the United States against all enemies, foreign and domestic; that I will bear true faith and allegiance to the same; that I take this obligation freely, without any mental reservation or purpose of evasion, and that I will well and faithfully discharge the duties of the office on which I am about to enter."

Governor of Massachusetts
and Others Chosen or Appointed:
Oaths of Office*

"I, (name to be pronounced here) do solemnly swear that I will bear true faith and allegiance to the Commonwealth of Massachusetts, and will support the Constitution thereof. So help me God."

"I, (name to be pronounced here) do solemnly swear and affirm, that I will faithfully and impartially discharge and perform all the duties incumbent on me as——: according to the best of my abilities and understanding, agreeably, to the rules and regulations of the Constitution, and the laws of this Commonwealth. So help me God."

Justices and Judges: Oath of Office†

Each justice or judge of the United States shall take the following oath or affirmation before performing the duties of this office:
"I,——do solemnly swear (or affirm) that I will administer justice without respect to persons, and do equal right to the poor and to the rich, and that I will faithfully and impartially discharge and perform all the duties incumbent upon me as——according to the best of my abilities and understanding, agreeably to the Constitution and laws of the United States. So help me God."

Police Officers, City of Boston: Oath of Office††

"I, (say your name) do solemnly swear / that I will uphold and defend / the Constitution of the United States of America / and the Commonwealth of Massachusetts/ and that I will oppose the overthrow / of the government of the United States of America / or of this Commonwealth / by force, violence / or by illegal / or unconstitutional method.

Table 7.1   Oaths of Office (*continued*)

Police Officers, City of Boston: Oath of Office†† (*continued*)

"I, (say your name), do solemnly swear / that I will faithfully and impartially discharge / and perform all the duties / incumbent on me / as a member of the Police Department of the City of Boston / and will obey / and be bound / by such rules and regulations / as are or may be, / from time to time / laid down for the government / or the Police Department of the City of Boston.

---

* Printed by the Office of the Secretary of State, Massachusetts.

† Title 28—Judiciary and Judicial Procedure, U.S. Code, 1988 ed., vol. 12, p. 146.

†† Boston Police Department, Office of Informational Services, "Form of Oath," emphasis added (/ = pauses).

Despite the fact that it makes sense to believe that the state is obligated to provide law and order by executing the laws, most constitutional scholars contend that people do not have an absolute right to state protection of the laws but only a contingent right, meaning that if the state acts to execute laws, it must do so in a way that does not deny equal protection of those laws to people who are similarly situated. According to this view, the state need not have a police department nor use its police power to protect anyone from murderers, rapists, kidnappers, or others who commit private, wrongful acts. But once the state uses its police power to protect some people from such wrongful acts, the state must protect other similarly situated victims.

The contingent view of equal protection guarantees is in the ascendancy. For this reason, most agree that once the state protects some people's fundamental rights, it must protect others' fundamental rights as well. In *Thornburgh v. ACOG,* Justice White observed that the only rights that might be considered fundamental are those that are "implicit in the concept of ordered liberty," which he interpreted to mean those that establish a "free, egalitarian and democratic society."[15] The rights to life and to liberty, therefore, can be said to be fundamental rights because without them there is no basis for a free and egalitarian, much less democratic, society. This means to the degree that the state protects anyone's right to life and liberty, it must protect others' right to life and liberty, even if we only think of the Equal Protection Clause in terms of contingent rights.

Equal protection jurisprudence has focused a great deal of attention on the contingent interpretation of the Equal Protection Clause when the state treats similarly situated people differently because of their race or gender.[16] The Court has ruled that race-based treatment triggers suspect classifications, to which the Court applies strict scrutiny to determine if there is a state interest sufficiently compelling and narrowly tailored to justify such unequal treatment.[17] Similarly, if the state treats people differently on the basis of their sex, the Court applies intermediate scrutiny to this semisuspect class to determine if there is a state interest sufficiently important and legitimate, as well as narrowly tailored, to justify such unequal treatment.[18] Because of this special scrutiny of policies that discriminate on the basis of race or sex, statutes with race or gender classifications are more likely to be struck down by the Court as unconstitutional on equal protection grounds.[19]

Pro-choice advocates, seeking to switch abortion-funding rights from negative due process rights to positive equal protection rights, therefore endeavor to show how the state, by failing to provide abortion funding, fails to protect some people's fundamental rights. They also attempt to show how the state's failure to provide abortion funding is an unconstitutional form of gender discrimination. One of the first to make such claims was Sylvia Law, who stated that although "[n]othing the Supreme Court has ever done has been more concretely important for women" than establishing the constitutional right to an abortion in *Roe*, that decision robbed women of the power of the law to secure full reproductive rights, including abortion funding, because "[d]espite the decision's overwhelming importance to women, it was not grounded on the principle of sex equality" and the Court "did not rely on the sex-specific impact of laws restricting access to abortion."[20] As a result, she points out that "literally hundreds of legal challenges to restrictive abortion laws have been brought, and only a very few of the cases have argued that the restrictions violated sex equality norms," thereby losing for women an important plank for securing guarantees of their reproductive rights.[21]

Before joining the Supreme Court, Justice Ruth Bader Ginsburg argued that restrictions on abortion funding violated the equal protection clause because they were a form of sex discrimination that deprived women of equal opportunities to education and employment.[22] Guido Calabresi located the comparison between men and women in terms of their equal right to engage in sexual intercourse without the aftermath of pregnancy. Prohibition of abortion funding, he argued, is an unconstitutional form of sex discrimination because it situates men and women unequally in relation to the reproductive consequences of sexual activity.[23]

Many others, including Guido Calabresi,[24] Deborah Rhode,[25] Cass Sunstein,[26] Laurence Tribe,[27] and Donald Regan,[28] also analyze abortion rights in terms of good or bad samaritan principles, arguing that the key point of comparison between men and women is their right to be bad samaritans by refusing to donate their bodies to others, including fetuses. As Laurence Tribe notes, "In my view, the most striking thing about governmental choices [to prohibit abortion funding] . . . is that they . . . require women to sacrifice their liberty, and quite literally their labor, in order to enable others to survive and grow."[29] To the extent that the state guarantees to men a right to refuse to donate their bodies or body parts to others, therefore, pro-choice advocates argue that it must do the same for women by providing abortion funding if women are too poor to afford an abortion themselves. This was the point made by Kathryn Kolbert, pro-choice lawyer in *Casey:* "Surely, if the Government cannot require individuals to sacrifice their lives or health for human beings who are born for other compelling purposes, they cannot do so for purposes of protecting potential fetal life."[30]

Yet these claims that the state's failure to provide abortions is a form of sex discrimination have run into a brick wall because the Court has declared, contrary to common sense, that discrimination on the basis of pregnancy is not sex discrimination. The Court has reasoned that pregnancy is not a condition that categorizes people into two groups, men and women, based on sex, but rather into two groups, pregnant women and nonpregnant people.[31] And while the first category contains only women, the second category contains both men and women. As the Court ruled in *Geduldig,*

> [while] it is true that only women can become pregnant, it does not follow that every legislative classification concerning pregnancy is a sex-based classification. . . . [Unless it can be shown] that distinctions involving pregnancy are mere pretexts designed to effect an invidious discrimination against the members of one sex or the other, lawmakers are constitutionally free to include or exclude pregnancy from the coverage of legislation . . . [because discrimination based on pregnancy does not divide people into two groups defined by sex, but rather] divides . . . [people] into two groups—pregnant women and nonpregnant persons. While the first group is exclusively female, the second includes members of both sexes.[32]

For this reason, the Court argues that one cannot claim that the state engages in sex discrimination when it treats pregnant women differently from other people because pregnancy does not differentiate between groups on the basis of sex. Discrimination on the basis of pregnancy, therefore, according to the Court, does not necessarily involve any type of suspect, or even semisuspect, classification. Consequently, the Court directs no special scrutiny on sex discrimination grounds to policies involving pregnancy, including prohibitions against public funding of abortions. This means that passage of an Equal Rights Amendment to the Constitution that prohibits states from discriminating against people on the basis of their sex would most likely, in the Court's view, fail to provide constitutional grounds for women's right to abortion funding since discrimination on the basis of pregnancy is not considered by the Court necessarily to be a type of gender discrimination.[33]

Once we identify the fetus as the cause of pregnancy, however, and as the cause of wrongful pregnancy if a woman does not consent to be pregnant, we see that current pro-choice efforts to switch from due process to equal protection grounds fail, not because the Court has ruled that pregnancy does not necessarily constitute sex discrimination, but rather because pro-choice advocates do not show how the fetus positions women similarly to other victims who suffer from wrongful intrusion of their bodily integrity and liberty. Once we reframe women's abortion rights in terms of their consent to be pregnant, the key constitutional issue becomes whether the state protects pregnant women as victims of private injuries committed by the fetus as state-protected human life to the same degree that the state protects others who are victims of private injury caused by human life.

With this perspective in place, we can see that current abortion-funding policies violate equal protection guarantees, even when established on contingent rather than absolute standards, not because those policies necessarily trigger gender discrimination as a semisuspect category but because they trigger unequal state protection of people's fundamental rights, including their right to the equal protection of laws that criminalize the intrusion of private parties on their bodily integrity and liberty. The Court has ruled that when state policies deny equal protection of fundamental rights, those policies are unconstitutional even if they invoke no suspect or semisuspect classifications.[34]

Unconstitutional Means

Applying equal protection analysis to abortion funding, therefore, need not founder on the shoals of sex discrimination precedents set by the Court. Even if pregnancy is not a form of sex discrimination, and even if sex discrimination is not elevated to the level of a suspect class, the Court must still apply strict scrutiny to determine if abortion funding restrictions are a means to protect the fetus that infringe on women's fundamental rights. This was the position the Court took in the 1992 *Casey* decision.[35]

In *Casey* the Court reaffirmed that it is legitimate for the state to protect the fetus as potential life, even though it has not declared the fetus to be a person under the protection of the Fourteenth Amendment.[36] As the plurality opinion noted, in 1973 in *Roe* the Court had ruled that the state had an "important and legitimate interest in protecting the potentiality of human life."[37] In *Casey* the position of the plurality was that this "portion of the decision in *Roe* has been given too little acknowledgment and implementation by the Court in its subsequent cases."[38] What primarily concerned the plurality in *Casey*, therefore, was not the legitimacy of the "substantial state interest in potential life throughout pregnancy,"[39] which they went overboard to affirm, but rather the means used by the state to protect potential life.

Identifying the central constitutional right in *Roe* to be women's right to choose an abortion, the plurality in *Casey* reasoned that any means undermining that right would be unconstitutional. Means, for example, posing an undue burden for a woman seeking to exercise her constitutional right of choice to have an abortion would be unconstitutional. As the plurality put it:

> A finding of an undue burden is a shorthand for the conclusion that a state regulation has the purpose or effect of placing a substantial obstacle in the path of a

woman seeking an abortion of a nonviable fetus. A statute with this purpose is invalid because the means chosen by the State to further the interest in potential life must be calculated to inform the woman's free choice, not hinder it.[40]

Although it is constitutional for the state to protect potential life, therefore, it is not constitutional for the state to use any means it chooses. Specifically, it is not constitutional for the state to use a means of protection that denies to a woman her constitutional rights. When the Court evaluated in *Casey* the means used by states to protect potential life, therefore, the Court found some of them to be constitutional and others to be unconstitutional because they violated women's constitutional rights. The Court upheld, for example, that it was constitutional for the state to require women to wait twenty-four hours before obtaining a requested abortion and to require "doctors to inform a woman seeking an abortion of the availability of materials relating to the consequences to the fetus, even when those consequences have no direct relation to her health"[41] because these means did not actually deprive a woman of her constitutional right to choose an abortion by placing an undue burden on her that would prevent her from obtaining one.

On the other hand, the Court ruled that it was unconstitutional for the state to require a woman to inform her husband that she seeks an abortion on the grounds that such a means, by exposing some women to the risk of physical harm, constituted an undue burden interfering with their constitutional right to choose an abortion. Citing domestic violence statistics that "one of every two women will be battered at some time in their life,"[42] the Court noted that "In a domestic abuse situation . . . [m]ere notification of pregnancy is frequently a flashpoint for battering and violence within the family."[43] For this reason, as the plurality opinion, speaking for a majority of the Court, stated, "women who fear for their safety and the safety of their children are likely to be deterred from procuring an abortion as surely as if the commonwealth had outlawed abortion in all cases."[44] Clearly, therefore, the constitutional issue at stake in women's abortion rights is neither the legitimacy of the state's interest and protection of potential life nor the suspect classification of gender as a category of strict scrutiny. Rather, it is the means the state uses to implement its interest in protecting potential life—specifically, whether those means violate fundamental constitutional rights, such as women's right to choose an abortion, by placing an undue burden on their exercise of that right. Reframing the key right in abortion as women's right to consent-to-pregnancy rather than merely choose-an-abortion, however, switches attention to a new fundamental right: women's right to equal protection by the state of their bodily integrity and liberty against harm imposed by human life. It is this fundamental right that the state must not hinder when it chooses means for protecting the fetus. Even if a woman's right to choose an abortion is secure, and even if gender is not elevated to the level of strict scrutiny, the Court's work is not done, for it must evaluate with strict

Table 7.2   Means Used by the State to Protect Potential Human Life

State Encouragement of Good Samaritan CONSTITUTIONAL	State Criminalization of Bad Samaritan CONSTITUTIONAL / UNCONSTITUTIONAL	State Failure to Protect Captive Samaritan UNCONSTITUTIONAL
State incentives to women to be good samaritans by giving their bodies to fetuses. E.g., Childcare support.	State criminalization of bad samaritan behavior by women refusing to give their bodies to fetuses. E.g., Prosecuting abortion providers.	State failure to protect women from captive samaritan status imposed by fetuses making them pregnant without consent. E.g., State failure to provide abortion funding.
Constitutional: Does not violate Due Process or Equal Protection Clauses.	**Constitutional** after viability in a medically normal pregnancy. **Unconstitutional** violation of Due Process Clause before viability or any time in a medically abnormal pregnancy.	**Unconstitutional** violation of Equal Protection Clause, if state protects others' integrity and liberty of others.

scrutiny whether the means the state used to protect potential life violate women's fundamental right to equal protection by the state of their bodily integrity and liberty when a fetus imposes pregnancy without consent.

There are basically three means the state can use to protect potential life, as table 7.2 summarizes. And for each, the key question is whether it is a means that interferes with a woman's constitutional right not only to choose an abortion but, more significantly, women's constitutional right to equal protection of her bodily integrity and liberty. One means the state currently uses to protect potential life, which surely is constitutional, is to offer women incentives to be good samaritans by voluntarily giving their bodies to the fetus. Public policies that support pregnancy and childbirth do just that, and they are constitutional as long as they do not interfere with women's constitutional rights, including the right to equal protection against private violence. As long as a woman has the right to decline such incentives, the state may offer them.[45] It is constitutional, therefore, for the state to protect potential life by means of offering childcare support to women who bear children, along with educational benefits and other facilities to make their childbearing and childrearing activities more attractive options.

Another means the state could use, but does not, to protect potential life would be to conscript women's bodies for pregnancy service by legislation requiring women to be good samaritans by remaining pregnant. No state, however, has passed this type of legislation. What is more, most likely the Court would rule that such a means for protecting potential life violates the Due Process Clause because it involves direct state interference in a woman's procreative activities, thereby violating her fundamental privacy right to be free of government involvement in her reproductive choices about her own body and life. While some states do require good samaritan behavior from people, such behavior does not include giving one's body or body parts to others, even when people's lives are at stake and even when people are related to each other by kinship ties. As the plurality opinion, speaking for a majority of the Court, noted in *Casey*, "It is settled now . . . that the Constitution places limits on a State's right to interfere with a person's most basic decision about family and parenthood."[46] It is difficult to imagine the crisis that would make it legitimate for the state to require women to give their bodies to fetuses, or that would justify state interference in the procreation decisions of either men or women.

On the other hand, states have been more successful in requiring women to be good samaritans by passing negative legislation criminalizing women's bad samaritan choices by prosecuting women who obtain abortions, health personnel who perform or assist with abortions, or both. Whether this means to protect a fetus is constitutional, of course, was the issue in *Roe*. Specifically, the Court examined whether the means used by the state to protect potential life—criminalization of abortions—violated women's due process guarantees, such as their fundamental right to make choices about their procreative activities, including the right to make the choice to be a bad samaritan by terminating pregnancy with an abortion.

The answer the Court gave was complex, if not confused. On the one hand, the Court ruled in *Roe* that it did violate women's fundamental right to due process if the state protected the fetus by criminalizing abortion before it was viable or at any point when the pregnancy in question was a medically abnormal one. On the other hand, the Court ruled that it did not violate women's fundamental right to due process if the state protected the fetus by criminalizing abortions after viability, provided the pregnancy in question was not a medically abnormal one threatening her with injury to her health or with death.

Roe, therefore, leaves us with a dubious sense of how the Due Process Clause limits the means the state may use to protect the fetus, generating much criticism. Since most likely it would be an unconstitutional violation of the Due Process Clause for the state directly to conscript a woman's body and require her to be or to remain pregnant, it is unclear exactly why it is constitutional for the state to prohibit her from terminating pregnancy at any point in pregnancy, which is, in effect, a prohibition that requires her to remain pregnant.

The Court's reference to the viability of the fetus as the standard determining women's right to terminate pregnancy does not clarify the situation. This is because most likely it would violate the Due Process Clause for the state to require born people to donate their bodies to other born people as a means for protecting the people in need of those body parts. This holds even when the people in question are related by kinship ties. If the state cannot protect born people by means of requiring other born people to donate their bodies to them, then it is unclear why it is constitutional for the state to require women to donate their bodies to preborn human life, as a means of protecting the fetus, when preborn human life, even when viable, may not yet be a person.

Critics of *Roe*, therefore, have concentrated attention on the inconsistencies it presents in relation to other applications of the Due Process Clause and to the arbitrariness of the viability standard itself. Missing from the discussion, however, is recognition of the extraordinary way the Court in *Roe* established that women's abortion rights are determined more by what the fetus does than by what the fetus is. While it has been common to think that *Roe* established viability as the ultimate criterion for determining women's abortion rights, in fact, *Roe* dramatically affirms that the most important criterion is what the fetus does to a woman.

Even if a fetus is viable, the Court in *Roe* established that no state may protect such a fetus by means of prohibiting an abortion, when what the fetus does to a woman threatens her health or her life. As Justice Blackmun, writing the opinion of the Court in *Roe*, stated:

> For the stage subsequent to viability, the State in promoting its interest in the potentiality of human life may, if it chooses, regulate, and even proscribe, abortion *except where it is necessary, in appropriate medical judgment, for the preservation of the life or health of the mother.*[47]

According to *Roe*, therefore, what the fetus does to a woman trumps what the fetus is in terms of a viability standard. Even if the fetus is viable and even if the state's interest in protecting the fetus at that point in its development is compelling, nevertheless, if what the fetus does to a woman sufficiently injures her, no state may protect a fetus by interfering with a woman's due process right to make a choice to be a bad samaritan by obtaining an abortion.

The Court was correct, of course, to rule in *Roe* that what the fetus does trumps what the fetus is. After all, the state's protection of born people follows that same logic. The state has a compelling interest in protecting born people, but that interest is trumped by what born people do. A born person who intrudes upon the bodily integrity and liberty of another person is stopped by the state from doing so, despite the state's compelling interest in protecting all born people, including perpetrators of privately imposed violence. In principle, this holds within kinship groups.

The flaw in the Court's reasoning in *Roe* and subsequent cases, therefore, is its failure to identify adequately what the fetus does. The Court failed to incorporate into abortion rights cases, for example, the law's recognition that all pregnancies, including medically normal ones, are serious injuries to a woman, if imposed upon her without her consent. What the fetus does, therefore, is not just injure women in medically abnormal pregnancies threatening her health or life, but in all pregnancies, including medically normal ones, if the fetus imposes pregnancy on a woman without her consent.

In addition, the Court in *Roe* mistakenly identified the fundamental right violated by the state when it protects the fetus by means of prohibiting abortion to be women's due process rights to make choices without interference from the state. In fact, the fundamental right at stake is women's equal protection right to be assisted by the state to stop preborn human life from intruding on their bodily integrity and liberty. To the degree that the state protects people from intrusion of their bodily integrity and liberty by born human life, the state must protect women from intrusion of their bodily integrity and liberty by preborn human life. To do otherwise violates women's equal protection guarantees.

The third means, therefore, the state could use to protect the fetus is unconstitutional: allowing fetuses to intrude on others' bodily integrity and liberty to take what they need for their own survival. Yet that is precisely the means currently employed by policies that prohibit the use of public resources to provide an abortion to a woman to stop a fetus from intruding upon her. Such policies prohibit the state from using its resources to stop a fetus from injuring a woman, even when its level of injury threatens to cripple her or to leave her brain dead in a coma for life. What the Court has yet to recognize, however, is how such state policies use an unconstitutional means to protect the fetus by denying to women their constitutional right to equal protection by the state of their physical security.

The state's protection of the fetus, of course, is based on its intrinsic value as a form of human life, not on a calculation of its utilitarian value. It is not because it costs the state too much money to perform abortions or because the state lacks the resources to perform abortions that it fails to stop a fetus from injuring a woman by imposing a wrongful pregnancy. To the contrary, when the state funds childbirth costs but not abortions, it costs the state more money to allow the fetus to continue its imposition of pregnancy. Nor does the state protect the fetus as a means to some other end. Currently, the state does not protect the fetus in order to avert a crisis caused by a diminishing population, for example, because we have no such population crisis. Rather, protection of the fetus is an end in itself, justified by the state's interest in the fetus as a form of human life.

Yet the state must also recognize the intrinsic value of the woman's bodily integrity and liberty. The state must recognize that there is no utilitarian calculation that can justify the fetus's intrusion in terms of a quantity of injury. Rather than waiting until the fetus causes so much damage to her health that she is permanently crippled or killed, therefore, the state and the Court must recognize instead that the fetus seriously injures a woman from the very moment it begins to intrude and transform her body from a nonpregnant to a pregnant condition against her will. Of course, the fetus cannot be held legally responsible for its wrongful acts since it lacks the mens rea of intentionality or the ability to control its actions. In this sense, its acts are similar to those of a born person under the influence of drugs or otherwise mentally incompetent who nevertheless imposes serious injury on another person. Just as the state protects people from injuries imposed by mentally incompetent born life, however, so, too, must the state protect women from injuries imposed by mentally incompetent preborn life.

Once the state removes abortion funding from welfare policies because it views the fetus as a form of human life under state protection, therefore, it becomes incumbent on the state not only to protect the fetus, as the plurality noted in *Casey*, but also to stop the fetus from causing harm to others, a point the plurality did not satisfactorily address in *Casey*. Even though the Court in *Casey* acknowledged the pain and burdens entailed in pregnancy, it failed to identify the fetus as the cause of those pains and burdens. As the Court noted, a pregnant woman "is subject to anxieties, to physical constraints, to pain that only she must bear."[48] This vision of immaculate pregnancy, however, blinded the Court from seeing the key legal issue: The fetus as the cause of those pains and burdens. As the consent-to-pregnancy approach reveals, however, without consent, a fetus's transformation of a woman's body from a nonpregnant to a pregnant condition constitutes serious harm and injury to her, even when the pregnancy in question is a medically normal one.

Losing Rights at Birth

As pro-life advocate Representative Lawrence J. Hogan (Maryland, R) states, his goal is to "give the child in the womb the same right to continue living as his older brother, with both of them, of course being governed by the even-handed application of the principles of due process and equal protection."[49] Pro-life advocates, therefore, do not expect that the fetus has more rights than a born person, only that it has the same rights. When born people intrude on the bodily integrity and liberty of others, the state stops them. If we do what pro-life advocates advise and evenhandedly apply the same principles to preborn life, the state must then stop the fetuses from intruding on women's bodily integrity without consent. To argue otherwise is to assume that fetuses may intrude on the bodily integrity of others in a way the state allows no born people to do. To so argue implies that fetuses have not equal, but more, rights than born people.

If the state allows the fetus to do what the state allows no born person to do, it becomes apparent that children lose rights at birth. But how can people have more constitutional rights before rather than after birth, when the Court has ruled that the Fourteenth Amendment does not even cover preborn life? How can it be constitutional for the state to deny to a pregnant woman equal protection against the private violence of a fetus intruding upon her body without consent, when the state provides protection against private violence to others? How can it be constitutional for the state to protect the fetus by sanctioning and allowing it to intrude on others' bodily integrity and liberty to meet its survival needs, when the state offers no such protection to born people, whatever might be their needs or kinship relations to others?

Let us imagine for a moment how Justice Antonin Scalia might answer such queries.[50] Perhaps he would propose that when a man and a woman engage in sexual intercourse, it is as if they have entered into a contract, and, most important, the fetus is the third party beneficiary to that contract. As such, the woman is obligated to let the fetus take her body to meet its survival needs. The question for Justice Scalia, however, is not just the validity of such a contractual construct;[51] even if one were to concede for a moment that it had legal standing, on what grounds would such a sexual-parental contract be voided by birth? If, by consenting to engage in sexual intercourse, parents incur an obligation to let their preborn children take their bodies at will, on what grounds could a born child—who needed a pint of blood, bone marrow, or other body part—be prohibited by the state from taking those body parts from a parent at will?

If Justice Scalia's preborn children, for example, have a right to take their mother's body as a consequence of her consent to engage in sexual intercourse with him, then why would not Justice Scalia's born children not only have a right to take their mother's body, but his body as well, to meet their survival needs? To engage in sexual intercourse as a factual condition preceding parenthood, therefore, would mean that consensual sexual intercourse entails a forfeit by men and women of all rights to be protected by the state against private violence inflicted by their children, as long as that violence serves their children's survival needs. On those grounds, the state would protect the right of a thirty-five-year-old child of Justice Scalia to capture him and his wife, coercively extract blood, bone marrow, or whatever was necessary to serve survival needs, even if the child's intrusions crippled the parents for life, all because thirty-five years earlier Justice Scalia and his wife consensually engaged in sexual intercourse.

Equal Protection of Women's Physical Security

Let us remember how these imaginative if not ludicrous scenarios connect with abortion funding. Currently, the Court has ruled that it is constitutional as a means to protect preborn life to allow potential life not only to coercively take a woman's body for its own use, but even to threaten a woman with crippling health injuries without employing state resources to stop the fetus. A woman could suffer permanent brain damage as a result of a pregnancy imposed upon her by a fetus against her will, and yet the Court has ruled that it is constitutional for the state to use, as a means for protecting the fetus, policies that allow it to cause that permanent brain injury. Of course, the Court has made it clear that a woman has a constitutional right to stop the fetus on her own, if she has the resources to do so, but it is constitutional for the state to protect the fetus by prohibiting the use of public resources to stop it on her behalf.[52] Most likely, the fetus could threaten to kill a woman, and, by extrapolation of current abortion funding reasoning, the Court would have to rule that it is constitutional for a state to allow the fetus to do so as a means for protecting it, a policy that has not yet been tested only because no state or the federal government has yet withdrawn public funding for abortions when women are threatened with death.

The state could view the fetus as unprotected life, of course, similar to a virus, a cancer, or a part of a woman's body, and then abortion funding would remain in welfare policies as a health benefit, much as other nations fund abortions. Yet, in the American system, the federal government and most states remove abortion funding from publicly funded health policies as a means to protect the fetus as human life. Abortion funding prohibitions, therefore, are an intentional and comprehensive state policy of failure to stop the fetus from intruding upon others without consent as a means for protecting preborn life. Such policies violate the Equal Protection Clause of the Constitution because they make pregnant women "completely ineligible" for state protection against "unjustified physical assault" by the fetus, a policy which constitutional law scholars declare to be one that everyone views as a form of state action which "would constitute a per se denial of the equal protection of the laws."[53]

Abortion funding restrictions, by allowing and permitting the fetus as state-protected human life to intrude upon a person without consent, render the victims of that intrusion, pregnant women, to be a "'class of persons' . . . completely ineligible for the protection of the [state] . . . from an entire category of mistreatment" by the fetus. As constitutional law scholars argue, if a state

> explicitly declares some people within its jurisdiction completely ineligible for the protection of its laws from some other form of mistreatment—from robbery, for example, or blackmail, or any other wrongful infliction of harm—no one would doubt that such discriminatory state action would "deny [such persons] the equal protection of the laws," regardless of the rationale the state might offer to defend it.[54]

While it is a legitimate state interest to protect potential life, therefore, the state may not implement that interest by using a means that makes pregnant women ineligible for state protection against harm caused by a fetus. As long as the state uses its police power to protect private people from violence imposed by others, abortion funding restrictions are an unconstitutional means of state protection of potential life because they cut women off from state protection against private violence imposed by preborn human life. If the state wishes to offer incentives to encourage women to be good samaritans in relation to fetuses, that is constitutional. And if the state wishes to conscript women's bodies for pregnancy service by directly forcing them to be good samaritans by giving their bodies to fetuses, it is dubious that such a means would be constitutional.

But it is clearly unconstitutional for the state to protect the fetus by a means that allows and permits it as a private party to harm a woman by making her its captive samaritan. Such a policy is state sanction of private violence, a virtual turning over of the police power of the state—the sole legitimate source of coercion—to a private party, the fetus, to serve its own needs. The state in effect protects the fetus by giving it complete leeway to impose whatever harm it may on a woman when it makes her pregnant to serve its own needs. The fetus can cripple a woman for life and leave her in a bedridden coma forever, and still the state protects the fetus by not stopping it from imposing such harm.

It is common to think of preborn human life as weak, dependent, and helpless. This characterization, however, while an accurate portrayal of a newborn baby, is not a factual depiction of preborn fetal life. A born infant lacks the power to intrude physically upon others, however powerful its vocal cries may be upon the ears and sensibilities of others when it screams for assistance with its physical and emotional needs. Newborn babies, therefore, do not ever pose a threat to others' physical security. No infant has the power to cripple a person for life, much less kill another. However dependent the infant is on others, it is truly helpless and powerless in relation to others. The opposite is true of preborn life. It does not cry out to others for help. To the contrary, it directly intrudes on and takes the bodies and liberty of others to meet its physical needs. While the survival of a born infant depends on others responding to its needs and giving to it, the survival of preborn human life depends on its brute force capability to take from others what it needs, regardless of whether there is consent to give.

While it is true that preborn human life is dependent on another person's body for its survival, therefore, it is hardly true that it is weak and helpless. To the contrary, preborn human life is a powerful intruder upon a woman's body and liberty which requires the use of deadly force to stop by removing it. The scope and power of what the fetus does to a woman when it makes her pregnant, in fact, ranks as one of the most invasive possible physical intrusions upon a person's body. Usually this intrusion does not kill a woman or pose a permanent threat to her health. Yet even in a medically normal pregnancy, the power of preborn human life to intrude upon and alter physically a woman's body as well as impose upon her liberty for the protracted period of nine months hardly renders the fetus as weak and helpless.

When we think of other types of physical intrusions, such as cancer, viruses, or other diseases, for example, we do not label them to be weak and helpless. To the contrary, the power and strength of cancer to take over a person's body and kill that person is the focus of intense medical research to find a way to stop cancer from doing so. The same is true of other forms of physical invasion of people's bodies by alien organic life. If we think of preborn life as a form of alien organic life, therefore, it is clear that it is not the case that it is weak and helpless. To the contrary, its effects on a woman are powerful in scope and duration, however dependent it is upon a woman's body for its own growth and survival.

Thinking of preborn life as a form of human life does not alter the fact that it is a powerful agent acting on a woman's body, rather than one that is weak and helpless. To the contrary, it is women, when they do not consent to the imposition of preborn life upon their bodies and liberty, who are then weak and helpless in relation to the fetus. Much as most born people require assistance to combat physical attacks upon their bodies and liberty by others, so, too, do women require assistance to combat the physical intrusion of preborn life upon their bodies and liberty. Without assistance, women remain at the mercy of intrusive preborn human life, unable to stop fetuses from crippling or even killing them.

The state, of course, exercises its police power precisely to provide assistance to people to stop intruders from violating their bodily integrity and liberties. To the degree that the state exercises its police power to stop such violations of people's physical security and liberty, so, too, must the state provide assistance to women when they are the weak and helpless victims of intrusion of their bodies and liberty by state-protected preborn human life. To do otherwise denies to women the equal protection by the state of their physical security and liberty. The move from choice to consent in the abortion debate, therefore, entails a parallel move from due process to equal protection as the fundamental right at stake. What is more, the equal protection guarantee at issue is not whether pregnancy is a form of sex discrimination or whether sex discrimination is an intermediate or strict scrutiny suspect classification.[55] To the contrary, the equal protection guarantee at issue is women's fundamental right to the equal protection of the state of their physical security against injuries imposed not only by born human life but also by unborn human life.

A consent-to-pregnancy foundation for abortion rights and abortion funding, therefore, establishes the state's obligation to provide equal protection of women's physical security and liberty. What is more, this right applies to all women, not just indigent women. The expenditure of funds by the state at the local and national level to protect the physical security of people whose bodies and liberty are imposed on by others applies to all people, not just those who cannot afford to pay to protect their own security. The state comes to the aid of victims whose bodily integrity and liberty is threatened by others, even if the victims in question could afford to pay for their own bodyguards and their own arsenals.

As long as the state protects preborn human life from harm, therefore, the state must stop preborn human life from causing harm, not just to indigent women who cannot afford to pay for their own protection, but to all women. This means that the state must come to the aid of all women who are the victims of wrongful pregnancy imposed upon them by state-protected preborn human life. To argue otherwise is to deny to women the equal protection of the state.

From Sex Discrimination to Fundamental Rights

Jurisprudence surrounding the Equal Protection Clause of the Fourteenth Amendment has proceeded along two tracks: suspect classification analysis and fundamental rights analysis. Claims that the state engages in sex discrimination when it restricts abortion funding fall into the first track. Recasting abortion rights in terms of women's right to consent-to-pregnancy rather than merely their right to choose-an-abortion, however, shifts equal protection analysis to the fundamental rights track. By so doing, the Court must consider anew the constitutionality of the means used by the state to protect potential life when those means violate women's fundamental right to equal protection of their physical security by the state.

When the state burdens people's fundamental constitutional rights, the Court applies strict scrutiny to that state policy, regardless of whether the people in question are members of a suspect classification group. Much jurisprudence controversy surrounds the question of which rights must be considered fundamental rights in equal protection analysis. The text of the Constitution defines explicit fundamental rights, most of which can be found in the Bill of Rights. The Court also has recognized other fundamental rights that are nontextual. Although the Court has ruled that even such basic rights as education[56] and welfare[57] need not be fundamental rights, on the other hand, it has established that there is a fundamental right to interstate travel,[58] to have offspring,[59] to vote,[60] and to have access to the judicial process.[61]

The Supreme Court of Colorado considered the constitutionality of a voter-initiated state constitutional amendment that would make it impossible for the state or its political subdivisions to pass a statute that makes sexual preference a protected class status.[62] If people refused to employ lesbians or to rent homes to homosexuals, for example, legislators would be prohibited from passing statutes that ban such discrimination, unless they repealed the amendment. The Colorado court ruled that such an amendment violated the federal Constitution because it deprived people of their fundamental right to participate in the political process; the Supreme Court upheld this Colorado court decision.[63]

The Colorado court did not rule that the state constitutional amendment violated the federal Constitution because it targeted homosexuals, lesbians, and bisexuals as a protected suspect class. To the contrary, sexual preference, along with age, marital or family status, poverty, and veterans' status, are not constitutionally suspect classifications. A state need not show a compelling state interest to discriminate on the basis of these characteristics in some contexts.[64] Rather, the issue was how this amendment denied to homosexuals, lesbians, and bisexuals their fundamental right "to participate equally in the political process," including the right of state legislators to pass, if they choose to, statutes that prohibit discrimination on the basis of sexual preference.[65]

Even though homosexuals are not a suspect class, therefore, the Colorado Supreme Court nevertheless ruled that since the constitutional amendment in question most likely involved a federally protected fundamental right, the state had to show a compelling state interest to justify that constitutional amendment and also to show that the state was using the least restrictive means to achieve it; otherwise the amendment violates equal protection guarantees. This the state could not do.[66] Thus the Colorado Supreme Court concluded that the amendment was unconstitutional because it denied equal protection of a fundamental right.

Generally, a "nontextual fundamental right is one that is 'implicit in the concept of ordered liberty' or 'deeply rooted in the Nation's history.'"[67] Certainly, the concept of ordered liberty includes the state's exercise of its police power to stop private people from physically intruding on the bodily integrity and liberty of others. For this reason, some of the most conservative legal scholars assert that the equal protection guarantees include the "right to the equal benefit of the laws protecting personal security."[68] According to Professor Raoul Berger, for example, known for his narrow approach to determining fundamental rights, there is nothing more basic in fundamental rights analysis than people's equal rights to "the full and equal benefit of all laws and proceedings for the security of person and property."[69] For this reason, basing women's claim on abortion funding on the grounds that women have an equal right to state protection of their physical security taps into the most basic of all rights deemed to be fundamental.

What is more, as Robin West notes, there are many ways to interpret equal protection guarantees, but the dominant one is the rationality model, which "seeks to ensure that legislators govern in a fair-handed and well-motivated way." This means that legislation violates the Equal Protection Clause if it either maliciously hurts some groups or in a biased way helps others.[70] Most pro-choice advocates who invoke this principle point to the way in which restrictions on abortion funding discriminate against women and hurt them.[71] This approach has not worked, however, because the Court ruled in *Washington v. Davis* that a facially neutral statute, that is, one that does not directly invoke race or gender categories in its formulation of policy, does not violate the Equal Protection Clause, even if it impacts differentially on different groups, as long as there is no intent to harm.[72] When legislators say, legitimately or not, that their intention is not to hurt women by restricting abortion funding but rather to protect potential life, they weasel out of equal protection guarantees, leaving women without the support of the state to obtain abortions, even when their health is in jeopardy.[73]

What we must do instead, therefore, is point to the way in which abortion-funding restrictions protect the fetus in a biased way, which is by allowing it to do what no born life is allowed to do. While it is constitutional to protect preborn life, it violates the Equal Protection Clause to protect preborn life by allowing it to impose serious injuries on a woman that the state stops born life from imposing. The injuries caused by preborn human life are just as serious and just as invasive as those caused by born human life. A woman who dies as a result of pregnancy caused by preborn human life is just as dead as a woman who has been killed by born human life. A woman who is bedridden for the rest of her life because a preborn fetus has caused a medically abnormal pregnancy that permanently damages her health is just as injured as if a born person had beaten her so severely that she would never fully recover. And a woman's bodily integrity and liberty is just as violated by preborn life that implants itself, using and transforming her body for nine long months without consent, as she is when a born person massively imposes on her body and liberty without consent, as in rape, kidnaping, slavery, and battery.

Whatever the legitimacy of the state's protection of preborn human life, that protection does not entitle human life to injure others before birth in ways in which the state does not allow human life to injure others after birth. There is nothing magical, therefore, about the status of preborn human life in terms of its entitlement to injure other people. When preborn human life injures a woman by imposing wrongful pregnancy, that injury situates her similarly to other victims of injuries imposed by human life. When two victims are situated similarly, because their injuries are similar and have been caused by human life, if the state protects one victim against those injurious wrongful acts, it must protect the other. To the degree, therefore, that the state protects people from injuries caused by born human life, it must protect people from injuries caused by preborn human life. To do otherwise violates the Equal Protection Clause, even interpreted conservatively in terms of contingent, rather than absolute, guarantees.[74]

Identification of the fetus as the cause of wrongful pregnancy identifies it as human life that is the cause of violent physical injuries on women, as well as the violator of women's liberty. Reframing women's right to consent to pregnancy as the foundation of abortion rights illuminates why the portrayal of abortion rights in terms of killing versus letting a person die misses the mark. The issue is not merely women's right to let the fetus die by not supporting it as a good samaritan nor merely her right to kill it in self-defense.[75] Rather, the key constitutional issue in abortion rights is a woman's right to state assistance to stop the fetus from imposing the injuries of wrongful pregnancy on her, to the degree that the state stops other human life from imposing injury on others.

We must go beyond securing for women merely the right to be bad samaritans by refusing to donate their bodies to fetuses, as many have argued. Rather it is women's rights as captive samaritans who need to be set free of their captors that is the key constitutional issue. From the standpoint of equal protection guarantees, the question is whether the state executes laws to protect pregnant women's bodily integrity and liberty against injuries inflicted by other private parties, including preborn private parties, to the same degree that it executes laws to protect others from private injury. The constitutional issue, therefore, is not merely a pregnant woman's due process right to be free of state policies that sanction the fetus's private wrongful acts or prefer its imposition of harm as a means for protecting it but also a pregnant woman's contingent equal protection right to affirmative state action to stop the fetus from imposing those injuries. To the degree that the state stops private parties, it must actively extend to pregnant women the equal protection of those laws by stopping the private injury of the fetus.

Thus, the state must fund abortions as a means for stopping the fetus from imposing the harm of wrongful pregnancy. What is more, the state must do so as quickly and expediently as its resources permit. The state may not tell a victim to wait for nine months before receiving assistance. While the state has some latitude and discretion in executing the laws, it may not subvert them by tactics that delay stopping aggressors or fail to stop them altogether. Abortions are the required technique for stopping the fetus, and to the extent that the state stops born people from intruding on others, it must fund abortions as the means necessary to stop preborn life from massively invading a woman's bodily integrity and liberty.

Application to the Fetus

The law already recognizes in contexts other than abortion that wrongful pregnancy imposes serious bodily injuries, whether in a normal or an abnormal pregnancy. What is more, laws criminalize the action of private parties who cause injuries to others. What we need to do is put these two components of the law together. We need to extend the legal scope of wrongful pregnancy to include the context of abortion by identifying the fetus as the cause of wrongful pregnancy when a woman seeks an abortion. And to the degree that laws expand to protect preborn human life from harm, laws must also expand to restrict preborn human life from causing harm.[76] This would then mean that when the fetus injures a woman by imposing a wrongful pregnancy, its action violates state laws that restrict private parties from injuring others.[77]

Of course, most laws that criminalize the action of private parties who cause injuries were not enacted with fetuses in mind. Yet the trend is to extend and apply such laws to protect the fetus. It is merely a symmetrical extension to expand such laws to restrict fetuses. There are many examples of how laws that formerly excluded fetuses from their application are today being reinterpreted to extend the same protection to fetuses as they offer to born people.[78] By 1946, for example, courts had begun to use existing laws to protect the personal rights of fetuses. In *Bonbrest v. Kotz*, a physician negligently removed an infant, thereby injuring a viable child, and her father sued. The Court ruled that a "non-viable foetus is not a part of its mother," and therefore a child after birth is entitled to the right of action for prenatal injuries.[79]

This principle was expanded in 1951 in *Woods v. Lancet*, in which the highest New York court observed,

> To hold, as a matter of law, that no viable foetus has any separate existence which the law will recognize is for the law to deny a simple and easily demonstrable fact. This child, when injured, was in fact, alive and capable of being delivered and of remaining alive, separate from its mother.[80]

In even more explicit language, the Ohio Supreme Court held in 1941, in *Williams v. Marion Rapid Transit*, that a viable fetus is a "person" within the meaning of the Ohio constitution.[81] On these grounds, after birth a child can sue for prenatal injuries caused by negligence.

This legislative protection extends to fetuses that are not yet viable. In 1956, for example, in *Hornbuckle v. Plantation Pipe Line Co.*, a fetus was injured in an automobile accident due to the alleged negligent operation by the defendant.[82] The fetus was born with serious deformities, and the Georgia Supreme Court held that a fetus need not be viable to recover damages for injuries sustained while in the womb.[83] Laws that protect people from injuries cover the fetus from the moment of its conception. As the court ruled, "If a child born after an injury sustained at any period of its prenatal life can prove the effect on it of a tort, it would have a right to recover."[84]

Even more recently, the California Supreme Court handed down a ruling with dramatic implications for abortion.[85] *People v. Davis* involved a pregnant woman who had been shot during a robbery and had lost so much blood that her fetus was stillborn the next day.[86] The robber was convicted of murder on the grounds that he had caused the fetus's death. His lawyer appealed, arguing that at the time of the shooting, the fetus was only twenty-three to twenty-five weeks old, and hence not viable and not a person; since the fetus was not a person, his client could not be convicted of murder.[87] The California Supreme Court upheld the murder conviction, holding that whether the fetus is viable or not does not matter because a fetus at even seven or eight weeks of age deserves protection under the law; thus its killing can be prosecuted as murder.[88]

Some courts include the unborn as a person by implication rather than by explicit legislative decree.[89] The Rhode Island Supreme Court in 1976, for example, held that the fetus from the moment of conception is a "person within the meaning of the [state's] Wrongful Death Act."[90] One justice on the Louisiana Supreme Court argued, in *Danos v. St. Pierre*, that a state statute about wrongful death should be interpreted so that the word "person" includes an "unborn child from the moment of fertilization and implantation."[91] The Michigan Court of Appeals ruled that the state's wrongful death statute extended coverage to fetuses because a "nonviable fetus not born alive" is a person within the meaning of the Michigan Wrongful Death Act.[92]

In other states, courts need not infer or make such requests because state legislatures have already explicitly conferred on an unborn fetus the legal rights of a person. In Missouri the legislature declared that "[t]he life of each human being begins at conception"; that "unborn children have protectable interests in life, health, and well-being"; and that "all Missouri laws [should] be interpreted to provide unborn children with the same rights enjoyed by other persons, subject to the Federal Constitution and [the U.S. Supreme] Court's precedents."[93] The law has shown great latitude for encompassing the fetus within its scope in order to protect it from harm, and what the law must also do is to show the same latitude for stopping the fetus from harming others.

Affirmative State Action

As James Madison, a founder of the American republic wrote, the interests of people must be connected with their constitutional rights. The great difficulty in framing a government, however, lies in this fact:

> You must first enable the government to control the governed; and in the next place, oblige it to control itself . . . . It is of great importance in a republic, not only to guard the society against the oppression of its rulers; but to guard one part of the society against the injustice of the other part.[94]

Clearly, the purpose of government is to guard one part of the society against the injustice of the other part while not creating new, state-based injustices in the process. To the extent that the state executes its purpose and does guard some people against injustices imposed by others, it must guard all people similarly situated as victims of injustice. This means that if the state executes the laws to protect some people from injury imposed by private wrongful acts, it must execute the laws to protect other people similarly situated.[95]

To the degree that the state recognizes the fetus as a form of human life, it is covered by statutes that not only protect it from harm by others but also that restrict it from harming others in turn. This means that to the degree that the state protects people from the wrongful acts of private aggression, the state must protect women from the wrongful acts of fetuses that impose pregnancy on them without consent as incompetent private actors. If the state does not do so, it denies to pregnant women their fundamental right to the equal protection of the law. This means that the state must fund abortions for women as the technique required for stopping fetuses from imposing wrongful pregnancy.

The Court currently interprets the state's failure to provide public resources for abortions in this way: if the state does not itself create the obstacle that prevents a person from implementing a constitutional right, the state is not obligated to remove that obstacle.[96] As applied to abortion rights, this means that if the state does not create the obstacle that prevents a woman from obtaining an abortion, the state need not remove that obstacle. Since the state does not create indigency, which prevents a woman from paying for an abortion, the Court reasons that the state is not obligated to remove indigency so that she may obtain one.[97]

The problem with this formulation of abortion-funding rights, however, is that it does not identify the relevant obstacle or the proper standard for evaluating the response of the state. The obstacle standing in the way of a woman's right to life and liberty is a fertilized ovum that is imposing the serious injuries of wrongful pregnancy. The proper equal protection standard for evaluating the response of the state to the removal of that obstacle is whether the state removes other such obstacles for other people whose bodily integrity and liberty is intruded on by private parties. If the state stops private parties from intruding on some people's right to bodily integrity and liberty, then it must stop fetuses from intruding on women's bodily integrity and liberty. If the state fails to stop the fetus when it provides public resources to stop other forms of private aggression, the state violates the Equal Protection Clause of the Constitution because it denies to women suffering from wrongful pregnancy the equal protection of the law.

This point is clear when we turn to other forms of intrusion in the context of abortion. When pro-life activists trespass on abortion clinics and vandalize them, for example, they successfully create obstacles to women's ability to exercise their right to procure abortions. The obstacles created by trespassers and vandals obviously are not creations of the state but rather the acts of private parties. Yet just because the state does not itself create trespassing and vandalism as obstacles, it does not follow that the state has no obligation to remove those obstacles by apprehending, prosecuting, and trying the people who have privately created them. If the state acts to protect some people from trespassing and vandalism, which it does, it then must act to protect all people similarly situated as victims. To do otherwise would violate the equal protection guarantees of the Constitution.

The state cannot withdraw from women the equal protection of the law by selectively failing to execute laws against trespassing and vandalism when the targets are abortion clinics, therefore, as a means for protecting preborn life. Rather, to the degree that the state protects any victims of trespassing, vandalism, and murder, it must not deny to abortion clinics the equal protection of laws that criminalize such private wrongful acts. This is starkly clear if we turn to the tragic example of the murder of abortion personnel. It surely creates obstacles to obtaining an abortion when pro-life fanatics murder people who provide abortion services. It would be unconstitutional, however, for the state to say that because it did not itself create those obstacles, it need not stop the murderers who do create those obstacles. To the contrary, as long as the state stops some private parties from murdering others, it may not selectively refuse to stop murderers of abortion clinic personnel as a means for protecting preborn life from the harm of abortions.

To date, even justices who vote against abortion rights in the Court, such as Justice Antonin Scalia, have not suggested in their opinions on access rights to abortion clinics that it would be constitutional for the state to encourage childbirth by failing altogether to stop harassers, vandals, and murderers. To the contrary, even the most ardent pro-life justices instead focus their attention on which law is applicable to the state's obligation to stop those who break laws concerning clinic access. In *Bray v. Alexandria Women's Health Clinic*,[98] for example, abortion clinics and abortion rights organizations sought to apply laws that prohibit conspiratorial action to deprive people of their civil rights to those who trespassed on, impeded, or obstructed entry to or exit from abortion facilities.[99] The Court's majority opinion, written by pro-life sympathizer Justice Antonin Scalia, declined to state or even insinuate that it would be constitutional for the state simply to fail to stop the harassment of the clinic's clients as a means for furthering the state's interest in encouraging childbirth.[100]

To the degree that the state executes laws to protect people from harassment, vandalism, and murder, the state must execute those laws to protect women who seek an abortion and abortion providers from harassment, vandalism, and murder. If the state apprehends and prosecutes people who vandalize property, for example, but not those who vandalize abortion clinics, the state fails to provide to those associated with abortion clinics the equal protection of the law. Failure to provide equal protection of the law to people who are similarly situated violates the Equal Protection Clause of the Constitution.

Even the most adamant pro-life advocates have not suggested that it would be constitutional for the state to fail to protect women from harassment, vandalism, and murder as a means for protecting the fetus from the harm of abortion. In the wake of the tragic killings of abortion clinic receptionists in Boston, for example, Cardinal Bishop Law of Boston, a leading abortion opponent, did not suggest that the state should simply let the murderer of abortion personnel go free as a means for protecting the fetus. He did not express outrage that tax dollars were being used to apprehend the murderer. To the contrary, he asked antiabortion activists to end their "prayerful presence" outside area clinics.[101] Moreover, when Massachusetts Governor Weld offered the services of state police to guard abortion clinics across the state, he voiced no objection to the use of tax dollars to support abortion clinics on the grounds that the state did not itself create the obstacles that were preventing women from obtaining abortions.

It would be unconstitutional for the state to refuse to use tax dollars to stop people from murdering abortion clinic personnel, to the degree that the state spends tax dollars to stop people from murdering people in other contexts. Similarly, to the degree that the state spends tax dollars to stop private parties from injuring others, it must spend tax dollars to stop the fetus from injuring a woman. Applying the equal protection guarantees to wrongful pregnancy itself, therefore, guarantees not merely the state's protection of abortion clinics and personnel but also the state's protection of a woman whose bodily integrity and liberty is being invaded by a fetus. The current expansion of the law to protect preborn life thus requires a symmetrical expansion to restrict preborn life. As long as the state endows preborn life with state-protected human status, it must also endow it with the restrictions that go with that status.

The key to the fetus's wrongful act is that it is already in progress. The first responsibility of the state, therefore, is to stop the wrongful act from occurring. In so doing, the state may not use more force than is necessary to accomplish that purpose. In the case of a wrongful pregnancy imposed by a fetus, the method required to stop it is an abortion, which entails the use of deadly force. The severity of the fetus's intrusion on a woman's body and liberty, if not life, justifies the use of deadly force to stop it.

This justification has always been clear when the fetus is threatening to kill a woman. Congress member Henry Hyde (Ill, R.) views the fetus as a "voiceless, voteless . . . tiny member of the human family,"[102] a little citizen in a woman's womb, if you will. Nevertheless, he supports not only the woman's right to use deadly force herself to stop the fetus but also the use of state funds to stop it on her behalf. He concurs, therefore, that the use of deadly force is justified because the fetus is in the process of injuring the woman and that an abortion is the only way to stop it. If there were some other way to stop it, surely that would be preferable. In the later months of pregnancy, for example, it is not necessary to kill the fetus to remove it from a woman's body, and an abortion, which by definition removes the fetus with no intention of keeping it alive, becomes a moot issue. In the future, new technologies may make it possible to remove a previable fetus without killing it, and then the use of deadly force becomes an option, not a necessity. At the moment, however, when a previable fetus is in the process of massively intruding on a woman's body and liberty, the technique for removing it entails destroying it. And the state's use of deadly force to stop the fetus, by means of funding the abortion, is necessitated by the state's provision of similar protection to other people when their bodily integrity and liberty are intruded on by private parties.

The state must stop the fetus in the same way that it stops any private aggression that is in progress. The state stops such wrongful acts by using the least amount of force necessary but enough force to get the job done. If one person is kidnapping another and holding that person hostage, the first task of the state is to free the captive. The state must do so with the least amount of force but nevertheless enough force to free the captive. When women are captured by a fetus, therefore, the first task of the state is to free them. This translates into state funding for abortions as the means necessary to free women from the captive status a fetus puts them in by imposing wrongful pregnancy.

While abortion-funding policies have been directed primarily to indigent women, equal protection analysis mandates public funding of abortions for all women. Such policies require a new recognition that society as a whole, through the state's use of tax dollars, must support the bodily integrity and liberty of all women, not merely those who lack the funds to defend themselves. Indigent women warrant state-provided abortions because they lack the funds to pay for one themselves and also because they are victims of nonconsensual intrusion of their bodily integrity and liberty. In this way, indigent women who are pregnant without consent are similarly situated to all other such pregnant women, and the state's obligation is to protect all women who are victims of private wrongful intrusion to the degree that the state protects any victims of such intrusion.

Recasting abortion-funding policies in this way highlights why it is not indigency that is the key constitutional issue. Rather, it is the state's response to the fetus's nonconsensual intrusion of women's bodily integrity and liberty that is the key constitutional issue. Equal protection guarantees obligate the state to stop the fetus as state-protected human life from imposing injury on any woman, to the degree that the state protects any victim of private injury.

Abortion Funding in a Minimalist State

To base women's right to abortion funding on their right to equal protection by the state from the private injury of the fetus rather than on their right to welfare benefits for health problems caused by natural forces harmonizes with a minimalist conception of the American state. That is, the size and authoritative scope of the state is kept to the minimum necessary for providing law and order by stopping private wrongful acts rather than expanded to cover such natural forces as disease, poverty, or the havoc wreaked by fires, earthquakes, floods, or hurricanes. The state is obligated to stop those private wrongful acts in order to secure law and order, the condition that underlies a civil society, as opposed to a state of nature governed by brute force alone.

According to this minimalist conception of the state, it is the obligation of the state to provide remedies to the victims of injuries imposed by other people, but it is only discretionary state action to provide aid to the victims of natural forces, including poverty.[103] The minimalist state, therefore, has no obligation to provide welfare benefits, such as food, shelter, clothing, or medical procedures, for people too poor to afford these necessities themselves. When the state does provide such benefits, it is a discretionary action. Attempts to expand the obligations of the American state to include welfare benefits, however, have been relatively unsuccessful, particularly when compared to other major Western industrial nations.[104] Not only does the American minimalist state turn its back on multitudes of people who are impoverished, homeless, and without health care, but also election results indicate that many Americans approve of such a state.

The liberal democratic theory that underlies the American state emphasizes rights. The claim of the rights holder does not depend on "beneficent treatment by others" but rather "dutiful actions by others," including the state, "that the rightsholder can demand without shame or embarrassment" because rights are entitlements.[105] Let one person steal money from another, therefore, and to the degree that the state provides law and order, the American state acts on behalf of the victim to stop the wrongful acts of the robber. To the extent that the state does take on this obligation, it must extend that protection to everyone who is a victim of private injury; to do otherwise violates equal protection guarantees. According to the standards of a minimalist state, which many conservatives in the United States embrace, injuries caused by other private parties are relevant to issues of law and order, but welfare benefits are not. Because the fetus injures a woman as a private party rather than as a natural force, even a minimalist conception of state action would designate abortion funding to be a fundamental obligation of the state as part of its obligation to provide law and order.

Grounds for Abortion Funding

Ironically, therefore, it is the very elevation of the fetus by the state to a status of state-protected human life that demands more, not less, state action to provide abortion funding, even when the state is conceptualized by using only the most minimalist standards. Although cancer cells can also impose tremendous physical damage on people and kill them, they do so not as entities that have any human standing but rather as a force of nature. Cancer cells are not protected by the state as human life, nor do courts interpret the laws to cover the well-being of cancer cells. For this reason, when cancer threatens to kill people, as devastating as its injury is, that injury raises no law-and-order issues. The state may, if it chooses, magnanimously extend welfare benefits to people suffering from cancer so they may obtain medical treatment to stop its injuries. And to some degree equal protection analysis would mandate that to the degree that the state extends welfare benefits to help victims deal with injuries caused by natural forces, it must extend those benefits to all such victims.

Yet the state has removed abortion funding from welfare benefits precisely on the grounds that the fetus is not a natural force but instead is state-protected human life. By so doing, the state does not lose its obligation to provide funds for abortions; it is merely that the grounds for that obligation shift. Rather than discretionary benefits by a maximalist welfare state, the grounds for abortion funding become the provision of law and order of a minimalist state. Even without the expansion of the state's role to cover areas of welfare benefits, therefore, the state is still required to fund abortions based on a principle of law and order. That is, abortion is a medical technique that stops one private party, the fetus, from imposing injury on another private party, the woman, not a medical technique that defends a woman against a force of nature, such as cancer. If the minimalist state restricts its role to providing only law and order in a society, therefore, it is still obligated to provide abortion funds to the degree that it provides funds to protect victims of private aggression. Abortion, rather than an alternative to pregnancy, is the state's remedy for stopping a fetus from imposing nonconsensual pregnancy on a woman.[106]

In this way, due process and equal protection guarantees mutually reinforce each other. People's rights to due process establish that it is unconstitutional for the state to use policies that allow private violence as a means for accomplishing state objectives. Yet this is precisely what the state does when it encourages childbirth by tolerating, allowing, or sanctioning the fetus's imposition of the private injuries of wrongful pregnancy. If the state wishes to encourage childbirth, it may use social constructions of maternity and voluntary incentive systems,[107] or it could try to do so directly by legislation that mandates that a woman maximize the probabilities that a fetus will make her pregnant and/or remain pregnant if that occurs. Such legislation, of course, would be subject to strict scrutiny by the Court as a form of state intrusion on people's bodily integrity and liberty. Leading constitutional law scholars, such as Charles Fried, think it would be unconstitutional for a state to intrude in this way and that such legislation would violate a woman's substantive due process rights, as would legislation that required women to have an abortion after so many children in order to further a state's interest in a severe overpopulation problem.[108] Other legal scholars, such as Dorothy Roberts, think it would be too invasive for the state to require even the insertion of the contraceptive Norplant to sustain constitutional challenges.[109]

Not only is it unconstitutional on due process grounds for the state to prefer the fetus's imposition of private violence as a means for accomplishing a state objective, but it is also unconstitutional on equal protection grounds for the state to fail to stop the fetus from imposing that injury, to the degree that the state stops other private parties from imposing injuries on others. Even a minimalist state, which offers no welfare benefits but only the promise to control private violence to establish law and order, must on those grounds stop the fetus from intruding on the bodily integrity and liberty of a woman.

A consent-to-pregnancy approach to abortion rights, therefore, solves the problems identified by legal scholar Kathleen Sullivan, who sees two constitutional visions of the abortion issue: the first is based on privacy as articulated by Justice Harry Blackmun in *Roe*, and the second is based on equal protection as proffered by Justice Ruth Bader Ginsburg's invocation of restrictions on abortion funding as a form of unconstitutional gender discrimination. Both, in Sullivan's opinion, are problematic because, some argue, due process privacy grounds guarantee only procedural entitlements without substantive content and equal protection guarantees are contingent. This argument has been used by the Court to claim that it is not treating men and women differently by denying funds for abortions because discrimination on the basis of pregnancy is not a form of sex discrimination.[110]

Reframing abortion rights in terms of women's right to consent to pregnancy, however, reveals in new ways how abortion-funding restrictions violate due process and equal protection guarantees even when contingently framed. Abortion funding guarantees no longer necessitate the proof of sex discrimination, nor do they rest on the discretionary option of the state to provide health benefits to people in need. Rather if the state chooses to remove abortion funding from welfare policies on the grounds that the fetus is state-protected human life, then abortion-funding rights rest squarely on the most conservative and minimalist conception of the state possible: a state that simply provides law and order by stopping private parties, including preborn ones, from intruding on the bodily integrity and liberty of others.

8

Right to Bodily Access

The Supreme Court in *Roe v. Wade* affirmed that women have the right of privacy to make choices about their own reproductive lives without state interference.[1] The flaw in this perspective, however, is that it is not the state that imposes wrongful pregnancy: it is the fetus. The obvious question is why in over twenty years of reasoning about abortion rights the Court has failed to see that the primary right at stake is a woman's right to be free of the fetus's intrusion of her bodily integrity and liberty and, concomitantly, the state's obligation to set her free to the degree that it does so for others whose bodily integrity and liberty has been imposed on by private parties. To find the answer to that question, we must turn not to the law but to the culture that the law reflects. As legal scholar Mary Ann Glendon notes, law can be thought of as a branch of rhetoric, a form of cultural hermeneutics and stories that interpret the world.[2] By so doing, as Laurence Tribe observes, the law too often reinforces the way in which culture disproportionately protects the rights of those more socially, economically, and politically powerful.[3] As a result, far from providing an oasis of neutrality in society, the law instead becomes a body of doctrine that is sluggish, to say the least, in extending equally to all persons guarantees of their bodily integrity and liberty.[4] The judicial support for slavery through much of U.S history is the most obvious and egregious example of the courts' failure to protect whole classes of persons.[5] The legal history of women's rights is another example of relatively late and still incomplete recognition of the need to protect women's bodily integrity and liberty from nonconsensual access by others.[6]

Coverture

From the inception of this country, our culture and law have supported the assumption that husbands have an automatic right of access to their wives' material assets, identities, and bodies.[7] As such, the law defined married women as a form of their husband's property, to be possessed and invaded by him at will. The common law principle of coverture, which states did not begin to abolish until the 1830s and 1840s, suspended a woman's legal existence, once she married, on the grounds that when a man and woman married they became one person, and that person was the husband. William Blackstone summarized this principle that subordinated wives to their husbands:

> By marriage, the husband and wife are one person in law: that is, the very being or legal existence of the woman is suspended during the marriage, or at least is incorporated and consolidated into that of the husband: under whose wing, protection and cover, she performs everything; and is therefore called in our law-french, a feme covert . . . and her condition during her marriage is called her *coverture* . . . . For this reason, a man cannot grant anything to his wife . . . for the grant would be to suppose her separate existence.[8]

As a result of coverture, until well into the nineteenth century married women in the United States could not in their own right sue or be sued, make contracts, draft wills, or buy or sell property. Their property and their earnings legally belonged to their husbands. Further, if they "owned property prior to marriage, any personal estate went fully into their husbands' hands and any real estate came under their spouses' sole supervision . . . [and] the children of the marriage fell entirely within the custody of the father."[9] The "husband *owned* the wife's person. Should she be injured in an industrial accident, he could sue for damages for loss of services. Should she rebel and run away, he could collect damages from whoever sheltered her."[10]

The American polity adopted this legal construction at the founding of this nation and has sustained it, in various forms and degrees, ever since. In the context of an American political tradition that stresses the values, if not the practice, of equality, independence, and civil rights, the founders' uncontested acceptance of coverture is even more startling. While there are many conspicuous exceptions to the universal application of new principles of governance, a primary distinction between slavery and coverture rests in part on the extraordinary attention and visibility accorded to the former and the all but invisible affirmation accorded to the latter.

Nowhere in the four-volume *Notes to the Constitutional Convention*, for example, did the founders refer to the odious principles of coverture as being at odds with the principles they were drafting into the new Constitution. In contrast, they waged long debates over the way in which slavery violated the precepts of the new state.[11] As political philosopher Susan Okin notes, although liberal theory regards the private institutions of marriage and the family as socializing citizens for their public roles in government, the irony is that it is these institutions, by legalizing the tyrannical rule of husbands over their wives, that epitomize the very antithesis of the virtues of equality, independence, and civil rights that they are supposed to foster.[12]

It was not until the mid-nineteenth century that states began to pass laws that freed married women from the oppressive legal practices of coverture, thereby enabling them to own their own property. Male legislators and male judges interpreted these laws so conservatively, however, that very little changed in the legal relationship between men and women.[13] As late as 1876, in *Seitz v. Mitchell*, the Supreme Court ruled that a District of Columbia statute that guaranteed to married women the right to property they had owned before marriage or acquired during marriage did not extend to their wage earnings.[14] As the Court decreed,

> [N]owhere, so far as we are informed, has it been adjudged that [a woman's] earnings or the product of them, made while she is living with her husband . . . . and engaged in no separate business, are not the property of the husband. . . . Her earnings while cohabiting with her husband are not made her property. She can have them only by the gift of her husband.[15]

This ruling derived from the idea that husbands owned the bodies, including the labor, of their wives. The legal requirement that a married woman take her husband's last name also reflects this vestige of a time when the law supported men's control of women's very identity in marriage. According to the highest court of the State of New York in 1881, common law dictated that when a woman married, "[H]er maiden surname is absolutely lost, and she ceases to be known thereby."[16] This legal requirement reflected married women's chattel status, allowing men to claim their children as their property and to render women's identities invisible,[17] and the enduring dictum that not only symbolizes "a merger in fact of [her] own personalit[y] in that of [her] husband" but also destroys "a major facet of her personality."[18]

The idea that husbands have a right of access to women's very identity as persons lasted legally well into the twentieth century.[19] As late as 1945, the Illinois Court of Appeals upheld such a requirement,[20] as did the Supreme Court as recently as 1972, in affirming the constitutionality of a state requirement that a married woman must use her husband's surname to apply for and receive a driver's license.[21] Some states still carefully regulate women's right to use their maiden names once married. Before 1981, for example, Iowa required spousal consent if a woman wished to use a surname other than her husband's, and to this day in Missouri, courts require that the interests of the husband be considered before a married woman is granted a name other than his.[22]

Domestic Violence

Cultural and legal disregard for the primacy of women's right to be free from private intrusion also is evident in the case of domestic violence. Society, if not the legal system, is just now beginning to recognize the magnitude of the problem. Though the exact incidence is difficult to determine, according to the Federal Bureau of Investigation, each year between three and four million women are beaten by their husbands or male partners, averaging one beating every fifteen seconds. Other experts estimate that the figure is as high as six million American women each year who are battered.[23] Over one million victims of such beatings seek medical help each year, and wives who are the victims of beatings by their husbands constitute 20 percent of hospitals' emergency room cases each year. Each year, husbands and male partners kill four thousand women, even though one-half of these victims were separated, divorced, or attempting to end the relationship at the time of their deaths. These deaths account for 30 percent of female homicide victims. Of battered women, 25 percent are pregnant. In addition, of the women who attempt suicide each year, 25 percent have been victimized by domestic abuse.[24]

Yet instead of supporting women's right to be free from private aggression, the law has sought to define the legally acceptable *amount* of intrusion and injury a husband may inflict on his wife. This legal disregard for women's bodily integrity and liberty is the basis of the infamous "rule of thumb" standard. As noted by William Blackstone, the common law confers on a husband the authority and right to correct his wife for "misbehaviour" in the same way that he has the power and authority "to correct his apprentices or children." As Blackstone notes, despite some doubt about whether a husband should have the "power of correction" over his wife, "the courts of law will still permit a husband to restrain a wife of her liberty, in case of any gross misbehaviour."[25] According to the common law, under coverture, therefore, it was not a crime for a husband to use moderate physical means of correction to discipline her.

Courts interpreted a husband's common law right to use physical force to discipline his wife as a rule of thumb principle: a husband could hit his wife with a stick to discipline her, as long as the stick was not wider that the width of his thumb. In the United States, this principle showed up in a North Carolina court decision in 1868.[26] Elizabeth Rhodes had been struck by her husband three times "with a switch about the size of one of his fingers (but not as large as a man's thumb)," even though there had been no provocation other than "some words uttered by her and not recollected by the witness."[27] The trial judge in the case ruled that the husband "had a right to whip his wife with a switch no larger than his thumb" and that "he was not guilty in law."[28] Upon appeal by the state, Judge Reade acknowledged that although anyone who inflicts such injury on another person "would without question" be guilty of battery,[29] the same is not true of a husband who beats his wife. The judge ruled that the husband was justified in beating his wife, that is, in committing battery. Although, nothing entitles a husband to beat his wife, in this particular case, the judge explained, the husband was justified because his wife had uttered "some slight words," and as the judge reasoned, "who can tell what significance the trifling words may have had to the husband? Who can tell what had happened an hour before, and every hour for a week? To him they may have been sharper than a sword."[30]

Judge Reade concluded that the duty of the courts was not to prevent a husband from intruding on his wife's bodily integrity and liberty by beating her but only to set a limit on the amount of injury he could inflict. The legal objective is to prevent a husband from grossly abusing his wife, but not to prevent him from abusing her at all. As long as the husband "does not inflict permanent injury" or "*grossly* abuse his powers," therefore, Judge Reade contended that courts should not concern themselves with the question of whether the "husband has the *right* to whip his wife much or little" or whether he uses a "stick larger than the thumb" or "a switch half the size."[31]

As the judge explained, "A light blow, or many light blows, with a stick larger than the thumb, might produce no injury; but a switch half the size might be so used as to produce death. The standard is the *effect produced*, and not the manner of producing it, or the instrument used."[32] In short, little more than a hundred years ago, the measure of physical violence permissible by husbands by law was the "effect produced," not women's absolute right to be free of private intrusion of their bodily integrity and liberty by others. If a husband neither permanently injured nor killed his wife, neither the state nor the courts were prepared to intervene.

Lord Matthew Hale, a seventeenth-century English jurist, may have been the first to assert the doctrine that forced sexual intercourse within marriage is not unlawful.[33] He wrote that

[the] husband cannot be guilty of a rape committed by himself upon his lawful wife, for by their mutual matrimonial consent and contract the wife hath given up herself in this kind unto her husband, which she cannot retract . . . [i]n marriage she hath given up her body to her husband.[34]

Though Hale provided no "supporting authority for his statement," his doctrine became "accepted as part of the common law without question by American legislatures, courts, and criminal law authorities."[35]

In 1905 a court ruled that "so far as we are aware all of the authorities hold that a man cannot himself be guilty of actual rape upon his wife."[36] Not surprisingly, feminists in the mid-nineteenth century frequently compared the status of American wives to slaves.[37] John Stuart Mill commented that although he was

far from pretending that wives are in general no better treated than slaves . . . no slave is a slave to the same lengths, and in so full a sense of the word as a wife is . . . . [A husband] can claim from her and enforce the lowest degradation of a human being, that of being made the instrument of an animal function contrary to her inclinations.[38]

Hillary Rodham Clinton's more recent comparison of the status of slaves and married women in the early periods of American history, therefore, was apt.[39]

Three decades after *Frazier*, courts in New Jersey and Massachusetts finally abandoned the Hale doctrine,[40] asserting that whatever might have been its status in the common law, the marital rape exemption has no place in today's society. As a New Jersey court said in 1981, in *New Jersey v. Smith,*

> The personal liberty of women and the recognition of them as independent citizens under the law had developed beyond question through legislative and judicial actions over more than a century . . . . No person in this State in 1975 could justifiably claim that a man had a legal right to impose his sexual will forcefully and violently on a woman, even if it was his wife, over her unmistakable objection.[41]

Yet the law has not yet completely guaranteed married women's right to bodily integrity and liberty, despite the fact that marital rape is the most common form of sexual assault reported by women, occurring twice as often as sexual assaults by strangers.[42] As of January 1984, twenty-eight states still expressly provided exemptions from prosecution for marital rape; only ten states expressly allowed the prosecution of husbands who rape their wives, but only eight of these states rejected outright the exclusion of husbands from the crime of rape.[43] The marital rape exemption is one of the more enduring vestiges of the cultural and legal heritage that views married women as the property of their husbands.

Sociologist Richard Gelles estimates that rape was a part of, or a sequel to, the battering of well over two million women by their husbands. More than a third of the residents of battered women's shelters admit that their abuse included sexual assault by their husbands.[44] The devastating effects of marital rape are sometimes even more traumatic than those of rape by a stranger. As David Finkelhor, assistant director of the Family Violence Research Program at the University of New Hampshire, explains,

> When you have been intimately violated by a person who is supposed to love and protect you, it can destroy your capacity for intimacy with anyone else. Moreover, many wife victims are trapped in a reign of terror and experience repeated sexual assaults over a period of years. When you are raped by a stranger, you have to live with a frightening memory. *When you are raped by your husband, you have to live with your rapist.*[45]

Yet the fact that not all states criminalize marital rape notifies husbands that a certain degree of injury to their wives is a right, not a crime. And women, caught in this web, are expected to submit to violence imposed by a husband as part of their wifely duty rather than to call on the state for help.[46] However natural heterosexual relationships might be construed, legislatures and courts have for too long used such notions of "nature" to endorse the dominance of men over women. The issue is not merely how much injury the law will allow men in general or husbands in particular to impose on women, but rather whether the law will recognize that all intrusions on women's bodily integrity and liberty are a serious crime.

The marital rape exemption is merely one of the more enduring vestiges of the cultural and legal heritage that has viewed married women as resources to which their husbands have an automatic right of access.[47] Today, after concerted efforts in the 1970s to reform the rape laws, the crime of rape is usually defined legally by reference to the victim, the woman, not to the man to whom she is related. The rapist's attack on the woman, not its ancillary effects on her marriage or other kinship relationships, constitutes the crime of rape. Even so, cultural attitudes often view male sexual aggression as natural and therefore see rape as merely the externalized expression of a natural aggression. In a society that fosters such views, the burden of preventing, if not proving, rape often falls on the victim. A chief goal of the rape reform efforts of the 1970s was therefore to shift the burden of preventing and proving rape from the victims to the perpetrators.[48] To do so, reform advocates established a woman's right to consent to sexual intercourse. They also distinguished implicit from explicit consent, arguing that a woman's consent to sex should not, and cannot, be implicitly assumed on the basis of past conduct, contextual setting, clothing, or even sexually suggestive behavior. Rather, consent means explicit consent. This requirement of consent extends to all women in all circumstances, including those who sell their sexual services as prostitutes. A prostitute is just as much a victim of rape as is any other woman if a man imposes sexual intercourse without her explicit consent.

Though heterosexual intercourse is commonly considered to be a natural relationship, the law now is more likely to recognize that naturalness does not negate the necessity of consent. Without consent, this "natural" relationship is a serious crime, which is reflected in current legal definitions of rape as "unlawful sexual intercourse with a female without her consent" and "unlawful carnal knowledge of a woman by a man forcibly and against her will."[49] The principle of consent was tested in the infamous 1988 New Bedford rape trial of two men for aggravated rape.[50] The victim, a young woman, entered Big Dan's Tavern in New Bedford, Massachusetts, ordered a drink; spoke with another woman; and watched a game of pool, where about fifteen men had gathered. As she prepared to leave, the young woman was knocked down from behind by two men, who removed her pants, dragged her along the floor as she furiously resisted, threw her onto the pool table, and with the help of other men restrained her while sexually penetrating her. Eventually, "clothed only in a shirt and one shoe, the victim escaped and ran into the street where she flagged down a passing truck."[51]

The question in the courtroom was whether the woman had "consented" to sexual intercourse. The judge disallowed as evidence of her consent the victim's past record of complaints about rape, psychiatric difficulties, and conversations about prostitution. Those pieces of evidence were ruled as neither relevant nor bearing on the issue of whether the defendants had a reasonable "belief that the victim consented" to sex in the bar, however "mistaken" that belief might actually have been.[52] The court upheld the woman's claim of rape, and the defendants were sentenced.[53]

While courts now acknowledge women's right to bodily integrity and liberty in the context of rape, the battle for women's right to consent to all such intrusions is still far from over. Of all of the remaining campaigns to be waged, the one that involves the most hidden and therefore most pernicious is the way our culture and law concede, rather than contest, a fetus's access to women's bodies. As long as the fetus's injury of a woman when it intrudes on her without consent does not exceed a certain level, the Court has seen no problem with its access per se. Such a view by the Court is nothing more than a resurrected "effects produced" test for injury, which harkens back to an antiquated "rule of thumb" mentality. To measure only the amount of physical harm a fetus imposes, and then only in terms of whether that amount threatens her with permanent damage to her health or with death, rather than a woman's right to be free from all private intrusion of her bodily integrity and liberty is to deprive a woman of her fundamental right to use the institutions of the state to protect her right to be let alone by others.

From Rule of Thumb to Rule of Law

Many view the principles of law in the American political system as forming the very substance of everyday human interaction. Even recently, at a drugstore counter in a middle-class suburb of Boston, I witnessed a remarkable exchange between a customer and the high school student who was tending the cash register just before closing time. The customer, who had come to pick up his photographs, explained that when leaving the film for processing, he had been asked for payment in advance, which he had paid. The student, doubting the story, demanded that he pay "again."

Quickly and predictably, tempers flared, and I observed an illustration of the primacy of law in American culture. At stake was $20, yet within moments, the customer delivered the peculiarly American challenge "I'll take you to court. I will go to court before I pay $20 again." The $20 were not the heart of the matter. Using the law and court systems would cost the customer far more, not just in dollars, but also in time and energy. The heart of that vignette is the litigiousness of Americans. Its lesson is that, in this culture, legal principles are likely to define the parameters of a controversy, if not its resolution.[54] As Ronald Dworkin says, "We live in and by the law. It makes us what we are; citizens and employees and doctors and spouses and people who own things."[55]

While many point to the liabilities of such a culture and legal system, few contest its reality. For this reason, some of the more difficult, contentious, and complex issues, such as abortion, find articulation in terms of where they fit within given frameworks of law. We might question, of course, how appropriate such a route is for solving social, if not moral, problems. Yet it is the route we are prone to use in this culture. To come to terms with the problems vexing our relationships with one another, we most often turn to legislation and court adjudication. Here we find that law provides "symbolic and ideological support for a system of stratification," and in order to make restructuring claims upon it, it is crucial "to see what values law proclaims" and "what doctrines it engenders."[56]

As law professor Frances Olsen notes, an "individual may be just as oppressed by the state's failure to protect him as by the state's restraint of his freedom for the sake of protecting another."[57] Another legal scholar, Mary Becker, voicing the same criticism, argues that the "Bill of Rights does less to solve the problems of women and nonpropertied men" than of other privileged groups.[58] She sees the Fourth Amendment, which guarantees the right to be secure in your person, house, papers, and effects against unreasonable governmental searches and seizures, as inadequate because the problem for women is to gain security in their own homes from husbands who rape and abuse them. As she observes, not only at the time when the Fourth Amendment was passed in the eighteenth century, but also "in many jurisdictions *today*, husbands and lovers could and can rape 'their' women without criminal consequences."[59]

That the law has oppressed women by failing to protect them from violation by private parties on the grounds that it is protecting the interests of the intruders is a lesson to be drawn from American political history as well. The historical continuity between legal manifestations of attitudes toward access to women's bodies and current governmental abortion-funding policies is alarming. Much as courts in the past did not contest the right of a husband's access to his wife's body, but only the degree of injury he inflicted, so current abortion policies address only the degree of injury inflicted by a fetus, rather than the presumption that it has an automatic right of access to a woman's body in the first place. It is only at the point where the effect produced by the fetus reaches medically abnormal proportions that the Court and most legislatures affirm women's constitutional right to preserve their health and life, rather than their right to autonomy.

Not only does the Court apply to abortion rights an outdated rule-of-thumb principle, focusing only on the effect produced by the fetus rather than on the woman's right to be free of all nonconsensual private intrusion of her body and liberty, but in so doing, the Court affirms only a woman's individual right of self-defense, not her right to state assistance in her self-defense. Currently the law's treatment of abnormal and normal pregnancy parallels what was characteristic of its earlier treatment of aggravated and simple rape.[60] An aggravated rape is one marked by extrinsic violence, such as the use of guns, knives, or beatings, or one involving multiple assailants or one in which there was no prior relationship between the victim and the defendant. A simple rape is one in which none of these aggravating circumstances is present. Predictably, researchers have found that juries are four times more likely to convict defendants in cases of aggravated rape.[61]

So, too, with wrongful pregnancy. In the context of abortion, it is not until the injuries of wrongful pregnancy are aggravated, that is, reach life-threatening or unusually severe health-endangering proportions, that our culture and our law can see that women are being injured. By contrast, even though the law recognizes that a "normal" wrongful pregnancy in other contexts is a serious injury, it has failed to see that injury in the context of abortion. Yet a normal wrongful pregnancy, as opposed to an abnormal (or aggravated) wrongful pregnancy—much as normal sexual intercourse imposed without consent—constitutes serious intrusion on a woman's bodily integrity and liberty.[62]

While it may be common to view what the fetus does as natural and therefore somehow beyond the reach of the law, the idea of what is natural in relation to women's bodily integrity has generally served as little more than a sham by which to legalize private intrusion into their bodies without their consent. This is obvious in the case of heterosexual intercourse, where cultural and legal assumptions about its naturalness did little more than justify husbands' and men's nonconsensual sexual intrusion of women's bodily integrity and liberty.[63] The same is true of wrongful pregnancy. The idea that pregnancy is natural transforms women into nothing more than passive components of what are considered automatic natural processes.

The Congressional Alternative

The Court, the president, and Congress can all be thought of as key institutional actors in the determination of public policy.[64] When fearful that the Court might overrule *Roe* and when frustrated with the failure of the Court to rule that women have the right to abortion funding, many people turned to Congress as an alternate route for securing women's reproductive rights. In 1989 after the *Webster* decision, for example, in which the Court had ruled that it was constitutional for a state to deny the use of public funds, facilities, and personnel for an abortion, people feared that this was merely the prelude to overturning *Roe* itself.[65] In response, feminist proponents of abortion rights stepped up their efforts to pass the Freedom of Choice Act (FOCA) in Congress, which would give women a legislative right to an abortion in case the Court overruled the constitutional right. Representative Les AuCoin (Ore., D) cosponsored the Reproductive Rights bill (H.R. 3700 and S. 1912), which provided that a "state may not restrict the right of a woman to choose to terminate a pregnancy before fetal viability or at any time, if such termination is necessary to protect the life or health of the woman."[66]

Yet Congress can never be an alternative path as long as the same cultural attitudes and assumptions that underlie the Supreme Court reasoning on abortion underpin the congressional analysis as well. Unfortunately, there is little reason to expect improvements over the Court's decrees, because Congress in its formulation of abortion rights uses exactly the same limited metaphors for pregnancy. As a result, the legislative branch merely perpetuates, rather than corrects, the flaws inherent in the representation by the Court of the right to an abortion and abortion funding.

What is missing from the congressional debate on the abortion issue is exactly what has been missing from the judicial debate: an understanding of the cause of pregnancy. Congress and the Court focus inordinate attention on what the fetus is, thereby failing to analyze what the fetus does to a woman when it makes her pregnant without her consent. Failure to recognize that the fetus causes pregnancy hides a woman's right to consent to pregnancy. As a consequence, debate focuses on a woman's right to choose an abortion without interference from the state, which misdirects attention from women's primary right to equal protection of the laws. To the degree that laws are interpreted to protect the fetus, so must they be interpreted to restrict the fetus.

The problem is that both Congress and the Court reflect a culture that has been slow to accord equal rights to women, and then only at minimum levels. For this reason, both institutions perpetuate and reinforce, rather than challenge and reframe, prevailing cultural assumptions that women's primary identity is to be of service to others. With premises such as these so firmly entrenched, those advancing women's rights within the institutional settings of both Congress and the Court identify a woman's right to refuse to sacrifice herself as the maximum possible way to conceptualize her autonomy and reproductive freedom.

Yet when a fetus causes wrongful pregnancy, it makes a woman a captive samaritan by imposing pregnancy without her consent. The key issue no longer is merely a woman's right to refuse to give her body to the fetus but also her even more primary right not to have her body and liberty taken by the fetus in the first place. It is the woman's status as a captive samaritan, not merely her right to be a bad samaritan, that must inform our cultural understanding of abortion rights and our institutional formulation of those rights in laws passed by legislatures and adjudicated by courts.

The power of cultural norms to set the parameters for institutional reasoning and override apparent differences is nowhere more evident than in the abortion debate. The Supreme Court is regarded as being insulated from public opinion, interpreting the Constitution free from the political pressures and social activism of the moment, whereas Congress is designed to represent public opinion, its institutional norms celebrating responsiveness to constituency pressure and political processes. Yet despite such institutional contrasts, both converge in their depictions of pregnancy and both reach the same conclusions about abortion rights. This commonality comes into focus in Congress and the Court's use of metaphorical depictions of pregnancy.

Congressional Metaphors

Four years before the *Roe* decision, as abortion was being hotly debated in the Ninety-first Congress, Rep. John R. Rarick (La., D.) prophesied that to discuss

this issue would be to open a "pandora's box."[67] The contents of the box actually opened by the legislative process reveal the same faulty definitions of pregnancy as those that structure the judicial branch's treatment of abortion rights,
namely, pregnancy defined variously as carrying a fetus, the development of a
fetus, the outcome of sex, a burden and sacrifice, and a value to society. In addition, the legislature came up with one more definition of pregnancy: as a punishment for sex.

Congressional debate has long fastened on the Court's view of pregnant
women as vessels who carry a fetus, sometimes depicted as a baby. As Rep. John
Dingell (Mich., R.) remarked,

> In assessing fetal health, the doctor . . . has learned that it is actually the mother
> who is a passive carrier . . . he [the unborn] is quite beautiful and perfect in his
> fashion, active and graceful. He is neither an acquiescent vegetable nor a witless
> tadpole . . . but rather a tiny human being as independent as though he were lying
> in a crib with a blanket wrapped around him instead of his mother.[68]

Pro-life Rep. John M. Murphy (N.Y., D.) introduced a "right to life" resolution
by saying that it would "insure, through law, that maternal rights are not superior to those of the child she carries."[69] Similarly, Rep. Robert K. Dornan (Calif.,
R.) observed that "it was not so very long ago that mothers who were pregnant
were said to be 'with child,'" and that, according to the Bible, "[a]t the sound of
Mary's greeting, the baby in Elizabeth's womb 'leapt for joy' . . . that infant of
course was St. John, the Baptist."[70]

The perceptions of a mother as an "incubator," "passive carrier," or "blanket"
for a fetus, which is itself portrayed as a "tiny human being," miss a crucial
marker: what the "tiny human being" does to a woman when it makes her pregnant. Some members of Congress have in fact tried to negate the view of women
as vessels. As Rep. Les AuCoin (Ore., D.) explained, "Surely, this Congress
should repudiate the mind set that views women as mere 'incubators' whose
rights and human spirit must be subordinated to their reproductive function."[71]
Yet such members have failed to identify explicitly the cause of pregnancy as the
fertilized ovum.

Fetal development, another key concept used by the Supreme Court, is also
present in congressional reasoning on abortion rights. As Henry Hyde (Ill., R.),
among others, has observed, when a woman is pregnant, her only choice is to
"kill" her "preborn child or [to] let nature take its course" until development is
complete and the child is born.[72]

Pro-life members of Congress also contend, along with the Court, that pregnancy is the result of sex, which allows them to support a woman's right to an
abortion subsequent to rape or incest, even when the pregnancy in question
poses no medical complications and hence the abortion is nontherapeutic. Representative Robert Michel (Ill., R.), for example, asserted that "victims of forced

rape or incest" are entitled to federal funds for "nontherapeutic abortions."[73] In 1980, when Congress legislated that no federal funds can be used for abortion even if pregnancy severely threatens women's health, the rape and incest exceptions remained.[74]

Most pro-life members of Congress agree with the Court that pregnancy can become a burdensome condition, and they affirm that when the fetus becomes life-threatening, a woman must have the right to an abortion. Some even specifically use the language of self-defense. As early as 1975, when pro-life Rep. Clement J. Zablocki (Wisc., D.) introduced a constitutional amendment to protect the unborn, he noted that when a mother's life is "seriously endangered by the continuation of pregnancy," abortion is permissible in "self-defense."[75] Two years later, when introducing a similar amendment, Rep. James Abdnor (S. Dak., R.) stated that it "shall not apply in an emergency when a reasonable medical certainty exists that continuation of the pregnancy will cause the death of the mother."[76] Representative Thomas Luken (Ohio, D.) stressed, in connection with the same amendment, that "nothing in this article shall prohibit a law permitting only those medical procedures required to prevent the death of the mother.[77] Similarly in 1976 when Rep. Henry Hyde's restriction on the use of Medicaid funds for abortion was being debated, pro-life Rep. Jim Santini (Nev., D.) stressed that it does not apply to those abortions necessary to save the life of the mother.[78] Yet Congress, like the Court, ignores the fetus as the cause of the burdens of a normal pregnancy, and, by so doing, casts a woman's right to terminate a normal pregnancy as the right to make decisions or to request an abortion rather than as the right to stop the fetus from imposing the extraordinary burdens of normal pregnancy on her.[79] Pro-life members reconstruct abortion as women's right to "abortion on demand," thereby ignoring that fetuses impose "pregnancy by demand" on women.[80]

Finally, some members of Congress who support funding for childbirth but not for abortion reflect the Court's interpretation of pregnancy as a value to society. Pro-life Rep. Robert K. Dornan (Calif., R.) observed that abortion is morally repugnant to many taxpayers, whereas childbirth is a value to be supported by public funds.[81] Similarly, as Rep. Martin Russo (Ill., D.) argued for cutting off Medicaid funds for abortion,

> Eliminating the source of funds [for abortion] may tip the balance toward bringing the child into the world and I believe in tipping the scale in favor of life almost every time . . . if Medicaid money were unavailable for this purpose [abortion] . . . [t]hat would save approximately 240,000 lives every year.[82]

In an even more startling pronouncement on the value of pregnancy to society, Rep. William Dannemeyer (Calif., R.) noted that unless women were pregnant and gave birth, no taxpayers would be born to pay off the national debt:

If we are going to pay off this debt, somebody has got to be born to pay it off. Now, since 1973, the decline in the birth rate per fertile female has reached the point where, as a civilization, we run the serious risk of disappearing from this planet. Right now . . . the rate of reproduction per fertile female is 1.8. Now, demographers tell us we need 2.1 to sustain a civilization . . . [or] by the year 2020, it will require a tax rate to pay social security benefits . . . between 25 percent and 32 percent.[83]

Congress has added an extracultural metaphor of its own to the mix of metaphors it shares with the Supreme Court, namely, pregnancy as a punishment for sex. Representative Donald M. Fraser (Minn., D.) expressed this view by saying that women "bear the responsibility for avoiding pregnancy. They must be punished if they do not."[84] Similarly, Rep. Larry McDonald (Ga., D.) decried the abortion policies at West Point, whereby "cadets who have illegitimate pregnancies are protected against dismissal and are kept in good standing as though they were honorable cadets . . . . All the female cadet needs to do in order to cover up her fornication is [to get an abortion]."[85] He deplored the fact that women cadets receive "no penalties" for their "promiscuity."

Most cultural metaphors for pregnancy are not so much wrong as incomplete.[86] Without an accurate analysis of the effects of the fetus on a woman, congressional debate perpetuates some serious distortions, such as equating abortion with slavery. Pro-life members of Congress have compared the abortion issue to the *Dred Scott* case, in which the Supreme Court affirmed in 1857 that slavery was constitutional. In 1973, only days after the *Roe* decision, Rep. Lawrence J. Hogan (Md., R.) declared the abortion decision to be even worse than the Court's "shameful Dred Scott decision which allowed slavery,"[87] and Rep. Angelo D. Roncallo (N.Y., R.) took the same tack in arguing for an antiabortion amendment:

On a shameful day in our history, the Supreme Court . . . rendered what has to be described as The Dred Scott Case of the 20th Century . . . . In jurisprudential terms, the Court's rulings have the same character as if the Court had defined an explicitly admitted human being as a nonperson. The 1973 abortion rulings, therefore, are based on exactly the same principle as the Dred Scott case, that an innocent human being can be defined as a nonperson and killed if his existence is inconvenient or uncomfortable to others or if those others consider him unfit to live.[88]

Pro-life Rep. Leonore K. Sullivan observed that just as Congress passed the Fourteenth Amendment "[w]hen the black man was deprived of his 'personhood' 100 years ago by the awful Dred Scott decision," Congress should pass a "right to life" amendment to negate women's rights to abortions.[89] Representatives Harold Volkmer (Mo., D.) and Richard Gephardt (Md., D.) together introduced a right-to-life amendment by declaring that abortion was the most important moral issue since slavery, and as we now reject slavery and Dred Scott, so, too, should we reject abortion.[90]

Other members of Congress, hostile to abortion rights and lacking understanding of the adversarial relation of the fetus and a woman when it coerces pregnancy, link abortion rights to the Hitlerite tactics of Nazi Germany. Even before the *Roe* decision, Rep. John R. Rarick (La., D.) predicted that if abortion were legalized, "euthanasia and mercy killings, [and the] killings of any unwanted—like the 'Third Reich' naziism," would follow.[91] In 1970 Rep. John G. Schmitz (Calif., R.) referred to abortion as the "rejection of traditional morality" in a nationwide campaign to get rid of people, which he termed "New Nazism."[92]

In the days following *Roe*, Rep. John Zwach (Minn., R.) compared the Court's decision to brutal euthanasia-eugenics policies. In his words, America was headed toward

an era of self-worship and selfishness never intended under our guarantee of life, liberty, and the pursuit of happiness . . . in the footsteps of Sodom and Gomorrah . . . If we are allowed today to kill the unborn, it will be but a small step to kill the infirm, the aged, or those of unsound mind.[93]

Similarly, Rep. Dominick V. Daniels (N.Y., D.) proposed a guarantee of the right to life of the "unborn, the ill, the aged, and incapacitated," on the grounds that they all were the targets of "utilitarian attitudes" that recalled those of proabortionists and Nazi scientists.[94] Furthermore, Rep. Angelo D. Roncallo (N.Y., R.) said that the right to an abortion rests on "the very same principle that underlay the Nazi extermination of the Jews . . . we have embarked upon the greatest slaughter of innocent human beings in any nation in the history of the world."[95]

Comments such as these reflect the same flaw present in the Supreme Court's reasoning on abortion, the failure to recognize the fetus as the cause of pregnancy. Without an adequate causal analysis, the aggressive way in which a fetus must intrude on a woman's body and liberty when making her pregnant remains invisible. The onus then falls on the woman, not the fetus, and Congress depicts the fetus as an innocent victim of the woman who chooses to stop its aggression. Although the fetus is innocent of conscious intention and cannot control its behavior, it is not innocent of massively intruding on a woman's body and liberty. Far from being the slave that is sacrificed in an abortion, the fetus is the one that enslaves the woman when it imposes a wrongful pregnancy.

9

The Politics of Consent

Good, Bad, and Captive Samaritans

Pro-life advocates have generally been responsible for making the personhood of the fetus the key issue in the abortion debate, the point on which women's right to terminate a pregnancy is presumed to stand or fall. Yet pro-choice advocates have also misdirected attention to what the fetus "is" rather than what it "does." This was evident at the very outset, in 1973, when the Court established the constitutionality of abortion rights in *Roe*. When pro-choice lawyer Sarah Weddington first argued the case before the Court in 1971, she linked the right to privacy to abortion rights precisely on the grounds that the "law had never treated the fetus as a person."[1] Later, when she reargued *Roe* in 1972, she spent most of her time dealing with the issue of "when life begins" as the key determinant of women's right to terminate pregnancy.[2]

In that reargument, Justice Stewart specifically asked Weddington, "[I]f—it were established that an unborn fetus is a person within the protection of the Fourteenth Amendment, you would have almost an impossible case, here [*sic*] would you not?"[3] Weddington responded, "I would have a very difficult case," and agreed that if the fetus were a person, abortion would be equivalent to killing a born child.[4] Not surprisingly, Assistant Attorney General of Texas Robert Flowers, who argued against *Roe*, emphasized that "it is the position of the State of Texas that upon conception we have a human being, a person within the concept of the Constitution of the United States and that of Texas, also."[5] He invoked the now familiar references to the fetus as part of a "silent minority, the true silent minority," declaring that fetuses have a right to "counsel" and to the "right to trial by jury."[6]

Justices Stewart and White concurred that if Flowers were right about the personhood of the fetus, then, as Justice Stewart stated, Flowers "can sit down; [because] you've won your case."[7] To underscore this point, Justice White asked Flowers the reverse, "You've lost your case if the fetus or embryo is not a person. Is that it?" Flowers replied, "Yes, sir, I would say so."[8]

The centrality of what the fetus "is" found its way into the majority opinion in *Roe*. As Justice Blackmun noted, even pro-choice advocate Sarah Weddington had agreed that if the fetus were a person, women would have no right to an abortion. As *Roe* states,

> The appellee [Wade] and certain amici argue that the fetus is a "person" within the language and meaning of the Fourteenth Amendment . . . . If this suggestion of personhood is established, the appellant's [Roe's] case, of course collapses, for the fetus' right to life would then be guaranteed specifically by the Amendment. The appellant [Weddington arguing for Roe] conceded as much on reargument.[9]

One of the legacies of *Roe*, therefore, is the focus of attention on what the fetus "is" rather than on what the fetus "does" as the foundation for women's right to terminate pregnancy. This view of abortion rights is shared by many pro-choice and pro-life advocates, who differ primarily in how they portray the fetus. On the one hand, pro-life advocates combine science and media techniques to construct the identity of a fetus as a child, a baby, a person, and even a citizen.[10] Pro-choice advocates, on the other hand, construct the identity of the fetus with sophisticated denials that it is a person. One of the most influential is Ronald Dworkin's analysis, in which he concludes that people who say the fetus is a person cannot believe that literally but are rather expressing sentiments for the belief in the value of life over a wide continuum, which includes the fetus.[11]

Yet, as this book has shown, abortion rights neither stand nor fall on whether the fetus is a person. Even Sarah Weddington now acknowledges that she made a mistake in *Roe* to say that abortion rights depend on what the fetus is.[12] In the intervening years, many pro-choice advocates have explored another line of reasoning, the "bad samaritan" foundation for abortion rights. By so doing, they follow the lead of moral philosopher Judith Jarvis Thomson, who in the early 1970s persuasively argued that even if the fetus is a person, and even if its life hangs in the balance as a needy recipient of a woman's body, a woman still has the right to be a bad samaritan by refusing to give her body to the fetus.[13]

This bad samaritan argument for abortion rights still does not go far enough. It claims only that women have a right to refuse to donate their bodies to a fetus. The state, by withholding funds for abortions for indigent women, coerces women to donate their bodies to fetuses by default and thus violates women's constitutional rights, because the state does not coerce any other class of people to donate their bodies to others in need. The flaw in this bad samaritan argument is that the state's failure to provide abortion funds can be seen not as a legislative decree by the state that mandates women to be pregnant, but merely as an expression by the state of its preference for pregnancy.

The insufficiency of the bad samaritan argument for abortion rights and funding stems from its failure to identify the fetus as the cause of pregnancy in general and as the cause of wrongful pregnancy in particular when a woman seeks an abortion. The issue is not merely that women have a right to be bad samaritans by refusing to give their bodies to a fetus. Rather, if a woman does not consent to pregnancy, the issue is that the fetus has made her its *captive samaritan* by intruding on her body and liberty against her will, and thus on the woman's right to be free from that status. Women must not only have a right of self-defense comparable to others in our society to use deadly force on their own behalf to stop fetuses from taking over their bodies, but also equal access to the resources of the state to provide for their defense against intrusions of their bodily integrity and liberty by means of abortion funding.

It might not be constitutional for the state itself to mandate that people donate their bodies to others in need or to conscript women's bodies for pregnancy service, but it is definitely unconstitutional for the state to tolerate, permit, or sanction one private person's capture of another person in order to take forcefully that person's body or body parts without consent. Yet this is what occurs when the state allows a fetus to impose the injuries of wrongful pregnancy. Clearly the state must not sanction the fetus's capture of a woman but instead must stop the fetus's imposition of wrongful pregnancy, to the same degree that the state executes its police power to stop other private intrusions of people's bodies and liberty. The class of people to compare with women seeking an abortion is therefore neither men nor the indigent nor racial groups but other victims of wrongful private intrusion. According to the equal protection standards set by the Constitution, if the state protects some victims of private wrongful acts, it also must exercise its police power to protect pregnant women from the wrongful private acts of a fetus imposing pregnancy upon them without their consent. This is the purpose of government according not only to the heritage of the American political system but also to the mandate of the Constitution.

For too long, however, the state has had it both ways, leaving women to suffer in the balance. The state omits abortion funding from health policies, on the grounds that abortion differs from killing cancer cells because abortion destroys potential human life under state protection. Yet once fetuses are put under state protection, the state does nothing to stop them as human life from injuring others, such as the women they make pregnant without consent in a medically normal pregnancy, much less the women they threaten to cripple for life in a medically abnormal pregnancy. By so doing, the state not merely protects preborn life but also privileges it in ways that the state entitles no born human life.

The captive samaritan basis for abortion rights, in contrast to the bad samaritan one, clarifies what is at stake in the issue, thereby gaining for women the right not only to an abortion but also to abortion funding. The issue is not how the state itself directly or indirectly conscripts women's bodies for pregnancy service, but rather how the state allows the fetus as state-protected preborn life to intrude on a woman's body and liberty in order to take from her what it needs, thereby conferring on the fetus an entitlement the state confers on no born people, regardless of their need or kinship relationships to others. Even if the state passed legislation that forced born people to donate their bodies or body parts to others as good samaritans, it is inconceivable that the state would support legislation that allowed one born person to capture another in order to take needed body parts. Yet current abortion-funding polices do just that, and the Court has yet to see the unconstitutional character of the state's failure to act to stop a fetus from imposing the injuries of wrongful pregnancy.

As Elizabeth Mensch and Alan Freeman argue, the language of rights is a language of membership in the moral community.[14] Much attention has been paid to whether abortion policies exclude the fetus from membership in a moral community. Yet women are the ones presently excluded from the moral community as defined by recognition of their rights.[15] It is time for the Court, Congress, and the public to recognize that the key issue in the abortion debate is not what the fetus "is," but rather what it "does" when it imposes wrongful pregnancy, and that whatever the definition of the fetus, its actions require appropriate state response. On the one hand, if the fetus is not a state-protected human life but merely a mass of alien cells that act as a natural force in a woman's body, then the state must make funds available for a woman to remove those cells intruding upon her body to the degree that it makes funds available for the removal of other forms of alien cellular intrusion, such as cancer. Or, if the fetus is a human life under state protection, then when it intrudes on a woman's body without her consent, the state must allocate public resources to stop the fetus to the degree that the state stops private parties from intruding on others.

Either way, the state is obligated to fund abortions based on what a fetus does. What the fetus is does not determine whether women have a right to abortion funding; it merely determines the principle mandating the state's obligation to fund abortion. If the fetus is a bunch of alien, nonhuman cells, then the state must not omit funds for abortions from health-benefit policies or if, however, the fetus is state-protected human life, then the state must fund abortions as part of its police power, which provides law and order, a power that includes stopping human life from causing harm by intruding on the bodily integrity and liberty of others, as well as protecting human life from harm. In either case, what the fetus does to a woman when it imposes wrongful pregnancy not only justifies her right to use deadly force herself to stop it but also justifies her right to expect state assistance in the form of public funding of abortion.

A Minimalist View

As nineteenth-century Justice Samuel F. Miller quipped, "Your argument is perfectly logical, but the result for which you contend seems to me absurd."[16] It may seem that the opposite could be said about the consent-to-pregnancy approach to abortion rights, and that the end, abortion funding, is a perfectly reasonable policy, endorsed by many Western nations,[17] but that the argument used to get to that policy, fetal intrusion if not aggression, is absurd. Yet this argument is no more absurd than positions already reached by the Court in abortion cases, much less the principles of the minimalist state on which the Court is based. If anything is absurd, it is not the idea of fetal aggression but rather the idea that discrimination based on pregnancy is not sex discrimination, as the Court has ruled, or that it is constitutional for the state to permit permanent injury to a woman's health from abnormal pregnancy in preference to stopping that injury by providing an abortion, as the Court has also ruled.

The underlying principle of a minimalist state is its police power, defined primarily in terms of the state's provision of law and order. The consent-to-pregnancy approach to abortion rights coopts, rather than contests, this principle. Taken at face value, the police power of the state argues for the public funding of abortion as a law-and-order remedy to a fetus's nonconsensual intrusion rather than as a welfare benefit to help a woman deal with a natural force, such as poverty.[18] The very definition of the American state presumes that it legitimately exercises power and coercion to establish law and order to protect people from aggression by others. To the degree that the state exercises its police power, it must therefore protect women, as well as others, from private wrongful acts. This duty includes protecting women against wrongful pregnancy imposed by a fetus.

Ultimately, as Gita Sen notes, all cultures socially construct the meaning of reproduction as one of the essential components of the social and political order of society.[19] The foundation for abortion rights presented here socially constructs pregnancy by drawing on one of the most fundamental principles of American culture, political traditions, and legal doctrines: consent. It does so by defining the abortion issue in terms of women's right to consent to pregnancy, not merely to choose an abortion. Its view of reproduction therefore challenges the most popular concept used by pro-life advocates to describe the fetus, its innocence. The fetus, according to a consent approach, is not innocent of causing pregnancy; it is only innocent of intentionality and the ability to control its behavior.

That the *Roe* decision failed to frame abortion rights in terms of women's right to consent to pregnancy reflects the tenor of those days, as yet unmarked by a feminist jurisprudence. At that time, Sarah Weddington could not even get credit in her own name without written permission from her husband because neither the culture nor the law had recognized that treating married women merely as extensions of their husbands' identity was an unconstitutional form of sex discrimination.[20] When she argued *Roe* before the Court, she was addressed as "Mrs." Weddington, not "Ms.," and presumably this was merely a symbolic expression of the many problems attending the subordination of women in the early 1970s.[21]

Little was then available, in terms of either feminist consciousness or legal perspective, to develop an alternative to the patchwork application of the right to use contraceptives or the right to obtain an abortion. Although contraception and abortion both involve reproduction, the similarity stops there. In principle, contraception prevents pregnancy from occurring, and abortion terminates a pregnancy already in progress.[22] The right to use contraceptives is similar to the right to expose oneself to the risk of mugging by walking down a deserted street at night. It is distinct from the right to abortion, which is similar to the right to stop a mugger from beating you as you walk down the deserted street, the right of self-defense. *Roe* and *Griswold* differ, therefore, not merely because *Roe* involves killing a fetus but also because a woman is justified in killing a fetus to prevent it from imposing the serious injuries of wrongful pregnancy.[23]

Concomitantly, although the state may fail to provide welfare benefits, such as street lights or contraceptives, to reduce the risk of injury, the same is not true of private violence. Once a mugging or a wrongful pregnancy is in progress, it is unconstitutional for the state to prefer that mugging or wrongful pregnancy as a means of protecting, respectively, the mugger or the fetus. Rather, to the degree that the state stops private violence against anyone, the state must stop the mugging and wrongful pregnancy on behalf of the victims.

In the early 1970s when *Roe* was decided, the law barely recognized women's right to consent to a sexual relationship with a man, so it is little wonder that the Court did not at that time frame abortion rights in terms of women's right to consent to a pregnancy relationship with a fetus. Yet even then the Court knew that there was a key difference between contraception and abortion, although it could not adequately specify that difference. After more than twenty years we can now see that abortion involves a relationship between two state-protected entities, the woman and the fetus, whereas the use of contraceptives, unless coerced by the state or another private party, involves only one individual. Abortion is the means necessary to stop the fetus as a private party from injuring a woman, whereas contraception is a means to reduce the risk that a fetus will injure a woman in the first place. John Hart Ely was right when he stated that "more than the mother's own body is involved in a decision to have an abortion,"[24] but he did not go on to identify the something else as the fetus's serious injury of a woman when it imposes itself without her consent and her right to state assistance to stop that injury in progress.

The Court implicitly recognized in *Roe* that a woman can be injured by a fetus when it noted a woman's constitutional right to an abortion whenever the fetus threatens her with a medically abnormal pregnancy. Yet the Court failed explicitly to recognize in *Roe*, not only that the fetus is the cause of that injury, but also that a fetus injures a woman in every pregnancy imposed on her against her will. The Court's failure to identify the fetus as the cause of wrongful pregnancy meant that there was no way to differentiate between state action in the case of such privacy rights as whom to marry or whether to use contraceptives, and the privacy right involved in abortion. Because the state is not obligated to help a person exercise his or her right to privacy by paying for that person's wedding or by funding the use of contraceptives, by extension the Court concluded that the state was not obligated to help a woman exercise her choice to have an abortion by funding it.

A major difference between weddings and contraception and abortion, however, is the element of coercion. A woman who is seeking an abortion is being
coerced by a fetus to be pregnant against her will. The appropriate analogy is not
people who choose to get married or to use contraceptives but rather people who
are being forced to marry or to use contraceptives against their will. The relevant
right of privacy is not the right to make choices about one's own life and body
but rather the right to be free of private intrusion. To the degree that the state
protects people against such private coercion, it must protect women against the
coercive intrusion of the fetus as a private party imposing the injuries of wrongful pregnancy against their will. Although the Court has held firmly, if reluc-
tantly, to the constitutional right of a woman to an abortion, its failure to identify what the fetus does to a woman when it causes pregnancy has resulted in
rulings that undermine women's rights by allowing the state to establish repressive regulations, such as twenty-four-hour waiting periods, and most serious of
all, prohibitions against the use of all public funds, facilities, and personnel for
the performance of abortions.[25]

Presumably there will be an uphill battle to establish women's right to consent to pregnancy, paralleling the uphill battle to establish women's right to consent to sexual intercourse. Opponents may argue that women bring pregnancy
on themselves by consenting to engage in sexual intercourse and are therefore
responsible for their own pregnancies. This is a familiar form of blaming the victim. Women were similarly held responsible for their sexual violation by men if
and when, from women's present or past behavior, it might be inferred that they
"wanted," or "expected" or "should have expected" sexual intercourse to occur—
in short were "asking for it." As the law now reads in most states, men may not
infer a woman's intention, much less her consent to sexual intercourse, from her
past behavior, current behavior, or setting. Rather, for sexual intercourse to be
legal, a woman must explicitly consent to engage in it.

The parallel to pregnancy has yet to be introduced into abortion cases, even
though the law has established wrongful pregnancy as a serious injury. Sexual
intercourse for fertile women always involves some risk that pregnancy will
occur. Yet a woman responsible for exposing herself to the possible risk that a fertilized ovum will act on her body is not responsible for the violation itself. A
woman who puts herself at risk by walking down a deserted street alone at night
or by behaving or dressing in ways that could be interpreted as sexually provocative, still retains the right to say no to sexual intercourse. So, too, with pregnancy.
A woman who engages in sexual intercourse without contraceptives may be ill
informed, irresponsible, stupid, or immature, but that does not entitle a private
party to intrude on her bodily integrity and liberty.

Consent clarifies what is at stake in the abortion debate. The key issue is not
the unwarranted intrusion of the state by restricting the right of women to make
private choices about how to live their own lives. To the contrary, the key issue
is women's right to consent to the physical intrusion of the fertilized ovum.

Should they say no, the issue is not only their right to self-defense but also their right to state intervention on their behalf to stop the fetus from intruding on them. When the state instead sanctions that private aggression, it violates the due process guarantees of the Constitution. And when the state simply fails to protect women from that private aggression in the same way that it protects others from private injury, it violates the equal protection guarantees of the Constitution. Reframing abortion rights in terms of women's right to consent to pregnancy thus provides a new route to abortion funding, even as it recasts many cultural, political, and legal assumptions about women, including their victimization, their association with self-sacrifice norms, and their relational rather than autonomous identities.

Women's Victimization

The consent-to-pregnancy foundation for abortion rights emphasizes the similarities between people, including men and women, rather than their differences. Although it is common to think of pregnancy as unique, this approach focuses instead on the similarities between pregnant women and other victims of nonconsensual intrusion.[26] It makes it possible to extend existing constitutional guarantees to women on the basis of the equality doctrine.[27] This approach harmonizes with Wendy Williams's view that "conceptualizing pregnancy as a special case permits unfavorable as well as favorable treatment of pregnancy. Our history provides too many illustrations of the former to allow us to be sanguine about the wisdom of urging special treatment."[28]

While many people labor to obtain autonomy and self-reliance for women by recasting their problems in nonvictimization terms, the consent approach takes another tack. Its identification of women's victimization by wrongful pregnancy imposed by a fetus justifies women's claims on the state to provide public resources for abortion. This approach does not make woman passive recipients of state aid or damsels in distress, waiting for the state in lieu of a traditional knight in armor to rescue them. To the contrary, it locates women's reproductive rights on the cornerstone of the foundation at the very construction of the American state. People expect the state to do many things, but its basic contribution is to protect people from private violence. When women are made pregnant against their will by state-protected fetuses, women are victims of private violence as much as anyone else in our society. To suggest that women must provide for their own protection against the private violence imposed by preborn human life, however unintentional that violence, while the state allocates resources to aid other people in distress does not empower women; it merely ostracizes them from the civil society defined by the very existence of the state.[29]

Feminist activists have had to define women as victims as a means of empowerment in other policy contexts, such as rape and sexual harassment. The concept of rape derives from the assumption that normal sexual intercourse is something that men *do* to women, and thus an experience that requires a woman's consent. This contrasts with the healthier view of heterosexual intercourse as a mutually shared experience between men and women.[30] But before that mutuality can occur, women must be considered equal partners in the relationship. And before that can occur, women must be recognized as victims in cases of sexual aggression, and removing their victimhood status is precondition to opening the door to equality.[31] So, too, with wrongful pregnancy. Before women can experience pregnancy as nonvictims, much less as partners in a mutually shared experience, both our culture and our law must recognize that women have a right to consent to a pregnancy relationship with a fetus as well as the right to receive the assistance of the state as a victim of wrongful pregnancy when a fetus imposes pregnancy against their will.

The same can be said of sexual harassment. Women had to be identified as the victims of this crime before it could even be defined legally as a crime. The identification of women as the victims of sexual harassment was then used to demand legal redress, thereby empowering women. Pregnancy is similar. Like sexual intercourse and other intimate relationships, it ranges from the most positive to the most negative of experiences. While victimization refers only to one pole of that continuum, it includes those women who experience bodily intrusion by a fertilized ovum against their will. The consent-to-pregnancy foundation for abortion rights does not imply that all pregnant women are victims, any more than that all women who experience sexual intercourse are victims, nor does it depend on stereotypes of women as being weaker than others.[32] Rather, it obligates the state to extend to pregnant women the same protections against private intrusion of their bodily integrity and liberty that everyone else in society takes for granted.

Feminists need not worry that labeling pregnant women as the victims of fetal intrusion, however uncontrollable it is, disempowers women, because as Drucilla Cornell, quoting Jean-François Lyotard, reminds us, "injustice is the crime combined with the perpetuation of silence that erases it." The only way the crime can become known as an injustice is to name it. For this reason, "Feminist jurisprudence seeks to make harms to women that do not 'exist' — as a harm that adequately expresses the experience and the actual suffering of women — within the current legal system. An abuse cannot be fought until it is understood as an abuse."[33]

As Faye Ginsburg notes, pro-choice and pro-life proponents often have similar ideas about marriage and the family, such as the vulnerability of women, but they reach opposite conclusions.[34] While many eschew a route that portrays women as victims, the consent-to-pregnancy view uses the abuse of women, not merely by the state or men, but also unintentionally by a fetus, as a starting point for dealing more effectively with women's vulnerability. Rather than being made responsible for their own vulnerability, women must have the right to claim the resources of the state to help them in defending themselves against nonconsensual intrusion by human life. Specifically, to the degree that the state protects all people from nonconsensual intrusion by private parties, it must provide abortions to all women as the necessary means for stopping a fetus from imposing wrongful pregnancy.

Self-defense or Self-sacrifice

Our failure to see women as the victims of fetal intrusion occurs because we overlay women's inherent right of self-defense with the opposing standard of self-sacrifice.[35] While it is of inestimable value for women to donate their bodies to fetuses, it remains a woman's right to be set free from a fetus that captures her by imposing pregnancy. To suggest otherwise is to tap into cultural attitudes about pregnancy and women rather than into legal precedents established in the law.

Women's close identification with their reproductive roles often makes it difficult to imagine a woman in terms of a personality independent of her identity as a mother, if not a wife.[36] Certainly Louis Brandeis and Samuel Warren did not do so in their classic article on the right to privacy. Using only masculine representations, they argued for expanding the notion of the right to privacy to include personality, but the personality they envisioned was a highly gendered one, based on the prerogatives of men only. They noted, for example, that the "common law has always recognized a man's house as his castle . . . . Man's family relations became a part of the legal conception of his life, and the alienation of a wife's affections was held remediable."[37] "[T]his development of the law was inevitable," they maintained, because the "intense intellectual and emotional life, and the heightening of sensations which came with the advance of civilization, made it clear to men that only a part of the pain, pleasure, and profit of life lay in physical things."[38] Men's right of privacy thus began with the inviolate character of their own bodies; then incorporated their "home as castle," inclusive of their wives and children along with their property; and eventually expanded to include immunity of their very personality. Quoting Lord Cottenham, the authors noted that "[A] man 'is entitled to be protected in the exclusive use and enjoyment of that which is exclusively his.'"[39]

This masculinized depiction of privacy as the right to be let alone from private intrusion has as its complement a masculinized depiction of the right to self-defense to protect that privacy. The right to self-defense is identified with male socialization patterns and the acquisition of skills, being defined as the "act of defending oneself, one's rights or position,"[40] as "Nature's eldest law,"[41] given content through the "noble and manly art" of fencing, pugilism, and boxing.[42] Men "who have studied the 'noble art of self-defence'" were viewed as being "peaceful in society."[43]

The right to self-defense is also grounded on gender stereotypes of masculinity in standard, contemporary legal doctrine, as found in the *Restatement of the Law (Second) Torts*. The castle doctrine is alive and well, and perhaps it will come as no surprise to learn that the person who is in charge of the castle is a man. A man is entitled to use deadly force to defend himself when attacked in his dwelling place, defined as "that part of the building or other habitation which is actually used for residential purposes . . . . Thus, a man's house is the dwelling place of himself, his family, his servants."[44] Although English common law required one to retreat, if possible, before using deadly force, that rule does not necessarily apply in the way in which American courts adjudicate the matter because in

> many parts of the country, the ideal of social manhood has included as one of its prime requisites courage and dignity. The interest of the actor in his personal dignity has been regarded as of greater importance than the social interest in the prevention of deadly affrays, and in the preservation of life and limb of those engaged in them . . . . Where the actor is attacked within his own dwelling place, or its curtilage, he may stand his ground and meet deadly force with deadly force . . . . In a few jurisdictions a man's business office or storehouse is regarded as partaking of the sanctity of his dwelling place, so that it becomes equally his "castle," and he need not retreat if attacked in it, although he might safely do so.[45]

The justification for allowing a man to use deadly force to defend his dwelling place stems from the "more or less instinctive feeling that a home is sacred, and that it is improper to require a man to run from his own house, or to submit to pursuit from room to room in it."[46]

If part of what a man defines as being "his" is his wife, who is ensconced within his castle, the question for women is what then belongs to the wife? What constitutes the wife's privacy according to the law? Is her home also "her" castle? Does her husband belong to her? Does she have things that are exclusively hers for her own use and enjoyment? Does the law even recognize that she has a personality of her own? Some feminist legal scholars say no. As Elizabeth Schneider's work shows, there is extraordinary evidence of sex bias in the laws of self-defense;[47] and in Catharine MacKinnon's view, the right to be let alone in the law comes to nothing more than the right of men to be let alone so that they may "oppress women one at a time."[48]

Yet to ask whether women have a personality of their own, which includes a notion of self-defense as an expression of one's autonomy, is akin to asking whether they have a fundamental right to personhood. As Laurence Tribe notes, when we talk about personhood, we mean the way in which "one's identity is constantly and profoundly shaped by the rewards and penalties, the exhortations and scarcities and constraints of one's social environment." We view the "personhood" that results from such complex processes as "sufficiently 'one's own' to be deemed fundamental in confrontation with the one entity that retains a monopoly over legitimate violence—the government."[49]

Self-defense is not a wanton right to kill; self-defense is rather the right to be let alone from intrusion that violates one's very identity as a person. This right extends not just to the security of one's body and liberty but also to one's personhood and personality. Yet rather than a personality parity between men and women, our culture and our law reflect a personality polarity, which assigns the right of self-defense to men as a defining component of their manhood, and assigns the duty of self-sacrifice to women as a component of their womanhood.

When an aggressor intrudes on a man's castle, much less his body, we do not expect him to donate his castle to the invader or sacrifice himself to the intruder, nor do we deny his right to refuse to donate his home and body to the intruder. Rather, we accept the man's right to defend his castle and his body, even with deadly force if need be. While the law protects the idea that a "man's home is his castle," women have long sought for merely the right to have a "room of one's own" within it. What is more, the struggle for merely a "room" precludes attention to the right to defend that room, once it is obtained.

It is time to recognize that a woman must have the right to a room of her own, but, even more fundamentally, the right to a body of her own and a personality of her own. Without a right to control one's body from intrusion by private parties, including a fetus, a woman does not have the prerequisites recognized by law as fundamental to her liberty and her very identity as a person. This does not require that we devalue the contributions made by either women or men who nurture, sustain, help, or give to others in need, only that we do not deny to people their legal rights on the grounds that they have the capacity to nurture.[50] As late as 1961, for example, the Court ruled that it was constitutional to exclude women from jury duty unless they explicitly wrote to request inclusion, on the grounds that their family roles took precedence, even for women who were not married or had no children. As the Court stated,

> Despite the enlightened emancipation of women from the restrictions and protections of bygone years, and their entry into many parts of community life formerly considered to be reserved to men, woman is still regarded as the center of home and family life. We cannot say that it is constitutionally impermissible for a state acting in pursuit of the general welfare to conclude that a woman should be relieved from the civic duty of jury service.[51]

The problem with such policies, which did not become unconstitutional until 1975,[52] was not their emphasis on the caretaking or family roles of women per se but rather their assumption that women's nurturance negates their basic legal rights.[53] As sociologist Carol Smart notes, the law tended to view the female body as a "conduit of disqualification" for such rights.[54] Applying to abortion the basic concept of privacy, the right to be let alone from private parties, includes women in the community of rights-holders from which they have traditionally been excluded. Women, as human beings with personalities of their own, cannot be squeezed into narrow confines that define them solely in terms of their nurturing and caring roles. However much we need and value those contributions, women also must be protected by the state from private parties who take their bodies and liberty without their consent.[55] This includes preborn as well as born human life.

The state's protection of fetal rights can lead to the state's invasion of women's privacy on behalf of the fetus.[56] Claims by the state that it can force a woman to deliver a baby by caesarean section or that a drug-addicted pregnant woman can be jailed in order to protect the developing fetus, are violations by the state of women's bodily integrity and liberty in the name of protecting the fetus. As Janet Gallagher notes, although it is legitimate for the state to support policies to ensure the birth of healthy children, such policies cannot ignore the fact that women possess fundamental rights that preclude the kind and degree of government intervention often proposed.

> A pregnant woman has a right to refuse medical intervention and a right to be free of any unique criminal or civil liability for her conduct during pregnancy and birth. This analysis relies less upon *Roe v. Wade*'s assessment of the legal personhood of the fetus in American law than upon the common law and constitutional rights of bodily integrity and personal decision making on which *Roe* itself was grounded.[57]

We must carefully monitor all state intrusions of women's bodies once they consent to be pregnant, making sure that the consent is not taken as a blank check for turning over women's bodies to the control of either the fetus or the state. Any intrusion of the state on women's bodily integrity when they consent to be pregnant demands the highest scrutiny of the Court. Conversely, when a woman does not consent to a pregnancy, the problem is not the state's intrusion on her bodily integrity but rather the state's failure to protect her bodily integrity from intrusion by the fetus.

Fear of state intrusion has all but blinded many pro-choice advocates from discerning this distinction. Susan Estrich and Kathleen Sullivan in their influential work on abortion rights, for example, speak of the need to keep the "state out of the business of reproductive decision-making," and of how the "[r]egimentation of reproduction is a hallmark of the totalitarian state, from Plato's Republic to Hitler's Germany."[58] Yet the problem with abortion funding is not that the state is too involved; it is not involved enough. The state stands by in order to protect the fetus as human life while it imposes serious injury on the woman. This is akin not to a totalitarian state but to a state of nature, void of government altogether. Estrich and Sullivan identify the state, not the fetus, as the agent of coercion in forced pregnancy. They claim that when the state restricts abortions, it impinges on a woman's bodily integrity just as much as if the state directly compelled a woman either to be pregnant or to have an abortion; "the state would plainly infringe its citizens' bodily integrity whether its agents inflicted knife wounds or its laws forbade surgery or restricted blood transfusions in cases of private knifings."[59] Yet the proper analogy with abortion is not state-restricted blood transfusions but the state's restriction of the knifer. Surely it would be unconstitutional for the state to refuse to stop private parties from slashing people on the grounds of protecting the aggressors.

The energies devoted to preventing the state from requiring pregnant women to be injected with drugs to prevent HIV-related maladies would be better directed toward mandating the state to provide abortion funding. State intrusions of pregnant women's bodies to protect either the women or the fetus, as long as these intrusions meet the standards already in place for state invasion of people's bodies, are not the main problem. If the state can coerce people to be vaccinated, it seems likely that it would be constitutional for the state also to invade pregnant women's bodies to this same minimal degree, and state policies that did so would not violate women's rights as much as do current abortion-funding policies. These policies strand women in a state of nature, at the mercy of fetal intrusion of their bodies without the assistance of the state to stop the fetus on women's behalf from imposing wrongful pregnancy.

A Utilitarian Basis for Abortion Rights

Pregnancy is a value central to each of our lives and to society as a whole. We are all the product of a woman's pregnancy, and each of us would like to think that our mother willingly took joy in nurturing our growth and development and experienced pregnancy as a union of interests between mother and child. After birth, as we grow to adulthood and struggle with the human condition, the pregnant relationship between mother and child often stands in stark contrast to the strife, despair, and loneliness of everyday life. As a result, our culture idealizes pregnancy, perhaps even more than it does heterosexual romance, as the oasis of love, joy, and communion.

Perhaps for this reason, in over twenty years of debate about abortion, the furthest we have come in understanding the right to terminate a pregnancy is to grant to women the right to be bad samaritans, who refuse to sacrifice their bodies to a fertilized ovum that needs nurture and support. We have not recognized that when a fertilized ovum makes a woman pregnant without her consent, it places her in the position of a captive samaritan, who has a right to be set free. What is more, we have allowed the state to exploit women's captive samaritan status rather than to correct it. This stands in dramatic contrast to the careful legislative monitoring of other forms of samaritan behavior so as to protect vulnerable donors from abuse by others. Policies that take advantage of people's poverty by using monetary incentives for them to disregard their own health needs, in contexts other than abortion, raise public concern. Payment for organ transplants is an example. In 1984 Congress passed the National Organ Transplant Act, which bans the sale of organs or vital human body parts, even those of victims of fatal accidents, which could provide lifesaving options for living people who are bound to die without them. Currently at least 31,000 people are on the waiting list for organ transplants, a demand that far exceeds the supply.[60] Yet as George Annas explains, Congress passed legislation prohibiting the sale and purchase of organs because its members were "sickened" by the notion of a brokerage system for selling human body parts.[61]

The sale of organs is not the only case of monetary incentives that undermine the right to life, particularly when poverty circumscribes someone's choices. Physicians maintain the lives of poor people on ventilators, for example, until there is no more hope, but even then they need the family's permission to take a patient off such a support. As Annas notes, "[I]t would be much easier to get the family's permission to withdraw treatment if you can say, 'Not only is this treatment futile, but we'll give you $30,000 if you stop treatment now and have your son or daughter be an organ donor.'"[62]

At issue here is the advisability of the state's use of monetary rewards to encourage people to disregard their bodily integrity and liberty as a means for advancing a legitimate state interest. The question is the ethics, much less the constitutionality of the state paying people to give up their organs if, by so doing, the state encourages people to allow intrusions on their bodily integrity and liberty that seriously threaten their own health. When the state encourages wrongful pregnancy, much less sanctions the imposition of wrongful pregnancy, the same question arises, for now the state is encouraging and sanctioning harm imposed by the fetus as a private party. Not only are such state policies unethical but also they violate the Constitution.

The ethical, as well as legal, justification for abortion rights has been compared to making choices on a lifeboat.[63] The Court often refers to a pregnant woman as "carrying a fetus," as if she were a lifeboat. In the utilitarian context of balancing the rights involved in abortion, as in the lifeboat, the goal of producing the greatest good for the most people entails the destruction of some. Lifeboat situations are described in the *Model Penal Code* as a "choice of evils," in which homicide is justified when it promotes "the very value [life] sought to be protected by the law of homicide."[64] Suppose a person,

> makes a breach in a dike, knowing that this will inundate a farm, but . . . [also that it is] the only course available to save a whole town. If he is charged with homicide of the inhabitants of the farm house, he can rightly point out that the object of the law of homicide is to save life, and that by his conduct he has effected a net saving of innocent lives. The life of every individual must be taken in such a case to be of equal value and the numerical preponderance in the lives saved compared to those sacrificed surely should establish legal justification.[65]

Lifeboat analogies with abortion are fallacious, however, because the people killed in the lifeboat are all truly innocent of creating the ethical dilemma, and the issue for the survivors is therefore one of sacrifice, not self-defense. It is justifiable homicide to sacrifice some people by killing them if there is no other way to save a "numerical preponderance" of other people. Abortion does not fit this lifeboat context, because the woman, though responsible for exposing herself to the risk that a fertilized ovum will implant itself, cannot control whether or not it will. If it does so, and she does not consent, then the fetus is imposing wrongful pregnancy. The analogy here is no longer to a lifeboat context, in which the fetus is sacrificed as an innocent party, but rather to a self-defense context, in which the fetus is stopped from harming a woman.

Abortion, therefore, invokes a principle of defense, not sacrifice. This point is too often lost because of a failure to identify the fetus as the cause of pregnancy. This failure perpetuates misunderstandings of women's right to an abortion, as illustrated by a colleague's response to the notion of women's right to consent to pregnancy: "If you invite someone to take a boat ride with you, you cannot all of a sudden just throw the person overboard." The problem with the boat ride as a metaphor for pregnancy, where presumably the woman's body is the boat and she invites the fetus to take a ride with her, lies in its many faulty assumptions. A woman who has not consented to pregnancy has not yet invited the fetus to take a ride in her body. To the contrary, the fetus is implanting itself in her body more like a stowaway, a private party to whom the woman has decidedly not given her consent. In addition, the fetus is not just a stowaway that is taking a ride in the woman's body, but rather a stowaway that is threatening the woman with serious intrusions on her liberty and massive physical injuries, if not death. Anyone faced with such a stowaway presumably has grounds for using deadly force to stop it, including calling for the Coast Guard to do so. It is legitimate, in short, for the state to protect what potential life is but not what potential life does when it coerces a woman to be pregnant. Even if the fetus were a person, it would have no right to intrude on and appropriate the body of a woman to serve its own needs. And if the fetus is not a person, any rights it might have are even more diminished.

As John Hart Ely notes, the state has a legitimate interest in protecting many entities that are alive but have no constitutional rights, such as potential life, animals, and wildlife.[66] The state protects animals from cruelty and wildlife from wanton destruction. Yet the protection of life is always limited by what life does, not just the value of what life is. The state mandates the destruction of animals when they inflict serious injury on people, and the protection of wildlife is contingent on the way wild creatures affect the property and physical security of human life. In order to sustain wildlife protection programs, conservationists must go to great lengths to demonstrate that protected forms of animal and plant life do not pose a threat to the economic livelihood, much less the lives, of people. The value of life, which our culture affirms and which the law protects, therefore, is best understood in terms of how protection of it is bounded by what life does.[67] As valuable as the fetus is as potential life, when it intrudes on a woman's bodily integrity and liberty against her will, the use of deadly force to stop it is justified, and stopping it is the job of the state.

A Relational Basis for Abortion Rights

To say that a woman is justified in obtaining an abortion and that the state is obligated to provide one is not to say that abortion is a good thing. As Mary Segers notes, "[I]n itself, abortion is a negative event, not something we joyfully celebrate with cigars and champagne, as we celebrate the birth of a baby."[68] And as Loretto Wagner, past president of Missouri Citizens for Life puts it, "[N]o one is ever going to convince me that it's all right to kill unborn babies, and I'm going to go on working to make abortion illegal."[69] Presumably most people would agree that it is not completely "all right" to kill life of any kind, particularly "babies." Advocates for basing abortion rights on choice are therefore forced to convince us that abortion is justified because it does not kill "unborn babies" but merely masses of cells that are not yet babies.

Yet according to its legal definition, a fetus is an "unborn child,"[70] and it is not uncommon for women who obtain abortions to testify to feelings of attachment to the fetus as if it were akin to a baby, even though they seek to terminate their relationship to it. As one pro-choice woman who sought an abortion stated, "I had this tiny little bit of a baby" inside of her.[71] And as another pro-choice woman stated, "I think it is entirely possible to believe that a fetus is a person—to absolutely accept that humanity of a fetus and still support abortion."[72] Still another pro-choice woman reported after having an abortion,

> I'll never forget being with three women, or six women actually. When three of them woke up, they had a general anesthesia, three of them said such things as, "Where's my baby. Is my baby dead? Will I ever have any other babies?" . . . I don't think we should minimize . . . [that] abortion does produce some concern on the part of women and we need to recognize it and say it "Yes, abortion kills a living human fetus." . . . And I think you have to call it for what it is and there's a sense of loss.[73]

Unfortunately, basing abortion rights on the notion of privacy defined by choice, rather than consent, treats abortion in terms of only one autonomous individual, making it impossible to think of pregnancy and abortion in terms of a relationship, though mounting evidence demonstrates the necessity to identify legal issues in exactly such terms.[74] Despite the profound relational reality of pregnancy and abortion, the law, as it now stands, establishes a woman's legal right to an abortion on the same individualistic grounds of decisional autonomy that guarantee her the right to read a book without interference from the state.

The current pro-choice argument could hardly be more antirelational and dissonant to communitarian ethics. Switching from a principle of choice to a principle of consent, however, recognizes that pregnancy necessarily involves a relationship between private parties, even while establishing stronger grounds for women's right not only to an abortion but also to state funding.[75]

Consent, in contrast to choice, is a relational principle. For consent to operate, there must be more than one entity. Basing abortion rights on privacy, defined as the right to consent to be pregnant, reframes those rights in relational rather than individualistic terms, compatible with the relational approach to other legal issues.[76] Laurence Tribe notes that pro-choice and pro-life forces are equally guilty of seeing only one party in the abortion debate, the woman or the fetus, respectively, while the vast majority of Americans see the complexity of an abortion picture with two beings.[77]

A consent-to-pregnancy foundation focuses on both the fetus and the woman, rather than on merely one of them. It is an example of how "legal rights are interdependent and mutually defining" when they "arise in the context of relationships among people who are themselves interdependent and mutually defining," so that "every right and every freedom is no more than a claim limited by the possible claims of others."[78] A consent-to-pregnancy foundation for abortion rights, therefore, invokes privacy as a right "to create and maintain different sorts of social relationships with different people" by exercising the right "to control who has access" to one's body and liberty.[79]

Legal scholar Mary Ann Glendon argues further that "rights talk encourages our all-too-human tendency to place the self at the center of our moral universe" and that "simplistic rights talk simultaneously reflects and distorts American culture. It captures our devotion to individualism and liberty, but omits our traditions of hospitality and care for the community."[80] Consent, however, as a relational principle offers a bridge between the individualistic self and others, thereby providing at least a bare minimum for operation of the traditions of hospitality and care for the community. We can value care, but not coerced care. Without consent, there can be no hospitality or care but only the injury of taking.

Reconfiguring rights involved in abortion shifts attention from the limits on what a woman can do to a fetus to the limits on what a fetus can do to a woman. Currently, a woman's right to choose is limited by the fetus's right to life. As a result, a woman cannot choose to have an abortion after fetal viability because of the state's protection of potential life. The fetus's right to life should rather be limited by a woman's right to defend herself against physical intrusions of her body and liberty. Such a limitation of the fetus's right to life holds even if it is a person. This approach avoids dehumanizing the fetus and isolating the pregnant woman as a totally independent individual whose only concern is to be free from state interference as she exercises her right to make choices about her own life. The consent-to-pregnancy principle for abortion rights recognizes and affirms the existence of another entity that is causing pregnancy, the fertilized ovum, and its humanity. However the fetus is socially constructed, the primary legal issue is not what it is but what it does.

We must guard against subverting the ethical dimension of pregnancy by socially constructing pregnancy as a natural physiological process. This robs abortion of its ethical component, because for an action to be ethical, a person must have the ability to consent to that act. To say that pregnancy is a natural process, even a beautiful natural process such as a sunset, implies that women should just relax and enjoy it and obviates consideration of what one human being does to another, thereby precluding consideration of the ethical relationship between a woman and a fetus. While it is certainly true that people can either enjoy or not enjoy natural processes, such as sunsets, it is not possible for a person to have an ethical relationship with a sunset.

So, too, with pregnancy. To the degree that we consider it to be something that happens automatically without human intervention, we strip it of the very component that makes it human: ethics. Like it or not, the reality is that abortion kills human life, however one constructs its stage of development and whether or not human life is synonymous with personhood. A woman's relationship with a fetus, however natural that may be, is also a relationship between two human beings. Whether women have good reasons or bad reasons for killing the fetus, their actions are justified, from an ethical vantage point, by what the fetuses do to them when they impose wrongful pregnancies, not what they are or are not in terms of a force of nature. Once the fertilized ovum is recognized as the agent responsible for the massive bodily transformations of pregnancy, the primary legal issue becomes a woman's right to consent to a relationship with this intruder, not its status as a person. Since women cannot escape from the intrusion in any other way, they are entitled to employ deadly force, as well as state assistance, to stop it, even if it the intruder acquires the highly charged label of "baby."

While *baby* may spark in all of us reflexes of nurturing and care, we must be cautious of our susceptibility to labels, including this one. As Martha Minow says, "We have tended to treat the categories we use [such as baby] as dictated by the essence of things rather than established by our decision to focus on one trait rather than another."[81] While it is not usual to focus on the fetus, much less a baby, as an intruder in relation to a woman, we need to follow Minow's advice and "reshape a category to accept or reject a new item" in order to integrate that reality into a new way of seeing the law.[82] In the case of abortion, we need to reshape our understanding of the category of fetus, and even baby, to recognize its physical intrusion on the body of a woman.

We do not need to dehumanize the fetus when basing abortion rights on a woman's consent to pregnancy because the personhood of the fetus is no longer the primary issue.[83] Rather, the fetus's agency in initiating and maintaining pregnancy is paramount. Even though a woman may decide to stop the fetus as an intruder, this does not mean that she must legally, psychologically, or emotionally negate all compassion and concern for it. Even when people are pitted against each other in what may be deadly combat, they can remain respectful of the dignity and value of the aggressor. This is preferable to the tactic of "psychic numbing," as Robert Jay Lifton terms it, whereby people rationalize aggressive action toward others by devaluing or dehumanizing the objects of their aggression, as in the Holocaust, Hiroshima, Vietnam, or war in general.[84] So, too, with abortion rights based on a consent to pregnancy, which affirm a woman's right of self-defense in relation to a fetus even while respecting the value, if not the humanity, of what is aborted. This approach is more consonant with the psychological and emotional anguish actually felt by many women when aborting a fetus.[85]

Many criticize classic liberal conceptions of individuals as autonomous agents who can freely choose their ends (values, goods, and goals) independent of their embeddedness in particular contexts from which they derive the meaning and significance of their lives.[86] A consent-to-pregnancy foundation for abortion rights avoids those pitfalls, thereby harmonizing with communitarians, who emphasize how each individual self is part of a complex set of relationships making up society and from which each person derives his or her values.[87] As a result, asocial individualism is replaced by social relationalism.[88] In the context of abortion rights, the classic liberal view denies any possible humanity of the "potential life" that is aborted.[89] A consent-to-pregnancy approach to abortion rights restores to pregnancy its inherent relational status, but not at the expense of sacrificing women's right to control their relations with others.

This approach is also more compatible with the growing concern for ecological relationships, termed eco-feminism.[90] One of its premises is that it is morally and ethically—and, it is hoped, will soon be politically and legally—wrong to view the environment, including such entities as third-world nations, as resources to be exploited at will by self-interested, autonomous individuals. Eco-feminists oppose putting women in the category of resources that are automatically available for use, if not exploitation. Pro-life arguments, which assume that a woman's body is a free good to be used and exploited by a needy fetus, lack respect for the woman whose body is so affected. The eco-feminist movement points to the danger, as well as immorality, of assuming that one may just take from the environment whatever one needs or wants. The ethical issues intensify when the environment in question is a human being's body, such as a pregnant woman's.

A consent-to-pregnancy foundation for abortion rights retrieves the reality that a woman's body is being used as a resource by a fetus. By denying the automatic right of that use, consent integrates a woman's right of self-defense against the nonconsensual use of her body with respect for her body as a valuable resource. It expands the term *wrongful pregnancy* to include those pregnancies imposed upon a woman without her consent, thereby giving more deference to the reproductive capacities of women's bodies and to the full range of their right of consent prior to any use of their bodies by fetuses, babies, or men. Religious traditions that focus on what the fetus is, therefore, miss the point. It is what the fetus does that makes a woman its victim and entitles her not only to the right to self-defense with deadly force but also to the assistance of the state to stop the fetus on her behalf.

Risks of Changing the Debate

Ellen Goodman, journalist, describes the abortion issue as one in which "every public person has staked out a position," yet one in which the "political arguments are frozen, and any movement off the mark is instantly seen as evidence — GOTCHA! — of hypocrisy or waffling. In such an atmosphere, the willingness to move is both risky and welcome."[91] The time is long overdue for moving the abortion debate from choice to consent . Many who have attempted to reframe abortion rights have refused to concede the initial premises of the opposition. Pro-life advocates claim, and some pro-choice advocates concur, that abortion rights are founded on the idea that the fetus is not a person and that were this premise to go, so, too, would abortion rights.[92] The personhood of the fetus has thus become the fulcrum around which many think the abortion issue teeters. Although the consent foundation meets these foes of abortion rights on their own ground by conceding the possibility that the fetus might be a person, this risks sinking women's rights under, with such alarmist headlines as the following:

PRO-CHOICE ADVOCATES AGREE:
THE FETUS IS A PERSON,
ABORTION IS MURDER

Yet even religious precepts, which are the main force behind the pro-life claim that the fetus is a person, fail to derail abortion rights on moral grounds once those rights are based on terms of women's right to consent to pregnancy. Religious norms generally prohibit murder, but they also generally recognize the right to self-defense.[93] Not only do Judaic precepts fail to equate full personhood with the moment of conception, but they even come close to applying the right of self-defense to the pregnant women who seek an abortion. Although the fetus is viewed as alive after forty days, it is regarded then neither as a person nor as a nonperson, but rather as "developing" life.[94]

More significantly, Moses Maimonides, the renowned medieval jurist and philosopher, applied the pursuer principle to abortion rights. According to him, the fetus is a pursuer and the pregnant woman is the pursued, and it is this element of the relationship that justifies a woman's use of deadly force. Support for this view is also found in the Jerusalem Talmud, where the argument is made for identifying the fetus as the pursuer of a pregnant woman, even though it lacks intent.[95]

Besides religious precepts and attitudes, a wide range of political views reflect how very large and diverse populations of this country have different feelings about the issue.[96] As Rosalind Petchesky and others note, public opinion on abortion is polarized in distinctive ways.[97] As one work shows, 59 percent of respondents in a national sample locate themselves in a centrist position with respect to whether the government should provide jobs, while 54 percent espouse extreme positions at either end of the approval scale on the abortion issue.[98] Yet in addition to attitudes and feelings about abortion and pregnancy, it is important to consider attitudes about consent. This book has shown how we must begin to focus on what we might call the politics of consent, and to reconceptualize women's relationship to a fetus to include a principle of consent, so that abortion represents not merely a woman's right as a bad samaritan to refuse to sacrifice herself to a fetus, but also her right as a captive samaritan to defend herself against it.

Betty Crocker versus Little Red Riding Hood

The woman's right to consent to pregnancy poses problems in seeming to undermine the standard pro-choice portrayal of abortion rights in the Betty Crocker model of motherhood.[99] Women generally decide to have an abortion on serious grounds.[100] They do not choose one in order to vacation in Bermuda or to go to beauty shops or on shopping sprees. This has been evident from the 1960s, when Sherri Finkbine, a mother and television celebrity specializing in children's programs, sought an abortion upon learning that she had taken the drug thalidomide during her current pregnancy. The impossibility of obtaining a legal abortion here led her to flee to Denmark for one, but in the process her plight and her struggle as the very embodiment of motherhood helped to educate a public reluctant even to discuss the issue.[101]

For such women, abortion stems from a desire to fulfill their traditional role as good mothers. They base their decision on whether they have the resources, emotional and economic, to be a good mother to children they already have and to children that will be born. When they feel they lack such resources, they would rather bring no child into the world than bear one that will jeopardize the lives of others or will suffer from a lack of attention and care.[102]

Yet invoking this Betty Crocker model of utilitarianism as a rationale for sacrificing a fetus to achieve a better life for other children, while emotionally appealing, has limitations. As pro-life advocates are quick to point out, a better answer to this situational problem is to provide more resources for pregnant women to sustain a pregnancy, and then, if the mother herself lacks the resources necessary to provide for the baby, to make the child available for adoption. Killing the fetus because you love it too much for it to be born becomes an unnecessary, if not illogical, solution to the goal of good mothering. In addition, the Betty Crocker argument provides no legal grounds for abortion funding, for the state is not obligated to fund a woman's choice of this method for mothering. Basing abortion rights on the justified use of deadly force to stop a fetus from imposing wrongful pregnancy runs the risk of going against the grain of most of our socialization about pregnancy. Instead of presenting pregnancy as a relationship of symbiotic beauty, it portrays it as a stark conflict between the woman and the fetus. Viewing the fetus as an aggressor runs counter to traditional family values, the harmony of family life, and women's traditional roles as wives and mothers. It might lead to attacks as:

THE AGGRESSIVE FETUS
WOMEN'S VICTIMIZATION BY FETUSES
FETAL AGGRESSION: SOCIETY'S HIDDEN VIOLENCE

Unlike the Betty Crocker approach to abortion rights, the consent foundation presents women as if they were Little Red Riding Hoods, threatened by the aggression of a fierce wolf who is camouflaged as an innocent form of life. Aside from the fact that wolves are not aggressive animals, people are unlikely to accept such a depiction of pregnancy. Few people are going to be comfortable with the idea that the fetus is not innocent but instead aggressively intrudes on a woman's body so massively that deadly force is justified to stop it.

This points to how policy change must involve change in culture and public opinion, not merely law, which ultimately is itself an interpretation of culture and public opinion.[103] As Martha Mahoney notes, culture and law are interactive,[104] so that changing policies about abortion funding require processes of education and communication combined with legal doctrine.[105] Martha Minow sees law as a community of interpreters, which includes more than courts alone.[106] To secure abortion funding on the basis of a consent-to-pregnancy approach therefore requires not only new legal arguments presented in courts but also discussions in the wide range of arenas that make up the human community. Since pregnancy, like all intimate experiences, means many things, for one of the meanings to involve the fetus as an aggressor does not rob pregnancy of its many other positive meanings. And a woman's right to consent to be pregnant acknowledges that the fetus exists with at least some attributes of a person, in lieu of the current depictions of the pregnant woman as a lone, autonomous decision maker with nothing but her own body to consider.

Self-defense and the Antimother

The consent-to-pregnancy foundation runs the final risk of portraying women as antimothers, or monsters who kill their children.[107] Viewing the fetus as a helpless baby opens the door to a dramatic portrayal of women's self-defense against that baby as a form of antimotherhood. It could lead to these headlines:

MOTHERS WHO KILL

FEMINISTS AS MURDERERS

SELF-DEFENSE: THE RIGHT TO MURDER YOUR BABY

Even pro-choice advocates sometimes find the self-defense justification for abortion distasteful. As one person said, "I am pro-choice. I'm satisfied with the way it is right now, and I don't like this idea of self-defense." Or as another pro-choice advocate once said, "I certainly didn't feel my baby was an aggressor attacking my body. I felt so close to my baby when I was pregnant that it is abhorrent to think of pregnancy the way you propose." Another person suggested "that whatever political value the notion of rights may have, the paradigm of conflicting rights seems singularly inappropriate to describe pregnancy, a condition of continuous connection and dependence."[108] Yet another person put it more bluntly, that this view of pregnancy "has nothing to do with human experience."[109]

Mary Becker, however, calls the inability or unwillingness to discuss the oppression and unhappiness of motherhood a taboo.[110] Although this particular experience of oppression and unhappiness can permanently injure a woman's health, the Court has ruled that it is constitutional for the state to protect the fetus by prohibiting the use of public resources to provide an abortion. For a woman too poor to afford an abortion herself, her experience of pregnancy is excruciating, and arguments that such a woman wishes to be a good mother or that the pregnant relationship between woman and child is beautiful do nothing to obtain for her the right to abortion funding.

The consent foundation for abortion rights does not discount the deep feelings engendered by birth and death and by pregnancy and abortion, nor does it characterize pregnancy only in aggressive, conflictual terms. While intrusive sensations are sometimes associated with pregnancy, in most cases these feelings pale beside the more pervasive feelings of togetherness with the new life. Yet the reality of the experience entailed by an abortion is that a woman does not want to be joined to the fetus. She seeks to be separated from the fetus, not to experience togetherness with it. Whatever her feelings toward the fetus, she seeks to end her relationship with it by using a technique that kills it. The issue in this context is not what pregnancy means when women celebrate their relationship with the fetus, nor even whether women have good or bad reasons for seeking an abortion. Rather, the primary question is what justifies an abortion and whether the state is obligated to pay for it.

A consent-to-pregnancy foundation answers that question on the grounds that abortion is justified by what the fetus does to a woman when it makes her pregnant, not what it is, or what her feelings might be about pregnancy, or whether she has good or frivolous reasons for seeking an abortion. However pregnancy may be represented in contexts other than abortion, the relevant context for abortion rights is the courtroom, not the nursery.[111] Legal principles guarantee that no fetus has a right to intrude on a woman's body and liberty by making her pregnant without her consent. Whatever the discomforts entailed in stretching the definition of pregnancy to include the fetus as an intruder, this definition establishes for women their right to terminate pregnancy, as well as the obligation of the state, to the degree that it stops other private parties from intruding on people's bodily integrity and liberty, to stop the fetus from imposing pregnancy without a woman's consent. We can feel compassion for the fetus, and we can even view it as a person. Nevertheless, the fetus as preborn human life does not have the right of automatic access to a woman's body, no more than does born human life. A woman's right to an abortion and to abortion funding ultimately rests most firmly on recognizing the fetus as an intruder should she not consent to the pregnancy that it imposes.

From Choice to Consent

Columnist William Safire considers abortion to be the perfect "wedge issue" for the Democrats, one that can open "a crack in the opposition's traditional support," which then allows the use of "a sledgehammer to split off a great segment of the other party's vote."[112] Certainly it was a decisive issue for voters in the 1992 presidential election. It was in Anna Quindlen's words a "stepping stone to elected office" in the midterm 1994 elections, and it is sure to be at the forefront in the 1996 presidential elections.[113] The advent of new abortion techniques, such as the drug RU486, does not reduce the centrality of the abortion issue in general. RU486, for example, brings with it both old and new problems. It can be used only within the narrowest of time frames, the side effects of cramps and bleeding may entail considerable pain and discomfort, it requires several visits to physicians, and of course there remains the issue of its public funding. Until we move from choice to consent as a foundation for abortion rights, there well be no grounds for obligating public funding of the use of RU486 as a new means for stopping preborn human life from invading women's bodily integrity and liberty. [114]

For this reason, despite the development of new technologies, we still need new ways to frame abortion rights that secure abortion funding. Even supporters of choice fall into the trap laid at the outset in *Roe*, that robs women of their full legal rights, including the right to abortion funding. The failure to see the fetus as the cause of pregnancy, and thus as the cause of the injuries of wrongful pregnancy, leads to the formulation of abortion rights in terms of the negative right to be free from state interference, rather than the positive right to receive state assistance to stop a fetus from injuring them. It influenced, for example, columnist Frank Rich, a pro-choice supporter, to define abortion rights in terms of women's right to be free of "policing uteri" policies, rather than their right to be protected by the state's police power through the public funding of abortion.[115]

Consent-to-pregnancy recasts the template of abortion rights by employing basic principles derived from the three interlocking dimensions of American politics: traditional culture, political philosophy, and legal doctrine. As Kristin Luker established, politics are founded on different conceptions of people's power relationships to each other.[116] At the heart of the abortion issue, she argues, was the "politics of motherhood." This book reframes the power issue to be the "politics of consent," the most basic principle and process underlying the American state. Despite the complexity of the American heritage of rights,[117] one of its most central and consistent features is the priority it places, both politically and legally, on people's right to consent to intrusions of their bodily integrity and liberty by others. It is time we applied these principles to abortion rights. Abortion does not stop the giving activity of the woman; it stops the taking activity of the fetus. To the degree that the state exercises its political power to stop private parties from taking the bodies and liberty of others, it must stop preborn parties from doing so by providing abortions to women who do not consent to be pregnant. With its emphasis on choice alone, *Roe* got us off the track, and it is time to get back on. Consent is a potent counterpunch to what has been the almost intractable appeal of the powerful slogan of the right to life. Hardly anyone, after all, can be against the right to life. To the extent that choice implies abortion, the advocates of choice are thus burdened with the task of deflecting the claim that they favor abortion over birth. For these and other reasons, choice has long been lamented by many of its advocates as a weak parallel to life, having less emotional, if not legal, appeal in the ensuing debates.

Conservatives, suspicious in general about the value of choice in comparison to the value of what is chosen, have held the labeling offensive for far too long. The right of choice provides no guarantees of what might be chosen. Women might choose abortion, individuals might choose to create art objectionable to some tastes, and people might choose to establish homosexual relationships — all choices that have been targets of vehement conservative attack. Consent, in contrast, not only is basic to the very conception of the American state but also is more resistant to conservative attack. Hardly anyone would support the right of one person to take things from another without the consent of the owner. Jesse Helms would hardly support legislation that allows the state to take a pint of his blood, much less legislation prohibiting the use of state resources to stop a private party from taking his body or depriving him of his liberty, without his consent, nor would Justice Antonin Scalia or Robert Bork.

The shift from a pro-choice to a pro-consent position as the legal counter to the pro-life position is also less vulnerable to attack because it uses the minimalist conceptions of the state that are endorsed by conservatives. That is, the basis of abortion rights is not women's right to be free from state interference but their right to be free from nonconsensual intrusion by the fetus as a private party. The fundamental job of the state is to stop private parties from intruding on others, and this translates into the obligation of the state to provide abortions to women as a mandatory remedy, not a discretionary benefit.

As George Bush once said, the "most compelling legacy of this nation is Jefferson's concept that all are created equal . . . . It doesn't say 'born.' . . . He [Jefferson] says 'created.' From the moment the miracle of life occurs, human beings must cherish that life, must hold it in awe, must preserve, protect, and defend it."[118] Missing from Bush's statement, as well as from statements by other pro-life advocates, is exactly how that miracle of life occurs. It occurs only on the basis of using another person's body. Yet the principle that using another person's body to preserve, protect, and defend one's own requires the consent of that other person is the basic precept of the American political system. Reframing women's reproductive rights on the basis of their right to consent to pregnancy, rather than merely their right to choose an abortion, thus draws on and activates the most cherished American political tenets. It is this move from choice to consent that gets us "from here to there," securing for all women the right both to an abortion and to abortion funding.

Notes

1 Where Do We Go From Here?

1. *Roe v. Wade*, 410 U.S. 113 (1973). For an excellent analysis of the *Roe* decision, see John Brigham, "The Supreme Court and the Laws: Reform and Reaction as Abortion Policy," *Making Public Policy* (Lexington, Mass: D.C. Heath, 1977).

2. Martha L. Minow and Aviam Soifer, "Brief Amicus Curiae," *Webster v. Reproductive Health Services, Supreme Court of the United States* (1988), p. 4. The abortion decision galvanized opposition, leading the *New Republic* to declare twelve years later that it was "the worst thing that ever happened to American liberalism [because] [a]lmost overnight it politicized millions of people and helped create a mass movement of social conservatives that has grown into one of the most potent forces in our democracy." Quoted in Lee Epstein and Joseph F. Kobylka, *The Supreme Court and Legal Change: Abortion and the Death Penalty* (Chapel Hill: University of North Carolina Press, 1992), p. 207. For an insightful analysis of how the abortion issue influences voter choices in primary and congressional electoral contests, see David Brady and Edward P. Schwartz, "Ideology and Interests in Congressional Voting: The Politics of Abortion in the U.S. Senate," *Public Choice* 84 (1995), pp. 25–48.

3. *Planned Parenthood of Southeastern Pennsylvania v. Casey*, 112 S. Ct. 2791 (1992), p. 2821 (plurality opinion reaffirming *Roe's* central premise).

4. See *Beal v. Doe*, 432 U.S. 438 (1977), p. 447 (ruling that a state did not violate federal statutory law by denying Medicaid benefits for "unnecessary" abortions); *Maher v. Roe*, 432 U.S. 464 (1977), p. 474 (upholding as constitutional a state's denial of Medicaid benefits for "unnecessary" abortions); *Poelker v. Doe*, 432 U.S. 519 (1977) (in which the Court ruled that a local law banning the performance of "unnecessary" abortions in publicly funded hospitals was constitutional); *Harris v. McRae*, 448 U.S. 297 (1980), pp. 316–317 (holding that it was constitutional for a federal law to provide benefits for maternity costs and general medically necessary services for indigent women but not for even medically "necessary" abortions).

5. See *Poelker v. Doe*, 432 U.S. 519 (1977), p. 521, and *Webster v. Reproductive Health Services*, 492 U.S. 490 (1989), p. 511 (upholding as constitutional a state's prohibition of the use of public facilities and public employees to perform abortions not necessary to preserve the life of the mother).

6. *Rust v. Sullivan*, 500 U.S. 173 (1991), pp. 192–193, 201–203 (upholding against constitutional challenges Title X regulations forbidding the use of family planning funds by any organizations that counseled, referred or encouraged abortion).

7. In a long line of cases, the Court has held that it is constitutional for a state to regulate abortions as long as the regulations did not pose an undue burden that absolutely

blocked a woman from obtaining one. See *Casey*, p. 2821 (plurality adopting the undue burden standard); *Webster*, p. 509; *Harris*, p. 314; *Maher*, pp. 473–474 (holding that *Roe* and its progeny stand for the idea that "the right protects the woman from unduly burdensome interference with her freedom to decide whether to terminate her pregnancy"); *Beal*, p. 446; *Bellotti v. Baird*, 428 U.S. 132 (1976), p. 147.

In *Casey*, the plurality summed up its view of "undue burden": "Numerous forms of state regulation might have the incidental effect of increasing the cost or decreasing the availability of medical care, whether for abortion or any other medical procedure. The fact that a law which serves a valid purpose, one not designed to strike at the right itself, has the incidental effect of making it more difficult or more expensive to procure an abortion cannot be enough to invalidate it. Only where state regulation imposes an undue burden on a woman's ability to make this decision does the power of the State reach into the heart of the liberty protected by the Due Process Clause." *Planned Parenthood of Southeastern Pennsylvania v. Casey*, 112 S. Ct. 2791 (1992), p. 2819 (plurality opinion of O'Connor, Souter, and Kennedy, JJ).

See George J. Annas, "The Supreme Court, Liberty, and Abortion," *New England Journal of Medicine* 327.9 (August 27, 1992), p. 653; Gillian E. Metzger, "Unburdening the Undue Burden Standard: Orienting Casey in Constitutional Jurisprudence," *Columbia Law Review* 94 (October 1994), pp. 2025–2040; David L. Faigman, "Reconciling Individual Rights and Government Interests: Madisonian Principles versus Supreme Court Practice," *Virginia Law Review* 78 (October 1992), pp. 1566–1571.

8. The Court held in *Casey* that the twenty-four-hour waiting period rule did not constitute an undue burden. As the Court stated, "A particular burden is not of necessity a substantial obstacle. Whether a burden falls on a particular group is a distinct inquiry from whether it is a substantial obstacle even as to the women in that group. And the District Court did not conclude that the waiting period is such an obstacle even for the women who are most burdened by it. Hence, on the record before us, and in the context of this facial challenge, we are not convinced that the 24-hour waiting period constitutes an undue burden." *Casey*, pp. 2825–2826 (overruling prior decision striking similar twenty-four hour waiting period). (Overruling, as to the twenty-four-hour waiting period, *Akron v. Akron Center for Reproductive Health, Inc.*, 462 U.S. 416 (1983).)

9. See *Casey*, p. 2843 (Stevens, concurring, objecting to the section of the plurality opinion upholding such consenting provisions where they force information upon women, regardless of each woman's informed status).

10. Though there has been some improvement recently, generally abortion training was more of an option than a requirement for medical students. Nearly one-third (31.2 percent) of American medical schools offer no training in abortion techniques, and from 1986 to 1991 the percentage of medical schools that do offer training dropped from 22.6 percent to only 12.4 percent, according to a study by Sara Rimer, "Abortion Clinics Search for Doctors in Scarcity," *New York Times* (March 31, 1993), p. A14.

11. Jerry Gray, "Republicans Agree to Back Restoration of Some Cuts," *New York Times* (March 3, 1995), p. A19.

12. See, e.g., *Eisenstadt v. Baird*, 405 U.S. 438 (1972), and *Griswold v. Connecticut*, 381 U.S. 479 (1965).

13. *Loving v. Virginia*, 388 U.S. 1 (1967).

14. *Pierce v. Society of Sisters*, 268 U.S. 510 (1925).

15. *Stanley v. Georgia*, 394 U.S. 557 (1969).
16. *Roe v. Wade*, 410 U.S. 153 (1973).
17. Ibid., p. 159.
18. Ibid., p. 158.
19. Ibid.
20. *Casey*, 112 S. Ct., p. 2821 (dispensing with *Roe's* trimester system, and thus allowing for greater regulation, but affirming viability/pre-viability distinctions).
21. Ibid.
22. See *Beal* (1977), *Maher* (1977), *Poelker* (1977), *Harris* (1980), and *Webster* (1989).
23. Roger Pilon, for example, eschews evaluating abortion rights primarily in terms of gender-based discrimination. Instead, he sees the issue as resting on the "question of whether a fetus is to be counted a person, and, more precisely, a person with rights." Pilon, "Ginsburg's Troubling Constitution," *Wall Street Journal* (June 17, 1993), p. A10. For perhaps the most philosophically complex and persuasive denial that the fetus is a person, see Ronald Dworkin, *Life's Dominion: An Argument about Abortion, Euthanasia, and Individual Freedom* (New York: Knopf, 1993).
24. Barbara Johnson, "Apostrophe, Animation, and Abortion," *Diacritics* (Spring 1986), p. 32; Jed Rubenfeld, "On the Legal Status of the Proposition that 'Life Begins at Conception,'" *Stanford Law Review* 43.3 (February 1991), pp. 599–635.
25. James L. Guth, Corwin E. Smidt, Lyman A. Kellstedt, and John C. Green, "The Sources of Antiabortion Attitudes: The Case of Religious Political Activists," in *Understanding the New Politics of Abortion*, ed. Malcolm L. Goggin (Newbury Park, Calif.: Sage, 1993), p. 44; Roger Wertheimer, "Understanding the Abortion Argument," in *The Problem of Abortion*, ed. Joel Feinberg (Belmont, Calif.: Wadsworth, 1984), pp. 49, 52.
26. Laurence H. Tribe, *Abortion: The Clash of Absolutes* (New York: Norton, 1990).
27. Technically, most medical texts consider a woman pregnant at the time of conception, and it is possible to detect the way a fertilized ovum affects a woman's body, before implantation, as early as five days after conception. For the purposes of this analysis, however, I consider the effects of the fertilized ovum on a woman's body after its implantation. Charles B. Clayman, ed., *The American Medical Association Encyclopedia of Medicine* (New York: Random House, 1989), p. 816.

As the fertilized ovum develops, it acquires a variety of labels, such as zygote, embryo, and fetus. Yet all terms share the commonality that the entity in question is making a woman pregnant, which is why its removal terminates her pregnant condition. For this reason, I often use the term *fetus* generically, rather than the specific term for its precise stage of development.
28. Legal scholar Reva Siegel makes the point that the "Court has never described the state's interest in protecting potential life as an interest in forcing women to bear children." Yet she views the source of coercion as the community, which expropriates women's bodies by restricting funds for abortions. She states that "women's lives are required to make potential life recognizable as a person," and for this reason "their labor in bearing life is a gift with which they can endow the community, not a resource the community can expropriate to its use." Siegel, "Reasoning from the Body: A Historical Perspective on Abortion Regulation and Questions of Equal Protection," *Stanford Law Review* 44.2 (January 1992), pp. 277, 371, 380. However, it is not the community that is expropriating a woman's body when she is pregnant; it is the fetus.

29. By general definition the word *fetus* refers to a "human offspring at any stage of its prenatal development, from conception to birth." In the more technical medical meaning of the term, however, *fetus* refers to the "unborn entity from roughly the eighth week of pregnancy (when brain waves can first be monitored) until birth, normally at nine months." Before eight weeks, the unborn entity is referred to medically as a fertilized ovum, a blastocyte, and later a zygote (covering the period from conception to about a week later, when it usually implants itself) and embryo (from the period when it could implant itself to eight weeks, if it does).

I follow the lead of Feinberg by using the general term *fetus* to cover the preborn entity, whatever may be its developmental stage, unless emphasis or technical reasons make other terms more appropriate. Joel Feinberg, "Abortion," *Freedom and Fulfillment: Philosophical Essays* (Princeton, N.J.: Princeton University Press, 1992), p. 37.

30. *Roe*, p. 119.

31. This is precisely the point of some pro-life advocates, such as Representative Henry Hyde, who would prohibit abortions virtually without exceptions, even for women impregnated by a fertilized ovum subsequent to rape or incest. "Now, rape and incest are tragedies," says Hyde. "Nobody says they are not. But why visit on the second victim, the unborn child that is the product of that criminal act, capital punishment?" Quoted in Adam Clymer, "Anti-Abortion Rally: Comeback Victory in Congress Sends a Warning to Pro-Choice Lawmakers," *New York Times* (July 3, 1993), p. A6.

32. Frances M. Kamm, *Creation and Abortion: A Study in Moral and Legal Philosophy* (New York: Oxford University Press, 1992).

33. Quoted in Donald P. Judges, *Hard Choices, Lost Voices: How the Abortion Conflict Has Divided America, Distorted Constitutional Rights, and Damaged the Courts* (Chicago: Ivan R. Dee, 1993), p. 287. According to Beverly Harrison, an "abortion is a negative, therapeutic, or corrective act, not an act of positive moral agency at all." Harrison, *Our Right to Choose: Toward a New Ethic of Abortion* (Boston: Beacon Press, 1983), p. 9.

34. Few, however, take the dramatic step of moving from a pro-choice to a pro-life position, as did Norma McCorvey, who was Jane Roe in *Roe v. Wade*. Sam Howe Verhovek, "New Twist for a Landmark Case: Roe v. Wade Becomes Roe v. Roe," *New York Times* (August 12, 1995), pp. A1, A9.

Some women do affirm that the process of making the decision to have an abortion helped them develop a sense of their own autonomy and self-worth, even if the abortion procedure itself holds no intrinsic value. Patricia Lunnenborg, for example, interviewed forty-seven abortion providers and fifty-seven women who had abortions and concluded that many women experience abortion in conjunction with feelings of personal growth, empowerment, and self-reliance. Lunnenborg, *Abortion: A Positive Decision* (New York: Bergin & Garvey, 1992), pp. 43, 93. In contrast, Rita Townsend and Ann Perkins describe the decision to have an abortion as one that creates isolation, shame, the desire for secrecy, and the feeling that none of the existing reasons for choosing an abortion are sufficiently good ones, testifying to the degree of concern for the values and the consequences of what is involved on the part of women who nevertheless do choose to have an abortion. Rita Townsend and Ann Perkins, eds., *Bitter Fruit: Women's Experiences of Unplanned Pregnancy, Abortion, and Adoption* (Alameda, Calif.: Hunter House, 1991).

35. Judith Jarvis Thomson, "In Defense of Abortion," reprinted in *Rights, Restitution, and Risk*, ed. W. Pavent (Cambridge, Mass.: Harvard University Press, 1986).

36. Donald H. Regan, "Rewriting *Roe v. Wade,*" *Michigan Law Review* 77 (1979), and F. M. Kamm, *Creation and Abortion: A Study in Moral and Legal Philosophy* (New York: Oxford University Press, 1992).

37. Philosopher Frances Kamm makes the same point from the perspective of moral rights and responsibilities. *Creation and Abortion*, pp. 173–175.

38. Tribe, *Abortion: The Clash of Absolutes.*

39. Mary Ann Glendon, "When Words Cheapen Life," *New York Times* OP-ED, (January 10, 1995), p. A19, and *Dred Scott v. Sandford*, 60 U.S. (19 How.) 393 (1856).

40. Ibid.

41. The Rev. Richard John Neuhause, "The Pro-Life Cause: How We Will Know When We Have Won," speech delivered at "The Future of the Pro-Life Movement: A Symposium," Harvard Law School (February 18, 1995), transcript pp. 1–4, 6.

42. Some state courts have allowed a "justification defense," which "argues that an action is justified when it prevents a greater harm, in this case, the killing of fetuses," in trials involving violence perpetrated by those opposed to providing or obtaining abortions, but these rulings have usually been reversed on appeal. Ronald Smothers, "Judge Won't Let Accused in Clinic Attack Argue that Killing Was Justified," *New York Times* (October 5, 1994), p. A18.

In the case of Paul Hill, a former Presbyterian minister and abortion protester, who was convicted on federal charges of killing two people and wounding a third while attempting to block the procurement of legal abortions, Judge Vinson gave wide latitude to develop a defense on the grounds that the fetus is a person; he ultimately ruled that "any such justification claim was 'strained at best'" on the grounds that "because abortion up to 26 weeks after conception is legal and not viewed by the law or society as a recognizable harm, there can be no justification for violence aimed at stopping it." Ronald Smothers, "Abortion Protester Is Guilty under Clinic Access Law," *New York Times* (October 6, 1994), p. A18.

43. The ethical issue between self-defense and lifeboat options is neatly presented in the work of Robert Jay Lifton. He points out that one technique for justifying the killing of people is simply to declare them to be subhuman, or not quite human. In his view, dehumanization destroys everyone—those who are the victims and those who are the perpetrators. To treat other people as if they were not persons desensitizes people not only to the humanity of others but also to their own humanity. For example, the institution of slavery victimizes not only those who are the slaves but also those who do the enslaving. While slaves are the obvious victims, so, too, are the masters of slaves, for they lose their humanity by perpetrating acts that negate the humanity of others. Robert Jay Lifton, *Death in Life: Survivors of Hiroshima* (Chapel Hill: University of North Carolina Press, 1991); Lifton, *The Genocidal Mentality: Nazi Holocaust and Nuclear Threat* (New York: Basic Books, 1990); Lifton, *Home from the War: Learning from Vietnam Veterans* (Boston: Beacon Press, 1991). See Michael Walzer for an exposition on why war need not entail dehumanization of the enemy. Walzer, *Just and Unjust Wars: A Moral Argument with Historical Illustrations* (New York: Basic Books, 1977).

44. As the work of Carol Gilligan and others show, women are more likely than men to frame issues in relational dimensions of care and responsibility rather than instru-

mental ones that emphasize their rights and boundaries. Gilligan, *In a Different Voice: Psychological Theory and Women's Development* (Cambridge, Mass.: Harvard University Press, 1982).

45. For a powerful pro-choice policy statement from a person who believes a "fetus is different from an appendix or a set of tonsils," and as potential life deserving of "respect, caution, indeed . . . reverence," see address by Governor Mario Cuomo of New York on "Religious Belief and Public Morality," September 13, 1984, Notre Dame University.

46. For an excellent analysis of marital rape exceptions in terms of Fourteenth Amendment equal protection guarantees, see Robin West, "Equality Theory, Marital Rape, and the Promise of the Fourteenth Amendment," *Florida Law Review* 42.1 (January 1990), pp. 45–79.

47. Anna Quindlen, "Going Nowhere," *New York Times* (June 23, 1993), p. A23.

48. As a prominent philosopher asserts, for example, "The fetus can hardly be portrayed as an aggressor." Kamm, *Creation and Abortion*, p. 176.

49. Kristin Luker, *Abortion and the Politics of Motherhood* (Berkeley: University of California Press, 1984).

50. *Casey*, p. 2859 (Rehnquist, concurring in part and dissenting in part) (quoting *Michael H. v. Gerald D.*, 491 U.S. 110 (1989), p. 124, n.4) (plurality opinion).

51. As one law scholar put it. Personal correspondence.

2   Immaculate Pregnancy

1. *Roe v. Wade*, 410 U.S. 113 (1973), p. 146.

2. Ibid., pp. 129–152, 160–163.

3. Ibid.

4. Leonard Glantz concurs that the primary reason the Court ruled that the fetus was not covered by the Fourteenth Amendment was because it was not yet born. Leonard Glantz, "Is the Fetus a Person? A Lawyer's View," *Abortion and the Status of the Fetus*, ed. William B. Bondeson, H. Tristram Engelhardt, Jr., Stuart F. Spicker, and Daniel H. Winship (Dordrecht, Netherlands: D. Reidel, 1983), pp. 107–108. See Susan R. Burgess, *Contest for Constitutional Authority: The Abortion and War Powers Debates* (Lawrence: University Press of Kansas, 1992), chap. 2, "Departmentalism and Judicial Activism: The Abortion Debate."

5. *Roe*, p. 157.

6. Ibid., p. 158.

7. Ibid.

8. *Beal v. Doe*, 432 U.S. 438 (1977), p. 443.

9. Ibid., pp. 444–445. Similarly, in a dissent from the *Harris v. McRae* ruling that a state may withhold Medicaid benefits to poor women who seek abortion costs even while funding pregnancy costs, Justices Brennan, Marshall, and Blackmun state, "A poor woman in the early stages of pregnancy confronts two alternatives: she may elect either to carry the fetus to term or to have an abortion." *Harris*, 448 U.S. 297 (1980), p. 333.

10. *Planned Parenthood of Southeastern Pennsylvania v. Casey*, 112 S. Ct. 2791 (1992), p. 2811 (plurality).

11. Ibid., p. 2817.

12. Ibid., p. 2824.

13. Ibid., p. 2830.

14. Ibid., p. 2831.

15. Ibid., p. 2842 (Stevens, J., concurring in part and dissenting in part).

16. See *Roe*, 410 U.S. 113, p. 159.

17. Ibid., p. 150.

18. Ibid., p. 158.

19. Ibid. Marriage, of course, is a relationship between two people, but in the context of the right to privacy, the right to choose whom to marry refers only to that of a single individual's right to choose whom to marry. Obviously, it is necessary that the person so chosen reciprocate in kind for a marriage actually to take place.

20. Ibid.

21. Ibid., p. 159.

22. Ibid.

23. In *Roe*, the definition of viability was connected to fetal development: a "fetus becomes 'viable'" when it is "potentially able to live outside the mother's womb, albeit with artificial aid." *Roe*, p. 160. The Court noted that "[v]iability is usually placed at about seven months (28 weeks) but may occur earlier, even at 24 weeks." *Roe*, p. 160. The Court thus initially in 1973 attached a trimester framework to the definition of viability. The Court eventually dropped the trimester framework, but not the viability standard. In *Webster v. Reproductive Health Services*, 492 U.S. 490 (1988), p. 518 (opinion of Rehnquist, J.), Chief Justice Rehnquist, along with Justices White and Kennedy, argued that the trimester system should be abandoned. In *Casey*, 112 S. Ct. 2791, p. 2818, Justices O'Connor and Souter joined Justice Kennedy in dispensing with the trimester framework. Chief Justice Rehnquist and Justices Scalia and Thomas did not join them, presumably because they wanted to overrule *Roe* altogether. See *Casey*, p. 2860 (Rehnquist, C.J., dissenting).

Thus, as it currently stands, a majority of the Court no longer supports the trimester system. As the plurality in *Casey* put it, "[w]e reject the trimester framework, which we do not consider to be part of the essential holding of *Roe*." *Casey*, p. 2818. The focus is now on what the *Casey* plurality viewed to be the key issue in *Roe*: viability. According to that opinion, "[t]he woman's right to terminate her pregnancy before viability is the most central principle of *Roe v. Wade*." *Casey*, p. 2817.

24. *Roe*, p. 160. The Court affirmed in *Webster* the definition of viability as "the point at which the fetus 'has the capability of meaningful life outside the mother's womb,'" *Webster*, p. 515. The problems involved in determining if a fetus actually is viable or not have not been solved by the Court.

25. See *Casey*, p. 2817.

26. *Roe*, p. 164.

27. Ibid., pp. 164–165.

28. *Webster*, p. 515, quoting *Colautti v. Franklin*, 439 U.S. 379 (1979), p. 386.

29. Ibid., p. 516.

30. *Casey*, p. 2803.

31. Ibid., p. 2804.

32. Ibid.

33. Ibid., p. 2811.

34. Ibid., pp. 2811–2812.

35. Ibid., pp. 2811–2812; emphasis added.

36. Ibid., p. 2849, citing *Webster*, pp. 553–554 (Blackmun, J., dissenting).

37. Ibid., p. 2816.

38. Ibid., p. 2817.

39. *Roe*, 410 U.S. 113, pp. 146–147 n.40.

40. *Doe v. Bolton*, 410 U.S. 179 (1973), p. 208; emphasis added.

41. *Harris v. McRae*, 448 U.S. 297, pp. 350–351 n.2 (1979) (describing *Bolton*).

42. Ibid., p. 340 (Marshall, J., dissenting).

43. *Simopoulous v. Virginia*, 462 U.S. 506 (1983), p. 520n. (Stevens, J., dissenting).

44. *Casey*, 112 S. Ct. 2791, p. 2826; emphasis added.

45. Ibid., p. 2870 (Rehnquist, C. J., concurring and dissenting).

46. Congress prohibited the use of federal funds for abortions either by means of an amendment to the annual appropriations bill for the Department of Health, Education and Welfare or by a joint resolution.

47. *Harris*, 448 U.S. 297, p. 302.

48. Ibid. (citing Pub. L. 96-123, § 109, 93 Stat. 926). This 1980 version of the Hyde Amendment also specifies that such rape or incest must have been reported promptly to a law enforcement agency or public health service. Ibid. The Court noted that there were three different versions of the Hyde Amendment, one of which was more restrictive because it did not include the rape and incest exception, and another that was broader because it included more exceptions based on danger to women's health. *Harris*, pp. 302–303. In *Harris*, the Court used the term "Hyde Amendment" to refer generically to all three versions of the Hyde Amendment, except where indicated otherwise (p. 303 n.4).

49. *Roe*, p. 152.

50. *Casey*, p. 2807.

51. Ibid.

52. *Harris*, p. 354. (Stevens, J., dissenting).

53. *General Electric v. Gilbert*, 429 U.S. 125 (1976), p. 130.

54. Ibid.

55. Ibid., p. 130.

56. Ibid., p. 142.

57. *Casey*, p. 2807.

58. See Justice Blackmun's dissent in *Beal*, 432 U.S. 438, pp. 448–449.

59. *Roe*, p. 125.

60. *Minor v. Happersett*, 88 U.S. (21 Wall.) 162 (1874), p. 167.

61. *Beal*, p. 446.

62. *Maher v. Roe*, 432 U.S. 464 (1977), p. 478.

63. Ibid., pp. 473–474; emphasis added.

64. Ibid., p. 478.

65. Henry Campbell Black, *Black's Law Dictionary*, 6th ed. (St. Paul, Minn.: West, 1990), p. 1179; emphasis added.

66. As I previously discussed (Chapter 1, note 27), a fertilized ovum begins to affect a woman's body from the moment of conception, and it is possible to detect its effects as early as five days after conception. Charles B. Clayman, ed., *American Medical Association Encyclopedia of Medicine* (New York: Random House, 1989), p. 816. For this rea-

son, most medical opinion considers a woman to be pregnant at the point of conception, assuming, of course, that conception occurs within her body. Most diagnostic tests for pregnancy, however, detect how the fertilized ovum affects a woman's body after the point of its implantation.

67. *Casey*, p. 2807; emphasis added.

68. Susan R. Estrich and Kathleen M. Sullivan, "Abortion Politics: Writing for an Audience of One," *University of Pennsylvania Law Review* 138.1 (November 1989), p. 126.

69. Ibid.

70. Ibid.

71. "Immaculate conception" in religious theology refers to the conception of Mary without original sin, not the virgin birth of Jesus, who was conceived without the physical agency of a man in relation to a virgin woman, Mary. Some theologians, such as Episcopal Bishop John Shelby Spong, point out, however, that the notion of Mary's immaculate conception developed in response to the Augustinian premise that the sin in life, evil, was "located in the flesh" and "transmitted through sex"; see Spong, *Born of a Woman: A Bishop Rethinks the Birth of Jesus* (New York: Harper, 1992), p. 216. As Spong characterizes Augustine's views, "The sins of the fathers and mothers were quite literally passed to the new life through sexual intercourse that resulted in conception" (p. 216).

The only way to equip Jesus with sinlessness, therefore, was to base his birth on the "virgin status" of his mother. This premise led inevitably backward to the "doctrine of the Immaculate Conception, which guaranteed that Mary's human flesh was not corrupted by Eve's sin," which meant that Mary also had been conceived without the agency of a human man and, therefore, that Mary was "pure" of original sin as a precondition for her preparation "to be the womb of the new creation [Jesus]" (pp. 216–217). As Spong notes, "When the dogma of the Immaculate Conception was promulgated in 1854 by Pius IX, Mary was said to have been 'preserved immaculate from all stain of original sin by the singular grace and privilege granted her by Almighty God'" (pp. 217–218).

The use of the term *immaculate pregnancy* in this context is meant to connote representations of biological conception that take place without the necessary involvement of physical agents.

72. *Casey*, p. 2821.

73. Ibid., pp. 2796–2797.

74. Viability does not mean deliverability but only that the fetus has some chance of surviving outside the womb with the aid of technological support. For this reason, viability is most accurately defined not in terms of the age of the fetus or its stage of development but rather in terms of the state of medical technology available to support the fetus outside the womb. The definition of what constitutes viability will change in the years to come as medical technology improves. Alan Zaitchik, "Viability and the Morality of Abortion," in *The Problem of Abortion*, ed. Joel Feinberg (Belmont, Calif.: Wadsworth, 1984), pp. 59–60.

75. Robert D. Goldstein, *Mother-Love and Abortion: A Legal Interpretation* (Berkeley: University of California Press, 1988), p. 105, n.2.

76. John Noonan, Jr., *A Private Choice: Abortion in America in the Seventies* (New York: Free Press, 1979), p. 124.

77. H. Tristram Engelhardt, "Introduction," in Bondeson et al., *Abortion and the Status of the Fetus*, p. xv.

78. Wayne R. LaFave and Austin W. Scott, Jr., *Criminal Law*, 2nd ed. (St. Paul, Minn.: West, 1986), p. 197.

79. Quoted ibid., p. 198, fn. 24.

80. W. Page Keeton, Dan B. Dobbs, Robert E. Keeton, and David G. Owen, *Prosser and Keeton on the Law of Torts*, 5th ed. (St. Paul, Minn.: West, 1984), pp. 1–26.

81. LaFave and Scott, *Criminal Law*, p. 13.

82. Ibid., p. 198, fn.

83. Ibid., p. 198.

84. Ibid.

85. Ibid., p. 399.

86. Ibid., p. 385.

87. If, for example, one person shoots another, that person is the objective cause of the other's death and, according to law, has committed homicide. Whether that person is held criminally responsible for the homicide, however, depends on the "absence or presence of legal justification or excuse for the shooting." To decide that question, the legal system asks three logically ordered questions: Did the defendant cause the death of the deceased? If yes, is the defendant criminally responsible for the homicide? If yes, what is the grade or degree of his guilt? The defendant must be acquitted if the answer to either the first or the second question is negative. Rollin M. Perkins and Ronald N. Boyce, *Criminal Law*, 3rd ed. (Mineola, N.Y.: Foundation Press, 1982).

88. Other statutes require that the person must know that the property received is stolen, and some legislation assumes that people are guilty of receiving stolen property if they had reason to know, even if they did not know, that the property was stolen. LaFave and Scott, *Criminal Law*, p. 213.

89. Ibid., pp. 212–213.

90. What is more, we must remember that the condition of pregnancy serves the immediate survival needs of the fetus, not the woman. It is the fetus whose development and continued existence depends on keeping a woman pregnant. While born people may wish to exercise the option to continue their presence in the form of offspring genetically and socially connected to them, the very fact that they are born signifies that their own immediate lives do not require the condition of pregnancy to sustain them. By contrast, the fetus does not merely intrude upon a woman's body as an incompetent actor, but as one who directly and specifically benefits from taking her body. As philosopher Frances M. Kamm notes, this gives the woman more rather than less justification for terminating pregnancy with an abortion. Kamm, *Creation and Abortion: A Study in Moral and Legal Philosophy* (New York: Oxford University Press, 1992), pp. 128–145.

91. For a powerful and insightful analysis of women's abortion rights from the perspective of the uniqueness of pregnancy, see Drucilla Cornell, *The Imaginary Domain: Abortion, Pornography and Sexual Harassment* (New York: Routledge, 1995), chaps. 1–2.

92. *Casey*, 112 S. Ct. 2791, p. 2806.

93. *Congressional Record*, 102nd Cong., H2845 (April 30, 1992).

94. Expanding the legal framework for what Catharine MacKinnon terms the "abortion controversy" (p. 1317) addresses her point that the "similarly situated" doctrine "continues to control access to equality claims" (p. 1297) that women are able to make. While

it is true that "[n]o men are denied abortions" (p. 1321), it has been difficult to show how women are "similarly situated" to men but treated differently. See MacKinnon, "Reflections on Sex Equality under Law," *Yale Law Journal* 100.5 (March 1991), pp. 1281–1328. Moving from choice to consent, however, recasts how we characterize women's situation compared to that of men. Reframing pregnancy as the right to consent to have one's body used by another person, including a potential person, situates men and women on similar ground, where pregnant women must have the same rights to bodily integrity currently available to nonpregnant women and men.

3   Separating Sex and Pregnancy

1. Most medical texts chart the way in which a fertilized ovum changes a woman's body from the moment of conception and, hence, consider a woman pregnant at conception. Laboratory pregnancy tests are designed to detect human chorionic gonadotropin (HCG), which greatly increases in production soon after the fertilized ovum implants itself in the cell lining of a woman's uterus, which is perhaps why it is reasonable to view implantation as the onset of pregnancy. Levels of HCG are accurate indicators not only of a woman's pregnant condition but also of the probability of a spontaneous abortion or ectopic pregnancy. Robert A. Hatcher, Felicia Stewart, James Trussell, Deborah Kowal, Felicia Guest, Gary K. Stewart, and Willard Cates, eds., *Contraceptive Technology, 1990–1992*, 15th rev. ed. (New York: Irvington, 1990), pp. 432–433.

2. As Joel Feinberg notes, by general definition the word *fetus* refers to a "human offspring at any stage of its prenatal development, from conception to birth." I will follow the lead of Feinberg by using the general term *fetus* to cover the preborn entity, whatever may be its developmental stage, unless emphasis or technical reasons make other terms more appropriate. Feinberg, "Abortion," *Freedom and Fulfillment: Philosophical Essays* (Princeton, N.J.: Princeton University Press, 1992), p. 37.

3. Edward J. Ozog, "When the Roof Falls In: Defining 'Occurrence' in Property Insurance," *Section of Tort and Insurance Practice of the American Bar Association* 19 (Winter 1990), brief 8, pp. 1–43.

4. As Guido Calabresi puts it, a causal link is "entirely predictive and empirical," meaning that the recurrence of an act or activity will "increase the chances that the injury will also occur." Calabresi, "Concerning Cause and the Law of Torts: An Essay for Harry Kalven, Jr.," *University of Chicago Law Review* 43 (1975–76), pp. 71–72.

5. W. Page Keeton, Dan B. Dobbs, Robert E. Keeton, and David G. Owen, *Prosser and Keeton on the Law of Torts*, 5th ed. (St. Paul, Minn.: West, 1984), p. 264.

6. Ibid.

7. Another term for legal cause is *proximate cause*, and the term *legal cause* is used here to mean proximate cause. Ibid., pp. 263–266.

8. Everyday opinion can usually identify the factual causes of an event. For this reason, courts usually assign to juries the task of defining the wide array of events that can be considered factually related to why an event occurred. The "classic test for determining cause in 'fact' directs the 'factfinder' to compare what did occur with what would have occurred if hypothetical, contrary-to-fact conditions had existed." The notion of cause implies that it is a "*necessary* antecedent" of an event, without which the event "would not have occurred." An act (or its omission) "is not regarded as a cause of an event

if the particular event would have occurred without it." The failure to put up a railroad crossing signal, for example, cannot be called a "cause" of a crash by an automobile into a train if the driver runs into the sixty-eighth car of the train. Similarly, a farmer cannot claim that the presence of a railroad embankment caused the flooding of his land during a cloudburst if his land would have been flooded anyway. Ibid., pp. 265–266.

9. Calabresi, "Concerning Cause and the Law of Torts," p. 71.

10. Ibid., p. 72.

11. Also termed the proximate cause. Keeton et al., *Prosser and Keeton*, p. 266. The legal or proximate cause of something, usually determined by juries, is that which the law decides is sufficient for liability. Ibid., p. 273. Hence it is a policy decision, not something the law identifies as an objective fact.

12. Henry Campbell Black, *Black's Law Dictionary*, 6th ed. (St. Paul, Minn: West, 1990), p. 1225. As the Court of Appeals of Louisiana defined proximate cause in *Hebert v. United Gas Pipe Line Co.*, 210 So.2d, 71, 74 (La. App. 1968) (quoting 65 C.J.S. Negligence § 103), it is the legal cause, or, that cause "which is involved [in] the idea of necessity . . . [the] one from which the effect must follow" as a matter of absolute necessity.

13. As discussed, some definitions of pregnancy define it as a condition commencing with the presence of a fertilized ovum in a woman's body, that is, with conception. And, to the degree that a woman's body does respond to the presence of a fertilized ovum before implantation, it is possible to extend the definition of pregnancy to include the period between conception and implantation. It is not until after implantation, however, that the changes in a woman's body resulting from a fertilized ovum reach the level necessary for the diagnosis of pregnancy. For this reason, the definition used here for pregnancy commences with implantation. From the standpoint of the law, this identification of the fertilized ovum as the initiator of a pregnant condition opens the door to its legal designation as the proximate cause of pregnancy.

14. When conception occurs inside a woman's body, we could define pregnancy as a condition commencing prior to implantation at the point when the fertilized ovum begins to affect her body. For purposes of analysis here, however, the effects of the fertilized ovum are considered at the point of implantation.

An appellate court in Louisiana distinguished proximate cause from remote cause in an often-cited tort case. A remote cause is necessary for the existence of the effect, ruled the court, but it "does not necessarily imply the existence of the effect." *Hebert*, 210 So.2d., p. 74 (quoting 65 C.J.S. § 103 at 1131). In *Hebert*, a gas pipeline company dug a canal in a pasture leased by a cattleman, after securing the cattleman's permission to do so. The work had the effect of isolating the lessee's cattle from fresh water and additional grazing land. All but two of the cattle subsequently died. The cattleman sued the gas pipeline company, claiming that the construction of the canal was the "proximate cause of the death of the cattle." *Hebert*, p. 74.

15. Ibid., pp. 74–75.

16. The Louisiana court noted that although a "person may be negligent in the performance or omission of some duty owed to the person injured, no liability attaches unless it appears that there was a causal connection . . . [which was] the proximate or legal cause of the injury, rather than a remote cause, or one merely causing a condition providing an opportunity for other causal agencies to act." *Hebert*, p. 74 (quoting 65 C.J.S. Negligence § 104, p. 1135).

17. Leon Speroff, Robert H. Glass, and Nathan G. Kase, *Clinical Gynecologic Endocrinology and Infertility*, 5th ed. (Baltimore: Williams & Wilkins, 1994), chap. 7, "Sperm and Egg Transport, Fertilization, and Implantation," pp. 231–250. Implantation of a fertilized ovum, of course, can occur in other places than a woman's uterus; these types of implantation cause a pregnant condition that is immediately life threatening to a woman. Implantation of a fertilized ovum in the uterus is what we mean by normal pregnancy, which usually does not involve a direct threat to a woman's life.

18. *Restatement (Second) of the Law of Torts* (Philadelphia: American Law Institute, 1965) (1963–1964 main vol.), chap. 16, § 442(a).

19. Prosser and Keeton et al., *Law of Torts*, p. 453.

20. Ibid.

21. These techniques are part of the explosion of expanding reproductive choices in the United States. Andrea L. Bonnicksen, *In Vitro Fertilization: Building Policy from Laboratories to Legislatures* (New York: Columbia University Press, 1989), p. 7.

22. Speroff et al., *Gynecologic Endocrinology*, p. 235.

23. James W. Knight and Joan C. Callahan, *Preventing Birth: Contemporary Methods and Related Moral Controversies* (Salt Lake City: University of Utah Press, 1989), p. 99.

24. Contrary to popular belief, sperm do not "swim" to the fertilization site. Sperm can swim only approximately one inch per hour. Given the anatomical distances involved, it would take sperm six to eight hours to reach an oviduct, and sperm do not have the energy required for such movement. Thus, sperm transport is achieved by the "contractile activity of the female reproductive tract, perhaps aided by prostaglandin F_{2a} present in the semen." The motile activity of the sperm is reserved for penetration of the egg at the fertilization site in the oviduct. Ibid., pp. 96–97.

25. Within ten to twenty-four hours after sperm enter the woman's uterus, for example, leukocytes appear in the uterus in large numbers to counteract their presence. Most of the sperm that die have not yet been transported through the uterus to the oviduct and so are removed by the leukocytes by means of phagocytosis. Ibid., p. 98.

26. C. W. H. Havard, ed., *Black's Medical Dictionary*, 37th ed. (London: A & C Black, 1992), p. 131.

27. Ibid., p. 131. Pregnancy is defined as the "period from conception to birth" by Charles B. Clayman, *The American Medical Association Encyclopedia of Medicine* (New York: Random House, 1989), p. 813. Pregnancy is defined as "the state of a female after conception and until termination of the gestation" by Edward C. Hughes, *The American College of Obstetricians and Gynecologists: Obstetric-Gynecologic Terminology* (Philadelphia: F. A. Davis, 1972), p. 327.

28. Speroff et al., *Gynecologic Endocrinology*, p. 241; Clayman, *American Medical Encyclopedia*, p. 816.

29. As Twiss Butler asks, what does pregnancy "show" us about a woman? She answers, "Pregnancy is a physical fact which precludes privacy . . . . [It shows] [t]hat a woman is manifestly not a virgin. Moreover, that she has been invaded by a man and visibly subjugated and colonized." Butler, "Abortion Law: 'Unique Problem for Women' or Sex Discrimination?" *Yale Journal of Law and Feminism* 4.1 (Fall 1991), p. 139. Our culture does assume that a pregnant woman is not a virgin and has been invaded by a man; however, the more accurate way to look at a pregnant woman is to assume that she has

been invaded by a fertilized ovum, which has transformed her body from a nonpregnant to a pregnant condition, and that she may or may not have been "invaded" by a man as a necessary, but not sufficient, cause of that process.

30. Barbara Katz Rothman's view that the fetus is a part of a woman's body, for example, establishes grounds for why children cannot sue their mothers for prenatal injuries. Rothman, *Recreating Motherhood* (New York: Norton, 1989). In Nancy E. Field's opinion, the fetus juridically is indistinguishable from other bodily tissue. See Field, "Evolving Conceptualizations of Property: A Proposal to De-commercialize the Value of Fetal Tissue," *Yale Law Journal* 99.1 (October 1989), p. 170. Laura R. Woliver notes that reproductive technologies, including IVF and surrogacy policies, have the potential for undermining abortion rights because they highlight views of the fetus as a separate entity from the woman and alter perceptions of fetal viability, which is a key principle on which current abortion rights are founded. See Woliver, "The Influence of Technology on the Politics of Motherhood," *Women's Studies International Forum* 14:5 (1991), pp. 483–485.

31. *Roe v. Wade*, 410 U.S. 113 (1972), p. 159.

32. Ibid., p. 158.

33. *Planned Parenthood of Southeastern Pennsylvania v. Casey*, 112 S. Ct. 2791 (1992), p. 2804.

34. Some might protest that separating a child from a mother during birth is a natural process, whereas severing a finger is not. Yet if a natural force such as lightning strikes a tree, separating it into two parts, we would not consider the two parts to be two separate trees merely because their separation occurred as a consequence of a natural process.

35. Some definitions of pregnancy include conception, and vice versa. According to some contemporary medical authorities, "[C]onception begins not with fertilization, but rather six to seven days later when the fertilized egg becomes implanted in the uterine wall." Quoted in Susan R. Estrich and Kathleen M. Sullivan, "Abortion Politics: Writing for an Audience of One," *University of Pennsylvania Law Review* 138.1 (November 1989), p. 128. For this reason, many accepted contraceptives operate after fertilization by foiling the process of implantation, as does RU486. Thus, many legal scholars note that there is no "bright physiological line" separating a before-and-after conception point, and the distinction between conception and abortion blurs. Ibid., pp. 126–127.

Yet the most significant legal point is that pregnancy is a condition *resulting from* what the fetus does to a woman when it makes her pregnant. From the standpoint of both law and medicine, however one defines conception, what makes a woman pregnant is when her body begins to change *as a result* of a fertilized ovum.

36. The law does not draw the distinction between probability and cause. Rather, the definition of cause includes "all antecedents which contribute to a given result." Rollin M. Perkins and Ronald N. Boyce, *Criminal Law*, 3rd ed. (Mineola, N.Y.: Foundation Press, 1982), p. 771. This means that the term *cause* "'includes all things which have so far contributed to the result as to be essential to it.'" Perkins and Boyce citing Prosser, "Proximate Cause in California," 38 *Calif. L. Rev.* 369 (1950), p. 375. By this standard, jogging in Central Park is a cause of mugging and rape since it is necessary to be in Central Park for attacks to occur there. Because the number of antecedent causes of any event

are legion, the law distinguishes between types of causes to identify those that are the primary ones. While jogging in Central Park is a factual cause, the muggers and rapists are the primary, or proximate, cause. For our purposes, we can think of factual causes as risks that set up the probability that primary causes will ensue.

37. There are some contexts in which a person's acceptance of the risk of injury may stand for his or her inability to claim damages for injury should it occur, but these contexts do not involve the intrusion of one's bodily integrity, liberty, or even property. If people agree to use a product that they know involves a risk to their health, for example, they may not be able to sue the makers of the product for injury should injury follow its use. For a definitive philosophical explanation of why the relationship between risk and responsibility in the context of pregnancy does not negate women's abortion rights, see F. M. Kamm, *Creation and Abortion: A Study in Moral and Legal Philosophy* (New York: Oxford University Press, 1992), chap. 5.

38. Stanley Holmes, "Pregnancy Law Covers Infertility, Suit Claims," *Chicago Tribune* (March 28, 1994), pp. 1–2.

39. Speroff et al., *Gynecologic Endocrinology*, p. 809.

40. Ibid., p. 810.

41. Ibid., p. 817.

42. Ibid., p. 811.

43. One woman is reported to have delivered a spontaneous pregnancy at the age of fifty-seven; another is reported to have delivered six children after the age of forty-seven, the last at the age of sixty-two. Ibid., p. 812.

44. Allen J. Wilcox, Clarice R. Weinberg, and Donnan D. Baird, "Timing of Sexual Intercourse in Relation to Ovulation: Effects on the Probability of Conception, Survival of the Pregnancy, and Sex of the Baby," *New England Journal of Medicine* 333.23 (December 7, 1995), p. 1517.

45. Ibid.

46. Ibid.

47. Ibid., p. 1519.

48. One day out of twenty-eight, 1/28, or .0357.

49. The probability of randomly selecting the one day of ovulation out of twenty-eight days is .0357 multiplied by .33, which is the probability that conception follows intercourse on the day of ovulation. This results in a maximum .0118 probability that intercourse on any random day of the ovulatory cycle will be followed by conception. The probability is .0036 for the fifth day prior to ovulation, using the probabilities associated with each day of the six-day fertile period provided by Wilcox et al. Ibid.

50. This figure is based on probabilities provided by Wilcox et al., who calculated that over the six-day fertile period of a woman's ovulatory cycle the following probabilities of conception, beginning with the fifth day before ovulation: .10, .16, .14, .27, .31, .33. The average probability of conception over the whole twenty-eight day period, therefore, is .0468 (these probabilities added and then divided by 28). Ibid.

51. After six months, the figure jumps to 72 percent; after one year, it is 85 percent. Speroff et al., *Gynecologic Endocrinology*, p. 817.

52. Ibid.

53. Ibid., p. 842.

54. Havard, *Black's Medical Dictionary*, p. 131.

55. L. Beil, "One-third of Pregnancies May Miscarry," *Science News* 134 (August 6, 1988), p. 86.

56. Allen J. Wilcox et al., "Incidence of Early Loss of Pregnancy," *New England Journal of Medicine* 319.14 (July 28, 1988), pp. 189–194.

57. Pierre Soupart estimates that it takes an average of four months of continual sexual activity to establish a pregnancy capable of producing a normal offspring because 16 percent of the ova fail to be fertilized at all, 42 percent of the embryos are lost within the first two weeks, leading to a loss of 69 percent of the total human ova exposed to spermatozoa by the expected time of birth. Though estimates vary somewhat, medical knowledge supports the contention that sexual intercourse alone is far from a necessary and sufficient condition for pregnancy. Soupart, "Present and Possible Future Research in the Use of Human Embryos," *Abortion and the Status of the Fetus*, ed. William B. Bondeson, H. Tristram Engelhardt, Jr., Stuart F. Spicker, and Daniel H. Winship (Dordrecht, Netherlands: D. Reidel, 1983), p. 79.

58. George P. Fletcher, *A Crime of Self-Defense: Bernhard Goetz and the Law on Trial* (New York: Free Press, 1988), p. 15.

59. Feinberg, *Freedom and Fulfillment*, pp. 69–70.

60. Laura R. Woliver, "Rhetoric and Symbols in the Pro-life Amicus Briefs to the *Webster* Case," paper presented at the Annual Meeting of the American Political Science Association, Chicago, 1992, p. 12. George J. Agich claims that the fetus generates a signal that terminates pregnancy, thereby supporting this view. See Agich, "Science, Policy, and the Fetus: Comments on Walters and Biggers," in *Abortion and the Fetus*, p. 45.

61. *Black's Law Dictionary*, pp. 608, 1207.

62. Ibid., pp. 184, 1013.

63. The complete definition of *mother* is "A woman who has borne a child. A female parent. The term includes maternity during prebirth period." The complete definition of *father* is "A male parent. He by whom a child is begotten. Natural father; procreator of a child." The term *beget* is defined as "To procreate as the father," for which there appears to be no counterpart for women. Ibid., pp. 155, 608, 1013.

64. *The Compact Edition of the Oxford English Dictionary*, vol. 1 (Oxford: Oxford University Press, 1971), p. 69.

65. Tennyson, *Love & Duty* 7 (1842), ibid., quoted p. 69.

66. Canne, *Necess. Separ.* (1849), 242 (1634), ibid., quoted p. 69.

67. Spurgeon, *Treas. Dav.* (1870) p. xliv; Heading, ibid., p. 969.

68. Scott, *Jrnl.* (1890), II.25 (1827), ibid., quoted p. 69.

69. Baring-Gould, *Bk. of West*, I, xii, 208 (1899), ibid., quoted p. 1858.

70. C. E. B., *Work for All* (1868), ibid., quoted p. 1858.

71. *Scribner's Magazine*, 15, 555/1 (1878), ibid., quoted p. 1858.

72. Sherry F. Colb, "Words that Deny, Devalue, and Punish: Judicial Responses to Fetus-Envy?" *Boston University Law Review* 72:1 (January 1992), p. 101.

73. Psychoanalysts suggest that the biological exclusion of men from such major phases of reproduction as pregnancy causes anxiety, which leads to compensatory customs that insert men into the reproductive process of giving birth. The "couvade" is such a custom. As Jacques Gélis writes, in the couvade, the woman leaves her bed immediately after birth, and "the man then takes her place in the bed and 'lives through' the birth: he writhes and moans; his face distorted with pain; when the 'labour' is over, the

baby is given to him to cuddle and soothe. . . . It is he who receives the congratulations of visiting friends—and the presents." Gélis notes that psychoanalysts attribute the couvade to "man's anxiety to procreate." As early as the seventeenth century, for example, some doctors assumed that "during the wife's pregnancy the man suffers the same indispositions as does she." Gélis, *History of Childbirth: Fertility, Pregnancy and Birth in Early Modern Europe*, trans. Rosemary Morris (Boston: Northeastern University Press, 1991), pp. 37–38.

74. Everett Carll Ladd, *The Ladd Report #8: Abortion: The Nation Responds* (New York: Norton, 1990), pp. 21–22.

75. Kathleen M. Sullivan, "The Justices of Rules and Standards," *Harvard Law Review* 106.1 (November 1992), p. 32.

76. Pierre Bourdieu argues that language is not merely a capacity to speak but also a tool for the social construction of value. The process of using language constitutes a linguistic marketplace, complete with competition for participation and the linguistic terms used for debate. It is a serious suggestion, therefore, that we reword questions on public opinion polls to reflect a new social construction of pregnancy, one that depicts the fetus as the aggressor who imposes injury as a basis for assessing women's right to stop it by means of an abortion. Bourdieu, *Language and Symbolic Power* (Cambridge, Mass.: Harvard University Press, 1991).

77. Colb, "Words that Deny," pp. 101–103.

78. Conversation with Jason Wittenberg.

79. For an excellent analysis of the impact of reproductive technology on the law's treatment of parenthood, see Marjorie Maguire Shultz, "From Informed Consent to Patient Choice: A New Protected Interest," *Yale Law Journal* 95.2 (December 1985), pp. 219–299.

80. Nancy Gibbs, "In Whose Best Interest?" *Time* (July 19, 1993), pp. 44–50.

81. Elizabeth Bartholet, "Blood Parents vs. Real Parents," *New York Times* (July 13, 1993), p. A19.

82. Some speak of *gestational pregnancy*, but that term refers to fetal development rather than the condition of pregnancy itself, which refers to a woman's body. For that reason, I prefer the term *pregnancy parenthood*. It is perhaps exactly because men have no control over whether a woman is made pregnant that cultural depictions of men's procreative powers are inflated as a way to compensate for men's lack of agency. We can speculate that the legal reification of men as the impregnators of women stems from a cultural necessity to include men in a phase of parenthood, pregnancy, from which they are profoundly excluded. Another effort to include men in "pregnancy parenthood" is reflected in the contemporary tendency for heterosexual couples to speak about "their pregnancies" and for men to refer to themselves and their female partners as "we" in the context of pregnancy, as in "we are pregnant." Conversation with Gwill York and Paul Maeder.

4   Consent to Pregnancy

1. Henry Campbell Black, *Black's Law Dictionary*, 6th ed. (St. Paul, Minn.: West, 1990), p. 305.

2. Ibid.

3. Ibid.

4. Ibid.

5. As Mary Anne Case notes, "Law is precisely that which fights nature. If something were all that natural, a law would not be needed to bring it about." Case, "Of Richard Epstein and Other Radical Feminists," *Harvard Journal of Law and Public Policy* 9.39 (April 25, 1995), p. 375.

6. Pro-life bumper sticker.

7. The preamble to the Missouri statute at issue in *Webster* declared the fetus to be a person from the moment of conception. *Webster v. Reproductive Health Services*, 492 U.S. 490 (1988), p. 501. The Court refused to rule on the constitutionality of a state's designation of the fetus since the question was not at issue. *Webster*, pp. 507–508. Michael S. Simon, "'Honey, I Froze the Kids': Davis v. Davis and the Legal Status of Early Embryos," *Loyola University Chicago Law Journal* 23.1 (Fall 1991), p. 136.

8. Ibid., pp. 136–137. A natural person is a living human being. A juridical person is an entity that may have rights and obligations, including the ability to sue and be sued; this term normally is used to describe the legal status of corporations.

According to the minutes of the meeting of the Louisiana Senate Judiciary Committee on May 13, 1986, under Louisiana law there are two types of persons: natural persons and juridical persons. The Louisiana statutes on IVF define an "in vitro fertilized human ovum" to be a "juridical person" and a "biological human being." As such, fertilized ova are entitled to sue and be sued, and curators may be appointed to protect their rights. If the egg and sperm donors "renounce their parental rights for in utero implantation," fertilized ova must be made available for "adoptive implantation." A fertilized ovum is considered "viable" after it develops over a thirty-six hour period, at which point it cannot be "intentionally destroyed." Finally, the state of Louisiana charges the physician or medical facility with the responsibility and duty of "safekeeping." Any disputes involving fertilized ova are to be resolved according to their "best interest." Patricia A. Martin and Martin L. Lagod, "The Human Preembryo, the Progenitors and the State: Toward a Dynamic Theory of Status, Rights, and Research Policy," *High Technology Law Journal* 5.2 (Fall 1990), pp. 270–271.

The Louisiana statutes declare that a fertilized ovum ceases to be a juridical person once implanted into a woman's uterus. Because the statute deals with IVF, and the woman's right to bodily integrity has not yet been implicated, the state may assert its interest in protecting the fertilized ovum. The statute revokes the juridical person status of the fertilized ovum at the point of implantation. Louisiana Senate Committee on Judiciary A, Minutes of Meeting of May 13, 1986, p. 8 (regarding Senate Bill No. 701).

9. Donald H. Regan, "Rewriting *Roe v. Wade*," *Michigan Law Review* 77.7 (August 1979), p. 1641.

10. Tristram Engelhardt notes that modern technology transforms what we might think of as the "blind forces of nature" into processes under the human control of the medical field. Engelhardt, "Concluding Remarks," in *Abortion and the Status of the Fetus*, ed. William B. Bondeson, H. Tristram Engelhardt, Jr., Stuart F. Spicker, and Daniel H. Winship (Dordrecht, Netherlands: D. Reidel, 1983), p. 335. Although Andrew Kimbrell reminds us that we need to strike a balance between social and biological nature and technological control, pregnancy primarily is a relationship between human beings, the fetus and the woman, not an automatic, natural, physiologic process. Kim-

brell, *The Human Body Shop: The Engineering and Marketing of Life* (San Francisco: Harper, 1993), pp. 295–296.

As Reva Siegal notes, "[H]uman reproduction is not simply a physiological process; like eating and dying, it is a social process, occurring in and governed by culture." To assume that reproduction is a form of "physiological naturalism" inhibits "judicial scrutiny of the social norms and practices that shape reproduction and its regulation." Siegel, "Reasoning from the Body: A Historical Perspective on Abortion Regulation and Questions of Equal Protection," *Stanford Law Review* 44.2 (January 1992), pp. 267–268.

11. Or entity, such as a corporation.

12. Kim Lane Scheppele and Jeremy Waldron, "Contractarian Methods in Political and Legal Evaluation," *Yale Journal of Law and the Humanities* 3.2 (1991), p. 196.

13. Daniel R. Ortiz, "Privacy, Autonomy, and Consent," *Harvard Journal of Law and Public Policy* 12.1 (Winter 1989), pp. 93–94.

14. Sanford Levinson, *Constitutional Faith* (Princeton, N.J.: Princeton University Press, 1988), p. 113; Nancy J. Hirschmann, *Rethinking Obligation: A Feminist Model for Political Theory* (Ithaca, N.Y.: Cornell University Press, 1992), p. 22. For a critical account of the rise of consent theory in seventeenth-century England, see Don Herzog, *Happy Slaves: A Critique of Consent Theory* (Chicago: University of Chicago Press, 1989).

15. Levinson, *Constitutional Faith*, p. 113.

16. We see this in the case of monetary incentives used by the government to encourage, some say to coerce, women to embed the contraceptive Norplant in their bodies. The economic vulnerability of poor women raises the question of whether their choice to accept economic inducements is in any real sense a choice between assent or refusal. Current debates over Norplant policies, therefore, reflect the significance we attribute to consent in our political system. Even when positive incentives are used to encourage women to implant Norplant, such as financial benefits, critics raise objections based on the idea that such financial inducements for women who are financially deprived are a form of coercion, which undermines their ability to consent to Norplant.

17. Carole Pateman, *The Sexual Contract* (Stanford, Calif.: Stanford University Press, 1988).

18. See Catharine MacKinnon, "Feminism, Marxism, Method, and the State: Toward a Feminist Jurisprudence," in *Feminist Legal Theory: Readings in Law and Gender*, ed. Katharine T. Bartlett and Rosanne Kennedy (Boulder, Colo.: Westview, 1991), pp. 187–195.

19. See Carole Pateman, *The Disorder of Women: Democracy, Feminism, and Political Theory* (Stanford, Calif.: Stanford University Press, 1989); Pateman, *The Problem of Political Obligation: A Critical Analysis of Liberal Theory* (New York: Wiley, 1979); Pateman, *Sexual Contract*.

20. Nancy J. Hirschmann, *Rethinking Obligation: A Feminist Method for Political Theory* (Ithaca, N.Y.: Cornell University Press, 1992), pp. 22–23. Don Herzog also notes that many situations are characterized as a combination of consensual and nonconsensual relations (Herzog, *Happy Slaves*, p. 230).

21. Carole Pateman, "Women and Consent," *Political Theory* 8.2 (May 1980), p. 157.

22. David J. Garrow, *Liberty and Sexuality: The Right to Privacy and the Making of Roe v. Wade* (New York: Macmillan, 1994). Others make similar points. See Rosalind

Pollack Petchesky, *Abortion and Women's Choice: The State, Sexuality, and Reproductive Freedom*, rev. ed. (Boston: Northeastern University Press, 1990), and Cass R. Sunstein, *The Partial Constitution* (Cambridge, Mass.: Harvard University Press, 1993).

23. Frauke Schnell, "The Foundations of Abortion Attitudes: The Role of Values and Value Conflict," in *Understanding the New Politics of Abortion*, ed. Malcolm L. Goggin (Newbury Park, Calif.: Sage, 1993), pp. 25–26.

24. In 1965 in *Griswold v. Connecticut*, 381 U.S. 479 (1965), p. 485, the Court ruled that a state may not prohibit the distribution, sale, or use of contraceptives to married couples. In 1972 the Court extended that ruling to include all single adults. *Eisenstadt v. Baird*, 405 U.S. 438 (1972), p. 453 (holding that "whatever the rights of the individual access to contraceptives may be, the rights must be the same for the unmarried and the married alike").

25. W. Page Keeton, Dan B. Dobbs, Robert E. Keeton, and David G. Owen, *Prosser and Keeton on the Law of Torts*, 5th ed. (St. Paul, Minn.: West, 1984), p. 113.

26. As Holly M. Smith contends, a woman does not waive her moral right to the use of her body by a fetus merely because she has consented to sexual intercourse. See, e.g., Smith, "Intercourse and Moral Responsibility for the Fetus," in Bondeson et al., *Abortion and the Status of the Fetus*, pp. 229–239. In contrast, many pro-life advocates believe that abortion starts with control over one's sexuality and that if women controlled their bodies sexually, they would not get pregnant. Donald G. Mathews and Jane Sherron De Hart, *Sex, Gender, and the Politics of ERA: A State and the Nation* (Oxford: Oxford University Press, 1990), p. 158. Although true to a point, this argument misses the most significant point: even if women do expose their bodies to the risk that a fetus will make them pregnant, that exposure does not stand for consent to the injuries of wrongful pregnancy. To the contrary, failure to control one's body in a relationship with a man does not stand for consent to engage in a pregnancy relationship with another entity, the fetus.

27. Keeton et al., *Prosser and Keeton*, p. 480.

28. Ibid., p. 481.

29. Ibid.

30. See, e.g., *Allstate Insurance Co. v. State Farm Mutual Automobile Insurance Co.*, 195 S.E.2d 711 (S.C.: 1973), p. 713; emphasis added.

31. Once people indicate their lack of consent, even when one might reasonably infer consent, the law no longer recognizes consent as being present. Once a woman indicates her lack of consent to engage in a sexual relationship with a man, one can no longer infer from her behavior an implicit consent to do so. Even though a "continued course of practical joking" between people, for example, "may permit the inference that there is leave to continue it further . . . [once] notice is given that all such conduct will no longer be tolerated," people are "no longer free to assume consent." Keeton et al., *Prosser and Keeton*, p. 114.

32. The law recognizes that "conditional or limited consent is no consent at all beyond the terms of the condition or the boundaries indicated." Rollin M. Perkins and Ronald N. Boyce, *Criminal Law*, 3rd ed. (Mineola, N.Y.: Foundation Press, 1982), p. 1076.

33. Consent to one thing does not necessarily signify implied consent to a "different or additional thing." For this reason, "consent even to prolonged kissing and hugging is not [in and of itself] consent to sexual intercourse," particularly when a woman explic-

itly indicates her lack of consent. Consequently, "[I]f a man forces sex upon an unwilling female, it is no defense to rape that she did not object to his lesser advances." Perkins and Boyce, *Criminal Law*, pp. 1076–1077, citing as an example *State v. Myers*, 606 P.2d 250 (Utah 1980) (holding that woman who engaged in "necking" with the defendant before he raped her did not "consent" to the rape).

34. *Planned Parenthood of S.E. Penn. v. Casey*, 112 S. Ct. 2791 (1992)(plurality), p. 2807.

35. Thomas C. Key and Robert Resnik, "Maternal Changes in Pregnancy," in *Obstetrics and Gynecology*, 5th ed., ed. David N. Danforth and James R. Scott (New York: Lippincott, 1986), p. 327.

36. At the point of implantation, the fertilized ovum is also called a blastocyst or trophoblast. In the text following, however, the term *fertilized ovum* will be used rather than the more technical terms that refer to specific stages in its development.

37. C. W. H. Havard, ed., *Black's Medical Dictionary*, 36th ed. (Savage, Mo: Barnes & Noble Books, 1990), p. 550.

38. Ibid.

39. Legally, an "aggressor" is the "party who first offers violence or offense," *Black's Law Dictionary*, p. 65.

40. Immediately after the ovum is fertilized, the zygote begins rapid cell division, though without growth, so that with each progressive division, "each of the cells (blastomeres) becomes smaller." James W. Knight and Joan C. Callahan, *Preventing Birth: Contemporary Methods and Related Moral Controversies* (Salt Lake City: University of Utah Press, 1989), p. 100. Once the conceptus, or zygote, has reached the sixteen- to thirty-two-cell state, it resembles a mulberry and, for this reason, is termed a *morula*. "In humans, the conceptus progresses to the morula stage while still *within the oviduct*, a process which requires approximately two or three days" (p. 100; emphasis added). The developmental requirements of the morula necessitate that it enter the uterus and implant itself on the lining.

41. Shortly after the blastocyst implants itself on the uterus, its inner mass of cells differentiates into three specialized layers of cells, which ultimately, if its implantation continues, pass through an embryo stage, during which time cells differentiate into such bodily components as neural tissue, epidermis of the skin, receptor cells of sense organs, and the epithelium of organs. Ibid., pp. 101–102.

42. The trophoblastic cells of the conceptus. Ibid., p. 101.

43. The blastocyst maintains its penetrating implantation by stimulating the corpus luteum to continue producing progesterone. Ibid., p. 101.

44. It is termed *trophoblast* at this point.

45. Harold Fox, "Placental Structure in Health and Disease," in *Modern Antenatal Care of the Fetus*, ed. Geoffrey Chamberlain (London: Blackwell Scientific, 1990), pp. 35–36.

46. Now termed *cytotrophoblast*.

47. "The circulation in this early placenta is necessarily sluggish and the pressure of blood extremely low. This is desirable because *penetration of an arteriolar* structure by the early trophoblast would presumably release blood into this primitive placenta at a pressure that might dislocate the ovum. The *perforation* of maternal blood vessels by the syncytiotrophoblast also allows human chorionic gonadotropin to be directly *injected into*

the maternal circulation." Irwin H. Kaiser, "Fertilization and the Physiology and Development of Fetus and Placenta," in Danforth and Scott, *Obstetrics and Gynecology,* p. 300.

48. Ibid., p. 311.

49. Ibid., pp. 304–305.

50. Peter J. McParland and J. Malcolm Pearce, "Uteroplacental and Fetal Blood Flow," in Chamberlain, *Modern Antenatal Care,* pp. 89–126.

51. Richard S. Abrams, *Handbook of Medical Problems during Pregnancy* (Norwalk, Conn.: Appleton & Lange, 1989), p. 113.

52. Kaiser, "Fertilization and the Fetus," p. 314.

53. Ibid., p. 316.

54. Ibid., pp. 311–312.

55. Abrams, *Handbook of Medical Problems,* p. 45.

56. When the fertilized ovum perforates the maternal blood vessels, for example, this perforation allows human chorionic gonadotropin to be "directly injected into the maternal circulation," as noted above. This chorionic gonadotropin "converts the corpus luteum in the ovary into a corpus luteum of pregnancy." This conversion prevents the "withdrawal of hormonal support from the endometrium," thereby "allowing the continuation of the pregnancy," which "results in failure to menstruate." Kaiser, "Fertilization and the Fetus," pp. 300–302.

57. At this stage, medically termed *trophoblast.*

58. Such as pregnancy-specific ß-1 glycoprotein (PSßG).

59. Kaiser, "Fertilization and the Fetus," p. 312.

60. Thomas C. Key and Robert Resnik, "Maternal Changes in Pregnancy," in Danforth and Scott, *Obstetrics and Gynecology,* pp. 327–328.

61. Ibid., pp. 329–334.

62. Ibid., pp. 334–338.

63. *Black's Law Dictionary,* p. 918. See, e.g., *Brazo v. Connecticut Real Estate Commission,* 418 A.2d 883 (Conn. 1979), p. 890.

64. *Black's Law Dictionary,* p. 918. The Court has used the way in which the Constitution guarantees the right to liberty in relation to the state as the foundation for the right to an abortion. The Fifth and Fourteenth Amendments prohibit the government from depriving people of their liberty without due process. The Court has interpreted this to mean that no state may use arbitrary procedures to interfere with a person's liberty or to interfere with certain basic, substantive liberties, however difficult it may be to define exactly what such basic liberties might encompass.

In 1973, the Court did rule that the constitutional right to privacy includes a woman's right to make decisions about the use of her own reproductive capacities, including her choice to terminate her pregnancy by means of an abortion prior to fetal viability. *Roe v. Wade,* 410 U.S. 113 (1973), p. 153. This means that prior to viability it is an unconstitutional infringement of a woman's liberty for the state to interfere with her decisional autonomy about her choice to have an abortion. Ibid., p. 164. The Court later ruled in *Casey* that it was constitutional for the government to regulate procurement of any and all abortions by means of regulations specifying twenty-four-hour waiting periods, elaborate informed consent procedures, and other such restrictions. *Casey,* 112 S. Ct., pp. 2822–2826.

For a comprehensive and incisive analysis of the constitutional right to privacy, see Laurence H. Tribe, *American Constitutional Law*, 2nd ed. (Mineola, N.Y.: Foundation Press, 1988), chap. 15, "Rights of Privacy and Personhood."

65. Samuel D. Warren and Louis D. Brandeis, "The Right to Privacy," *Harvard Law Review* 4.5 (December 15, 1890), pp. 193–196.

66. Tribe, *Constitutional Law*, p. 1302.

67. Black, *Law Dictionary*, p. 919.

68. Christopher Wolfe, "Natural Law," in *The Oxford Companion to the Supreme Court of the United States*, ed. Kermit Hall et al. (New York: Oxford University Press, 1992), p. 581.

69. Tribe, *Constitutional Law*, p. 1688(n. 18-1).

70. Black, *Law Dictionary*, p. 1388.

71. Ibid.

72. Nicky Hart, "Procreation: The Substance of Female Oppression in Modern Society," *Contention: Debates in Society, Culture and Science* 1.1 (Fall 1991), pp. 89–101, 109. For another excellent analysis of how coerced pregnancy constitutes severe qualitative intrusion, see Robert P. Goldstein, *Mother-Love and Abortion: A Legal Interpretation* (Berkeley: University of California Press, 1988).

73. David Haig, "Genetic Conflicts in Human Pregnancy," *Quarterly Review of Biology* 68.4 (December 1993), p. 496.

74. Ibid.

75. While some have noted the analogy between slavery and pregnancy, the role of the fetus as the enslaver remains obscure. For a superb analysis of the application of the Thirteenth Amendment to the abortion issue, see Andrew Koppelman, "Forced Labor: A Thirteenth Amendment Defense of Abortion," *Northwestern University Law Review* 84.2 (Winter 1990), pp. 485, 487, 493–494. Koppelman, however, does not place weight on *who* is the enslaver, the fetus or the state; it is sufficient for his purposes to say simply that the woman is serving the fetus involuntarily by invoking a victim-based, rather than perpetrator-focused, interpretation of the Thirteenth Amendment. While some African-American feminists' sensibilities may find offensive the equation of slavery with coerced pregnancy, the National Black Women's Health Project views abortion rights, including funding, as a "matter of survival" for poor women. Byllye Avery, "A Question of Survival / A Conspiracy of Silence: Abortion and Black Women's Health," in *From Abortion to Reproductive Freedom: Transforming a Movement*, ed. Marlene Garber Fried (Boston: South End Press, 1990), p. 76.

76. An exception is Koppelman's fine analysis of the slavery argument application to abortion rights in "Forced Labor," pp. 480–535.

77. I am indebted to an anonymous reviewer for pointing out this objection to the use of slavery as a principle in the abortion debate.

78. Abrams, *Handbook of Medical Problems*, pp. 46–47.

79. Acute "renal failure can result from volume contraction due to prolonged nausea and vomiting," and in later pregnancy, blood loss "from concealed or overt uterine hemorrhage" can result in acute renal failure. Ibid., pp. 65–67.

80. Ibid., p. 114.

81. Ibid., p. 137.

82. Ibid., p. 145.

83. While donation of one's body lies outside the "duty to care," the same is not true of material resources. Grounds that guarantee women's right to consent to the donation of their bodies in pregnancy, therefore, do *not* extend to fathers a right to consent to donate their economic resources in support of their offspring. See Monique Vinet Imbert, "The Golden Egg: In Vitro Fertilization Produces Adjudication," *Rutgers Computer and Technology Law Journal* 17.2 (1991), pp. 504–512; Susan Moller Okin, *Justice, Gender and the Family* (New York: Basic Books, 1989); and Martha Fineman, "Dominant Discourse, Professional Language, and Legal Change in Child Custody Decisionmaking," *Harvard Law Review* 101.4 (February 1988), pp. 727–774.

84. Nor has any state or the federal government passed a law that requires parents to donate body parts to born children, even in the case of such minimally invasive parts as a pint of blood. It is open to speculation whether such legislation, if ever passed, would pass as constitutional after scrutiny by the Supreme Court. In the case of fetuses, however, there is no law that obligates women to give their bodies to them, so the situation is one in which the fetus takes a woman's body without her consent. While it might be constitutional for a state to require parents to donate their bodies to their offspring, it is inconceivable that it would be constitutional for a state to mandate that offspring may take parts of their parents' bodies without consent.

85. Richard A. Posner, *The Problems of Jurisprudence* (Cambridge, Mass.: Harvard University Press, 1990), p. 350.

86. Sissela Bok, "Ethical Problems of Abortion," in *The Problem of Abortion*, 2nd ed., ed. Joel Feinberg (Belmont, Calif.: Wadsworth, 1984), p. 191.

87. Donald Regan makes the point that the key to all duty-to-aid cases is that the relationship is entered into on a voluntary basis. For example, a common carrier has a duty to aid in relation to passengers, the master of a ship to members of the crew, a jailer to his prisoner, innkeepers to their guests, storeowners to their customers, employers of all kinds to their employees, schools to their pupils, and so forth. There is no duty to aid, however, without first establishing the voluntary nature of the relationship on a principle of consent; without consenting to engage in a relationship in the first place, there is no relationship. Regan, "Rewriting *Roe v. Wade*," *Michigan Law Review* 77 (1979), p. 1593.

88. *Black's Law Dictionary*, p. 551.

89. See *Roe*, 410 U.S., p. 146 n.40 (quoting from the ABA's Uniform Abortion Act).

90. Judith Jarvis Thomson, "In Defense of Abortion," reprinted in *Rights, Restitution, and Risk*, ed. W. Parent (Cambridge, Mass.: Harvard University Press, 1986), p. 19.

91. Laurence H. Tribe, *Abortion: The Clash of Absolutes* (New York: Norton, 1992), p. 103.

92. Richard A. Posner, *Sex and Reason* (Cambridge, Mass.: Harvard University Press, 1992), p. 333.

93. Ian A. Hunter, "The Canadian Abortion Quagmire: The Way In and a Way Out," *Canadian Family Law Quarterly* 6 (1990), pp. 57, 76.

94. Emily Martin, "The Egg and the Sperm: How Science Has Constructed a Romance Based on Stereotypical Male-Female Roles," *Signs* 16.3 (1991), pp. 485–501, and Martin, *The Woman in the Body: A Cultural Analysis of Reproduction* (Boston: Beacon Press, 1992).

95. Robert Baker, "'Pricks' and 'Chicks': A Plea for 'Persons,'" in *Sexist Language: A*

Modern Philosophical Analysis, ed. Mary Vetterling-Braggin (Totowa, N.J.: Littlefield, Adams, 1981).

96. Perhaps the work of David Haig develops such masculine perspectives most fully. He argues that there is competition and conflict at all stages of the reproductive process, including the immune reaction of the woman's body at the gamete transport phase, when sperm are deposited in her body. As he notes, "[I]t is common to assume that pregnancy is a cooperative enterprise between mother and child. But there is very little evidence for that." Instead, Haig sees a competition, if not conflict, between the mother and the fetus in which the "fetus benefits by extracting as much nutrition as it can use from the woman," and the woman responds by striking "a balance between nourishing the fetus and keeping resources for herself and her future children." Marc Lipsitch, "Genetic Tug-of-War May Explain Many of the Troubles of Pregnancy," *New York Times* (July 20, 1993), p. C3. See also Haig, "Genetic Conflicts in Human Pregnancy," *Quarterly Review of Biology* 68.4 (December 1993), p. 495.

Barbara Duden also makes the point that the social construction of the fetus has commonly involved aggressive metaphors. She notes that the August 1990 issue of *Life* magazine, for example, uses language that implies agency to the fertilized ovum (blastocyst), as if it "attempt[s]" to do things, "feel[s] its way for a comfortable home," is "free to attach itself anywhere," "is picky" and "decide[s]" where to implant itself, and "communicate[s]" with the woman. As the text reads, "The blastocyst is attempting to pass through the narrowest opening of the fallopian tube just before entering the uterus . . . . Gliding into the uterus . . . feeling its way for a comfortable home to spend the next 39 weeks. . . . Although now free to attach itself anywhere, the blastocyst is picky and may take as many as three days to decide on a spot, usually near the uterine ceiling . . . . The blastocyst has landed! Like a lunar module, the embryo facilitates its landing on the uterus with leg-like structures composed of sugar molecules on the surface." Quoted in Barbara Duden, *Disembodying Women: Perspectives on Pregnancy and the Unborn*, trans. Lee Hoinacki (Cambridge, Mass.: Harvard University Press, 1993), pp. 13–14.

97. We find such relational and mothering language in the work of Barbara Katz Rothman, who sees the nurturing bond between mother and child as a basis for analyzing reproductive rights. See Rothman, *Recreating Motherhood: Ideology and Technology in Patriarchal Society* (New York: Norton, 1989). Similarly, the work of Jennifer Nedelsky exemplifies efforts to recast the language of autonomy and individualism, if not conflict, into that of responsible relational norms. See Nedelsky, "Reconceiving Autonomy: Sources, Thoughts and Possibilities," *Yale Journal of Law and Feminism* 1.1 (Spring 1989), pp. 7–36, and Nedelsky, "Reconceiving Rights as Relationships," paper delivered at University of Alberta Law School, 1992.

98. Lynn Paltrow, the Director of Special Litigation of the Center for Reproductive Law and Policy, for example, considers it an "anti-choice" position to assert that "fetuses have rights separate from and hostile to the woman." Letter to the Editor, *New York Times* (December 22, 1993), p. A22. See also, Cynthia R. Daniels, *At Women's Expense: State Power and the Politics of Fetal Rights* (Cambridge, Mass.: Harvard University Press, 1993).

99. The case of assisted suicide hovers on the borderline of what the law allows. Generally, the law does not condone suicide, yet the law also recognizes the right to die. These two policies collide head on when terminally ill patients seek death by suicide

rather than merely the refusal of medical treatment. See Seth F. Kreimer, "Does Pro-Choice Mean Pro-Kevorkian? An Essay on Roe, Casey, and the Right to Die," *American University Law Review* 44.3 (February 1995), pp. 830–840; Julia Pugliese, "Don't Ask—Don't Tell: The Secret Practice of Physician-assisted Suicide," *Hastings Law Journal* 44.6 (August 1993), p. 1293.

100. Some might argue that the definition of pregnancy proffered here resurrects old-fashioned legal reasoning premised on rigid principles of boundaries, ownership, and individual power, a tactic of dubious merit just when legal reasoning that appeals to relational, contextual references is making some inroads. Joseph William Singer, "Sovereignty and Property," *Northwestern University Law Review* 86.1 (Fall 1991), pp. 1–56; Singer, "Property and Coercion in Federal Indian Law: The Conflict between Critical and Complacent Pragmatism," Southern California Law Review 63.6 (September 1990), pp. 1821–1841; Jack M. Beermann and Joseph William Singer, "Baseline Questions in Legal Reasoning: The Example of Property in Jobs," *Georgia Law Review* 23.4 (Summer 1989), pp. 911–995; Martha Minow, *Making All the Difference: Inclusion, Exclusion, and American Law* (Ithaca, N.Y.: Cornell University Press, 1990).

101. Others, such as Daniel Ortiz, while noting the gains to be made by relational feminism that eschews "autonomy-talk," make the point that relational feminism "cannot well achieve much of what the feminist legal agenda demands" on the abortion issue. As a result, feminists must smuggle in autonomy-talk to resolve inherent tensions between relational feminism and abortion rights as the only response that can work. See Ortiz, "In a Diffident Voice: Relational Feminism, Abortion Rights, and the Feminist Legal Agenda," paper presented at Cornell Law School, April 1992.

102. For some, this involves viewing prenatal and postnatal life in terms of their behavioral and psychological continuities, in which the fetus is like a newborn baby. John T. Noonan, Jr., *A Private Choice: Abortion in America in the Seventies* (New York: Free Press, 1978), pp. 160–161.

103. See Dorothy E. Roberts, "Motherhood and Crime," *Iowa Law Review* 79.1 (October 1993), pp. 96–97, 100; and Martha L. A. Fineman, "Feminist Theory and Law," *Harvard Journal of Law and Public Policy* 18 (Spring 1995), p. 349.

5 Wrongful Pregnancy

1. *Roe v. Wade*, 410 U.S. 113 (1973), p. 163.

2. Henry Campbell Black, *Black's Law Dictionary* 6th ed. (St. Paul, Minn.: West, 1990), p. 1612.

3. *Harris v. McRae*, 448 U.S. 297 (1980), p. 354 n.7 (Stevens, J., dissenting).

4. *Michael M. v. Superior Court of Sonoma County*, 450 U.S. 464 (1981).

5. Ibid., pp. 471, 473.

6. Currently, "sterilization is the most popular method of birth control in the United States." Lisa A. Podewils, "Traditional Tort Principles and Wrongful Conception Child-Rearing Damages," *Boston University Law Review* 73.3 (May 1993), p. 407.

The use of sterilization as a method of birth control is ridden with race and class biases. Historically, some connect it to early eugenics efforts to combat white elite fears of "race suicide." See Angela Davis, "Racism, Birth Control, and Reproductive Rights," in Marlene Gerber Fried, ed., *From Abortion to Reproductive Freedom: Transforming a*

Movement (Boston: South End Press, 1990), p. 19. For another view, see Ellen Chesler, *Woman of Valor: Margaret Sanger and the Birth Control Movement in America* (New York: Simon and Schuster, 1992).

7. Podewils, "Traditional Tort Principles," pp. 407–408. Usually, the doctor is not held responsible for the costs of raising the child. In "thirty-six jurisdictions . . . [where] wrongful conception suits have been allowed, twenty-eight have denied child-rearing damages as a matter of law." As Podewils notes, however, this is beginning to change. Ibid.

8. *Marciniak v. Lundborg*, 450 N.W.2d 243 (Wis. 1990), p. 245, cited in Krista Mirhoseini, "Torts—The Wisconsin Supreme Court Addresses Wrongful Pregnancy Causes of Action *Marciniak v. Lundborg*, 153 Wis.2d 59, 450 N.W.2d 243 (1990)," *Marquette Law Review* 74.3–4 (Spring/Summer 1991), pp. 575–576.

9. Ibid. Perhaps we can assume from this ruling that if the benefits of having a child do not outweigh the damage caused by a wrongful pregnancy, neither would exercising an option to obtain an abortion offset the damage entailed by a pregnancy that is coerced since the damage stems from the coercion, not from a calculus of utility that evaluates the context of that coercion per se. Some see a trend in the way in which courts are willing to include the costs of child rearing in wrongful pregnancy damages. A. Lynne Wiggins, "*Marciniak v. Lundborg*: Physicians as Surrogate Parents? Rolling the Dice for Recovery in Wrongful Conception Cases," *American Journal of Trial Advocacy* 16.3 (Spring 1993), p. 856.

10. *Shessel v. Stroup*, 316 S.E.2d 155 (Ga. 1984).

11. Ibid., p. 157.

12. *Black's Law Dictionary*, p. 785.

13. A failed abortion, or failure to inform a woman of information that may be relevant to her decision to choose an abortion, also constitutes in the law the injury of wrongful pregnancy. In this case, no medical emergency stems from the pregnancy itself but rather from tangential factors, such as the health of the fetus and child that may be born. While the woman faces no unexpected medical threats to herself, normal pregnancy nevertheless is considered an injury to the woman if she would have chosen an abortion had she known about fetal abnormalities or other information relevant to her decision to continue her pregnancy. In Ohio, for example, in *Flanagan v. Williams*, 623 N.E.2d 185 (Ohio App. Dist. 1993), a husband and wife filed wrongful birth and wrongful life claims, charging that attending doctors had failed to provide them with timely information that their fetus suffered from spina bifida, even though an ultrasound technician had notified one of their doctors of this possibility early in the woman's pregnancy. Consequently, by the time they had learned the sad facts, too much time had passed for the woman to be eligible for an abortion. In this case the Ohio Supreme Court defined several types of injuries. These included normal pregnancies subsequent to failed sterilization and abortions, although this type of injury was not at issue in this case. *Flanagan*, p. 188. In particular, the court affirmed that a "'wrongful pregnancy' cause of action is a lawsuit filed by a parent on his or her own behalf for damages resulting from the birth of a healthy, normal child following a failed sterilization . . . and in the case of a failed abortion." Ibid. (citations omitted). The Ohio Supreme Court has recognized a cause of action by parents who claimed "wrongful pregnancy" and has awarded damages for a normal pregnancy, but not for the child-rearing expenses of a normal, healthy child. See

ibid. The court has upheld the awarding of damages for child-rearing expenses in the event of "wrongful pregnancy" only if and when the child that is born is disabled. See ibid.

14. Ibid., pp. 189–190 (citations omitted).

15. *Kush v. Lloyd*, 616 So.2d 415 (Fla. 1992), p. 417 n.2.

16. *Keel v. Banach*, 624 So.2d 1022 (Ala. 1993), p. 1029.

17. Wisconsin, Rape Shield Law, § 972.11, stats., which reads in part,

(b) If the defendant is accused of a crime under § 940.225 [sexual assault], 948.02 [sexual assault of a child], 948.05 [sexual exploitation of a child] or 948.06 [incest with a child], any evidence concerning the complaining witness's prior sexual conduct or opinions of the witness's prior sexual conduct and reputation as to prior sexual conduct shall not be admitted into evidence during the course of the hearing or trial, nor shall any reference to such conduct be made in the presence of the jury, except the following, subject to § 971.31(11) [motions before trial]:

1. Evidence of the complaining witness's past conduct with the defendant.

2. Evidence of specific instances of sexual conduct showing the source or origin of semen, pregnancy or disease, for use in determining the degree of sexual assault or the extent of injury suffered.

18. In these cases, the California courts use "consent to sex" as a proxy for "consent to pregnancy." That is, they assume that a woman who does not consent to sexual intercourse also does not consent to a subsequent pregnancy. See following discussion for case citations.

19. Rape Shield Law.

20. *People v. McIlvain*, 130 P.2d 131 (1942).

21. Ibid., pp. 132–133.

22. Ibid., p. 137.

23. Ibid.

24. Ibid.

25. As the Court put it, "Surely [normal] pregnancy as a result of forcible rape is great bodily injury." *People v. Cardenas*, 48 Cal. App. 3d 203, 121 Cal. Rptr. 426 (Cal. App. 2 Dist. 1975), p. 428. This view was confirmed in *People v. Superior Court (Lozano)*, 69 Cal. App. 3d 57, 137 Cal. Rptr. 767 (Cal. App. 2 Dist. 1977).

26. *People v. Caudillo*, 21 Cal. 3d 562, 580 P.2d 274, 146 Cal. Rptr. 859 (1978), p. 873, fn. 20.

27. Ibid., p. 870, fn. omitted.

28. Ibid., p. 872.

29. Ibid., pp. 870–871.

30. *People v. Sargent*, 86 Cal. App. 3d 148, 150 Cal. Rptr. 113 (Cal. App. 4 Dist. 1978), pp. 115–116.

31. Ibid. As the court put it, the injuries of "[a] pregnancy resulting from a rape . . . are not injuries necessarily incidental to an act of rape."

32. Ibid.

33. Ibid.

34. *People v. Superior Court (Duval)*, 198 Cal. App. 3d 1121, 244 Cal. Rptr. 522, 9 Cal. App. 3 Dist. (1988).

35. Ibid., p. 527.

36. Ibid. The appeals court also ruled, however, that the vice principal could not be held responsible for the substantial bodily injury of Sonia's pregnancy because he had not "intended" that she would become pregnant. To be held legally responsible for a crime, one must have intended to cause the injury. The court maintained in this case, "Nothing in the record even remotely suggests that defendant consciously desired that Sonia become pregnant. Indeed, if speculation could serve for evidence, the circumstances of this illicit relationship strongly suggest it is far more likely that pregnancy was a consequence defendant devoutly wished would not be consummated . . . . On this record, the most that can be said is that defendant negligently, even recklessly, ignored the possibility that his conduct might lead to pregnancy." Ibid., pp. 528–529, fn. omitted. This language affirms that even when courts see the connection between sex and pregnancy, they recognize their disaggregation as well. The court's reference to a man's "impregnating" a woman is combined with acknowledgment that sexual intercourse only sets up the "possibility" that pregnancy will ensue. Embedded in the statement that a man's conduct "might lead to pregnancy" is recognition that something else is necessary to make a pregnancy occur. As discussed, that something else is the fertilized ovum when it implants itself on a woman's body.

37. *People v. Brown*, 495 N.W.2d 812 (Mich. App. 1992).

38. Ibid., p. 813.

39. Ibid., p. 815 (quoting M.C.L. § 750.520a(j); M.S.A. § 28.788(1)(j)).

40. See, e.g., *In the Interest of Michael R.B.*, 499 N.W.2d 641 (Wis. 1993), p. 644 n.2 (quoting Wisconsin's Rape Shield Law); *State v. Wooten*, 1993 WL 61317 (Wis. App.) (unpublished); *State v. Jennerjahn*, 1993 WL 414603 (Wis. App.) (unpublished).

41. *State v. Kindrick*, 619 A.2d 1,2 n.2 (Ct. 1993)(quoting Conn. Gen'l. Stat. § 5486(f)); *State v. Christiano*, 617 A.2d 470 (Conn. App. 1992)(quoting same statute). It is worth noting that in Connecticut the admission of evidence of pregnancy, injury, disease, and semen is to determine if the defendant is the "source" of these conditions. See ibid. While we must take issue with the idea that a man is the "source of pregnancy" instead of a fertilized ovum, the relevant point here is the law's recognition that normal pregnancy is relevant to the woman's claims of injury, if and when she does not consent to be pregnant.

42. See *Smith v. Commonwealth*, 1993 WL 129604 (Va. App. 1993) (unpublished).

43. See *Heflin v. Mississippi*, 1993 WL 361355 (Miss. 1993) (unpublished). For superseding opinion, see *Heflin v. State*, 643 So.2d 512 (Miss. 1994).

44. See *State v. Vining*, 609 So.2d 984 (La. App. 4 Cir. 1992)(reaffirming *State v. Bell*, 377 So.2d 303 (La. 1979)(holding that state's interest in protecting minors from pregnancy justifies statutory rape law).

45. Thomas C. Key and Robert Resnik, "Maternal Changes in Pregnancy," in *Obstetrics and Gynecology*, 5th ed., ed. David N. Danforth and James R. Scott (New York: Lippincott, 1986), p. 327.

46. W. Page Keeton, Dan B. Dobbs, Robert E. Keeton, and David G. Owen, *Prosser and Keeton on the Law of Torts*, 5th ed. (St. Paul, Minn.: West, 1984), p. 112.

47. Nonhuman "natural" forces, such as fires, earthquakes, floods, and hurricanes, can also impose absolute, quantitative, and qualitative injuries because the presumption is that no one can consent to the changes wrought by such forces. We can have

other types of relationships with nature, but it does not make sense to talk about whether we "consent" to let the rain fall or "consent" to an earthquake. Note, however, that what defines a crime differs somewhat from what defines an injury. In a criminal prosecution, generally it is not an adequate defense to say that the victim consented to the crime. As LaFave and Scott note, criminal offenses are wrongs against the general public, not merely the particular individual. A person charged with homicide, for example, cannot use as a defense that the victim furnished the gun and ammunition used to do the killing. Similarly, when charged with the statutory offense of fraternity hazing, it is not a defense to say that the "pledges consented to the activity." Wayne R. LaFave and Austin W. Scott, Jr., *Criminal Law*, 2nd ed. (St. Paul, Minn.: West, 1986), pp. 477–479.

There are limits, therefore, "to the extent to which the law will recognize a privilege based upon . . . consent. . . . One may permit an amputation made necessary by accident or disease, but he who struck off the hand of a 'lustie rogue' to enable him to beg more effectively was guilty of mayhem despite the other's request." Similarly, "The fact that a masochist consented to a severe beating by a sadist was not a defense to a charge of aggravated assault." Rollin M. Perkins and Ronald N. Boyce, *Criminal Law* (Mineola, N.Y.: Foundation Press, 1982), pp. 1075–1076.

48. Black, *Law Dictionary*, p. 785.

49. Marjorie Maguire Shultz, "From Informed Consent to Patient Choice: A New Protected Interest," *Yale Law Journal* 95.2 (December 1985), pp. 219, 224.

50. Keeton et al., *Prosser and Keeton*, p. 112.

51. Michael D. Bayles, "Harm to the Unconceived," *Philosophy and Public Affairs* 5.3 (Spring 1976), p. 293. Joel Feinberg defines harm more broadly to include passive inaction as well as invasive action. Feinberg, "Wrongful Conception and the Right Not to Be Harmed," *Harvard Journal of Law and Public Policy* 8.1 (Winter 1985), pp. 57–64. By this standard, passively allowing the fetus to injure a woman by imposing wrongful pregnancy is a form of harm to her in addition to the active invasion by the fetus of her body and liberty.

52. Bayles, "Harm to the Unconceived," pp. 294–295.

53. *Zepeda v. Zepeda*, 190 N.E.2d 849 (1963).

54. *Curlender v. Bio-science Laboratories*, 106 Cal. App. 3d 811 (1980).

55. *Turpin v. Sortini*, 643 P.2d 954 (1982).

56. The Washington Supreme Court ruled similarly in *Harbeson v. Parke-Davis, Inc.*, 656 P.2d 483 (1983), as did the New Jersey Supreme Court in *Procalnik v. Cillo*, 478 A.2d 755 (1984).

57. *Walker v. Mart*, 790 P.2d 735 (1990).

58. *Roe*, 410 U.S. 113, pp. 154, 162–164.

59. People have a right to preserve their life and health when threatened with viruses, bacteria, cancers, and such natural forces as fires, earthquakes, hurricanes, and floods. Constitutional law scholars assume it would be unconstitutional for the state to deny people the right to call on physicians to remove cancers. Personal communication with Professor Kathleen Sullivan, Stanford Law School. The state may regulate the medical profession to ensure that it is meeting the health needs of people in a responsible way, but it would be unconstitutional to deny to people the right to protect their health by consulting and working with physicians.

60. See Richard A. Rosen, "On Self-Defense, Imminence, and Women Who Kill Their Batterers," *North Carolina Law Review* 71.2 (January 1993), p. 374.

61. Any injury, of course, can involve all three dimensions of injury, as if someone raped, brutally inflicted many physical injuries, and then killed another person, thereby qualitatively, quantitatively, and absolutely injuring them.

62. For a compilation of state-level self-defense statutes, see Eileen L. McDonagh, "Self-Defense Norms," working paper.

63. *Statutory rape* is sexual intercourse with a male or female under statutory age, with or without the victim's consent, and *forcible rape* is the "unlawful carnal knowledge of a woman by a man forcibly and against her will." Black, *Law Dictionary*, p. 1260. *Aggravated rape* usually refers to forcible rape committed with the imposition of injuries additional to those of the rape itself.

64. See McDonagh, "Self-Defense Norms."

65. *Model Penal Code and Commentaries*, part I (Philadelphia: American Law Institute, 1985), § 3.04, pp. 30–31.

66. John A. Pirko, "Defining the Crime of Excessive Self-Defense: Voluntary Manslaughter in Illinois," *Northern Illinois University Law Review* 3.1 (Winter 1982), p. 231. States vary in duty-to-retreat standards, but the minority rule requires "a lawful occupant of a dwelling to avail himself of any reasonable means of escape from the dwelling before defending himself by inflicting bodily injury or death upon an intruder." Yolanda R. Mitchell, "Criminal Law—No Longer a Duty to Retreat—Chapter 696 of Mass. Acts of 1981," *Massachusetts Law Review* 67.2 (Spring 1982), p. 89. The duty to retreat applies to intrusion on property, however, not direct intrusion on one's body.

The right of battered women to self-defense includes the controversial principle that they have a right to defend themselves after attacks have occurred, rather than only during those attacks. See Mira Mihajlovich, "Does Plight Make Right: The Battered Woman Syndrome, Expert Testimony and the Law of Self-Defense," *Indiana Law Journal* 62.4 (1986–1987), p. 1270.

67. *Model Penal Code*, § 3.04, p. 33.

68. Legislators and other proponents of abortion laws, of course, did not frame them in terms of a woman's right to self-defense, and many view early-nineteenth-century statutes that criminalize abortion as attempts to discourage white, middle-class women from terminating their pregnancies as part of eugenic concerns about the birthrate of other groups in society. As such, abortion was seen as a crime against society and against womanhood. Lawrence M. Friedman, "American Legal History: Past and Present," in *American Law and the Constitutional Order: Historical Perspectives*, ed. Lawrence M. Friedman and Harry N. Scheiber (Cambridge, Mass.: Harvard University Press, 1988), p. 230. Nevertheless, even in this repressive, xenophobic context, state laws permitted abortions when a woman's life was in danger, attesting to the implicit recognition of women's right to self-defense as well.

69. *Roe*, 410 U.S. 113, p. 175 (Rehnquist, J., dissenting).

70. When we examine these thirty-six state statutes, we see that they all affirm a woman's right to kill a fetus when it threatens her with the absolute injury of death. Some statutes, even in the late nineteenth century, also acknowledged even greater latitude for a woman's justified use of deadly force against a fetus that made her pregnant against her will.

71. Cf. *Roe*, p. 177 (Rehnquist, J., dissenting). Viewed in this way, these statutes embody common ground in the abortion debate: that a woman has a right to self-defense, which includes the right to stop the fetus with deadly force when it intrudes on her sufficiently. From the very beginning of the legislative history of abortion rights, even as early as 1843 in Alabama, lawmakers acknowledged a woman's right to bodily integrity and liberty by legislatively guaranteeing that she could use deadly force to stop a fetus from killing her. While many have searched in vain for principles that could unite pro-life and pro-choice advocates, it is this principle of self-defense that does the trick, a principle that has been there since the start of the abortion debate in the nineteenth century, was affirmed in *Roe*, and has been reconfirmed in abortion cases since then. Acknowledgement of women's right to kill the fetus when it threatens her with death affirms the most primary right of privacy in the American political system: the right to be let alone from other private parties.

72. Jane English, "Abortion and the Concept of a Person," in *The Problem of Abortion*, ed. Joel Feinberg, (Belmont, Calif.: Wordsworth, 1984), p. 151.

73. Lawyers refer to an aggressor who is innocent of intentionally causing harm as one who imposes "excused but unjustified aggression," and it is the fact that the aggression is unjustified that entitles the victim to use deadly force to stop it. Joel Feinberg, "Abortion," *Freedom and Fulfillment: Philosophical Essays* (Princeton, N.J.: Princeton University Press, 1992), p. 63.

Feinberg correctly classes the fetus as innocent by virtue of its immaturity and because it does "not choose to threaten its mother," yet he then makes the mistake of asserting that the "fetus is not only innocent but also not an aggressor" because "[i]t did not start the *trouble* in any fashion" (p. 63, emphasis added). Medically and legally, it is incorrect to say that the fetus did not start pregnancy; the fetus is the only party capable of starting, much less maintaining, pregnancy. As the legal definition of pregnancy states, it is a condition "resulting from a fertilized ovum," and medical texts chronicle the massive changes that result from the very conception of a fertilized ovum to the maintenance of its implantation in her body for nine months.

While the fetus is innocent of an intentionality, it is not innocent of causing pregnancy. To the contrary, it is an aggressor upon a woman's body if she does not consent to being pregnant. Feinberg is mistaken, therefore, to assert, "There is simply *no interpersonal 'aggression'* involved at all in the *normal pregnancy*" (p. 64; emphasis added). To the contrary, all nonconsensual pregnancy, whether medically normal or not, involves interpersonal aggression since, by definition, it involves one private party, the fetus, that directly and concretely intrudes on the body and liberty of another private party, the woman.

74. Some, such as Nancy Davis, claim that "it is doubtful that we can defend abortion—even in cases in which the woman's life is clearly at stake—by appealing to the right to self-defense." Davis, "Abortion and Self-Defense," in *Abortion: Moral and Legal Perspectives*, ed. Jay L. Garfield and Patricia Hennessey (Amherst: University of Massachusetts Press, 1984), p. 187. Yet, if born human life does not have entitlement to impose such injuries on another person, surely preborn human life has no such entitlement, and a woman's right to self-defense in relation to a fetus that imposes even a medically normal pregnancy is justified.

75. Some might object to a woman's right to self-defense on the grounds that she

provokes the fetus to make her pregnant by allowing sperm into her body, which sets up the probability that a fertilized ovum will be conceived and make her pregnant, which might be construed as a form of causing the conditions of her self-defense. See Paul H. Robinson, "Causing the Conditions of One's Own Defense: A Study in the Limits of Theory in Criminal Law Doctrine," *Virginia Law Review* 71.1 (February 1985), pp. 1–63.

It is true that self-defense does not apply as a justification for the use of deadly force if the victim of aggression has provoked that agression. In *Ayer v. Robinson*, 329 P.2d 546 (Cal. App. 2 Dist. 1958), p. 547, for example, it was "alleged as a defense that any violence committed by defendants was provoked by plaintiff's vile and abusive language and by his unlawful 'interference'" with the defendant. Although in this case the court made a judgment in favor of the plaintiff (ibid., p. 549), in *Illinois v. Smith*, 522 N.E.2d 1061, p. 1064 (Ill. App. 1990) (quoting *People v. Fleming*, 507 N.E.2d 954 (Ill. App. 1987), p. 959), the court affirmed that "a person may not provoke the use of force and then retaliate claiming self-defense." Similarly, in *Fontenelle v. Waguespack*, 90 So. 662 (La. 1992), p. 663, the court ruled that "Unless the defendant provoked the difficulty by insults, abuse, threats, or other conduct, he would be entitled to recover, if plaintiff, without legal excuse, committed an assault and battery upon him."

Yet if we are to consider this possibility in the context of pregnancy and abortion, it is apparent that it is not that a woman provokes a fetus but that her body is attractive to a fetus, much as a woman might be sexually attractive to a man. Being attractive to a private party, however, does not give that party the right to intrude on one's body, liberty, or even property. Owning an attractive house, car, or personal items, for example, does not give private parties who are attracted to them the right to take them from you. Nor does a woman's sexual attractiveness give a man the right to impose himself sexually on her. So, too, with the fetus, if we were to pursue this line of reasoning. Even if we think of a woman's body as attractive to a fetus, that attractiveness does not give the fetus the right to take a woman's body without her consent.

76. What is meant by *inalienable* is that their natural rights cannot be taken away from them, either by the state or by a private person. To say that rights are inalienable, therefore, is to say that they cannot be surrendered or transferred either to the state or to another private person without the consent of the person who possesses those rights. In the American context, people's possession of inalienable rights in relation to the state, as embodied in the Bill of Rights, includes freedom of speech, religion, due process, and equal protection of the laws. *Black's Law Dictionary*, p. 759. See *Morrison v. State*, 252 S.W.2d 97 (Mo. App. 1952), p. 101.

As the Declaration of Independence, a classic natural rights document, states, "When in the course of human events, it becomes necessary for one people to dissolve the political bands which have connected them with another, and to assume among the powers of the earth, the separate and equal station to which the laws of nature and of nature's God entitle them, a decent respect to the opinions of mankind requires that they should declare the causes which impel them to the separation. We hold these truths to be self evident, that all men are created equal, that they are endowed by their creator with certain unalienable rights, that among these are life, liberty and the pursuit of happiness."

77. The Declaration of Independence was the first formal expression of people's belief that an organized political community has the right to choose its own form of gov-

ernment in order to protect natural rights. As it proclaims, "to secure these [self-evident natural rights to life, liberty, and the pursuit of happiness], governments are instituted among men, deriving their just powers from the consent of the governed." The Declaration of Independence, therefore, explicitly asserts that if government becomes destructive of its purpose to secure natural rights, the people retain the right "to alter or to abolish it, and to institute new government, laying its foundation on such principles and organizing its powers in such form, as to them shall seem most likely to effect their safety and happiness."

We must note the gap between a theory of natural rights and practice, however, evident in the very founding of the American state. Thomas Jefferson, author of the Declaration of Independence, for example, originally included a passage denouncing the slave trade, for the obvious reason that the institution of slavery was directly at odds with natural law principles, which assert that all people are created equal with inalienable rights to their life, liberty, and pursuit of happiness. Southern delegates to a committee appointed by the Continental Congress to draft the Declaration of Independence, however, were offended by the denouncement of slavery, and so it was amended both by the committee and by the Congress by striking out the antislavery passage. The Continental Congress adopted the Declaration of Independence on July 2, 1776; it was proclaimed on July 4, 1776. Vernon Bogdanor, ed., *The Blackwell Encyclopedia of Political Institutions* (Oxford: Basil Blackwell, 1987), pp. 163–164.

78. Clarence Thomas is perceived by some to endorse natural law principles as a way of supporting a fetus's right to life. Russell Hittinger, "Natural Law after the Thomas Nomination Hearings," paper presented at Harvard University, Department of Government, Spring 1992. We could also say, of course, that natural law principles support a woman's right to defend herself against another private party that seriously injures her. Judith A. Baer and others, however, remind us that there is a distinction between natural law and the Constitution and that preferences differ on how to relate them to each other. See Baer, "What We Know as Women: A New Look at *Roe v. Wade*," *National Women's Studies Association Journal* 2.4 (Autumn 1990), p. 580.

Michael J. Perry also cautions against using the traditions of the American people as a source of norms for constitutional adjudication since that tradition encompasses so much diversity that it is little help in resolving human rights conflicts in particular contexts. See Perry, "Noninterpretive Review in Human Rights Cases: A Functional Justification," *New York University Law Review* 56.2–3 (May–June 1981), p. 283. This is not to say, however, that there is no connection between the American natural law heritage and the rights established in the Constitution, only that the translation between the two is complex and to some degree unpredictable.

79. Sheldon Gelman, "'Life' and 'Liberty': Their Original Meaning, Historical Antecedents, and Current Significance in the Debate over Abortion Rights," *Minnesota Law Review* 78.3 (February 1994), p. 588.

80. Society is now governed by a rule of law that the people themselves, or through their representatives, legislate, implement, and adjudicate by a government apparatus set up by the people.

81. The Constitution, which represents the creation of the state in the American case, becomes an instrument to be used by the people to solve the vexing problems of a state of nature void of law and institutions. People created the Constitution to establish

justice, ensure domestic tranquility, promote the general welfare, and secure liberty. The Preamble to the Constitution states, "We the People of the United States, in Order to form a more perfect Union, establish Justice, ensure domestic Tranquility, provide for the common defense, promote the general Welfare, and secure the Blessings of Liberty to ourselves and our Posterity, do ordain and establish this Constitution for the United States of America." These are general directives, but it is safe to say that at the least the Constitution establishes a state that is obligated to execute the laws to stop private people from unlawfully taking the lives, liberty, and property of other private people and that the provision of benefits is discretionary state action. Some argue that such benefits are discretionary state action, some that they should be obligations of the state, but only a few that they already are obligations of the state.

82. The First Amendment forbids the federal government from interfering in a person's exercise of religion, freedom to speak (this includes journalistic forms of speech, such as the press), the right to assemble peaceably, and the right to petition the government for a redress of grievances. The Second Amendment forbids the federal government from preventing the people from keeping and bearing arms; the Third Amendment from quartering soldiers in peacetime in a person's house without consent; the Fourth from searching or seizing people or their houses, papers, and effects in an unreasonable manner; and the Fifth from depriving any person of life, liberty, or property without due process of law. The Fifth Amendment also forbids the federal government from compelling people to be witnesses against themselves and sets up rules to protect people from the state when they are involved in criminal proceedings. The Sixth Amendment checks the power of the federal government in criminal proceedings by requiring speedy trials by jury and the guarantee of defense counsel; the Seventh guarantees the right to trial by jury in civil proceedings in which the value of the controversy exceeds $20; the Eighth forbids the federal government from setting excessive bail or fines and from inflicting cruel or unusual punishment; the Ninth states that rights not specifically enumerated in the Constitution are retained by the people; and the Tenth states that power not delegated to the federal government nor prohibited to the states is reserved to the states or to the people.

83. Though initially this amendment covered only the relation between people and state-level governments, interpretations by the Supreme Court gradually added to its power to guarantee to people the same types of protection in relation to state-level government that the Bill of Rights guaranteed in relation to the federal government. If the state itself becomes too intrusive, people have a right of self-defense, not only against private intrusion but also against the state as expressed by their right to rebel. Justification for the American Revolution rested on such an understanding of a minimalist state, one whose only obligation was to provide law and order within prescribed boundaries so as not to intrude on the very right to privacy to be let alone that the state itself is brought into being to ensure. Natural law doctrine entitles people to use deadly force against the state when disengaging from it if the state has impermissibly intruded on their inalienable rights.

84. *Black's Law Dictionary*, p. 1156
85. Ibid.
86. *Rochin v. People of California*, 342 U.S. 165 (1952).
87. Cf. ibid., pp. 166–167. Rochin claimed that the method used to extract evi-

dence violated the Due Process Clause, the same clause currently at issue in abortion rights.

88. Ibid., p. 172. Frankfurter based his opinion directly on the Due Process Clause of the Fourteenth Amendment. In this case, the compelling state interest in controlling crime by obtaining evidence to convict criminals did not override the fundamental right of a suspected criminal to be free from state intrusion of his body in the form of a stomach pump. Kermit L. Hall, James W. Ely, Jr., Joel B. Grossman, and William M. Wiecek, eds., *The Oxford Companion to the Supreme Court of the United States,* (New York: Oxford University Press, 1992), p. 739.

89. *Rochin,* p. 172. In concurring but separate opinions, Justices Hugo Black and William O. Douglas agreed that the conviction of Rochin should be overturned but thought that the Due Process Clause of the Fourteenth Amendment provided grounds that were too "nebulous." Ibid., p. 175 (Black, J., concurring). For this reason, they thought the reversal of opinion should be based on Rochin's Fifth Amendment right not to be forced to incriminate himself. Ibid., pp. 175, 179. Ironically, it was Douglas himself who gave constitutional "substance" to the due process clause in his famous opinion in *Griswold v. Connecticut,* 381 U.S. 479 (1965). Hall et al., *Oxford Companion to the Supreme Court,* p. 739.

90. The following discussion of the constitutionality of state intrusion into the bodies of people suspected of criminal activity is drawn from Laurence H. Tribe. *American Constitutional Law,* 2nd ed. (Mineola, N.Y.: Foundation Press, 1988), pp. 1331–1334.

The Court ruled, for example, that it violated the bodily integrity rights of suspected criminals in the context of their right against unreasonable searches and seizures, as guaranteed by the Fourth Amendment, to search a person's rectum under nonmedical conditions. *Huguez v. United States,* 406 F.2d 366 (9th Cir. 1968), cited ibid.; moreover, the Court also ruled that the search itself violated the Fifth Amendment's guarantee against inhumane treatment.

A border search of a woman's vagina is unconstitutional unless there is clear indication that evidence will be found. *Henderson v. United States,* 390 F.2d 805 (9th Cir. 1967), cited ibid., p. 1331 n.6. Yet the Court upheld as a "reasonable search" under the Fourth Amendment the constitutionality of a compelled blood test to determine alcoholic content for a victim of an automobile accident while he was in a hospital bed. *Schmerber v. California,* 384 U.S. 757 (1966), cited ibid., p. 1331 n.4; the Court also has upheld the constitutionality under the Fourth Amendment of state searches of the rectal cavity of suspected criminals in a number of cases, such as *Rivas v. United States,* 368 F.2d 703 (9th Cir. 1966), *cert. denied* 386 U.S. 945 (1967); and a search by a doctor in a hospital, using scientific procedures, of a suspect's anal cavity, despite the suspect's violent objections, *Blackford v. United States,* 247 F.2d 745 (9th Cir. 1957); and of a search at the border of a man's rectum and stomach, *Blefare v. United States,* 362 F.2d 870 (9th Cir. 1966), cited ibid., p. 1331 n.6.

The Court also ruled that the surgical removal of a bullet from the arm of a suspected criminal did not constitute an invasion of his bodily integrity under the Fourth Amendment as long as it was done in a hospital with full procedural safeguards. *United States v. Crowder,* 543 F.2d 312 (D.C. Cir. 1976)(en banc), cited ibid., p. 1331 n.7. The Court also supported this position by refusing to hear a case dealing with the constitutionality of removing a bullet lodged just under the skin in the side of the chest of a suspected criminal. Accord, *Creamer v. State*, 192 S.E.2d 350 (Ga. 1972), *cert. dismissed* 410 U.S. 975 (1973), cited ibid., p. 1331 n.7.

Generally, however, the Court tends to draw the line at surgical intrusion, ruling that the state may not so directly intrude on a suspected criminal where surgery would seriously infringe upon the defendant's privacy right and where the state already possessed independent substantial evidence against the suspect. *Winston v. Lee*, 470 U.S. 753 (1985), p. 765.

91. Tribe, *American Constitutional Law*, p. 1332.

92. The Constitution also empowers the state to intrude on people's property in the form of eminent domain, which entitles the state to take property from private parties to serve the public welfare as long as appropriate compensation is made to the private parties and proper procedures for the taking of property are in place.

93. In *Jacobson v. Massachusetts*, 197 U.S. 11 (1905), pp. 26–27, the Court ruled that it was constitutional for a state to require smallpox vaccinations despite the religious objections of some people.

94. Where there is no compelling state interest, however, the Court has been reluctant in more recent decades to allow the state to intrude on the bodily integrity of individuals. The most poignant cases are those dealing with the bodily integrity rights of institutionalized individuals in nonpenal contexts. The rights of the mentally incompetent, for example, were not protected by the Court in *Buck v. Bell*, 274 U.S. 200, 207 (1927). The Court upheld the sterilization of mentally incompetent individuals, or "imbeciles" in the immortally insensitive words of Justice Holmes in his majority opinion. The state of Virginia sterilized two women under this statute—Carrie and Doris Buck—neither of whom "would be classified as mentally incompetent by today's standards." Tribe, *Constitutional Law*, p. 1339, quoting Stephen Jay Gould, *The Mismeasure of Man*. As Tribe notes, the upholding of this statute by the Supreme Court made it constitutional for nearly fifty years to sterilize people deemed mentally incompetent. The Court ruled in *Skinner v. State of Oklahoma*, 316 U.S. 535 (1942), however, that it was unconstitutional to sterilize prisoners against their will. In Virginia alone more than 7,500 involuntary sterilizations were performed between 1924 and 1972. Ibid., p. 1339, n.15. Such policies are no longer constitutional.

95. Samuel D. Warren and Louis Brandeis, "The Right to Privacy," *Harvard Law Review* 4.5 (December 15, 1890), pp. 193–220.

96. Mary Ann Glendon, *Abortion and Divorce in Western Law* (Cambridge, Mass.: Harvard University Press, 1987), p. 36

97. Daniel R. Ortiz, "Privacy, Autonomy, and Consent," *Harvard Journal of Law and Public Policy* 12.1 (Winter 1989), p. 92.

98. Ibid.

99. Richard F. Hamm, "Common-Law Court," in *Oxford Companion to the Supreme Court*, p. 171.

100. The source of common law is "universal custom, reason, or natural law," and we can think of it as law that is in effect even though it has not been explicitly legislated by the state. The authority for common law includes the natural law assumption that people have inalienable rights, which are embedded in customs, traditions, and court-created precedents when the judicial system adjudicates the rights of one person in relation to another. Ibid., p. 171; Richard Posner, *The Problems of Jurisprudence* (Cambridge,

Mass.: Harvard University Press, 1990), chap. 8; Melvin Aron Eisenberg, *The Nature of the Common Law* (Cambridge, Mass.: Harvard University Press, 1988), chaps. 1–5.

101. For this reason the most practical impact of common law crimes is in the "area of common law misdemeanors, public mischief, and indecency offenses." *Model Penal Code*, § 1.05, pp. 78–79; quoted in LaFave and Scott, *Criminal Law*, p. 69, n.42. Common law crimes in the United States, which are recognized by courts as constituting criminal behavior in the absence of legislative statutes declaring them to be so, include, for example, a person who conspires to injure the business of another; a person who incites others to harm people by beating them, destroying their property, or murdering them; a person who offends others by "uttering obscene language in public"; a person who discharges a gun near a sick person; a person who libels another; and a person who eavesdrops on another. Ibid., pp. 68–69.

102. Some exception is made for property in cases of emergency.

103. *Curran v. Bosze*, 566 N.E.2d 1319 (Ill. 1990).

104. Ibid., p. 1323 (quoting *Union Pacific Ry. v. Butsford*, 141 U.S. 250 (1891)).

105. *Strunk v. Strunk*, 445 S.W.2d 145 (Ky. 1969). *Strunk* was extensively cited by the court in *Curran*. *Curran*, 566 N.E.2d, pp. 1326–1327.

106. *Curran*, p. 1326 (quoting *Strunk*).

107. *Strunk*, p. 149. The key to this affirmation lies in the court of appeals' ruling that "the operative procedures in this instance are to the best interest of [the ward]," based on the substitute judgment of his guardian. Ibid.

108. Lance Morrow, "When One Body Can Save Another," *Time* (June 17, 1991), p. 57; survey in article done by Yankelovich, Clancy, Shulman.

109. Harriet F. Pilpel, "Hyde and Go Seek: A Response to Representative Hyde," *New York Law School Law Review* 27.4 (1982), pp. 1101–1123.

110. For this reason, S. I. Benn's suggestion that a pregnant woman acquires a duty to care for the fetus, that is, to sustain its life, is flawed because the process of sustaining a fetus's life, in contrast to what is involved in sustaining the life of aged parents, entails massive uses of one's body. See Benn, "Abortion, Infanticide, and Respect for Persons," in *The Problem of Abortion*, 2nd ed., ed. Joel Feinberg (Belmont, Calif.: Wadsworth, 1984), p. 136.

111. Alison McIntyre. "Guilty Bystanders? Reflections on Good Samaritan Laws," paper presented at Bunting Institute Colloquium Series, April 15, 1992.

112. Donald H. Regan, for example, is not sure that it would be unconstitutional for states to pass a law "requiring parents to donate needed organs to their children." Regan, "Rewriting *Roe v. Wade*," *Michigan Law Review* 77.7 (August 1979), p. 1620.

113. Marcia Angell, "The Right to Die," keynote speech delivered to the American Academy of Arts and Sciences, May 14, 1992; Philip J. Prygoski, "Abortion and the Right to Die: Judicial Imposition of a Theory of Life," *Seton Hall Law Review* 23 (1992), pp. 99–111.

114. *Cruzan v. Director, Missouri Department of Health*, 497 U.S. 261 (1990).

115. *Refusal of Treatment Legislation: A State by State Compilation of Enacted and Model Statutes* (New York: Society for the Right to Die, 1991), p. 1.

116. Eileen P. Flynn, *Your Living Will: Why, When, and How to Write One* (New York: Citadel Press, 1992), p. 16.

117. *Refusal of Treatment*, p. 1. In addition, Congress passed the Patient Self-

Determination Act in 1990 as part of the Omnibus Budget and Reconciliation Act. It took effect December 1, 1991, and requires that health care professionals have in place institutional policies that instruct patients to provide advance directives and inform patients about their rights to die under state law and to require documentation about whether a patient did provide an advance directive. In response to this legislation, several states have passed laws that mirror this one (pp. 3–4).

118. The one telling exception in "living wills" are precedents and legislation that prohibit a woman from controlling a medical decision when she is "both severely ill and pregnant." In practice, living wills are overridden only by close relatives of the deceased. Marcia Angell, personal conversation.

119. Cynthia R. Daniels, *At Women's Expense: State Power and the Politics of Fetal Rights* (Cambridge, Mass.: Harvard University Press, 1993), pp. 31–32. See also Marie Ashe, "Zig-Zag Stitching and the Seamless Web: Thoughts on 'Production' and the Law," in E. Kelly Weisberg, ed., *Feminist Legal Theory* (Philadelphia: Temple, 1993), pp. 582–593.

120. *UAW v. Johnson Controls*, 111 S. Ct. 1196 (1991).

121. See Daniels, chap. 3, and Sally J. Kenney, *For Whose Protection? Reproductive Hazards and Exclusionary Policies in the United States and Britain* (Ann Arbor: University of Michigan Press, 1992). Courts have been more willing, however, to intrude upon the rights of drug-addicted pregnant women. See Daniels, chap. 4.

122. The Court should complete that task by securing for women the same latitude for self-defense as is operable for others in society.

123. Brande Stellings shows how victims of private violence, such as rape, when not defended by the state against that violence, not only are metaphorically stranded in a state of nature but also are concretely deprived of their public persona, or citizenship. See Stellings, "The Public Harm of Private Violence: Rape, Sex Discrimination and Citizenship," *Harvard Civil Rights–Civil Liberties Law Review* 28.1 (Winter 1993), p. 189.

124. See Carole Pateman for analysis of how theorists depicting the state of nature use patriarchal norms. Pateman, "Women and Consent," *Political Theory* 8.2 (May 1980), p. 152.

125. Modern political thought is distinguished by its "reliance on the logical fiction of a state of nature, assumed as a starting hypothesis." Adriana Cavarero, "Equality and Sexual Difference: Amnesia in Political Thought," in *Beyond Equality and Difference: Citizenship, Feminist Politics, Female Subjectivity*, ed. Gisela Bock and Susan James (London: Routledge, 1992), p. 35.

6   Abortion Funding and Due Process

1. Prior to *Roe v. Wade*, 410 U.S. 113 (1973), the Supreme Court considered the abortion issue in *United States v. Vuitch*, 402 U.S. 62 (1971), which reversed a lower court ruling that had overturned an abortion law in Washington, D.C. The Supreme Court, while ruling that the law was constitutional, nevertheless said that the statute would have been unconstitutional if it had placed the burden of proving that an abortion was necessary for a woman's life or health on a physician rather than on the prosecution. This encouraged pro-choice litigants to believe that they might find a favorable

reception in the court system. Lee Epstein and Joseph F. Kobylka, *The Supreme Court and Legal Change: Abortion and the Death Penalty* (Chapel Hill: University of North Carolina Press, 1992), pp. 162–167.

2. The Fourteenth Amendment applies to state level government, and the Fifth Amendment to the federal government. The Fifth Amendment reads, "No person shall . . . be deprived of life, liberty, or property, without due process of law."

3. See *Griswold v. Connecticut*, 391 U.S. 479 (1965) and *Eisenstadt v. Baird*, 405 U.S. 438 (1972) (right to use contraceptives); *Loving v. Virginia*, 388 U.S. 1 (1967) (right to marry); *Stanley v. Georgia*, 394 U.S. 557 (1969) (First Amendment right to read in privacy); *Pierce v. Society of Sisters*, 268 U.S. 510 (1925); *Meyer v. Nebraska*, 262 U.S. 390 (1923) (right to rear children).

4. *Roe*, p. 153.

5. James C. Mohr, *Abortion in America: The Origins and Evolution of National Policy, 1800–1900*, (New York: Oxford University Press, 1978), pp. 247, 259–260. As Robert W. Bennett notes, "*Roe v. Wade* has few rivals as the most controversial constitutional decision of the Burger Court years." Bennett, "Abortion and Judicial Review: Of Burdens and Benefits, Hard Cases, and Some Bad Law," *Northwestern University Law Review* 75.6 (February 1981), p. 981.

Janet Benshoof considers *Roe* to have been the most important Supreme Court decision for women's right to liberty, equality, and health in the history of the United States. Benshoof, "The Legacy of *Roe v. Wade*," in *Abortion: Moral and Legal Perspectives*, ed. Jay L. Garfield and Patricia Hennessey (Amherst: University of Massachusetts Press, 1984), p. 35.

6. Laurence H. Tribe, *Abortion: The Clash of Absolutes* (New York: Norton, 1990), pp. 81–90. Some, such as Walter Dellinger, believe that Court decisions subsequent to *Roe* actually changed the right to an abortion from fundamental to nonfundamental. Walter Dellinger and Gene B. Sperling, "Abortion and the Supreme Court: The Retreat from *Roe v. Wade*," *Pennsylvania Law Review* 138.1 (November 1989), p. 83. For an insightful analysis of abortion funding decisions, see Susan Frelich Appleton, "Beyond the Limits of Reproductive Choice: The Contributions of the Abortion-Funding Cases to Fundamental-Rights Analysis and to the Welfare-Rights Thesis," *Columbia Law Review* 81.4 (May 1981), pp. 721–758.

7. However, as Appleton notes, "if state action deprives an individual of something that otherwise belongs to him [or her], [that person] has been penalized" in distinction to state action that merely refuses to provide a subsidy to engage in a protected activity. Appleton, "Beyond the Limits of Reproductive Choice," p. 733.

8. *Harris v. McRae*, 448 U.S. 297 (1980), pp. 316–318, 326.

9. Ibid., p. 324 (Stevens, J., dissenting), (emphasis added). As Justice Stevens noted, the solicitor general had suggested as much in oral argument before the Court. The reason this issue has not yet come before the Court is because even pro-life advocates, such as Henry Hyde, believe not only that a woman has a right to an abortion when the fetus threatens her life but also that the state should fund abortions to save a woman's life. Congress, therefore, allows federal funds to be used for abortions to save a woman's life, thereby obviating the need for the Court to rule on whether women have a constitutional right to such funds.

10. *Beal v. Doe*, 432 U.S. 438 (1977).

11. *Maher v. Roe,* 432 U.S. 464 (1977).
12. *Poelker v. Doe,* 432 U.S. 519 (1977).
13. *Harris,* p. 353 n.5 (Stevens, J., dissenting).
14. Ibid.
15. *Webster v. Reproductive Health Services,* 492 U.S. 490 (1989). See Gayle Binion, "*Webster v. Reproductive Health Services:* Devaluing the Right to Choose," *Women and Politics* 2.2 (1991), pp. 41–59.
16. *Webster,* p. 500.
17. *Rust v. Sullivan,* 500 U.S. 173 (1991).
18. See *Harris,* p. 324 (Stevens, J., dissenting) (describing the government's argument, which the majority essentially adopts).
19. For this reason, abortion advocates turned to state-level courts where there was evidence of greater latitude accorded to constitutional guarantees for abortion funding. The first abortion funding case to reach a state's highest court was decided favorably in Massachusetts, *Moe v. Secretary of Admin. and Finance,* 471 N.E.2d 387 (S. Jud. Ct. Mass. 1981), where the court ruled that Massachusetts must provide for medically necessary abortions if it provides other medically necessary health services. California, Connecticut, New Jersey, and Oregon followed suit, but efforts to obtain abortion funding guarantees at the state level failed in Pennsylvania. J. Ralph Lindgren and Nadine Taub, *The Law of Sex Discrimination* (St. Paul, Minn.: West, 1988), pp. 404–405.
20. *Harris,* p. 315.
21. Ibid.; emphasis added.
22. Ibid.
23. *Webster,* p. 509.
24. *Roe,* p. 159.
25. *Harris,* p. 325.
26. As Jed Rubenfeld notes, we must examine not merely what the state forbids but also what its laws produce. Even negative rights affirmed by the Due Process Clause have a positive aspect, which he defines as "the real effects that conformity with the law produces at the level of everyday lives and social practices." Rubenfeld, "The Right of Privacy," *Harvard Law Review* 102.4 (February 1989), p. 783.
27. As a legal scholar notes, personhood often connotes a distinctive conception of private life free from intrusion, as idealized, for example, by the home. Stephen J. Schnably, "Property and Pragmatism: A Critique of Radin's Theory of Property and Personhood," *Stanford Law Review* 45.2 (January 1993), pp. 347–407.
28. An exception to this rule would be if private people enslaved you, which would violate the Constitution.
29. Susan R. Estrich and Kathleen M. Sullivan, "Abortion Politics: Writing for an Audience of One," *University of Pennsylvania Law Review* 138.1 (November 1989), pp. 126–127.
30. Thomas O. Sargentich, "Due Process, Procedural," in *The Oxford Companion to the Supreme Court of the United States,* ed. Kermit L. Hall, James W. Ely, Jr., Joel B. Grossman, and William M. Wiecek (New York: Oxford University Press, 1992), p. 236. The degree of procedural protections against state action varies by the type of deprivation involved. When the state takes people's property, as in the case of eminent domain, or affects one's economic livelihood, as by imposing regulatory procedures, the due process

guarantee of the Constitution requires that the state do so in ways that are free from bias and do not unjustly treat the individuals involved. The state may regulate the licensing of optometrists, for example, by requiring that they be certified for approval by a board of professionals in their field appointed by the state. But the state cannot allow its board to be made up of optometrists who, because of their financial interests, are predisposed in hearings for misconduct to revoke the licenses of competing optometrists; then the procedures used by the state to implement its regulation of the practice of optometry would be unconstitutional on procedural due process grounds. See *Gibson v. Berryhill*, 411 U.S. 564 (1973), and *Mathews v. Eldridge*, 424 U.S. 319 (1976), p. 335, which established the three-part balancing test that the court uses in determining "how much process is due" when people are deprived of liberty or property. When the state intrudes not only on people's property but also on their lives and liberty, then how the state may proceed is even more restricted by due process guarantees. See Laurence H. Tribe, *American Constitutional Law*, 2nd ed. (Mineola, N.Y.: Foundation Press, 1988), pp. 629–632, 663–768.

31. Ibid., pp. 553–586, 1302–1435.

32. As long as the person is of the opposite sex. The Supreme Court has ruled that although there is a constitutional right to marry a person of the opposite sex, there is no constitutional right to marry a person of the same sex. Katharine T. Bartlett, *Gender and the Law: Theory, Doctrine, Commentary* (Boston: Little, Brown, 1993), pp. 457–462.

33. *DeShaney v. Winnebago County Dept. of Social Services*, 489 U.S. 189 (1989).

34. Ibid., p. 193.

35. Ibid., pp. 192–193. The child had been in the temporary custody of the state only briefly, and some argued that the state abrogated its obligation to protect Joshua by returning him to the custody of his father. Yet personnel involved in Joshua's case at this time did not find sufficient evidence to remove him permanently, nor did they subsequently, thereby leaving Joshua to the mercy of his situation and the eventual tragedy.

> The Winnebago County authorities first learned that Joshua DeShaney might be a victim of child abuse in January 1982, when his father's second wife complained to the police, at the time of their divorce, that he had previously "hit the boy causing marks and [was] a prime case for child abuse." . . . The Winnebago County Department of Social Services (DSS) interviewed the father, but he denied the accusations, and DSS did not pursue them further. In January 1983, Joshua was admitted to a local hospital with multiple bruises and abrasions. The examining physician suspected child abuse and notified DSS, which immediately obtained an order from a Wisconsin juvenile court placing Joshua in the temporary custody of the hospital. Three days later, the county convened an ad hoc "Child Protection Team"—consisting of a pediatrician, a psychologist, a police detective, the county's lawyer, several DSS caseworkers, and various hospital personnel—to consider Joshua's situation. At this meeting, the Team decided that there was insufficient evidence of child abuse to retain Joshua in the custody of the court. Ibid., p. 192 (citations omitted).

See Thomas A. Eaton and Michael Wells, "Governmental Inaction as a Constitutional Tort: *DeShaney* and Its Aftermath," *Washington Law Review* 66.1 (January 1991), pp. 107–167.

36. *DeShaney*, p. 196.

37. *Webster*, p. 507 (citing, among other cases, *Harris*).

38. *DeShaney*, p. 195.

39. See Jack M. Beermann, "Administrative Failure and Local Democracy: The Politics of *DeShaney*," *Duke Law Journal* 1990.5 (September 1990), pp. 1078–1112, and Steven J. Heyman, "The First Duty of Government: Protection, Liberty, and the Fourteenth Amendment," *Duke Law Journal* 41.3 (December 1991), pp. 507–571.

40. Susan Bandes, "The Negative Constitution: A Critique," *Michigan Law Review* 88.8 (August 1990), p. 2274.

41. This leaves the question, of course, of how we would know that the state even existed if anarchy reigned.

42. The constitutionality of permissible state action and inaction requires that once the state grants a right to some, it must not deny that right to others, either through affirmative action or through inaction. If the state grants some people access to its institutions to redress private wrongs, therefore, it must grant that access to everyone, and failure to do so, either by overt state action or passive state inaction, violates the Constitution. William E. Nelson, *The Fourteenth Amendment: From Political Principle to Judicial Doctrine* (Cambridge, Mass.: Harvard University Press, 1988), p. 196.

43. Civil Rights Act of 1875, 18 Stat. 336.

44. Tribe, *Constitutional Law*, p. 1693, n.10 (citing H. Friendly, "The Dartmouth College Case and the Public-Private Penumbra" 12 *Tex. Q.* 123, 13 (1968)). "Facially unconstitutional" refers to the actual words or wording used in a statute that in and of itself constitutes a violation of the Constitution. Henry Campbell Black, *Black's Law Dictionary*, 6th ed. (St. Paul, Minn.: West, 1990), p. 590.

45. Tribe, *Constitutional Law*, p. 1693; emphasis added. To be unconstitutional, such a state policy "need not be either a formal writing or facially unconstitutional" but simply a practice that "reflects deliberate indifference to or reckless disregard for protected rights." Susan Shoemaker, "*D.T. v. Independent School District*: Limiting Liability under 42 U.S.C. Sec. 1983," *Urban Lawyer* 24.2 (Spring 1992), p. 396.

46. A wrongful act is one to which the perpetrator is not entitled. Sometimes it is difficult to determine whether an act is wrongful. A case in point is whether it is a wrongful act of negligence for a parent to use prayer to aid a sick child to the exclusion of medical treatment. Some states include prayer-treatment exemptions in child abuse and neglect statutes in deference to parents who wish to exercise their right to raise their children as they choose. Eric W. Treene, "Prayer-Treatment Exemptions to Child Abuse and Neglect Statutes, Manslaughter Prosecutions, and Due Process of Law," *Harvard Journal on Legislation* 30.1 (Winter 1993), pp. 135–199.

In the case of a fetus that imposes wrongful pregnancy, however, it has no comparable right to do so. The state is not depriving a fetus of a right by stopping it from imposing wrongful pregnancy; although it may be legitimate for the state to protect the fetus, that protection does not rest on any entitlement of the fetus to another person's body.

47. *DeShaney*, p. 193: "In March 1984, Randy DeShaney beat 5-year-old Joshua so severely that he fell into a life-threatening coma. Emergency brain surgery revealed a series of hemorrhages caused by traumatic injuries to the head inflicted over a long period of time. Joshua did not die, but he suffered brain damage so severe that he is expected to spend the rest of his life confined to an institution for the profoundly retarded. Randy DeShaney was subsequently tried and convicted of child abuse."

48. This includes not only the state's failure to act as a form of state action having the force of law but also the state's acceptance of custom when it acquires the force of law. See *Adickes v. Kress & Co.*, 398 U.S. 144 (1970), p. 171 (holding that private refusal of service based on state-enforced custom of segregation in restaurants would violate the Fourteenth Amendment).

49. *Civil Rights Cases*, 109 U.S. 3 (1883), p. 17; emphasis added.

50. I base this typology on a reading of Tribe's *Constitutional Law*, chap. 18, "The Problem of State Action." Analyses of cases and points of law in reference to state action draw predominantly on Tribe's work.

51. For this reason, examples involving state statutes that directly delegate authority to private parties are not as relevant to the fetus's imposition of wrongful pregnancy as are cases that involve state tolerance or sanction of injurious private acts in the absence of legislation that authorizes such acts. In *Lugar v. Edmondson Oil Co.*, 457 U.S. 922 (1982), p. 941, for example, the Court ruled that a private party acts as if it is a state actor if the state passes a statute that authorizes such action, permits the private party to act without judicial supervision, and assists the private party by providing state officials to implement the private action. In the case of wrongful pregnancy, however, the state does not pass legislation that directly authorizes the fetus as a private party to impose the injuries of wrongful pregnancy to serve its own needs, but rather it passes legislation that prohibits the state from stopping the fetus as a private party from imposing the injuries of wrongful pregnancy.

52. *Lynch v. United States*, 189 F.2d 476, pp. 479–480 (5th Cir. 1951), *cert. denied*, 342 U.S. 831 (1951).

53. *Reitman v. Mulkey*, 387 U.S. 369 (1967).

54. The amendment, Proposition 14, in California read as follows: "Neither the State nor any subdivision or agency thereof shall deny, limit or abridge, directly or indirectly, the right of any person, who is willing or desires to sell, lease or rent any part or all of his real property, to decline to sell, lease or rent such property to such person or persons as he, in his absolute discretion, chooses." Cited in Tribe, *Constitutional Law*, p. 1700 n.9. The purpose of this amendment, and its immediate effect, was to invalidate two California statutes passed by the legislature that made it unlawful to prohibit certain types of private housing discrimination. A consequence of the amendment, therefore, would be to encourage private discrimination in housing, and for this reason the California Supreme Court ruled that it was unconstitutional since the state itself was involved in that private discrimination by virtue of the amendment that now protected it.

55. Ibid., p. 1697 (citing *Reitman*, p. 381).

56. Ibid., p. 48 n.26 (citing *NAACP v. Alabama*, 357 U.S. 449 (1958), pp. 462–463).

57. Ibid., p. 1701.

58. "There is a sufficiently close nexus between the State and the challenged action of the regulated entity so that the action of the latter may be fairly treated as that of the State itself." Leon Friedman, "New Developments in Civil Rights Litigation, and Trends in Section 1983 Actions," *Practising Law Institute/Litigation and Administrative Practice Course Handbook Series* 484 (1993), p. 10.

59. A third way is when the private party exercises powers that are traditionally the exclusive prerogative of the state. Ibid.

60. *Burton v. Wilmington Parking Authority*, 365 U.S. 715 (1961).

61. Ibid., p. 721 (quoting Chief Justice Vinson in *Shelley v. Kraemer*, 334 U.S. 1, 13 (1948)).

62. Ibid., p. 725.

63. As the Court noted, for example, the land and building were publicly owned; public funds paid for the land, acquisition, construction, and maintenance for the building; and, indeed, it was the intention of the state to fund the operation of this building. The Court stated, "It cannot be doubted that the peculiar relationship of the restaurant to the parking facility [state building] in which it is located confers on each an incidental variety of mutual benefits. Guests of the restaurant are afforded a convenient place to park their automobiles, even if they cannot enter the restaurant directly from the parking area. Similarly, its convenience for diners may well provide additional demand for the Authority's parking facilities." Ibid., p. 724. Some constitutional law scholars consider this case to be a correct, though unrepresentative, decision by the Court.

64. Ibid., p. 725.

65. Ibid.; emphasis added.

66. *Shelley v. Kraemer*, 334 U.S. 1 (1948).

67. Ibid., p. 19.

68. Ibid.

69. Ibid.

70. Ibid.

71. *Marsh v. Alabama*, 326 U.S. 501 (1946), pp. 508–509.

72. *Jackson v. Metropolitan Edison Co.*, 419 U.S. 345 (1974).

73. *Flagg Brothers, Inc. v. Brooks*, 436 U.S. 149 (1978). In addition, the Court ruled in *Polk County v. Dodson*, 454 U.S. 312 (1981), pp. 318–319, that an inadequate defense by a state-paid public defender is not an example of state action since the function of providing counsel is essentially a private function for which the state office and authority are not needed. The Court ruled in *Blum v. Yaretsky*, 457 U.S. 991 (1982), that decisions to transfer or discharge Medicaid patients from nursing homes against their will did not constitute unconstitutional state action because such judgments were the product of private medical personnel to which the state merely adjusted Medicaid benefits accordingly. Similarly, the Court ruled in *Rendel-Baker v. Kohn*, 457 U.S. 830 (1982), that the decision of a school to fire one of its teachers who opposed school policy did not constitute state action despite the fact that the school received substantial funding from the state, operated according to strict state regulations, and had a contract with the state to teach troubled students.

As Laurence Tribe notes, however, in each of these cases, the issue before the Court was not a rule but rather individual decisions to which some people objected. That is, no state rule was being challenged in *Polk County*, in *Rendel-Baker*, or in *Blum*. Rather, individual people in each case objected to how they had been treated or to particular decisions that affected them. It is less likely that the Court will find evidence of state action when there is no rule or systematic policy involved in the issue. Tribe, *Constitutional Law*, pp. 1716–1717.

The *DeShaney* decision can be seen as an example of how the Court distinguishes between an individual decision and a state policy; it was a specific judgment that was at issue in *DeShaney*, not an operating rule of the state or a systematic state policy. The state policy was to stop child abuse, not sanction it, even though in the tragic example of *DeShaney*, the state had failed to do so. Of course, it is precisely rules and policies that are involved in the state's failure to fund abortions. For this reason, it is more likely that the Court would rule that policies that systematically prohibit the state from acting to stop the fetus from imposing the injuries of wrongful pregnancy would constitute a form of state action that unconstitutionally sanctions the fetus's imposition of private wrongful acts on a woman.

74. Tribe, *Constitutional Law*, p. 1694 n.15 (citing *United States v. Cruikshank*, 92 U.S. 542 (1876), p. 555).

75. Ibid., p. 1694.

76. Ibid. (citing *United States v. Hall*, 26 Fed. Cas. 79 (Cas. No. 15, 282) (C.C.S.D. Ala. 1871), p. 81).

77. *Black's Law Dictionary*, pp. 24, 115.

78. Ibid., p. 24.

79. Ibid., p. 1488.

80. *Harris*, p. 315.

81. Ibid., p. 325.

82. *Maher v. Roe*, 432 U.S. 464 (1977), p. 474.

83. Substantive due process guarantees restrict the type of deprivations that the state may constitutionally impose. Regardless of how evenhanded the state's procedures may be, the Constitution restricts the state from making certain types of deprivations of life, liberty, and property unless there is an overriding need and the means used by the state are the narrowest necessary for achieving its compelling state objective. Rights that are not fundamental, but nonetheless fall under the due process protection of the Constitution, need only be rationally related to accomplishing a legitimate interest of the state. See Tribe, *Constitutional Law*, pp. 553–586, 629–632, 663–768, 1302–1435. Tribe also discusses structural due process rights on pp. 1673–1687.

It is difficult to pinpoint people's substantive, or fundamental, rights because they are not specifically enumerated in the Constitution, but over the years the Court has identified many of them to be in the area of reproductive activity, such as the right to engage in sexual intercourse with the use of contraceptives, the right to choose whom to marry, the right to bear children, and the right to make educational decisions for one's children. Protection of the substantive due process guarantees means that, regardless of the state's adherence to strict due process procedures, some actions by the state can still be unconstitutional simply because of the type of deprivation involved.

84. Robert W. Bennett, "Abortion and Judicial Review: Of Burdens and Benefits, Hard Cases, and Some Bad Law," *Northwestern University Law Review* 75.6 (February 1981), p. 999.

85. Procedural guarantees require the state to use fair and just processes when it imposes burdens on individuals. If the state needs to barge into your home, for example, in all but extraordinary cases it must first have a search warrant. If the state must restrict your liberty by imprisonment, it must do so in a way that assures you of procedural guarantees, such as informing you of the charges, giving you a chance to respond, and making sure that state officials engage only in appropriate conduct. Thomas O. Sargentich, "Due Process, Procedural," in Hall et al., *Oxford Companion to the Supreme Court*, p. 236.

The procedural guarantees in place when the state takes people's lives or liberty, for example, require that the government grant not only such protections as "the right to call witnesses, the right to counsel, the right of cross-examination, and the right of judicial review" but also the right of appeal and other such mechanisms that allow people to question or challenge the state. See Tribe, *Constitutional Law*, pp. 663–768.

86. Such a scenario is reminiscent of the scarcity/coerced reproduction after nuclear war that was depicted so dramatically and graphically in Margaret Atwood's *Handmaid's Tale* (New York: Ballantine Books, 1987).

87. Tribe, *Constitutional Law*, p. 1692.

88. This is termed the ends-means test.

89. *McCulloch v. Maryland*, 17 U.S. 316 (1819).

90. Ibid., p. 421, quoted in Craig R. Ducat and Harold W. Chase, *Constitutional Interpretation*, 4th ed. (St. Paul, Minn.: West, 1988), p. 150. Also see Tribe, *Constitutional Law*, pp. 301–302.

91. Tribe, *Constitutional Law*, p. 303; italics in original.

92. Ibid., p. 561.

93. Ibid., pp. 560–561.

94. Ibid., p. 1310.

95. Ibid.

7 From Due Process to Equal Protection

1. "[E]verybody knows perfectly well, economically advantaged white women in the United States, including the wives and daughters of those political and economic leaders who are gaining political mileage by opposing legal abortion, will have access to medically safe abortions, legal or not." Beverly Wildung Harrison, *Our Right to Choose: Toward a New Ethic of Abortion* (Boston: Beacon Press, 1983), p. 3. Sonia Corrêa and Rosalind Petchesky argue that the right to privacy, if defined as private liberties or choices, is meaningless for the poorest and disenfranchised. Rather than abandon the language of rights, what we need to do instead, they argue, is to reconstruct the right to an abortion so that it secures protection for the wide range of people defined by gender, class, cultural, and other differences. Corrêa and Petchesky, "Reproductive and Sexual Rights in Feminist Perspective," in *Population Policies Reconsidered: Health, Development, and Human Rights*, ed. G. Sen, A. Germain, and L. Chen (Cambridge, Mass.: Harvard University Press, 1994). A consent-to-pregnancy approach to abortion rights does just that by reconstructing a framework for the right to an abortion based on the fundamental right to be free of other private parties.

2. A conservative estimate is that 15,000 women annually bear unwanted children as a result of federal restrictions on abortion funding, and another 3,000 resort to illegal abortions. Mark A. Graber, "The Ghost of Abortion Past: Pre-*Roe* Abortion Law in Action," *Virginia Journal of Social Policy and the Law*, 1.2 (Spring 1994), pp. 368–369. In the wake of the failure to successfully challenge the constitutionality of abortion funding restrictions, litigators at the state level have responded by challenging state abortion laws, using their state constitutions. As a result, courts in Massachusetts, California, New Jersey, Connecticut, Oregon, and Pennsylvania "have recognized the discriminatory nature of a non-neutral funding scheme and have enjoined the regulations by relying on

state law." See Ellen Relkin and Sudi Solomon, "Using State Constitutions to Expand Public Funding for Abortions: Throwing away the Carrot with the Stick," *Women's Rights Law Reporter* 9.1 (Winter 1986), pp. 29–32.

3. See Charles Fried, on behalf of Appellants, in oral argument before the Supreme Court in *Webster v. Reproductive Health Services*, 492 U.S. 490 (1989), Doc. No. 88-605, p. 20 (April 26, 1989).

4. Reliance on the private right of self-defense is tantamount to evidence that the "public order is not working." John Q. Lafond, "The Case for Liberalizing the Use of Deadly Force in Self-Defense," *University of Puget Sound Law Review* 6.2 (Spring 1983), p. 284.

5. Although at times people must defend themselves, even with deadly force, the official attitude is outrage when people "usurp the state's task of keeping law and order." George P. Fletcher, *A Crime of Self-Defense: Bernhard Goetz and the Law on Trial* (New York: Free Press, 1988), p. 4.

6. "Privacy is too limited a concept to capture what is at stake for women, either as individuals or as a group." Deborah L. Rhode, *Justice and Gender: Sex Discrimination and the Law* (Cambridge, Mass.: Harvard University Press, 1989), p. 212. Lilian R. BeVier thinks that defining the right to privacy as freedom from government interference is positively misleading in the abortion debate. BeVier, "What Privacy Is Not," *Harvard Journal of Law and Public Policy* 12.1 (1989), pp. 101–102. As Cass R. Sunstein notes, "there appears to be a mounting consensus that equality arguments are better than liberty arguments with respect to abortion generally." Sunstein, *The Partial Constitution* (Cambridge, Mass.: Harvard University Press, 1993), p. 395, n.21. Robert W. Bennett asserts that abortion could have been decided on equal protection grounds just as readily as on due process grounds. Bennett, "Abortion and Judicial Review: Of Burdens and Benefits, Hard Cases and Some Bad Law," *Northwestern University Law Review* 75.6 (February 1981), p. 986.

7. This clause is more pro-active than the due process clause because it also specifies that the state shall actively do something to extend to every person the equal protection of the laws.

8. Jacobus tenBroek, *Equal under Law* (originally *The Antislavery Origins of the Fourteenth Amendment*, 1951) (New York: Collier, 1965), pp. 53, 56, 117; Joseph Tussman and Jacobus tenBroek, "The Equal Protection of the Laws," *California Law Review* 37.3 (1949), pp. 341, 364–365.

9. tenBroek, *Equal under Law*, p. 119.

10. Ibid. This interpretation of the equal protection clause attributes substantive content, securing government protection of fundamental, that is, natural, rights. The idea of equality is a "modifying condition," meaning that "[e]qual denial of protection, that is, no protection at all, is accordingly a denial of equal protection." Ibid., p. 237.

11. Joseph Tussman and Jacobus tenBroek view the doctrine of equality as embodied in the Declaration of Independence to be incorporated into the Fourteenth Amendment. As such, the Equal Protection Clause was "designed to impose upon the states *a positive duty* to supply protection to all persons in the enjoyment of their natural and inalienable rights—especially life, liberty, and property—and to do so equally" (emphasis added). Though one might think that the injunction that no state "shall deny to any person within its jurisdiction the equal protection of the laws" is a demand sim-

ply for administrative fairness, they claim that the equal protection clause was much more. What Justice Matthews said in *Yick Wo v. Hopkins*, 118 U.S. 356 (1886), p. 369—that "the equal protection of the laws is a pledge of the protection of equal laws"—the authors interpret as being "abundantly clear that the quality of legislation as well as the quality of administration comes within the purview of the clause." Tussman and tenBroek, "Equal Protection of the Laws," pp. 341–342.

12. See table 7.1.

13. Ibid.

14. Table 7.1 documents a few oaths of office administered to executives in the federal, state, and local levels of government, all of which testify that to be an executive of the state necessarily entails the solemn promise to uphold and execute the laws of the state.

15. *Thornburgh v. ACOG*, 476 U.S. 747 (1986), p. 790 (White, J., dissenting)(quoting *Palko v. Connecticut*, 302 U.S. 319 (1937), pp. 325–326).

16. Donald H. Regan has argued that although we "need to bring in the equal protection value" into the right to an abortion, he tends to think that the Court decided the "public facilities and public funding cases . . . correctly . . . [because] what is objectionable is the state's compelling a woman to serve the fetus, a compulsion which is absent once abortion is no longer forbidden." Regan, "Rewriting *Roe v. Wade*," *Michigan Law Review* 77 (August 1979), pp. 1644–1645. This view misses the crucial point, however, that it is not merely a woman's right to refuse to give her body to a fetus but also a woman's right not to have her body taken by a fetus.

17. A suspect class refers to the categorization of people on the basis of those demographic characteristics that are relatively immutable features acquired at birth and which have a history of being used for invidious discrimination and social stereotyping. Two suspect classifications recognized by the Court are race and national origin. Generally it is impossible for a state to show a compelling reason for treating people differently solely because of race or national origin, and for this reason, legislation that facially discriminates on the basis of race or national origin generally will be struck down by the Court as unconstitutional. In *Korematsu v. United States*, 323 U.S. 214 (1944), for example, the Court considered whether it was constitutional in the aftermath of Pearl Harbor for the state to intern in "war relocation centers" people who were of Japanese origin or ancestry and resided within a depth of forty miles inland on the West Coast. Ibid., p. 221. The Court applied strict scrutiny, but nonetheless upheld the internment as necessary to the United States' military security. Ibid., pp. 223–224.

A more recent example is the landmark decision of *Brown v. Board of Education*, 347 U.S. 483 (1954). Race is a suspect class and education, when and if the state chooses to provide it, is a "right which must be made available to all people on equal terms." Ibid., p. 493. For a provocative interpretation of the ineffectiveness of the *Brown* decision as a catalyst for the 1960s, see Gerald N. Rosenberg, *The Hollow Hope: Can Courts Bring about Social Change?* (Chicago: University of Chicago Press, 1991). See Gerald Gunther, "Foreword: In Search of Evolving Doctrine on a Changing Court: A Model for a Newer Equal Protection," *Harvard Law Review* 86.1 (1972), p. 1; Michael Klarman, "An Interpretive History of Modern Equal Protection," *Michigan Law Review* 90.2 (November 1991), p. 213; Kenneth L. Karst, "Foreword: Equal Citizenship under the Fourteenth Amendment," *Harvard Law Review* 91.1 (1977), pp. 1–68.

18. Gender also is a demographic characteristic acquired at birth that is relatively immutable and certainly associated with invidious discrimination. Yet there are problems with applying equal protection analysis on the basis of suspect classes to abortion rights because the Court has not elevated gender to the level of a suspect class but only to the level of a semisuspect, or intermediate, class. Consequently, if the state chooses to discriminate on the basis of gender, it need only show an important reason for doing so, not a compelling reason, thereby making it less likely that policies that discriminate on the basis of gender will be declared unconstitutional. Even with this limitation, however, the Court has ruled that some discrimination on the basis of gender is unconstitutional. The first case to establish this view was *Reed v. Reed*, 404 U.S. 71 (1971). In this case, for which then judge and now Justice Ruth Bader Ginsburg helped prepare the brief, the Court struck down an Idaho statute that automatically made fathers, rather than mothers, the executors of their children's estates (p. 76). The Court ruled that such a policy did not serve a rational state interest as required since gender is a semisuspect classification (p. 76). Some have suggested that now that Ruth Bader Ginsburg has joined the Court as a justice, her view that sex discrimination should be a suspect class may prevail. See *Harris v. Forklift Systems*, 114 S. Ct. 367, 373 (1993); Ginsburg concurs on p. 304, where she calls for the Court to reexamine the standard of scrutiny applied to gender discrimination. Even if sex does become a suspect classification, however, a remaining problem is the Court's ruling that discrimination on the basis of pregnancy is not necessarily a form of sex discrimination. See *Geduldig v. Aiello*, 417 U.S. 484 (1974) and *General Electric v. Gilbert*, 429 U.S. 125 (1976).

19. Racial inequality was the crucible of the Fourteenth Amendment, not sex inequality. For this reason, it was not until as late as 1971 in *Reed v. Reed* that the Court concluded that "unequal treatment of women on the face of the law could violate the constitutional guarantee of equal protection of the laws." Catharine A. MacKinnon, "Reflections on Sex Equality under Law," *Yale Law Journal* 100.5 (March 1991), p. 1284.

20. Sylvia A. Law, "Rethinking Sex and the Constitution," *University of Pennsylvania Law Review* 132.5 (1984), pp. 973–975. Some consider that the decision in *Reed* signaled that although the Court would no longer automatically uphold sex-based classifications as constitutional, a majority on the Court was only willing to declare sex a semisuspect, not a suspect, classification. Sally J. Kenney, *For Whose Protection? Reproductive Hazards and Exclusionary Policies in the United States and Britain* (Ann Arbor: University of Michigan Press, 1992), p. 165.

21. Law, "Rethinking Sex and the Constitution," pp. 981, 985.

22. As Ruth Bader Ginsburg wrote in 1985, "[T]wo related areas of constitutional adjudication" are "gender-based classification" and "reproductive autonomy," both of which influence "the opportunity women will have to participate as men's full partners in the nation's social, political, and economic life." She criticizes the Court's doctrinal separation of women's reproductive autonomy under substantive due process from gender classifications under equal protection guarantees. As a result, the "Court's gender classification decisions overturning state and federal legislation, in the main, have not provoked large controversy," in contrast to the "Court's initial 1973 abortion decision, *Roe v. Wade*," which "became and remains a storm center," sparking both "public opposition and academic criticism." Ginsburg, "Some Thoughts on Autonomy and Equality in Relation to *Roe v. Wade*," *North Carolina Law Review* 63 (1985), pp. 375–376. What

is more, Ginsburg believes that if the right to an abortion had been based on equality, the "Court probably would have ruled unconstitutional Congressional prohibitions on financing abortions for poor women." Neil A. Lewis, "A New Era In Abortion: End of Litmus Test for Court Nominee," *New York Times* (July 19, 1993), p. A13.

23. Guido Calabresi, *Ideals, Beliefs, Attitudes, and the Law: Private Law Perspectives on a Public Law Problem* (Syracuse, N.Y.: Syracuse University Press, 1985), p. 97. He identifies the danger inherent in *Roe* as the Court's failure to recognize sufficiently the value placed by some on the personhood status of the fetus. As he notes, the "gravitational pull of the law" from early English law up to the present has been to accord a fetus the protection of our law, at least for some purposes (p. 94). Calabresi thinks that it is "ironic" that the Supreme Court ignored this pull in *Roe* "when it made its misguided . . . statement . . . that fetuses are not persons for purposes of due process" (p. 94). The result was a "disaster," and the consequence of *Roe* was that it was "impossible for the opposing views [on abortion] to live with each other" (p. 97). "Suppose we described the [abortion] clash, more accurately, as one between values and beliefs which would give *primacy to equality* (among men and women as to participation in sex) even occasionally *at the cost of life-values*, and values and beliefs which would give primacy to life-preservation (even of not fully developed life) over equality . . . . [I]s that an accurate way of describing the abortion conflict? I think it is" (p. 99; emphasis added).

Calabresi, therefore, advocates that credence be given to both the personhood status of the fetus and the equality of men and women, rather than merely to women's right to make choices about how to live their lives. Privacy arguments may be inadequate as guarantees for abortion because "We have not in our law had any consistent pattern of constitutional rights to our own bodies or to privacy in sexual matters that seems to exclude governmental regulations . . . . Sales of hearts and body parts are not allowed. Laws against homosexual practices among consenting adults are, absurdly but regularly, held constitutional" (p. 100). For this reason, he seeks to base abortion rights on guarantees of equality between men and women, rather than on a woman's right of privacy. "For me, the essence of the argument in favor of abortion is an equality argument. It is an equal protection rather than a due process argument. It is a *women's rights versus fetal life debate*. It is based on the notion that without a right to abortion women are not equal to men in the law" (p. 101; emphasis added).

24. Calabresi, for example, evokes these grounds when he states, "There is in American law no general duty to be a good samaritan, to save lives . . . our legal system would rather let some people die unnecessarily than impose duties on others to save them!" Ibid., pp. 102–103. Calabresi locates the moral right to be a bad samaritan in relation to the legal right to obtain an abortion in his contention that a law that would require "only women, or only blacks, to save people who are drowning . . . would surely be unconstitutional" (p. 103).

25. "Even if the fetus were assumed to be a person, it would not follow that its interests must assume primary importance. Just as we do not compel individuals to serve as Good Samaritans in other contexts, we ought not to expect women at all stages of pregnancy to sacrifice their own destiny to embryonic life. State efforts to coerce childbirth do violence to the values of care and commitment that should underpin mother-infant attachments." Rhode, *Justice and Gender*, pp. 212–213.

26. Cass Sunstein says that "abortion should be seen not as murder of the fetus but

instead as a refusal to continue to permit one's body to be used to provide assistance to it." Sunstein, *Partial Constitution*, p. 273.

27. Women are "uniquely vulnerable to [the] imposition" of the "burden of self-sacrifice on behalf of the unborn because women must call on others for assistance if they would choose not to make such a sacrifice." Laurence H. Tribe, *American Constitutional Law*, 2nd ed. (Mineola, N.Y.: Foundation Press, 1988), p. 1355.

28. Donald H. Regan wants to clarify the grounds on which women have a right to an abortion, not extend their reproductive rights to include abortion funding. He thinks that the fundamental right underlying the right to an abortion is not merely the right to make a choice but rather the right not to be compelled by the state to "serve the fetus"; "once abortion is no longer forbidden," therefore, his view is that the compulsion is absent. Since there is no longer a problem once the state desists from compelling a woman to serve a fetus, there are no grounds for requiring a state to fund an abortion. Regan, "Rewriting *Roe v. Wade*," pp. 1644–1645.

29. Laurence H. Tribe, "The Abortion Funding Conundrum: Inalienable Rights, Affirmative Duties, and the Dilemma of Dependence," *Harvard Law Review* 99.1 (November 1985), p. 337.

30. Kathryn Kolbert, oral argument before the Court in *Planned Parenthood of Southeastern Pennsylvania v. Casey*, 112 S. Ct. 2791 (1992), April 22, 1992, transcript pp. 10–11.

31. *Geduldig v. Aiello*, 417 U.S. 484 (1974).

32. Ibid., pp. 396–397 n.20.

33. The controversial nature of the abortion issue is one reason that states failed to ratify the Equal Rights Amendment, yet even if the ERA were now to pass, subsequent rulings by the Court that pregnancy discrimination is not a form of sex discrimination most likely would blunt the impact of the ERA for abortion-funding entitlement. Jane J. Mansbridge, *Why We Lost the ERA* (Chicago: University of Chicago Press, 1986).

34. Legal scholar Lori Rankin terms discrimination on the basis of race and sex a "statutory classification" equal protection claim based on a "fundamental right" equal protection claim. Rankin, "Ballot Initiatives and Gay Rights: Equal Protection Challenges to the Right's Campaign against Lesbians and Gay Men," *University of Cincinnati Law Review* 62.3 (Winter 1994), p. 1062.

35. *Planned Parenthood of Southeastern Pennsylvania v. Casey*, 112 S. Ct. 2791 (1992).

36. *Roe v. Wade*, 410 U.S. 113 (1973), p. 158.

37. *Casey*, p. 2791, citing *Roe*, pp. 162–163.

38. Ibid.

39. Ibid., p. 87, citing *Webster*, p. 519 (opinion of Rehnquist, C.J.).

40. Ibid., p. 2820.

41. Ibid., p. 2823.

42. Ibid., p. 2826.

43. Ibid., p. 2827.

44. Ibid., p. 2829.

45. Kathleen M. Sullivan, "Unconstitutional Conditions," *Harvard Law Review* 102 (1989), pp. 1413–1506.

46. *Casey*, p. 849.

47. *Roe*, pp. 164–165; emphasis added.

48. *Casey*, p. 2807.

49. *Congressional Record*, House of Representatives, 93rd Congr., 2nd Sess. (1974), vol. 120, p. 399.

50. I am grateful to Judge Guido Calabresi, Second Circuit, Federal Court of Appeals, for suggesting the following line of reasoning and discussion. Personal conversation, February 5, 1996.

51. Some states still view a marriage contract, for example, as entailing marital rape exemptions which make it impossible to claim legally that one's bodily integrity and liberty have been violated by the imposition of nonconsensual sexual intercourse by one's spouse. This is tantamount to obtaining the right to intrude sexually upon the body of one's spouse as a condition of the marriage contract. The trend, however, is for marital rape exemptions to be dropped by states, not instituted by states. For this reason, marital rape exemptions do not bolster contentions, even in their highly speculative form, that consent to sexual intercourse would imply contractual obligations to allow one's bodily integrity to be violated by fetuses conceived or by children born subsequent to that sexual intercourse.

52. *Harris v. McRae*, 448 U.S. 297 (1980).

53. *Romer v. Evans*, 882 P.2d 1335 (1994), *Amici Curiae Brief* of Laurence H. Tribe, John Hart Ely, Gerald Gunther, Philip B. Kurland, and Kathleen M. Sullivan.

54. *Amici Curiae Brief* of Tribe et al.

55. The fact that fetuses only intrude upon women is relevant if one were to claim abortion restrictions were a form of sex discrimination, and that sex discrimination required strict scrutiny by the Court. A fundamental rights, rather than a sex discrimination, approach to abortion rights, however, by-passes the issue of how the state discriminates against men and women by pointing to the way the state discriminates against victims of private injury. Whatever the group characteristics of those victims, the state violates the Constitution if it offers protection to some victims of private violence but not to others similarly situated.

56. *San Antonio Independent School District v. Rodriguez*, 441 U.S. 1 (1973), in which the Court ruled that the right to education is not expressly or implicitly guaranteed in the Constitution, and, thus, education is not a fundamental right.

57. In *Dandridge v. Williams*, 397 U.S. 471 (1970), the Court ruled that there was no fundamental right to welfare and that classification schemes for receipt of welfare benefits were constitutional.

58. *Shapiro v. Thomson*, 394 U.S. 618 (1969), in which the Court struck down a law denying welfare assistance to those who had been in residence for less than one year on the grounds that although the "right to travel" was found nowhere in the text of the Constitution, it nevertheless was a right "fundamental to the concept of our federal union" (p. 630). In *Sosna v. Iowa*, 419 U.S. 393 (1975), however, the Court upheld a one-year residency requirement for divorce actions.

59. *Skinner v. Oklahoma*, 316 U.S. 535 (1942), in which the Court ruled that "one of the basic civil rights of man" is to reproduce (p. 541).

60. *Harper v. Virginia State Board of Elections*, 383 U.S. 663 (1965), in which the Court struck down a poll tax on the grounds that the right to vote is so fundamental that any classifications burdening its exercise must receive strict scrutiny.

61. *Griffin v. Illinois*, 351 U.S. 12 (1956). The Court ruled that although there is no fundamental right to appeal a criminal conviction, if the state allows an appeal, it must

provide a trial transcript to an indigent criminal defendant if such a transcript is necessary for an "adequate and effective appellate review" (pp. 19–20). Similarly, in *Douglas v. California*, 372 U.S. 353 (1963), the Court ruled that a state must appoint a defense counsel for all appeals to which criminal defendants are entitled.

62. *Evans v. Romer*, 882 P.2d 1335 (1994). The state constitutional amendment states that "homosexual, lesbian or bisexual orientation, conduct, practices or relationships could not provide the basis for protected class status." The Supreme Court struck down this state constitutional amendment in *Romer v. Evans*, 1996 WL 262293 (U.S.).

63. Ibid., p. 1339, and *Romer*, 1996 WL 262293.

64. Poverty does not constitute a discriminatory class, according to the Court, in cases where equal protection analysis applies. Donald W. Jackson, *Even the Children of Strangers: Equality under the U.S. Constitution* (Lawrence: University Press of Kansas, 1992), p. 189. Also, there is no constitutional right to be a homosexual. In *Bowers v. Hardwick*, 478 U.S. 186 (1986), for example, the Court ruled that there is no constitutional right to engage in homosexual sodomy. If the issue in this case had been whether it were constitutional for Colorado to prohibit homosexual conduct, the Court would either have had to rule that it was constitutional or it would have had to overrule *Bowers*. The issue in this case, however, was whether homosexuals had a right to be treated equally compared to other groups—that is, whether it would be constitutional to prohibit legislation that mandated equal state protection of homosexuals compared to other groups.

65. *Romer*, 832 P.2d (quoting earlier opinion), p. 1339. As a federal district court considering a similar amendment stated, "relevant Supreme Court precedent support[s] the proposition that '[s]tates may not disadvantage any identifiable group, whether a suspect category or not, by making it more difficult to enact legislation on its behalf,'" such as prohibiting a group from participating in the political process. *Equality Foundation of Greater Cincinnati v. Cincinnati*, 838 F.Supp. 1235 (S.D. Ohio 1993) (citations omitted). Also see *Romer v. Evans*, 1996 WL 262293 (U.S.).

66. *Evans*, p. 1349. As the Supreme Court has ruled, "States have no compelling interest in amending their constitution in ways that violate fundamental federal rights." *Evans*, p. 1350 (citation omitted). In *Evans*, the Colorado Supreme Court held that the state's objectives, such as "[e]nsuring that certain racial, gender, or ethnic groups receive undiminished funds for civil rights enforcement could easily be accomplished by earmarking funds to cover the costs of such enforcement" (p. 1346).

67. Thomas E. Baker, "Can Voters Exclude Homosexuals and Their Interests from the Legislative Process?" *Preview of the United States Supreme Court Cases* (American Bar Association), no. 1 (September 29, 1995), p. 15.

68. Anthony S. Winer, "Hate Crimes, Homosexuals, and the Constitution," *Harvard Civil Rights–Civil Liberties Law Review* 29 (1994), pp. 389–390, 395.

69. Ibid., p. 401.

70. Robin West, "Equality Theory, Marital Rape, and the Promise of the Fourteenth Amendment," *Florida Law Review* 42.1 (January 1990), p. 52.

71. For an in-depth and classic analysis of how restrictions on abortion funding discriminate against women, see Reva Siegel, "Reasoning from the Body: A Historical Perspective on Abortion Regulation and Questions of Equal Protection," *Stanford Law Review* 44.2 (January 1992), pp. 261–381.

72. *Washington v. Davis*, 426 U.S. 229, 239, 241–242 (1976).

73. Similarly, policies that treat pregnant women as if they are nothing more than vessels or containers for fetuses while treating the welfare of the fetus as more significant than that of the women have the effect of devaluing pregnant women, reducing them to little more than an "inert incubator, or a culture medium for the fetus." George J. Annas, "Pregnant Women as Fetal Containers," *Hastings Center Report* (December 1986), pp. 13–14. What we must begin to recognize is that current restrictions on abortion funding treat the welfare of the fetus not only as more significant than that of any woman but also as more significant than any born person. What merits legal scrutiny, therefore, is the biased way in which abortion policies elevate protection of the fetus.

74. As Robin West notes, state passivity in relation to some victims of private violence but not others is "paradigmatic violation of the constitutional guarantee of equal protection of the law." West cites the example of a "southern state's refusal to grant a common law cause of action to black travelers to protect them against southern white innkeepers' refusals of service" and the example of states' "refusal to protect black citizens from homicidal attacks by whites or a state's passivity in the fact of widespread lynching and private violence." West, "Equality Theory," p. 62.

75. N. Bernard Nathanson with Richard N. Ostling, *Aborting America* (Garden City, N.Y.: Doubleday, 1979), p. 220.

76. Joanna K. Weinberg notes that the Court itself, particularly Justice Scalia and Justice O'Connor, appear "to approve dating the origin of the state's interest in the fetus from conception." Weinberg, "Review Essay: The Politicization of Reproduction," *Berkeley Women's Law Journal* 5 (1989–1990), p. 206.

77. In contemporary American consciousness, "fetuses are *becoming* persons" and along with this trend is a "new-found legal status of fetuses as persons"—that is, as "rights-bearing entities under the law." Deirdre Moira Condit, "Constructing Fetal 'Personhood': An Examination of Law and Language," paper presented at the Annual Meeting of the Midwest Political Science Association, Chicago, April 18–20, 1991, p. 3. Patricia A. King contends, "There is today no inherent legal obstacle to giving viable fetuses legal protection fully equivalent to that given the newborn." King, "The Juridical Status of the Fetus: A Proposal for Legal Protection of the Unborn," in *Abortion: Moral and Legal Perspectives*, ed. Jay L. Garfield and Patricia Hennessey (Amherst: University of Massachusetts Press, 1984), p. 74.

78. In the past, few laws were written with the fetus in mind, and initially, therefore, courts refused to apply to unborn fetuses the laws written to cover injuries. In 1891, for example, after a pregnant woman and a fetus were seriously injured in a train accident, the child was born crippled and deformed. In *Walker v. Railway Co.*, 28 L.R.Ir. 69 (1891), an Irish court ruled that the child could not sue for negligence because at the time of the accident she was "not a person, or a passenger, or a human being." Cited in Robert H. Blank, *Mother and Fetus: Changing Notions of Maternal Responsibility* (New York: Greenwood, 1992), p. 54.

In 1900 the Illinois Supreme Court in *Allaire v. St. Lukes Hospital*, 56 N.E. 638 (1900), ruled that a fetus injured when its mother was hurt in an elevator accident had "no separate legal existence," even though once born the child was "sadly crippled for life." *Allaire* (cited in Blank, *Mother and Fetus*, p. 54). One reason the Court refused the fetus's claim was to avoid setting a precedent that could be used by children in subsequent cases to sue their mothers.

In a dissent that proved prescient, however, Judge J. Boggs noted that at some point of "viability," even if the mother is killed, the fetus might not be, and for this reason, he argued, the law must recognize that two parties are involved when a pregnant woman is injured and that the fetus is "capable of independent and separate life." *Allaire*, p. 641 (Boggs, J., dissenting). Accordingly, although the fetus is "within the body of the mother, it is not merely a part of her body, for her body may die in all of its parts and the child remain alive and capable of maintaining life." Ibid. (quoted in Blank, *Mother and Fetus*, p. 55). The infant that survived an accident that occurred while it was a fetus should, therefore, he concluded, be allowed the same right to recover damages as its mother. Common law also has supported the fetus's property and contract rights (p. 55).

79. *Bonbrest v. Kotz*, 65 F.Supp. 138, 140 (D.D.C. 1946); cited in Blank, *Mother and Fetus*, pp. 55–56.

80. *Woods v. Lancet*, 102 N.E.2d (1951), pp. 691, 695; quoted in Blank, *Mother and Fetus*, p. 56.

81. *Williams v. Marion Rapid Transit, Inc.*, 87 N.E.2d 334, 340 (Ohio 1949), p. 503. Following this line of reasoning, the New Jersey Supreme Court held that a fetus that sustained injuries when its mother was in a car accident had a right to sue for the wrongful conduct that caused its injuries while in its mother's womb. As the court put it, "Regardless of analogies to other areas of the law, justice requires that the principle be recognized that a child has a legal right to begin life with a sound mind and body. If the wrongful conduct of another interferes with that right, and it can be established by competent proof that there is a causal connection between the wrongful interference and the harm suffered by the child when born, damages for such harm should be recoverable by the child." *Smith v. Brennan*, 157 A.2d (1960), pp. 497, 503. Quoted in Blank, *Mother and Fetus*, p. 56. In *Smith*, p. 503, the Court explicitly stated that using existing laws to cover the fetus in order to protect it did not mandate that the fetus actually must be a person. It is irrelevant to recovery for prenatal injury, the court ruled, whether "an unborn child is a 'person in being.'" As Robert Blank notes, respected legal commentator William L. Prosser considers this trend to allow laws designed to protect born people against negligent injuries to cover injuries to unborn fetuses to be "the most spectacular abrupt reversal of a well settled rule in the whole history of the law of torts." Blank, *Mother and Fetus*, pp. 56–57.

82. *Hornbuckle v. Plantation Pipe Line Co.*, 93 S.E.2d (Ga. 1956), p. 727; cited in Blank, *Mother and Fetus*, pp. 57–58.

83. Ibid.

84. Ibid., p. 728. Similarly, a Rhode Island appellate court in *Sylvia v. Gobeille*, 220 A.2d (R.I. 1966), pp. 222, 224, 226, ruled, "We are unable logically to conclude that a claim for injury inflicted prior to viability is any less meritorious than one sustained after." Quoted in Blank, *Mother and Fetus*, p. 58. This ruling exemplifies a trend, notes Robert Blank, toward the abolition of the viability rule. This means that states and courts are using existing laws, which were not written with a fetus in mind and which earlier were not used to cover protection of fetuses, to now protect fetuses by including them in the coverage of those laws.

85. *People v. Davis*, 872 P.2d (Cal. 1994), p. 591.

86. Ibid., p. 593.

87. "Lawyers Discuss California Fetus Murder Case," on "All Things Considered," National Public Radio, May 21, 1994.

88. *People v. Davis*, p. 593. As the prosecuting attorney for the case pointed out, the Court reached this conclusion because the California statute did not make a distinction between viable and nonviable fetuses. California's murder statute simply read that it is "unlawful to kill a human being or a fetus," which the Court interpreted as meaning any and all fetuses, viable or not. "Lawyers Discuss California Fetus Murder Case," NPR.

89. Blank, *Mother and Fetus*, p. 61; see *Group Health Association v. Blumenthal*, 453 A.2d (Md. 1983), p. 1198 (holding that a child born alive and who then dies of injuries sustained while a fetus can maintain a wrongful death action), and *Justus v. Atchison*, 565 P.2d (Ca. 1977), p. 122; *Egbert v. Wenzl*, 260 N.W.2d (Neb. 1977), p. 480.

90. *Presley v. Newport Hospital*, 365 A.2d 748 (R.I. 1976), p. 754; cited in Blank, *Mother and Fetus*, p. 61.

91. *Danos v. St. Pierre*, 402 So.2d 633 (La. 1981) (concurring opinion); cited in Blank, *Mother and Fetus*, p. 61. See also *O'Grady v. Brown*, 645 S.W.2d 904 (Mo. 1983) (holding that the statutory term *person* includes the fetus).

92. Blank, *Mother and Fetus*, p. 62; *Fryover v. Forbes*, 439 N.W.2d 284 (Mich. App. 1989)(Weaver, D. J., dissenting), pp. 284–285.

93. *Webster v. Reproductive Health Services*, 492 U.S. 490 (1989), pp. 490, 500.

94. James Madison, *The Federalist*, ed. Jacob E. Cooke (New York: Meridian Books, 1961), no. 51, pp. 349, 351.

95. Earl M. Maltz notes that the most basic function of government is the protection of life, liberty, and property, and debates over the Fourteenth Amendment center on what level of government should have jurisdiction: federal or state. Maltz, *Civil Rights, the Constitution and Congress, 1863–1868* (Lawrence: University Press of Kansas, 1990), p. 57.

96. *Harris v. McRae*, 448 U.S. 297 (1980), pp. 316–317.

97. Ibid.

98. *Bray v. Alexandria Women's Health Clinic*, 113 S. Ct. 753 (1993).

99. For insightful analyses of *Bray*, see Sherri Snelson Haring, "*Bray v. Alexandria Women's Health Clinic*: 'Rational Objects of Disfavor' as a New Weapon in Modern Civil Rights Litigation," *North Carolina Law Review* 72.3 (March 1994), p. 764, and J. Paige Lambdin, "Civil Rights = Abortion Protests = 42 U.S.C. § 1985(3) Does Not Provide a Federal Cause of Action against Protesters Who Obstruct Access to Abortion Clinics—*Bray v. Alexandria Women's Health Clinic*, 113 S. Ct. 753 (1993)," *Seton Hall Law Review* 24.4 (1994), p. 2096.

100. The Court only ruled in *Bray* that the particular law in question, the Ku Klux Klan law, did not apply to anti-abortion activists because these people did not harbor an invidiously discriminatory intent toward women in general, evidenced by the fact that many anti-abortion activists are women; that there was only an incidental effect on women who needed to travel across state lines to obtain abortions, not a conspiratorial intent on the part of anti-abortionists to deprive such women of their right to interstate travel; and anti-abortionists did not intend to deprive women seeking abortions of the equal protection of the law, so this claim was not suitable for review by the Court.

101. Kevin Cullen and Brian McGrory, "Abortion Violence Hits Home," *Boston Globe* (December 31, 1994), p. 1.

102. *Congressional Record*, House of Representatives, 102nd Congr. (1992), vol. 138, p. H2834; 103rd Congr. (1993), vol. 139, p. H4322.

103. "Modern American governments, both state and federal, build roads, employ workers, and grant licenses; they distribute tax exemptions, medical care, food stamps, and cash grants. They have, in short, enormous wealth and power." Yet there is no "clear constitutional entitlement" to benefits provided by the government, which raises serious constitutional questions. Lynn A. Baker, "The Prices of Rights: Toward a Positive Theory of Unconstitutional Conditions," *Cornell Law Review* 75.6 (September 1990), p. 1189. See Frank I. Michelman, "Welfare Rights in a Constitutional Democracy," *Washington University Law Quarterly* 1979.3 (1979), p. 659; Michelman, "The Supreme Court, 1968 Term—Foreword: On Protecting the Poor through the Fourteenth Amendment," *Harvard Law Review* 83 (1969), p. 7.

104. The literature is vast, but see Theda Skocpol, *Protecting Soldiers and Mothers: The Political Origins of Social Policy in the United States* (Cambridge, Mass.: Harvard University Press, 1992), who argues that the American state was a pioneer in providing maternalist benefits to mothers and children but a laggard compared to western Europe for providing old age insurance and health and worker benefits.

105. Robert Blank and Janna C. Merrick, *Human Reproduction, Emerging Technologies, and Conflicting Rights* (Washington, D.C.: Congressional Quarterly Press, 1995), pp. 2–3.

106. Malcolm L. Goggin views abortion as a redistributive, not a distributive, policy issue, by which he means that abortion rights pit competing claims against each other, and one side's gain is the other side's loss. See Goggin, "Introduction: A Framework for Understanding the New Politics of Abortion," in *Understanding the New Politics of Abortion*, ed. Malcolm L. Goggin (Newbury Park, N.J.: Sage, 1993), pp. 15, 18 fn.15. Yet a consent-to-pregnancy approach to abortion rights redefines it not so much as a redistributive policy but rather as a state's remedy for private, wrongful imposition of the fetus on a woman. The loss of the woman's body to the fetus is a loss of that to which it has no entitlement in the first place, unless she consents to pregnancy.

107. Jane Jenson notes that the concern of the capitalist state about its national population fosters particular social constructions of maternity as an area of state activity. See Jenson, "Gender and Reproduction: Or, Babies and the State," *Studies in Political Economy* 20 (Summer 1986), p. 15.

108. Charles Fried, argument before the Court in *Webster*, Doc. No. 88-605, pp. 21–22 (April 26, 1989). Some also think it would be unconstitutional for the state to mandate directly that a woman either be pregnant or have an abortion. George J. Annas, Leonard H. Glantz, and Wendy K. Mariner, "Amici for Appellees in *Webster v. Reproductive Health Services*: Brief for Bioethicists for Privacy as *Amicus Curiae* Supporting Appellees," *American Journal of Law and Medicine* 15:2–3 (1989), p. 172.

109. Dorothy E. Roberts, "The Only Good Poor Woman: Unconstitutional Conditions and Welfare," *Denver University Law Review* 72 (1995), pp. 931–948.

110. Kathleen M. Sullivan, "Law's Labors," book review of *Liberty and Sexuality: The Right to Privacy and the Making of Roe v. Wade* by David J. Garrow, *New Republic* (May 23, 1994), pp. 42–45.

8 Right to Bodily Access

1. *Roe v. Wade*, 410 U.S. 113 (1973).

2. Mary Ann Glendon, *Abortion and Divorce in Western Law* (Cambridge, Mass.: Harvard University Press, 1987), pp. 6–9.

3. Laurence H. Tribe, "The Curvature of Constitutional Space: What Lawyers Can Learn from Modern Physics," *Harvard Law Review* 103.1 (November 1989), pp. 13–14, 38–39. Legal scholar Jane Rutherford makes the same point, viewing the Due Process Clause in terms of a myth that is simultaneously true and fictional. Rutherford, "The Myth of Due Process," *Boston University Law Review* 72.1 (January 1992), pp. 3–4.

4. For an excellent collection of essays that explores the ways in which the law is anything but neutral, see Austin Sarat and Thomas R. Kearns, eds., *The Fate of Law* (Ann Arbor: University of Michigan Press, 1991).

5. Lea S. VanderVelde notes that women were omitted from those gains acquired by African-American men following the Civil War. Reconstruction debates failed to apply the Thirteenth Amendment's ban on involuntary servitude to "wives' servitude to their husbands" because the rationale for freeing slaves was that this "was necessary 'to return to them their manhood,' a phrase that notably omitted the emancipation of women, whether wives or servants, slave or free. The Reconstruction Congress viewed slave women in relation to men and never afforded them the full range of rights and benefits accorded freedmen." VanderVelde, "The Gendered Origins of the *Lumley* Doctrine: Binding Men's Consciences and Women's Fidelity," *Yale Law Journal* 101.4 (January 1992), pp. 831–832.

6. The *Brief Amicus Curiae of American Historians*, filed in *Webster v. Reproductive Health Services*, 492 U.S. 490 (1989)(Doc. 88-605), carefully demonstrates how legal justifications of discriminatory attitudes toward women were established throughout the nineteenth century and into the twentieth.

In no small measure, the discriminatory, differential treatment of women's right to bodily integrity and liberty stems not from anatomical differences between men and women but from differences in attitudes toward permissible access to one's body. The word *access* usually connotes something people value as a means to their empowerment, such as access to education, economic resources, or other such goods. In the case of women, however, the word *access* denotes just the opposite because the law has viewed women's bodily integrity and liberty as resources to be accessed automatically by others. Rather than empowerment, access has stood for women's disempowerment. The history of women's emancipation, therefore, is in large part a history of gaining freedom from the assumption that classes of people have an automatic right of access to women's bodies and liberty. Far from a singularly Western cultural problem, women's subordination in other contexts is of concern as well. According to the Yoruba tribe in Nigeria, for example, "a woman is supposed to slavishly follow the man's wishes and she is not considered a rational, autonomous being." A husband is viewed as "the owner of her head," not merely her body. Temisanren Ebijuwa argues that a woman must be viewed as a "fully rational autonomous agent" whose right to health "overrides the so-called fetus' 'right to life.'" Ebijuwa, "Abortion, Women and National Development: The Nigeria Experience," *Ahfad Journal: Women and Change* 10.1 (June 1993), p. 33. Anthony Ewing makes the point that international protection for women against gender-specific acts of violence needs to be developed in "Establishing State Responsibility for Private

Acts of Violence against Women under the American Convention on Human Rights," *Columbia Human Rights Law Review* 26 (Spring 1995), pp. 752–754. Violence against women is a universal that transcends any particular culture, class, ethnicity, or nation. Rhonda Copelon, "Recognizing the Egregious in the Everyday: Domestic Violence as Torture," *Columbia Human Rights Law Review* 25 (Spring 1994), p. 292.

7. Susan Estrich notes that husbands have traditionally been guaranteed by the law sexual access to their wives. Estrich, *Real Rape* (Cambridge, Mass.: Harvard University Press, 1987), p. 37.

8. William Blackstone, *Commentaries on the Laws of England*, Bk. 1 (Chicago: University of Chicago Press, [1765] 1979), p. 430.

9. Mary Beth Norton, *Liberty's Daughters: The Revolutionary Experience of American Women, 1750–1800* (Boston: Little, Brown, 1980), pp. 45–46.

10. William J. Crotty, *Political Reform and the American Experiment* (New York: Crowell, 1977), p. 20; emphasis in text.

11. Eileen L. McDonagh, "Gender Politics and Political Change," in *New Perspectives on American Politics*, ed. Lawrence C. Dodd and Calvin Jillson (Washington, D.C.: Congressional Quarterly Press, 1994). The one exception is Abigail Adams's attempt to draw attention to the illiberal bases of coverture marriage, penned in her famous plea to her husband, John, in 1776: "Remember the ladies" since "all Men would be Tyrants if they could . . . why then, not put it out of the power of the vicious and lawless to use us with cruelty and indignity with impunity?" Quoted in Norton, *Liberty's Daughters*, p. 50).

12. Susan Moller Okin, *Justice, Gender and the Family* (New York: Basic Books, 1989). Similarly, Nancy Cott cogently argues that the definition and regulation of marriage is involved in the formation of all nation-states and, in that sense, integral to construction of the public sphere. Cott, "The Dewey Lecture," lecture delivered at Harvard Law School, Cambridge, Mass., Fall 1994.

13. Norma Basch, *In the Eyes of the Law: Women, Marriage, and Property in Nineteenth-Century New York* (Ithaca, N.Y.: Cornell University Press, 1982), p. 30.

14. *Seitz v. Mitchell*, 94 U.S. 580 (1876), p. 584.

15. Ibid., pp. 584–585; cited also in Kevin C. Paul, "Private/Property: A Discourse on Gender Inequality in American Law," *Law & Inequality: A Journal of Theory and Practice* 7.3 (July 1989), p. 406.

16. *Chapman v. Phoenix National Bank of the City of New York*, 85 N.Y. 437, 449 (1881); quoted ibid., p. 407.

17. William Coyle, "Common Law Metaphors of Coverture: Conceptions of Women and Children as Property in Legal and Literary Contexts," *Texas Journal of Women and the Law* 1 (1992), pp. 315–336, esp. p. 315.

18. Leo Kanowitz, *Women and the Law: The Unfinished Revolution*, quoted ibid., p. 331.

19. Paul, "Private/Property," p. 407.

20. *People v. Lipsky*, 327 Ill. App. 63, 67, 63 N.E.2d 642, 644 (Ill. App. 1945); cited ibid., p. 407.

21. *Forbush v. Wallace*, 341 F.Supp. 217 (M.D. Al. 1971), *affirmed by* 405 U.S. 970 (1972) without a written opinion; cited ibid.

22. Ibid., p. 408. Legal scholar Mary Ann Glendon notes that occasionally it is a

woman who seeks to use her husband's name against the wishes of her spouse or former spouse. In this case, courts must consider whether married women have a right to use their husbands' names. Usually courts have held that an ex-husband cannot prohibit his former wife from using his name, as long as the use is nonfraudulent. Glendon, *The Transformation of Family Law: State, Law, and Family in the United States and Western Europe* (Chicago: University of Chicago Press, 1989), p. 106.

23. Susan D. Appel, "Beyond Self-defense: The Use of Battered Woman Syndrome in Duress Defenses," *University of Illinois Law Review* 1994.4 (1994), p. 956.

24. Katharine T. Bartlett, *Gender and Law: Theory, Doctrine, Commentary* (Boston: Little, Brown, 1993), p. 527.

25. Blackstone, *Commentaries on the Laws of England*, Bk. 1, pp. 444–445; quoted ibid., p. 19.

26. *State v. Rhodes*, 61 N.C. 453 (1868).

27. Ibid., p. 454, quoted in Bartlett, *Gender and Law*, p. 19.

28. Ibid., p. 454.

29. Ibid.

30. Ibid., p. 458, quoted in Bartlett, pp. 20–21.

31. Ibid., p. 459.

32. Ibid., p. 458, quoted in Bartlett, pp. 21–22; emphasis in text.

33. Joanne Schulman, "Battered Women Score Major Victories in New Jersey and Massachusetts Marital Rape Cases," *Clearinghouse Review* 15.4 (1981) (New York: National Center on Women and Family Law, 1981), p. 344.

34. Quoted ibid.

35. Ibid. Schulman notes that several English justices criticized Hale for lack of substantiation for his claim.

36. *Frazier v. State*, 86 S.W. 754 (1905), p. 755; quoted in Schulman, "Battered Women," p. 344.

37. Michael N. Salveson, "Sexism and the Common Law: Spousal Rape in Virginia," *George Mason University Law Review* 8.2 (Spring 1986), pp. 369–387.

38. Quoted in Carole Pateman, "Women and Consent," *Political Theory* 8.2 (May 1980), p. 156.

39. Hillary Rodham, "Children under the Law," *Harvard Educational Review* 43.4 (November 1973), pp. 487–514.

40. In doing so, they left open the question of whether it ever had been correctly categorized as a part of common law. Schulman, "Battered Women Score Major Victories," p. 344.

41. *New Jersey v. Smith*, 426 A.2d 38, 46–47 (N.J. 1981)(citations omitted); quoted in Schulman, "Battered Women Score Major Victories," p. 344.

42. Monica Rickenberg and Joanne Schulman, "Florida, New York, and Virginia Courts Declare Marital Rape a Crime," *Clearinghouse Review* 18.7 (1984), p. 745; Judith A. Lincoln, "Abolishing the Marital Rape Exemption: The First Step in Protecting Married Women from Spousal Rape," *Wayne Law Review* 35.3 (Spring 1989), pp. 1219–1250; Rene I. Augustine, "Marriage: The Safe Haven for Rapists," *Journal of Family Law* 29.3 (1990–1991), pp. 559–590.

In 1977, for example, at least 14 percent of married men raped or attempted to rape their wives. This figure is based on Dianna E. H. Russell's survey, *Rape in Marriage*, in which she defined rape as forced oral, anal, or vaginal penetration; cited in "To Have and To Hold: The Marital Rape Exemption and the Fourteenth Amendment," *Harvard Law Review* 99.6 (April 1986), p. 1258.

43. Ibid., pp. 1258–1259; Rickenberg and Schulman, "Marital Rape a Crime," p. 745.

44. Schulman, "Battered Women Score Victories," p. 344.

45. Ibid., pp. 344–345; emphasis in text.

46. Ibid., p. 345.

47. The law has also affirmed men's proprietary rights over all aspects of women's reproductive labor, sexual intercourse being only one manifestation of that proprietorship. As scholar Kevin Paul notes, "the legal distinction between 'sex' and 'rape' reveals the principles of domination and subordination that yet permeate American law as it relates to women . . . . Laws prohibiting rape were created in early Western societies to protect the property interests men held in their wives and daughters. The crime a man committed in raping a woman was that of stealing another man's property, or of diminishing its value through 'unlawful' sexual intercourse." Paul, "Private/Property," pp. 410–411. Specifically, the law protected the virginity of a daughter as a prerequisite to her marriageability, and it protected the "husband's interest in his wife's fidelity" to secure his role as head of his family and as biological male progenitor. "To Have and To Hold," pp. 1256–1257. For an analysis of how the relationship between force and consent is socially constructed in the context of rape, see Dorothy E. Roberts, "Rape, Violence, and Women's Autonomy," *Chicago-Kent Law Review* 69.2 (1993), pp. 359–388.

48. Leigh Bienen, "Rape III—National Developments in Rape Reform Legislation," *Women's Rights Law Reporter* 6.3 (Summer 1980), pp. 170–213; Ronald J. Berger, Patricia Searles, and W. Lawrence Neuman, "The Dimensions of Rape Reform Legislation," *Law and Society Review* 22.2 (1988), pp. 329–357.

49. Henry Campbell Black, *Black's Law Dictionary* (St. Paul, Minn.: West, 1990), 6th ed., p. 1260.

50. See *Commonwealth v. Viera* and its companion case, *Commonwealth v. Silvia*, 519 N.E.2nd 1320 (Mass. 1988).

51. See ibid., p. 1321.

52. See ibid., pp. 1327–1328.

53. Three received sentences of from nine to twelve years and one from six to eight years. We must note, however, that the victim suffered serious trauma as a result of the crime. The publicity of the event and trial forced her to move to Florida, where she died a year later in a car crash. Ed Quill, "Convictions Appealed in Big Dan's Rape Case," *Boston Globe* (November 4, 1987), pp. 29, 31.

54. For an analysis of the importance of law within the Western tradition, see Harold J. Berman, *Law and Revolution: The Formation of the Western Legal Tradition* (Cambridge, Mass.: Harvard University Press, 1983).

55. Ronald Dworkin, *Law's Empire* (Cambridge: Mass.: Harvard University Press, 1986), p. vii.

56. Lawrence M. Friedman, "American Legal History: Past and Present," in *American Law and the Constitutional Order: Historical Perspectives*, ed. Lawrence M. Friedman and Harry N. Scheiber (Cambridge, Mass.: Harvard University Press, 1988), p. 467. As Daniel R. Ortiz notes, "law is indeed one of our most important cultural activities."

Ortiz, "The Myth of Intent in Equal Protection," *Stanford Law Review* 41.5 (May 1989), pp. 1150–1151.

57. Frances Olsen, "Statutory Rape: A Feminist Critique of Rights Analysis," *Texas Law Review* 63.3 (November 1984), p. 388.

58. David L. Faigman also questions whether the Bill of Rights protects anyone but majorities in society in "Reconciling Individual Rights and Government Interests: Madisonian Principles versus Supreme Court Practice," *Virginia Law Review* 78.7 (October 1992), pp. 1520–1529.

59. Mary E. Becker, "The Politics of Women's Wrongs and the Bill of 'Rights': A Bicentennial Perspective," *University of Chicago Law Review* 59.1 (Winter 1992), p. 454.

60. Although the worst forms of overt sexism in the legal treatment of rape are gone, sexism is still apparent. Kim Lane Scheppele, "Just the Facts, Ma'am: Sexualized Violence, Evidentiary Habits, and the Revision of Truth," *New York Law School Law Review* 37.1–2 (1992), pp. 124–125.

61. Susan Estrich, *Real Rape* (Cambridge, Mass.: Harvard University Press, 1987), pp. 4–5.

62. In the case of fetuses, however, the state and the Court not only refer to nonconsensual pregnancy as normal but go even further by passing legislation that actively forbids the state from stopping the fetus by means of abortion funding on the grounds that the state prefers the fetus's simple injury of a woman to a policy of stopping it, in spite of the fact that there is no issue concerning proof of her consent. If a woman seeks an abortion, by definition she does not consent to an ongoing pregnancy, thereby avoiding the pitfall that too often accompanies simple rape: trying to prove after the fact that a woman did not consent to sexual intercourse.

63. Grounds that heterosexual relationships are "natural" form in some part the Supreme Court's reasoning that homosexual relationships are "unnatural" and, hence, not constitutionally protected. Bartlett, *Gender and Law*, pp. 429–471.

64. Lee Epstein and Joseph F. Kobylka, *The Supreme Court and Legal Change: Abortion and the Death Penalty* (Chapel Hill: University of North Carolina Press, 1992), p. 22.

65. Frances Olsen, "Unraveling Compromise," *Harvard Law Review* 103.1 (November 1989), pp. 105–135; Samuel W. Buell, "Criminal Abortion Revisited," *New York University Law Review* 66.6 (December 1991), pp. 1774–1831.

66. Barbara Hinkson Craig and David M. O'Brien, *Abortion and American Politics* (Chatham, N.J.: Chatham House, 1993), p. 310.

67. *Congressional Record*, 91st Cong., 1st Sess. (1969), vol. 115, p. 35421.

68. Ibid., p. 37378.

69. *Congressional Record*, 96th Cong., 2nd Sess. (1980), vol. 126, p. 522.

70. *Congressional Record*, 97th Cong., 2nd Sess. (1982), vol. 128, p. 21802.

71. *Congressional Record*, 98th Cong., 1st Sess. (1983), vol. 129, p. H7319.

72. Ibid., p. H7317.

73. *Congressional Record*, 95th Cong., 1st Sess. (1977), vol. 123, p. 39392.

74. *Congressional Record*, 96th Cong., 2nd Sess. (1980), vol. 126, p. 309. Other prolife members of Congress, however, would deny all abortions, whether intercourse was consensual or not. Speaking against the rape and incest exceptions to abortion funding,

Rep. Thomas J. Bliley, Jr. (Va., R.), stated that the "mother's lack of responsibility for the conception does not remove the child's right to life." *Congressional Record*, 98th Cong., 1st Sess. (1983), vol. 129, p. E3700.

What follows in Rep. Bliley's remarks is a fascinating analogy of pregnancy to the personal sacrifice required of those who must defend a nation against unjust aggression: "Lack of fault for being pregnant does not justify denying another innocent human being his/her life. Where preservation of basic rights is at stake, society has the right to require of its members personal sacrifice. An individual would not personally be responsible for his country being attacked by an unjust aggressor, but he is still bound to oppose that aggression at great personal sacrifice and risk" (p. E3701). Bliley asserts that a person not only has a right but also an obligation to oppose "unjust aggression." The key question, obviously, is whether he would apply that principle to wrongful pregnancy. If a woman does not consent to the intrusion and appropriation of her body by a fetus, its implantation is the kind of "unjust aggression" that, according to Bliley, warrants opposition. Such a view of wrongful pregnancy would justify abortion rights for women, as well as public funding.

75. *Congressional Record*, 94th Cong., 1st Sess. (1975), vol. 121, pt. 4, p. 4189.

76. *Congressional Record*, 95th Cong., 1st Sess. (1977), vol. 123, p. 2489.

77. Ibid., p. 9532. Pro-life Representative Robert A. Young (Mo., D.) echoed the exception when he introduced his "Human Life Amendment": "Nothing in this Article shall prohibit medical procedures which physically verifiable facts establish as necessary to prevent the death of a pregnant woman" (p. 9540).

78. *Congressional Record*, 94th Cong., 2nd Sess. (1976), vol. 122, pt. 24, p. 31452.

79. In the words of Dr. Jane Hodgson, "'[M]edically necessary' means any abortion that was requested by a woman." *Congressional Record*, 95th Cong., 1st Sess. (1977), vol. 123, p. 31039.

80. Representative Robert K. Dornan (Calif., R.), ibid. The tendency of some members of Congress, particularly pro-life advocates, is to reduce pregnancy to a laundry list of aches and pains. By so doing, they not only trivialize the reasons that women obtain abortions but also obscure the principle justifying them. As Rep. Hyde said, if women were allowed to have abortions because of how pregnancy affects their health, they could be allowed to have abortions because of migraine headaches, fatigue, debilitation, depression, or morning sickness. *Congressional Record*, 98th Cong., 2nd Sess. (1984), vol. 130, p. H7187.

81. *Congressional Record*, 95th Cong., 1st Sess. (1977), vol. 123, p. 19703.

82. Ibid., p. 19714.

83. *Congressional Record*, 98th Cong., 1st Sess. (1977), vol. 129, p. H7319.

84. *Congressional Record*, 95th Cong., 1st Sess. (1977), vol. 123, p. 38398.

85. *Congressional Record*, 97th Cong., 2nd Sess. (1982), vol. 128, p. 804.

86. An exception, however, is pregnancy as a "punishment for sex," which I classify as simply "wrong" rather than merely "incomplete."

87. *Congressional Record*, 93rd Cong., 1st Sess. (1973), vol. 119, p. 23996.

88. *Congressional Record*, 93rd Cong., 2nd Sess. (1974), vol. 120, pt. 13, p. 17092.

89. *Congressional Record*, 94th Cong., 1st Sess. (1975), vol. 121, p. 30744.

90. *Congressional Record*, 95th Cong., 1st Sess. (1977), vol. 123, p. 2462.

91. *Congressional Record*, 91st Cong., 1st Sess. (1969), vol. 115, p. 35421.

92. *Congressional Record,* 91st Cong., 2nd Sess. (1970), vol. 116, p. 28370.
93. *Congressional Record,* 93rd Cong., 1st Sess. (1973), vol. 119, p. 23996.
94. Ibid., p. 24238
95. *Congressional Record,* 93rd Cong., 2nd Sess. (1974), vol. 120, p. 17092.

9 The Politics of Consent

1. Sarah Weddington, A *Question of Choice* (New York: Grosset/Putnam, 1992), p. 64.
2. Ibid., pp. 136–137.
3. Transcript of oral argument before the Court, *Roe v. Wade,* 410 U.S. 113, Doc. No. 70-18, p. 20.
4. Transcript in *Roe,* pp. 20–21. When asked the following question by a justice (not identified on the transcript): "So . . . you'd have to say that this [having an abortion when the fetus has the protection of the Fourteenth Amendment] would be equivalent after the child was born if the mother thought it bothered her health [by] . . . having the child around, she could have it killed. Isn't that correct?" Weddington responded, "That's correct." Ibid., p. 21.
5. Ibid., p. 23.
6. Ibid., p. 33.
7. Ibid., p. 30; Weddington, *Question of Choice,* p. 141.
8. Transcript in *Roe,* p. 30.
9. *Roe,* pp. 156–157; emphasis added.
10. "Anti-abortionists in both the United States and Britain have long applied the principle that a picture of a dead fetus is worth a thousand words." Rosalind Pollack Petchesky, "Fetal Images: The Power of Visual Culture in the Politics of Reproduction," reprinted in *Women and the Law,* ed. Mary Joe Frug (Westbury, N.Y.: Foundation Press, 1992), p. 483; Deirdre Moira Condit, "Constructing Fetal 'Personhood': An Examination of Law and Language," paper presented at the 1991 Annual Meeting of the Midwest Political Science Association, Chicago, April 18–20, 1991; Celeste Michelle Condit, *Decoding Abortion Rhetoric: Communicating Social Change* (Urbana: University of Illinois Press, 1990); Laura R. Woliver, "The Influence of Technology on the Politics of Motherhood: An Overview of the United States," *Women's Studies International Forum* 14.5 (1991), pp. 479–490.
11. Ronald Dworkin, *Life's Dominion: An Argument about Abortion, Euthanasia, and Individual Freedom* (New York: Knopf, 1993). For a masterful critique of Dworkin's position, see Frances M. Kamm's review, "Abortion and the Value of Life: A Discussion of *Life's Dominion,*" 95 *Columbia Law Review* (1995), pp. 160–221.
12. Personal communication with Sarah Weddington, in answer to a question I asked at a talk given February 1994, Planned Parenthood League of Massachusetts.
13. Over the years since Thomson's article, this argument has been effectively developed by a large number of scholars, such as Donald Regan, Frances Kamm, Sylvia Law, Deborah Rhode, Cass Sunstein, Laurence Tribe, and Kathryn Kolbert (who used this argument when she argued *Casey* before the Court).
14. Elizabeth Mensch and Alan Freeman, "The Politics of Virtue: Animals, Theology and Abortion," *Georgia Law Review* 25.4 (Spring 1991), p. 1123, and Mensch and

Freeman, *The Politics of Virtue: Is Abortion Debatable?* (Durham, N.C.: Duke University Press, 1993).

15. Mensch and Freeman, *Politics of Virtue*, p. 132.

16. Quoted in William H. Rehnquist, *The Supreme Court: How It Was, How It Is* (New York: William Morrow, 1987), p. 184.

17. For an excellent examination of Canadian policy, see Janine Brodie, "Health versus Rights: Comparative Perspectives on Abortion Policy in Canada and the United States," in *Power and Decision: The Social Control of Reproduction*, ed. Gita Sen and Rachel C. Snow (Boston: Harvard School of Public Health, March 1994).

18. I thank Karen Orren for highlighting this comparison in a personal conversation.

19. Gita Sen, "Reproduction: The Feminist Challenge to Social Policy," in Sen and Snow, eds., *Power and Decision*.

20. Sarah Weddington, *A Question of Choice* (New York: Putnam, 1992), p. 24.

21. Ibid., pp. 115–119.

22. In practice, because some forms of contraception terminate a pregnancy in progress, the boundary between contraception and abortion can dissolve. In *Griswold v. Connecticut*, 391 U.S. 479 (1965), however, the Court established the foundation for the right to use contraceptives as if their use did not entail destruction of potential life; the opposite is true in *Roe*, when the Court established the constitutional grounds for the right to have an abortion. In that sense, therefore, we can and must distinguish between the constitutional principles that underlie the right to use contraceptives from those that underlie the right to terminate pregnancy by an abortion.

23. William Van Alstyne, "Closing the Circle of Constitutional Review from *Griswold v. Connecticut* to *Roe v. Wade*: An Outline of a Decision Merely Overruling *Roe*," *Duke Law Journal* 1989.6 (December 1989), pp. 1677–1688.

24. John Hart Ely, "The Wages of Crying Wolf: A Comment on *Roe v. Wade*," *Yale Law Journal* 82.5 (April 1973), p. 931.

25. See Andrew Koppelman's masterful application of the Thirteenth Amendment to compulsory pregnancy. Koppelman, "Forced Labor: A Thirteenth Amendment Defense of Abortion," *Northwestern University Law Review* 84.2 (Winter 1990), p. 503. Implementation of one's right to state assistance to free oneself from such impositions, however, presumably also invokes equal protection guarantees of the Fourteenth Amendment.

26. This addresses the issue raised by Frances Olsen and others that privacy doctrine based on decisional autonomy alone "reinforce[s] sexism by treating abortion and childbirth as central to women's identity as women." Olsen, "Unraveling Compromise," *Harvard Law Review* 103.1 (November 1989), pp. 112, 117–121.

27. Mary Joe Frug, *Postmodern Legal Feminism* (New York: Routledge, 1992), pp. 4–5. Patricia J. Williams also underscores the value of a rights approach for securing better outcomes. She thinks that "rights are to law what conscious commitments are to the psyche. This country's worst historical moments have not been attributable to rights-*assertion*, but to a failure of rights-*commitment*. From this perspective, the problem with rights discourse is not that it is constricting, but that it exists in a constricted referential universe." Williams, "Alchemical Notes: Reconstructing Ideals from Deconstructed Rights," in *A Less than Perfect Union: Alternative Perspectives on the U.S. Constitution*, ed. Jules Lobel (New York: Monthly Review Press, 1988), pp. 59–61.

Similarly, Mary Poovey thinks that the political capital generated by the discourse of rights in the United States means that it should not be jettisoned but rather reworked to achieve feminist goals. Poovey, "The Abortion Question and the Death of Man," in *Feminists Theorize the Political*, ed. Judith Butler and Joan W. Scott (New York: Routledge, 1992). See Laura W. Stein, "Meshing Equality and Privacy to Advance Feminist Goals: A Proposal for Tinkering," paper delivered at Feminism and Legal Theory Workshop, directed by Martha Fineman, Columbia University School of Law, New York, March 1993.

Mary Becker explores formal equality as applied to two concrete legal issues, child custody and same-sex relationships, using three alternatives to formal equality theory: Catharine MacKinnon's dominance approach, Robin West's hedonic approach, and Margaret Radin's pragmatic approach. See Becker, "Strength in Diversity: Feminist Theoretical Approaches to Child Custody and Same-Sex Relationships," *Stetson Law Review* 23.3 (Summer 1994), pp. 701–742. For a discussion of difference versus sameness as an approach to women's legal rights, see Joan C. Williams, "Dissolving the Sameness/Difference Debate: A Post-modern Path beyond Essentialism in Feminist and Critical Race Theory," *Duke Law Journal* 1991.2 (April 1991), pp. 296–323.

28. Wendy W. Williams, "The Equality Crisis: Some Reflections on Culture, Courts, and Feminism," *Women's Rights Law Reporter* 7.3 (Spring 1982), p. 196. Others, however, search for solutions to the particularity of women's experience against a principle of its universality. For a classic treatment, see Elizabeth V. Spelman, *Inessential Woman: Problems of Exclusion in Feminist Thought* (Boston, Mass.: Beacon Press, 1988). Others decry strategies that seek to achieve women's emancipation by repressing sexual difference, what Adriana Cavarero terms "claiming homologization with the male subject." Cavarero, "Equality and Sexual Difference: Amnesia in Political Thought," in *Beyond Equality and Difference: Citizenship, Feminist Politics and Female Subjectivity*, ed. Gisela Bock and Susan James (London: Routledge, 1992), p. 39.

"In any culture, the construction of motherhood carries the mixed messages of the experience of that culture with life, death, sex and gender. Such experience is not universal . . . it is a historical phenomenon subject to development and change." Clarissa W. Atkinson, *The Oldest Vocation: Christian Motherhood in the Middle Ages* (Ithaca, N.Y.: Cornell University Press, 1991), p. 6.

Although there are many ways in which class, race, and nationality particularize pregnancy as an experience, the consent-to-pregnancy approach draws on what Ann Ferguson terms two cross-cultural constants: that women are or can become biological mothers and that the experience of the vast majority of women everywhere is one of primarily being mothered rather than fathered. By "mothered" and "fathered," Ferguson refers to who socially cared for a person in infancy and early childhood. Ferguson, *Sexual Democracy: Women, Oppression, and Revolution* (Boulder, Colo.: Westview Press, 1991), p. 67.

"Reproduction affects women as women, in a way that transcends class divisions and that penetrates everything—work, political and community involvements, sexuality, creativity, dreams." Rosalind Petchesky, "Reproductive Freedom: Beyond 'A Woman's Right to Choose,'" *Signs* 5.4 (Summer 1980), p. 666.

29. This approach draws on what some feminists term *dominance feminism*—that is, the identification of how women are subordinated by forces of domination. Although

there are critics of it, dominance feminism has been in the ascendancy in recent years. Kathryn Abrams, "Sex Wars Redux: Agency and Coercion in Feminist Legal Theory," *Columbia Law Review* 95.2 (March 1995), pp. 304–376.

30. Nancy Gager and Cathleen Schurr, *Sexual Assault: Confronting Rape in America* (New York: Grosset & Dunlap, 1976), pp. 169–175.

31. Cynthia V. Ward somewhat critically thinks there is no inherent contradiction between radical feminism and liberalism; in fact, she locates the power of the theory of domination as emanating from the principles of liberalism itself by showing that radical feminists, such as Catharine MacKinnon, are really "closet liberals." Ward, "The Radical Feminist Defense of Individualism," *Northwestern University Law Review* 89.3 (Spring 1995), pp. 871–899.

32. Mona Harrington, *Women Lawyers: Rewriting the Rules* (New York: Knopf, 1994), p. 264.

33. Drucilla Cornell, *Beyond Accommodation: Ethical Feminism, Deconstruction, and the Law* (New York: Routledge, 1991), pp. 19–20.

34. Faye D. Ginsburg, *Contested Lives: The Abortion Debate in an American Community* (Berkeley: University of California Press, 1989), p. 191.

35. As Caroline Whitbeck notes, women's roles are regarded as important to the extent that those roles enhance the experiences of others, but not of women themselves. As a consequence, "the subjects of women's needs and women's moral integrity and bodily integrity are omitted regularly, as is the issue of matching women's responsibilities with the authority to carry them out." Whitbeck, "The Moral Implications of Regarding Women as People: New Perspectives on Pregnancy and Personhood," in *Abortion and the Status of the Fetus*, ed. William B. Bondeson, H. Tristram Engelhardt, Jr., Stuart F. Spicker, and Daniel H. Winship (Dordrecht, Netherlands: D. Reidel, 1983), p. 247.

36. Even to claim such a persona for women, according to some critics, is to masculinize women and destroy the significant difference between men and women, thereby robbing women of the very difference that should be their leverage for making claims on the state. Many women tend to see autonomy and compassion as if they were polar opposites. The goal, however, is to construct autonomy in terms of relationships with others. Kenneth L. Karst, "Woman's Constitution," *Duke Law Journal* 1984.3 (June 1984), pp. 450–479.

37. Samuel D. Warren and Louis D. Brandeis, "The Right to Privacy," *Harvard Law Review* 4:5 (December 15, 1890), pp. 194, 220.

38. Ibid., p. 195. When Brandeis and Warren begin to talk about the instruments by which privacy is invaded, they again speak of the individual only in masculine terms, such as how "his" reputation can be lowered in the "estimation of *his fellows*" (p. 197). They state that the "common law secures to each individual the right of determining, ordinarily, to what extent *his* thoughts, sentiments, and emotions shall be communicated to others" (p. 198). Yet they cite as an example that when "*man* records in a letter to *his son*, or in *his diary*, that *he did not dine with his wife* on a certain day," no one can "publish them to the world, even if possession of the documents [letters or diaries] had been obtained rightfully" (p. 201). As they continue, "A *man* writes a dozen letters to different people. No person would be permitted to publish a list of the letters written" (p. 201; emphasis added throughout).

39. Ibid., p. 205.

40. *Oxford English Dictionary* (Oxford: Oxford University Press, 1971), compact edition, p. 417.

41. Ibid., p. 1681: Dryden, *Abs. & Achit.*, I, p. 458.

42. Ibid.

43. Ibid., p. 1849; Corden, *Speeches*, p. 76.

44. *Restatement of the Law (Second), Torts* (St. Paul, Minn.: American Law Institute, 1965), vol. 1, § 65, p. 112.

45. Appendix, vol. 1, pp. 78–81.

46. Ibid.

47. Elizabeth M. Schneider, "Describing and Changing: Women's Self-Defense Work and the Problem of Expert Testimony on Battering," *Women's Rights Law Reporter* 14.2–3 (Spring–Fall 1992), p. 214; Schneider, "The Violence of Privacy," *Connecticut Law Review* 23.4 (Summer 1991), pp. 973–999.

48. Catharine A. MacKinnon, *Feminism Unmodified: Discourses on Life and Law* (Cambridge, Mass.: Harvard University Press, 1987), p. 102.

49. Laurence H. Tribe, *American Constitutional Law* (Mineola, N.Y.: Foundation Press, 1988), pp. 1305–1306.

50. Mary Frances Berry is driven to despair by the definition of women as primarily responsible for child care, which creates a mother-care tradition that undermines women's ability to claim equal rights and access to power. See Berry, *The Politics of Parenthood: Child Care, Women's Rights, and the Myth of the Good Mother* (New York: Viking, 1993), pp. ix, 85ff.

51. *Hoyt v. Florida*, 368 U.S. 57 (1961), pp. 61–62. This ruling was not overturned until 1975 in *Taylor v. Louisiana*, 419 U.S. 522, 537 (1975).

52. *Taylor*, p. 537.

53. As Katharine T. Bartlett notes, "feminists define progress in opposition to tradition and the past . . . [because] tradition . . . represents patriarchal gender role norms, the elimination of which is feminism's primary goal. Deepening the contemporary feminist hostility towards tradition has been its association with 'family values.'" Bartlett, "Tradition, Change, and the Idea of Progress in Feminist Legal Thought," *Wisconsin Law Review* 1995.2 (1995), p. 304.

54. Carol Smart, *Feminism and the Power of Law* (London: Routledge, 1989), p. 96. As Judith Resnick notes, the identification of women with family roles results in women's lack of a "juridical voice" and a concomitant resistance by federal judges "to resist jurisdiction over civil rights claims motivated by gender." Resnik, "'Naturally' without Gender: Women, Jurisdiction, and the Federal Courts," *New York University Law Review* 66.6 (December 1991), p. 1750.

55. Virginia Held seeks to contrast the social contract tradition, including premises of rationality, with a mothering tradition in which the mother-child relationship is paradigmatic. Held, "Mothering versus Contract," in *Beyond Self-interest*, ed. Jane J. Mansbridge (Chicago: University of Chicago Press, 1990), p. 288. Yet before we can contrast these two, we must join them by guaranteeing to women the right to consent to pregnancy.

56. The literature is vast, but for excellent analyses and critiques, see Daniels, *At Women's Expense*; Sally J. Kenney, *For Whose Protection? Reproductive Hazards and Exclusionary Policies in the United States and Britain* (Ann Arbor: University of Mich-

igan Press, 1991); Beth Driscoll Osowski, "The Need for Logic and Consistency in Fetal Rights," *North Dakota Law Review* 68.1 (1992), pp. 171–208.

57. Janet Gallagher, "Prenatal Invasions and Interventions: What's Wrong with Fetal Rights," *Harvard Women's Law Journal* 10.9–58 (Spring 1987), p. 12.

58. Susan R. Estrich and Kathleen M. Sullivan, "Abortion Politics: Writing for an Audience of One," *University of Pennsylvania Law Review* 138.1 (November 1989), p. 130.

59. Ibid., p. 127.

60. For this reason, Duke University economist Frank Sloan advocates the sale of organs, at least by families of fatal accident victims. Boston University medical ethicist George Annas disagrees. National Public Radio, "Morning Edition," July 6, 1993.

61. Ibid.

62. Ibid.

63. For a discussion of utilitarian ethical rules in the context of mortal combat and other philosophical perspectives, see Marshall Cohen, Thomas Nagel, and Thomas Scanlon, eds., *War and Moral Responsibility* (Princeton, N.J.: Princeton University Press, 1974).

64. *Model Penal Code* (Philadelphia: American Law Institute, 1965), p. 14.

65. Ibid., pp. 14–15. Also see Eric Rakowski, "Taking and Saving Lives," *Columbia Law Review* 93.5 (June 1993), pp. 1063–1156.

66. Ely, "Wages of Crying Wolf," p. 926.

67. We can have moral obligations to living entities, such as our pets or wildlife, which are not people. Patricia D. White, "The Concept of Person, the Law, and the Use of the Fetus in Biomedicine," in Bondeson et al., *Abortion and the Status of the Fetus*, p. 127. What is more, the law regulates relationships between people and other living beings.

68. Mary C. Segers, "Abortion and the Culture: Toward a Feminist Perspective," in *Abortion: Understanding Differences*, ed. Sidney Callahan and Daniel Callahan (New York: Plenum, 1984), p. 231.

69. Quoted in the *New York Times* (February 17, 1992), p. A10.

70. *Black's Law Dictionary*, p. 621.

71. Kristin Luker, Interview 102 (pro-choice), p. 7. Interviews are archived at the Murray Research Center, Radcliffe College, Cambridge, Mass.

72. Ibid., Interview 111 (pro-choice), p. 11.

73. Ibid., Interview 118 (pro-choice), p. 21.

74. Martha Minow, *Making All the Difference: Inclusion, Exclusion, and American Law* (Ithaca, N.Y.: Cornell University Press, 1990), chaps. 8–11, pp. 8–9.

75. Emily Gill sees no contradiction between a language of rights and a language of community. She agrees with Martha Minow that "[r]ights provide a language that depends upon and expresses human interconnection at the very moment when individuals ask others to recognize their separate interests." Gill, "Autonomy and the Encumbered Self," in *Radical Theories of Law*, ed. Stephen Griffeth and Robert C. L. Moffat (Lawrence: University Press of Kansas, forthcoming).

For a discussion of the place of love, compassion, and wisdom in the context of abortion rights, see Ruth Colker, *Abortion and Dialogue: Pro-choice, Pro-life, and American Law* (Bloomington: Indiana University Press, 1992).

76. For a dimensional analysis of personhood defined as freedom, identity, and con-

textuality, see Margaret Jane Radin, "Market-inalienability," *Harvard Law Review* 100.8 (June 1987), pp. 1904–1905. Consent to pregnancy supports those who seek to include an ethic of care and responsibility in the abortion debate. See Linda C. McClain, "'Atomistic Man' Revisited: Liberalism, Connection, and Feminist Jurisprudence," *Southern California Law Review* 65.3 (March 1992), pp. 1242–1243. For an excellent analysis of relational feminism in the context of abortion rights, see Pamela S. Karlan and Daniel R. Ortiz, "In a Different Voice: Relational Feminism, Abortion Rights, and the Feminist Legal Agenda," *Northwestern University Law Review* 87.3 (Spring 1993), pp. 858–896.

77. Laurence H. Tribe, *Abortion: The Clash of Absolutes* (New York: Norton, 1990), pp. 137–138.

78. Minow, *Making All the Difference*, p. 277. Consent between the woman and the fetus, of course, leaves open the nature of consent that operates between the mother and the father of the fetus.

79. James Rachels, "Why Privacy Is Important," *Philosophy and Public Affairs* 4.4 (Summer 1975), p. 326.

80. Mary Ann Glendon, *Rights Talk: The Impoverishment of Political Discourse* (New York: Free Press, 1991), pp. xi, xi–xii.

81. Minow, *Making All the Difference*, p. 233.

82. Ibid.

83. This is contrary to those who believe, as Mary Anne Warren does, that "it is not possible to produce a satisfactory defense of a woman's right to obtain an abortion without showing that a fetus is not a human being." To the contrary, it is precisely to the degree that the state protects the fetus as human life that it must restrict the fetus as human life from imposing a wrongful pregnancy. See Warren, "On the Moral and Legal Status of Abortion," in *The Problem of Abortion*, 2nd ed., ed. Joel Feinberg (Belmont, Calif.: Wadsworth, 1984), p. 102.

84. Robert Jay Lifton, *Death in Life: Survivors of Hiroshima* (Chapel Hill: University of North Carolina Press, 1991); Lifton, *The Genocidal Mentality: Nazi Holocaust and Nuclear Threat* (New York: Basic Books, 1990); Lifton, *Home from the War: Vietnam Veterans—Neither Victims Nor Executioners* (New York: Simon & Schuster 1991). See M. Walzer for an exposition for why war need not entail dehumanization of the enemy, *Just and Unjust Wars: A Moral Argument with Historical Illustrations* (New York: Basic Books, 1977).

85. Barbara Johnson, "Apostrophe, Animation, and Abortion," *Diacritics* (Spring 1986), pp. 29–39; Angela Bonavoglia, ed., *The Choices We Made: Twenty-five Women and Men Speak Out about Abortion* (New York: Random House, 1991).

86. Stephen Mulhall and Adam Swift, *Liberals and Communitarians* (Oxford: Blackwell, 1992).

87. Ibid., p. 13.

88. See particularly Michael Sandel, *Liberalism and the Limits of Justice* (Cambridge: Cambridge University Press, 1992).

89. Barbara Katz Rothman, *Recreating Motherhood: Ideology and Technology in Patriarchal Society* (New York: Norton, 1989).

90. J. Ann Tickner, *Gender in International Relations: Feminist Perspectives on Achieving Global Security* (New York: Columbia University Press, 1992).

91. Ellen Goodman, "'Prolife'—and 'Prochoices'—in Maine," *Boston Globe* (September 17, 1992), p. 17.

92. Probably the most powerful denial that the fetus is a person is to be found in the work of Ronald Dworkin, who thinks that opposition to abortion is based on views that the fetus stands for the sanctity of life, not literally on the presumption that it is a person. Dworkin, *Life's Dominion*.

93. Similar to Christianity, Judaism strongly believes that "no one has the right to put one life before another life." Scott Aaron, "The Choice in 'Choose Life': American Judaism and Abortion," *Commonweal* 119.4 (February 28, 1992), p. 15. Judaism, however, interprets "choose life," found in Deuteronomy 30:19, differently than Christians do because Jews believe that life fully begins only when one is born (Ibid.). For the first forty days of gestation, Jews consider the fetus to be in a liquid or unformed state; after the fortieth day and up until birth, the fetus has the status of a limb; but it is not until birth that one acquires a soul (pp. 15–16).

94. Ibid., p. 16. One needs to understand the way in which Judaism defines the beginning of life to comprehend its position on abortion. As long as a child is in utero, the mother's life takes precedence because the mother is fully alive. After birth, the child's and the mother's lives are given equal value since the offspring is now considered fully alive (p. 15). These beliefs about when a fetus becomes a person stem from the *Mishna*, *Ocholot*, chap. 7, 6th Halacha, according to Rabbi David Ellenson (p. 15).

95. Daniel B. Sinclair, "The Interaction between Law and Morality in Jewish Law in the Areas of Feticide and Killing a Terminally Ill Individual," *Criminal Justice Ethics* 11.2 (Summer/Fall 1992), pp. 78–79.

96. Kristin Luker, *Abortion and the Politics of Motherhood* (Berkeley: University of California Press, 1984).

97. Rosalind Pollack Petchesky, *Abortion and Women's Choice: The State, Sexuality, and Reproductive Freedom* (Boston: Northeastern University Press, 1990); Michele McKeegan, *Abortion Politics: Mutiny in the Ranks of the Right* (New York: Free Press, 1992), p. 11; Wendy Kaminer, *A Fearful Freedom: Women's Flight from Equality* (Reading, Mass.: Addison-Wesley, 1990), p. 211.

98. Sidney Verba, Kay Lehman Schlozman, and Henry E. Brady, *Voice and Equality: Civic Voluntarism in American Politics* (Cambridge, Mass.: Harvard University Press, 1995). Moreover, the authors found that although more than twice as many respondents registered extremely pro-choice views as registered extremely pro-life views, the latter tend to concentrate all of their energies on this one issue; pro-choice advocates have a wider range of concerns, thereby dissipating the attention they can devote to the abortion issue alone.

99. Betty Crocker, as a registered trademark, is used here to refer to the traditional homemaking values associated with it.

100. Margaret G. Farrell, "Revisting *Roe v. Wade*: Substance and Process in the Abortion Debate," *Indiana Law Journal* 68.2 (Spring 1993), pp. 269–362.

101. Lee Epstein and Joseph F. Kobylka, *The Supreme Court and Legal Change: Abortion and the Death Penalty* (Chapel Hill: University of North Carolina Press, 1992), p. 143.

102. This ultimately utilitarian orientation meshes with what Roger Rosenblatt describes as the need to look at the social context in which the sanctity of life, repre-

sented by the fetus, is embedded as grounds for justifying abortion. Rosenblatt finds many historical precedents that justify abortion on contextual grounds, particularly when such issues are at stake as "[r]ape, incest, illegitimacy, protecting the woman's life," or even the need to "preserv[e] the milk for children already born." Rosenblatt, *Life Itself: Abortion in the American Mind* (New York: Random House, 1992), pp. 6, 71.

103. "[I]t is now widely accepted that law, particularly adjudication, is fundamentally an interpretive process." Drucilla L. Cornell, "Institutionalization of Meaning, Recollective Imagination and the Potential for Transformative Legal Interpretation," *Pennsylvania Law Review* 136.4 (April 1988), p. 1136. For an analysis of the subversive consequences of changing interpretative stories and narratives, see Patricia Ewick and Susan S. Silbey, "Subversive Stories and Hegemonic Tales: Toward a Sociology of Narrative," *Law and Society Review* 29.2 (1995), pp. 197–226.

104. Martha R. Mahoney, "Legal Images of Battered Women: Redefining the Issue of Separation," *Michigan Law Review* 90.1 (October 1991), p. 2.

105. The recognition of the problem of domestic violence required not merely changes in the law but also public recognition. Elizabeth M. Schneider, "Epilogue: Making Reconceptualization of Violence against Women Real," *Albany Law Review* 58.4 (1995), pp. 1245–1252. The same can be said of abortion-funding policies.

106. Martha Minow, "Interpreting Rights: An Essay for Robert Cover," *Yale Law Journal* 96.8 (July 1987), pp. 1860–1862.

107. This runs the risk of fueling those who already depict abortion in murderous terms. Linda C. McClain, "Equality, Oppression, and Abortion: The Use of Equality Arguments by Women's Organizations that Oppose Abortion Rights," paper delivered for the Feminism and Legal Theory Workshop, directed by Martha Fineman, Columbia University School of Law, New York, April 1993.

108. Harvard Law Review Note, "Rethinking (M)otherhood: Feminist Theory and State Regulation of Pregnancy," *Harvard Law Review* 103.6 (April 1990), p. 1337.

109. Comment offered by a panel member at the Annual Meeting of the Law and Society Association, Toronto, June 1995. As Marie Ashe's work has shown, there is resistance to the depiction of women as bad mothers who deviate from norms of self-sacrifice and connective nurturing of children. Ashe, "The 'Bad Mother' in Law and Literature: A Problem of Representation," *Hastings Law Journal* 43.4 (April 1992), pp. 1017–1018.

110. Mary Becker, "Maternal Feelings: Myth, Taboo, and Child Custody," *Southern California Review of Law and Women's Studies* 1.1 (Winter 1992), p. 164.

111. For an excellent critique of the privacy doctrine in relation to abortion rights, see Linda C. McClain, "The Poverty of Privacy?" *Columbia Journal of Gender and Law* 3.1 (1992), pp. 119–174.

112. William Safire, "The Double Wedge," *New York Times* (February 23, 1995), p. A23.

113. Anna Quindlen, "Polls, Not Passion," *New York Times* (November 9, 1994), p. A27. As early as 1973, pro-life advocates used the abortion issue to influence political elections. For example, in the New Jersey gubernatorial election of 1973, Brendan Byrne had to denounce publicly his support for abortion in order to run successfully as a candidate. William Lasser, *The Limits of Judicial Power: The Supreme Court in American Politics* (Chapel Hill: University of North Carolina Press, 1988), p. 217.

114. We have yet to consider fully how the use of RU486 could entail liabilities due to damage to children who were exposed to it prior to birth. Gary M. Samuelson, "DES, RU-486, and Deja Vu," *Journal of Pharmacy and Law* 2.1 (1993), pp. 64–70.

115. Frank Rich, "Their Own Petard," *New York Times* (February 23, 1995), p. A23.

116. Kristin Luker, *Abortion and the Politics of Motherhood* (Berkeley: University of California Press, 1984). For an insightful analysis of the relationship between problem definition and problem solving, see David A. Rochefort and Roger W. Cobb, *The Politics of Problem Definition: Shaping the Policy Agenda* (Lawrence: University Press of Kansas, 1994).

117. Michael W. McCann, *Rights at Work: Pay Equity Reform and the Politics of Legal Mobilization* (Chicago: University of Chicago Press, 1994).

118. Quoted in *New York Times* (January 23, 1992), p. A1.

Index